LIBERATION SOCIOLOGY

2ND EDITION

by

Joe R. Feagin
Texas A&M University

and

Hernán Vera
University of Florida

Paradigm Publishers
Boulder • London

Copyright © 2008 by Paradigm Publishers

Published in the United States by Paradigm Publishers, 3360 Mitchell Lane Suite E, Boulder, CO 80301 USA.

Paradigm Publishers is the trade name of Birkenkamp & Company, LLC, Dean Birkenkamp, President and Publisher.

Library of Congress Cataloging-in-Publication Data

Feagin, Joe R.
    Liberation sociology / Joe R. Feagin, Hernan Vera. — 2nd ed.
        p. cm.
    Includes bibliographical references and index.
    ISBN-13: 978-1-59451-604-7 (hardcover: alk. paper)   1. Social justice.   2. Social ethics.   3. Sociology—Moral and ethical aspects.   4. Sociology—Political aspects. 5. Applied sociology.   6. Critical theory.   I. Vera, Hernan, 1937–   II. Title.
    HM671.F43 2008
    303.3'72—dc22

                                                                          2008005959

Printed and bound in the United States of America on acid-free paper that meets the standards of the American National Standard for Permanence of Paper for Printed Library Materials.

Designed and Typeset by Straight Creek Bookmakers.

To Derek, Nicolás Bastián, Natasha María, Marcos Antonio, and all the world's other children and grandchildren. May the world you inherit be much more just than ours.

CONTENTS

PREFACE AND ACKNOWLEDGMENTS

Not long after the first edition of this book, the New York City and Washington, D.C., events of 9/11 changed the world in which we live. Soon thereafter, a U.S. military effort led by President George Bush began aggressive preemptive invasions against the governments of Afghanistan and Iraq. Rather quickly, the myths of U.S. innocence and moral superiority were no longer tenable in the face of revelations about torture by U.S. soldiers in Iraqi prisons, about so-called rendition episodes in which agencies of the U.S. government secretly move U.S. prisoners abroad to places where torture is less visible or politically acceptable, and about the support given to extreme torture tactics banned by international agreements by no less than the U.S. president, vice president, and other high government officials.

One major U.S. television network soon began a very popular and propagandistic television series called *24,* which compressed a day's events into an hour TV drama, with the plot line usually involving a fantasy about evil "terrorists" who, when aggressively tortured, at the last minute provided accurate information needed to avert terrible events that would involve many deaths. Under this worst-case scenario set by the television show's producers, and given the tension induced by a plot compressed into an hour, average viewers likely find it hard to think of constitutionally allowed alternatives to the aggressive torture applied before their eyes. Yet, these media-contrived events do not reveal that such torture is usually counterproductive, because people admit to anything under torture. Such programs desensitize the public to the horrors of torture and thereby subvert the protections against totalitarianism provided by the U.S. constitutional tradition.

Soon after our first edition, a media "feeding frenzy" was generated by the 9/11 events and the subsequent Iraqi invasion, and the media often provided the world with haunting images of a sharpened racial divide in the United States. Americans of color, especially those with Middle Eastern backgrounds, were routinely stereotyped and mocked in the mainstream media, discriminated against in the workplace and malls, and violently attacked on the streets. Moreover, travelers within the United States are now constantly reminded that the U.S. government views itself as "at war with terrorism" every time that they are forced to dispose of their mouthwash, perfume, and hand lotion bottles in passing through mandatory security searches at airports. Such extreme security measures constantly insure that the average American will make a personal connection between life in the United States and the military invasions in the Middle East. In addition, offering a rationale of expanding "homeland security," numerous governmental officials and private groups have inaugurated a renewed "war" against undocumented immigrants from Latin American countries, such as in the effort to build a tall security fence on the México border. In spite of this xenophobic effort to wall out needed workers—who are in fact economic refugees from countries where U.S. corporations play a key role in creating economic crises—few U.S. citizens see the irony in continuing to brag about the U.S. role in the destruction of the Berlin wall in Germany and the end of a Soviet political system that routinely blocked and persecuted immigrants.

In the first edition of this book we predicted an increase in the aggressive international posture of a still imperialistic United States. At that time, very few U.S. sociologists had ever systematically examined this U.S. imperialism or colonialism in mainstream publications. This is still the case. We still see no articles in the *American Sociological Review* or books in the book list in *Footnotes,* the newsletter of the American Sociological Association, that indicate major research by U.S. sociologists on this country's continuing overseas invasions and continuing international imperialism. In our view such social science research is much needed if this country is ever to achieve its celebrated ideals of "liberty and justice for all."

Today sociology ignites the imagination of countless students who choose to take sociology courses or elect sociology as a major in colleges and universities around the world. Indeed, we, the coauthors, share the experience of having our imaginations ignited when each of us, on separate continents, first encountered sociology in university courses. Joe Feagin decided to become a sociologist after attending his first lectures in sociology at Harvard University. Hernán Vera, at about the same time in Chile, became enamored with sociology when he first read C. Wright Mills's vision of sociology in *The Sociological Imagination.* Students today continue to be attracted to sociology because of its promise to contribute to their political, social, and moral understanding of themselves and their social worlds—and often because they hope it will help them participate in building a better society. For generations now, not just college students but all who learn to read the world through sociological ideas have shared in the excitement and insight of being empowered by their newly acquired mindfulness. Community activists, union leaders, teachers, social workers, journalists, lawyers, politicians, theologians, and many others the world over have found sociology to be enlightening, challenging, and useful in their careers and lives.

However, all too often sociologists choose to forget the activist and radical traditions of the discipline that they actively practice. Sociological theories are frequently taught as disembodied ideas on the margins of one's education. The passion and social change commitments of the many great thinkers and activists in social science are too frequently forgotten or ignored. The ideas and works of pathbreaking and adventurous sociologists such as Jane Addams and W.E.B. Du Bois—to mention but two of the giants whose research and commitment to a better world have shaped our society and discipline—are only occasionally taught. In this state of collective amnesia, it is easy to go with the flow and accept conventional approaches and ideas that circulate because of their immediate utility. New ideas and approaches are frequently seen as distractions from career work. We once asked a colleague what he thought of the work of the great European analyst of society, Michel Foucault, whose work was then beginning to have a significant impact in sociology. Naively, he said, "I have not read that work because I have had no need to quote it."

Yet new ideas are extraordinarily important to human progress. In 1905 a modest European graduate student wrote his doctoral dissertation and three research papers that, with one more research paper written in 1915, articulated the revolutionary ideas that constitute what is today referred to as "Einstein's Universe." Photoelectric cells and lasers, fiber optics, space travel, semiconductors, our view of the birth and expansion of the cosmos, and nuclear power are just a few parts of the huge new Universe that Albert Einstein's ideas created. Einstein was, to use the term we employ in this book, a *countersystem thinker.* Einstein did not work alone; he was gregarious and passionate about his scientific ideas. In his early days he worked with Milena Maric, a scientist whom he married and later divorced. Throughout his life, he shared and developed his scientific ideas in discussions with friends and colleagues. Moreover, over his lifetime Einstein wrote and published hundreds of articles, many of them in scientific journals, but many others in various liberal outlets on such progressive causes as pacifism and international human rights.[1]

In sociology today, a countersystem thinker is likely to research and document empirically such social phenomena as the increasing inequality among class, gender, and racial groups in this and other contemporary societies. Such a countersystem sociologist may on the basis of that research challenge the established and inegalitarian societal order on which many private and government policies are built. There is no question that those countersystem sociologists who believe that a better world is possible, and who have oriented their teaching and research to that viewpoint, often have a harder time going through required hiring and promotion rituals in the private marketplace, in government agencies, and in academia. Today, the idea that social justice and democracy are the better future for our society and our world is far from being a matter of general consensus. For example, just in the week before we concluded this preface a "liberal" Democratic Party candidate for the U.S. presidency was asked by a journalist, if he had to choose between security and democracy, what would he choose? He responded "security," and not "democracy." Indeed, he could have rejected this false dichotomy, but did not do so. If this difficult political reality should deter readers of this book from orientating their careers and lives toward participation in research on and construction of a much more egalitarian and democratic society, then they will miss out on one of the most exciting aspects of the discipline of contemporary sociology.

The amnesia surrounding the roots of sociology and an uncritical acceptance of conventional theories and methods influence the ways in which sociology is taught in the undergraduate curriculum and in courses for new sociologists in graduate schools. Conventional theoretical ideas and instrumental-positivistic methods (see below for a definition) are too frequently taught as if they constitute the essential core of the discipline and the only way of doing a legitimate sociology. There is too much emphasis in graduate education on learning how to conceal from others, and from oneself, one's own cultural, class, racial, political, and gender biases. In many sectors, the most respectable sociology is that which takes a position of apparent social neutrality, yet one often uncritical of or unaware of its moral and political impact on other human beings.

Nonetheless, sociology remains a valuable social science, for it has great potential to assist in progressive social change. It has both the craft and the intellectual perspective to contribute to a deeper understanding of how society works. Sociologists have the potential to probe the social complexity of life in ways that their colleagues in numerous other disciplines cannot. Indeed, in terms of significant ideas, sociology already has had an important impact on U.S. society and the world. Today, politics, business, social work, and government would be difficult to conduct without the vocabulary and concepts borrowed from sociology. Ideas and terms such as role, institution, ritual, variable, model, correlation, social class, social environment, social consensus, status, prestige, privilege, conflict, integration, social function, and so on have often migrated from sociology into everyday life and popular discourse.

Like the other social sciences, sociology has the potential to yield an image of a better world for all but also a potential for assisting in continuing oppression. It is the potential for social improvement that we want to support and reawaken with this book. This book is not a treatise on all one needs to know about the societal-liberation potential of sociology. Instead, it includes many sociological ideas and much data organized in such a way as to render its readers mindful of the moral and political dimensions of the craft and vocation of sociology. An awareness of these dimensions is the indispensable precondition for a critical understanding of social science and for contributing by means of that social science to the betterment of society.

We wrote this book with sociology and other social science teachers and students in mind. Indeed, we provide throughout the book, and especially in the epilogue, some specific advice and suggestions for such teachers and students. Still, we believe this book to be useful for all those who want to learn how to understand the social dilemmas and future potential of the planet we live on—and for all those who would like to play a part in improving and saving the human species. Science and technology have moved at a blinding speed in the past century, but scientific knowledge and techniques will be only as liberating as our ability to put them to use for the common good. Otherwise, they will be used to construct more sophisticated systems of human oppression that will likely benefit a few, while degrading the overall human condition.

We also wrote this book to assure young sociologists and other social scientists that a social science that openly acknowledges its moral concerns, its own biases and limitations, and its hopes and fears for the future is not only possible and worthwhile but also essential for the country's and planet's survival. The pressures placed on graduate students and new faculty members to do conventional teaching, to conduct mainstream instrumental-positivistic research, or to obtain extramural funding for its own sake can make it appear that sociology can no longer be practiced without giving up humanistic goals and intellectual independence.

Indeed, some graduate students at major universities have recently noted that some of their professors no longer see room for idealism and activism in contemporary sociology. We have a rather different view. The examples in the pages that follow will clearly dispel the impression that such idealism and activism no longer have a place in sociology. Just to mention one expression of such new activism, we can note Sociologists Without Borders (Sociólogos Sin Fronteras), organized in Spain in 2001 and the next year in the United States. This is a transnational organization of sociologists, faculty, and students with these stated goals from its website (www.sociologistswithoutborders.org): "That all people have equal rights to political freedoms and legal protections, to socioeconomic security, to self-determination, and to their personality. That is, old or young, regardless of where they live, their faith, and whether they are male or female, gay or straight, and regardless of their skin color they have the same universal rights, including their rights to their own particular cultures. . . . SSF is thus perfectly in synch with public sociology that advocates that sociologists be engaged and committed, and also reflective and critical. Besides SSF-US, there are chapters in Brazil, Chile, Iran, Canada, and Spain." This statement was prepared by its current U.S. president, sociologist Judith Blau. The organization has a new journal, *Societies Without Borders,* and made a significant impact in 2003 by putting a resolution against the Iraq invasion on the annual American Sociological Association ballot. With members in fifty countries, the organization has partnered with international human rights groups at the World Social Forum and the U.S. Social Forum. As we move into a new millennium, grassroots organizations across the globe are undertaking field research projects designed for community betterment, projects for which sociological and other social science knowledge and research are indispensable. In numerous countries, nongovernmental organizations are mushrooming to assist community groups in struggles for better lives for their peoples, and these organizations frequently use the talents of sociologists. Many sociologists wishing to pursue broad human rights ideals and activism will need to educate or reeducate themselves in the innovative methods, ideas, and practices that will enable them to contribute to the goals of these community and grassroots organizations. Although the ability to cross-tabulate data from old survey data sets may seldom be useful to people seeking more just communities and societies, there are many other sociological research strategies that can be quite useful. The latter can assist in the understanding of the social worlds that local people need in their struggles to transform and improve their lives. It is for those seeking a career in a change-oriented sociology, for those seeking a fulfilling life working as social scientists on behalf of human betterment, that we have written this book.

As numerous physical and social scientists are currently demonstrating (see especially Chapters 6 and 8), the human species may be running out of time. The evidence now suggests that within the next century major environmental crises, such as global warming and ozone depletion, and the trend of increasing global income and wealth inequality along racial and class lines, will likely threaten a significant destruction of human societies across the planet.

Today we need a new generation of visionary social researchers and activists who can think clearly and deeply about building a better human society now and in the near future. Frederick Polak, a pioneer in social-future studies, strongly urged social scientists, political leaders, and ordinary citizens to ask what our vision of the human future is. Although sociological research and ideas can help us understand our societal dreams and decide which to accept or reject, such analysis is beneficial only if it allows us to choose a better social future. Let us conclude by closely paraphrasing Polak's final words: *We human beings have the ability to dream better futures than we have yet succeeded in dreaming. We have the ability to create a much better society than we have yet succeeded in creating.*[2]

ACKNOWLEDGMENTS

We are greatly indebted to many supportive social science colleagues. Although we cannot name them all, we would particularly like to thank Diana Kendall, Anne Rawls, Sidney Willhelm, Jennifer Mueller, Claire Renzetti, Ken Bolton, Nestor Rodriguez, Stan Bailey, T. R. Young, Gideon Sjoberg, Nijole Benokraitis, Noel Cazenave, Carl Jensen, Phil Nyden, Walda Katz-Fishman, Jerome W. Scott, Mary Jo Deegan, Barbara Finlay, Michael Hill, Kendal Broad, Paul Johnston, Maxine Baca Zinn, Bob Newby, Tony Orum, Leslie Houts Picca, David McBride, Bernice M. Barnett, and Frank Lindenfeld for their help, comments, and suggestions on earlier drafts of this manuscript. Alfonso Arrau, Raúl Urzúa, Daniel Chernilo, and Juan Enrique Opazo provided insightful feedback on some of our ideas. We are especially indebted to our Paradigm editor, Dean Birkenkamp, for his enthusiastic support for this project.

CHAPTER I

What Is
Liberation Sociology?

INTRODUCTION: CRITICAL APPROACHES TO SOCIETY

In the spring of 1845 one of the founders of the liberation social science tradition, the young Karl Marx, wrote that "the philosophers have only *interpreted* the world, in various ways; the point, however, is to *change* it."[1] Sociologists centrally concerned about human emancipation and liberation take this insight seriously. The point of liberation sociology is not just to research the social world but to change it in the direction of expanded human rights, participatory democracy, and social justice.

Liberation sociology is concerned with alleviating or eliminating various social oppressions and with creating societies that are more just and egalitarian. Liberation from *what* is linked to liberation for *what*. An emancipatory sociology not only seeks sound scientific knowledge but often takes sides with, and takes the outlook of, the oppressed and envisions an end to that oppression. It adopts what Gideon Sjoberg and his associates have called a *countersystem* approach. A countersystem analyst consciously tries to step outside her or his own society in order to better view and critically assess it. A countersystem perspective often envisions a society where people have empathetic compassion for human suffering and a commitment to reducing that suffering. It envisions research and analysis relevant to everyday human problems, particularly those of the socially oppressed. The countersystem standard is broader than that of an existing society or nation-state. Using a broader human rights standard, such as the UN Universal Declaration of Human Rights, the liberation sociologist accents broader societal and international contexts and assesses existing social institutions against a vision of more humane social arrangements.[2]

The consequences of taking this standpoint are explored throughout this book. We are unabashedly eclectic in our approach and are influenced by Enlightenment, modernist, and postmodernist theorists. Neo-Marxist, feminist, and antiracist conceptions have had their impact on our thinking. Moreover, the liberation theology of Latin America and Africa and recent developments in the way we think about the mind and the body—no longer a viable dichotomy—have also been influential (see Chapter 2).

We do not propose here another abstract or doctrinaire approach but rather an emancipatory way to practice good sociology. Taking sides with, and understanding the outlook of, the socially oppressed can have profound consequences for the stages of social research: on how we know what we know, on what we choose to research, on the nature of our scientific endeavor, on the methods we choose, and on the conclusions we can draw from research.

A sociologist's, or a social research team's, choice of what to study is a consciously goal-oriented decision. This always *subjective* choice is not made in social isolation but according to personal and collective tastes and convictions, and often in response to enticements such as grant monies, career prestige, or job security. Thus, many sociologists choose to deeply research U.S. society with an eye to changing it for the better, whereas others choose to narrowly research certain social topics whose description or analysis is mainly sought by leading agents of the status quo. Some social scientists choose to go into the field and examine critically the impact of powerful nation states or large corporations on people's everyday lives and provide that information critically to proponents of change, whereas other researchers limit their research to less critical descriptions of the views or attitudes of the general population for an establishment funding agency. Some choose to dig deeply into a society's foundations, including its systems of social control and information distribution, whereas others choose to do surface-level research that helps those who head existing institutions to perform their roles more successfully. A concern for greatly expanding human rights frequently guides the research of liberation-oriented social scientists who seek major social improvements, whereas many other social scientists choose to mainly ignore the oppressive values and discriminatory practices of the status quo.

Some social science research emphasizes its policy relevance for those at the helm of the nation state or large corporations. The research of liberation sociology, in contrast, is generally defined by its usefulness to those who are oppressed and struggling for their liberation.

Commitments to alleviating human suffering—or to peace, human rights, social justice, and real democracy—politicize the practice of sociology no more than the commitments that assert indifference, value-free methods, or neutral knowledge.

One of the exciting developments since the 1960s has been the emergence of an array of critical social theories in the humanities and social sciences. These include, among others, feminist theory, postmodern theory, queer theory, antiracist theory, and a variety of Marxist theories, including the critical theory of Germany's Frankfurt School. Since the 1960s the social sciences in Europe and the United States have become more accepting of Marxist thought, as well as of the other critical approaches. Numerous sociologists have joined progressive organizations such as the Sociology Liberation Movement. Since the 1960s, critical social theory and research have frequently been published in new books and new social science journals.[3] As sociologist Berch Berberoglu has noted, "This new generation of critical scholars—envisioning a society without exploitation, oppression, and domination of one class, race, sex, or state by another—helped provide the tools for analysis for the critical study of social issues and social problems that confront contemporary capitalist society."[4]

A common theme in critical social theories is the centrality of social oppression and domination. In their research and analysis, most critical social analysts press for the liberation of human beings from oppressive and alienating social conditions. Most research the larger institutional contexts and macrostructures of oppression, domination, and exploitation and yet also view such structures as crashing into the everyday lives of human beings. The daily *experiences* of oppressed and subjugated peoples are a central focus and concern.

As a rule, critical social theorists do not focus only on the negative realities and consequences of oppression but often target issues and strategies of human liberation from that oppression (see Chapter 7). These theoretical frameworks generally see resistance to oppression and domination as beginning "at home, in people's everyday lives— sexuality, family roles, workplace."[5] These critical social thinkers support the action of human beings in their own liberation.

EMPOWERING PEOPLE

One Effort at Liberation Sociology: Project Censored

Let us briefly examine an example of sociological effort toward societal liberation—a project that has had a significant impact. This research effort is called Project Censored. Carl Jensen, a sociologist at Sonoma State University, launched this national research effort in the 1970s to explore whether there was systematic omission of important and newsworthy events and issues in the mainstream media.

In discussions with us, Jensen has noted that his quest was stimulated in part by bewilderment over the reelection of Richard Nixon by a landslide only five months after the news of the Watergate break-in, one of the most sensational political crimes in U.S. history—in which Nixon's campaign organization was then known to be involved.[6] Jensen's knowledge of the mainstream press was useful in explanation: "While there was substantial information available tying the administration in with the Watergate burglary, the media did not put the issue on the national agenda until after the presidential election in November 1972."[7] Therefore, the American people who went to the polls in that fateful November were generally "uninformed about the true significance of Watergate." In effect, the mass media fostered the reelection of a criminal politician, Richard Nixon.

Jensen's bewilderment is an attitude toward events that has propelled the research of many generations of scientists. Galileo, Isaac Newton, Alfred Einstein, Karl Marx, W.E.B. Du Bois, Charlotte Perkins Gilman, and many others also refused to accept what was happening before their eyes as unproblematic, routine, or natural. They asked, "Why?" "How?" and "Under what conditions?" As in other countersystem sociology projects, this attitude was coupled with a desire to change the world, to make a difference. Jensen imagined a world with more democracy, and one with a freer flow of information. He also thought about the way that sociological research could bring it about.

An attitude of curiosity and concern about what happens in the world is not easy to translate into actual research. Many other people may be looking at the same happenings and seeing something ordinary, something not worth significant research effort. Jensen had come to understand an important issue but quickly learned as well that "no one else seemed to share that knowledge."[8] He queried many sociology departments at California universities, seeking advice and counsel, yet received no response. Alfred McClung Lee, a past president of the American Sociological Association, whose work we will examine later, was one of the few who initially encouraged this innovative mass media project.

Interestingly, Jensen's main support and encouragement came from the lower-middle-class and working-class students who took his annual seminar on mass media censorship issues. In 1976 this seminar began to conduct the research he had in mind, and Project Censored was born. For Jensen this project became "a personal crusade" that eventually led him to cut his teaching activities in half in the mid-1980s, with a consequent cut in pay. Sociology departments around the country seldom have resources or the inclination to finance internal research projects, particularly those with such a progressive intent. Jensen's wife, Sandra, became a full-time partner in his research enterprise. It was not until 1989 that Jensen got a grant from the CS Fund, one of few foundations that support innovative boat-rocking research projects. This major breakthrough allowed Jensen to hire a part-time research assistant and permitted the project to better produce and disseminate its research results. Slowly, an international reputation developed, and other grants followed. In the twenty-first century, Project Censored continues to have an impact on domestic and global public access to mass media information. After Jensen retired from the project in 1996, Peter Phillips, another sociologist, was brought in to shepherd the operations of Project Censored.

According to Project Censored's mission statement, its main objective is "the advocacy for and protection of First Amendment free press in the United States. Through a faculty, student, community partnership, Project Censored serves as a national press/media ombudsman by identifying important national news stories that are underreported, ignored, misrepresented, or censored by media corporations anywhere in the United States. We also encourage and support journalists, faculty, and student investigations into First Amendment issues through our annual censorship yearbook and nationwide free press advocacy."

To identify the underreported or ignored news stories, Project Censored relies on numerous researchers, especially college students participating in the annual Project Censored seminar at Sonoma State University. These students analyze the many nominations received from journalists, educators, librarians, researchers, and the general public. The students carefully examine the nominations and after a discussion decide which stories can be considered censored in the mainstream media. This is a process of classification of and comparison with the stories that made the mainstream media. The research offers students an opportunity to learn by participating in field research.

Every year, Project Censored publishes a list of the twenty-five most censored news stories. Final selections are made by a panel of distinguished journalists, educators, and authors, who volunteer their efforts. By ranking ignored or censored news stories and disseminating the details about the stories, Project Censored de-censors them and better informs the public. For example, in 1995 the media ignored a story about sixty-eight elderly men and women who were dumped in a mass grave in Chicago. Most of these were poor elderly people who died alone and unknown during that year's heat wave. For Jensen, "the traditional hallmark of a responsible press is that it should afflict the comfortable and comfort the afflicted; it would seem that today's press has turned that measure on its head."[9]

Over the years, Project Censored's Top 25 list has called the attention of the public to the suppression of very important stories. In 2007, for example, the leading story among the most-censored stories was the debate on the future of the Internet. Supreme Court decisions and proposed congressional legislation, which the mainstream media largely ignored, would, according to the Project, result in the reality that "No longer will everyone enjoy an equal voice in the freest and most comprehensive democratic forum ever devised by humankind."[10] At issue is a struggle between cable companies on the one side, and consumers and Internet service providers (ISPs) on the other. The latter are in favor of "net neutrality" and claim that in the absence of evenhanded government regulation the powerful cable companies will regulate their lines against the public interest. ISPs will have to pay for the right to use the cable lines, thereby making Internet access more expensive and unequal in access for ordinary consumers. Cable companies might also decide, as they have in the past, to control Internet content. Cable companies claim that allowing ISPs free access to cable lines denies cable companies significant profits on their investments. They also claim that not allowing cable owners to charge would discourage innovation and new investments.

On June 27, 2005, the United States Supreme Court ruled that cable companies like Comcast and Verizon were not required to share their lines with rival ISPs in the way telephone companies have to do for phone lines. Cable modem service, according to the FCC, is a one-way information service in contrast to phone lines that carry two-way communications. Telephone companies claim that such a decision gives an unfair advantage to cable companies and are requesting to be released from their common carrier requirement as well.

Internet neutrality advocates say that the passage of certain legislation being considered in Congress would forever compromise the Internet. Giant cable companies would attain a monopoly on high-speed cable Internet access. This would likely prevent moderate-income citizens from broadband access, while monitoring and controlling the content of much information that can be accessed. The aforementioned Court decision marks the beginning of the end for a robust, more democratic Internet. Yet there has been a virtual media blackout in covering this very important story. As a result of this Supreme Court decision, the legal stage has been set for further corporate control of the Internet.

In 2007 also among the most-censored stories (in fourteenth place) was how Homeland Security has contracted with a major company (KBR) to build U.S. detention camps (a contract for $385 million). As reported on the web site of Halliburton (KBR's parent company), "The contract, which is effective immediately, provides for establishing temporary detention and processing capabilities to augment existing Immigration and Customs Enforcement (ICE) Detention and Removal Operations (DRO) Program facilities in the event of an emergency influx of immigrants into the U.S., or to support the rapid development of new programs. The contingency support contract provides for planning and, if required, initiation of specific engineering, construction and logistics support tasks to establish, operate and maintain one or more expansion facilities."[11]

What little coverage the announcement received focused on concerns about Halliburton's reputation for overcharging U.S. taxpayers for substandard services. The crucial phrase "rapid development of new programs" received little attention. It is anyone's guess what "new programs" might require rapid expansion of detention centers capable of holding 5,000 people each.[12] Project Censored notes that among the few independent journalists who have explored what the Bush administration might actually have in mind, Peter Dale Scott has speculated that the "detention centers could be used to detain American citizens if the Bush administration were to declare martial law." Scott recalls that during the Reagan administration, National Security Council aide Oliver North organized the Rex-84 "readiness exercise," which contemplated the Federal Emergency Management Agency rounding up and detaining 400,000 "refugees" in the event of "uncontrolled population movements" over the Mexican border into the United States. North's exercise reportedly contemplated suspension of the U.S. Constitution. At the Iran-Contra Hearings into North's and others' secret actions, concerns that the ideas for expanded internment and detention facilities would not be confined to "refugees" were publicly articulated. Independent journalists have observed that after September 11 the Bush administration implemented a number of interrelated programs that were planned in the 1980s under President Reagan. Among these was the so-called Continuity of Government (COG) proposal—a classified plan for keeping a secret "government-within-the-government" running during and after an event like a nuclear disaster. Apparently, the White House would determine what constitutes such a situation.[13]

Project Censored has publicized statistical figures little known to the public, but which constitute vital information for those who vote on political candidates and programs. For example, the United States, contrary to the rhetorical emphasis on equality, has become the most unequal of all industrialized nations—with the wealthiest 1 percent of households holding least 40 percent of the country's wealth. [14] The growing inequality in the country is a story not centrally covered by mainstream media corporations, which are usually controlled by white executives in the 0.1 percent at the top of the country's economic pyramid.

Walter Cronkite, the famous journalist who wrote the introduction for a 1996 Project Censored yearbook, noted that ideological diversity "is the strength of the free press, and since the nation's founding it has been so perceived by those who love democracy." [15] Project Censored counters to an extent what Cronkite calls "the awesome power" of mainstream media executives deciding what news is worth exposing. Cronkite explains that the news stories that reach major television journalists like him "have been culled and re-culled by persons far outside our control." People at local newspapers or at the wire services, such as the Associated Press, decide which news items are passed to television network news centers in the big cities, where producers and anchor people then decide what actually goes on the air. Colorful or violent stories tend to get the most attention. As some journalists say, "if it bleeds, it leads." Often this decision "involves which items can be illustrated—which we freely acknowledge gives the item far greater impact than the paragraph recited by the broadcaster." The result is that a small elite of professional journalists make the "significant judgments on the news of the day, and it is a lot of power for a few men." [16]

Those sociologists and others guiding Project Censored make it clear that they are not just concerned with overly zealous governmental officials who intentionally censor news, as when U.S. military officials have severely limited press access to the theaters of war. This is but one type of censorship. There are other forms, including business-oriented actions that are in effect self-censoring. Peter Phillips, director of Project Censored, has explained that "media owners and managers are motivated to please advertisers and upper-middle-class readers. Journalists and editors are not immune from management influence. Journalists want to see their stories approved for print or broadcast, and editors come to know the limits of their freedom to diverge from the bottom-line view of owners and managers." [17]

In addition to identifying bypassed news stories, Project Censored keeps an eye on developing trends. One trend is the continuing concentration of media ownership. A democracy cannot survive without a free flow of information. The managing editor of the *New York Times* once confided as much: "Year after year, newspapers have become concentrated into fewer and fewer organizations. Those organizations have become more and more centralized, less and less concerned about the flow of information to the public and more occupied with the flow of profits to the central corporation."[18] In the first decade of the 2000s fewer than two hundred top executives and directors on boards of the largest and most-influential media corporations have become the media elite of the world, yet they would fit in a medium-sized college classroom. Although these executives and directors may not agree on all major issues, "they do represent the collective vested interests of a significant proportion of corporate America and share a common commitment to free market capitalism, economic growth, internationally protected copyrights, and a government dedicated to protecting their interests."[19] With still increasing concentration, only a narrow corporate-sanctioned version of the major news will likely be presented. Moreover, as this concentration and censorship are placed in the hands of executives and directors at ever fewer multinational corporations, we will see ever more global media control and a narrowing of the news available to the majority of people on the planet. The consequences of this information control deserve much more social science study.

The sociologists and others working on Project Censored show us how the sociological imagination can be applied for the common good. Without a strong commitment to participatory democracy and a vision of the importance of an educated citizenry, the research conducted in this project would not have been possible. Carl Jensen and his social science colleagues have thus been engaged in a type of liberation sociology, with a critical and countersystem approach to research and analysis.

Sociology and Societal Betterment

The sociology of liberation is part of a long tradition that aims at both studying and rebuilding society. Auguste Comte, the French physicist and philosopher who coined the word "sociology" in the nineteenth century, viewed the new science as laying bare the reality of society and thereby helping to transform it (see Chapter 2). However, Comte was not a progressive philosopher of social science. The new directions for societal change that he envisioned were rather protective of the status quo. In a draft of his book on the civil war in France, Karl Marx noted that Comte "was known to the Paris workers as the prophet of personal dictatorship in politics, capitalist rule in political economy, hierarchy in all spheres of human activity, even in science, the creator of a new catechism, a new Pope, and new saints to replace old ones."[20] Interestingly, Comte gave private lectures on his "positive philosophy" (later called "positivism"), but was never given an academic position in a French university.

In the 1930s, in one of the first probing analyses of the meaning of what sociologists were doing, Robert Lynd proposed that the knowledge produced by a *critical* sociology is required so that democracy can "continue to be the active guiding principle of our culture."[21] In his major book *Knowledge for What?*, which began as a set of lectures at Princeton University, Lynd argued that sociology should focus on practical problems in need of societal reform. Operating with an interdisciplinary focus that questioned the building of self-perpetuating academic traditions, Lynd called for research oriented toward truly democratic principles.

In this book we call for the practice of more emancipatory and liberation sociology, but we do not seek an end to all conventional sociological research linked to funding by the nation-state or by mainstream foundations. In the present moment, these latter research efforts often do generate some valuable knowledge about the structure and reality of U.S. society, such as in sociological research projects dealing with the corporate abandonment of central cities.[22] Nevertheless, many traditional social science research projects directly or indirectly reinforce the oppressive structures of society, if only by not challenging those social structures with strong alternatives going beyond the limits of present-day elite-controlled U.S. politics. We also call here for greater democratic access to all social science knowledge. Social scientific knowledge is regarded by some in our day as a commodity that confers the power to control nature, to shape other human beings, and to improve ourselves. Knowledge is power, and some, like Michel Foucault, use one word, power/knowledge, to describe the two aspects of the same phenomenon.[23]

We call for the reassertion of a sociological practice designed to *empower* ordinary people through social science research and knowledge. By having better access to critical sociological knowledge, people will be in a better position to understand their personal and familial troubles, make better sense of the world we live in, plan their individual and collective lives, and relate in egalitarian and democratic fashions to others within and outside their own nation state. This includes being in a better position to struggle for individual and collective human rights. A broad-based democracy can be fully developed in our era only if key types of knowledge are made available to all, not just to those at the top of the socioeconomic pyramid and their professional servants.

We envision here much more egalitarian access to relevant scientific knowledge. Too much social science today is top-down research that neglects the experiences, realities, and concerns of those who are socially marginalized and oppressed. We believe that a renewed social science commitment to human liberation and social justice—a shift to the "for whom" and "for what" relevance of social science research and writings—can significantly reshape the scientific practice and product that sociology and other social scientific disciplines regularly generate.

As we have seen in the case of Project Censored, a major aim of a countersystem research project is to raise both the researchers' and the people's consciousness of the oppressive structures of the society in which we live. A related goal is to stop, or at least to reduce significantly, that human oppression and suffering. As we will make clear in subsequent chapters, liberation sociology follows in the paths of early sociologists like Jane Addams and W.E.B. Du Bois, who connected their sociological ideas to social activism, and of later sociologists like C. Wright Mills, who proposed that a sociological imagination allows people "to grasp what is going on in the world and to understand what is happening in themselves as minute points of the intersections of biography and history within society."[24]

OPPRESSION: A CENTRAL SOCIOLOGICAL PROBLEM

Questioning Social Hierarchy

The questioning and researching of the hierarchies of class, gender, and racial power are major elements in a sociology of liberation and emancipation. Liberation sociology is concerned with the oppression of various groups in society, including those who are poor or are discriminated against because of their physical appearance, their alternative lifestyles, or their sexual orientations. Everyday life involves social interaction, with most people coming into contact with others every day. Our relationships are shaped by societal structures and forces, including racism, patriarchy, heterosexism, class exploitation, and other processes of domination. Such social forces are expressed in both informal networks and bureaucratic organizations. Sociologists have long observed what the effects of these and other social forces are on people enmeshed in them—much in the way physicists infer the existence of the forces of gravity and electromagnetism.

Since early in the history of the discipline, many progressive sociologists have questioned the major inequalities in the distribution of socioeconomic resources in the societies where they have lived, as well as across the world. However, at least since the 1920s, mainstream sociology has too often avoided or tiptoed around major issues of elite power and coercion, especially in regard to class, racial, and gender exploitation and oppression. In recent decades, when mainstream sociologists have treated power, they have often preferred to research legitimate power (sometimes called "authority") rather than illegitimate power. In addition, they have substantially ignored the ruling class at the helm of society. For example, most social scientists who have researched social class and social mobility in U.S. society have limited themselves to social classes below the level of the ruling class, the top elite. This can be seen in classical studies of social mobility such as *Opportunity and Change* by David Featherman and Robert Hauser.[25] Clearly, the social sciences sometimes play a very traditional role in society. A glaring example is the once widely discussed book *The Bell Curve,* by social scientists Richard Herrnstein and Charles Murray. This book, which had a half million copies in its first printing, explicitly argues against the ideal of social equality considered to have been conceived in the U.S. Declaration of Independence. By its defense of the meaningfulness of so-called intelligence test differentials between white and black (and Latino) students for U.S. government educational policy, this social science book further attempts to legitimize racial oppression in the United States.[26] As Alvin Gouldner once noted, social science has a "dialectical character and contains both repressive and liberative dimensions."[27]

In the United States, deeply critical analyses of power and hierarchy are resisted by most captains of industry, politicians, and mainstream intellectuals and by much of the general (especially white) public. The country's traditionally white and male leadership resists such probing analyses because these will likely make more obvious the unfairness of the existing distribution of social positions and material and symbolic rewards. Since most leaders and much of the public do not ask for such critical analyses of power, it is easy for many sociologists to take the position that it is not their responsibility to research or correct the large-scale power and resource inequalities. In contrast, the sociology of liberation embraces concerns about social inequality and about the illegitimacy of the powers that be, and it takes the additional step of choosing the societal processes and institutional arrangements that produce this deepening inequality as its central problem. In this book we underscore the act of choosing what should be studied because this is a crucial and indispensable decision in much sociological practice. Injustice should be examined not just in its maldistribution of goods and services but also in the deep-lying social relations responsible for making that distribution possible. These social relations, among which oppressive power relations are a key part, are responsible for the way in which important societal goods are distributed. They also determine whether individuals, families, and other groups are integrated into or excluded from society's important decisionmaking processes. And they can also shape the development of human identities and the sense of belonging and dignity. In the end social justice is more than a question of redistribution of power, more than a matter of resolving within existing relations the justice in how goods are distributed. It is a matter of totally restructuring the larger framework of social relations for the greater good.

As we have already noted, important among the major social oppressions are racism, patriarchy, heterosexism, and class exploitation. A leading feminist sociologist, Dorothy E. Smith, has argued that mainstream sociology is linked to the dominant ideological apparatus of U.S. society, which accounts for its historical emphasis on research issues primarily of concern to (white) men. For the most part, mainstream sociology's themes, she notes, are "organized by and articulate the perspectives of men—not as individuals ... but as persons playing determinate parts in the social relations of this form of society."[28] For many decades now, feminist sociologists and others representing traditionally subjugated groups have pressured social scientists to research the social world from the perspectives of the oppressed and to take their experiences seriously as a source of understanding and knowledge (see Chapter 7).

Structures of domination and oppression are not social phenomena to be examined among the other parts and processes of a static "social system," because the term "social system" is laden with the assumption that societal arrangements are more or less harmonious and that change in one element brings about change in other elements and in the general organization of the system (see discussion of Talcott Parsons in Chapter 3). Although some relations in society exhibit an equilibrating or harmonious character, many relations do not show any such character. Expropriation, exploitation, domination, and oppression are processes that produce and reproduce the way Western societies like the United States are arranged. To characterize a social arrangement as a social system without explaining how it was initially created and how it is now being reproduced takes for granted as immutable and beyond our reach what we need to actively observe and change.

Many sociologists—particularly those who have the best-paying, most-stable jobs—have been white men, and if they wish they can live so that they are relatively isolated from the more severe consequences of much social oppression in society. C. Wright Mills once cogently noted that "most social scientists have had little or no sustained contacts with such sections of the community as have been insurgent; there is no left-wing press with which the average academic practitioner in the course of his career could come into mutually educative relations."

Such isolation has had significant impacts on both the social sciences and on society.[29]

What Is Social Oppression?

In a probing analysis, political scientist Iris Young has suggested that oppression and domination are disabling constraints that affect the "institutional conditions necessary for the development and exercise of individual capacities and collective communication and cooperation." Domination involves "institutional conditions which inhibit or prevent people from participating in determining their actions or the conditions of their actions."[30] Loving parents, for example, who make a practice of routinely making important decisions without consulting their children when they are old enough to make their own choices, disable them through their everyday domination. In like fashion, various benevolent dictators have disabled and disempowered the people whose good they have claimed to seek.

Oppression consists of "systematic institutional processes which prevent some people from learning and using satisfying and expansive skills in socially recognized settings or institutionalized social processes which inhibit people's ability to ... communicate with others or to express their feelings and perspective on social life in contexts where others can listen."[31] The persecution and killing of Jews and Gypsies in Nazi Europe, the exploitation of farm laborers in the United States, the pillage of aboriginal people's lands in the name of progress, the enslavement of Africans in the Americas, and the sweatshops still found in U.S. and other Western cities are examples of this oppression. Those who must work for less pay on account of their class, racial, ethnic, sexual orientation, or gender status are thereby socially oppressed. Although oppression often includes material deprivation, the issues involved go beyond an unequal distribution of goods and resources. Oppression eliminates or reduces human dignity and the capacity to express oneself and participate in the larger society as effectively as those who are more privileged.

The oppression of women has been a central issue of the current era. For example, in her famous 1960s book *The Feminine Mystique*, Betty Friedan wrote of the troubled North American housewife, especially the white suburban housewife, as being in a state of recurring personal distress. Though most such women lived in enviable circumstances by international standards, they often felt cheated and suffered from numerous gendered afflictions that came to be known as "housewives' fatigue." Friedan did not write her book merely to engage the reader's sympathy but to show that these women were being prevented from self-realization through gendered oppression and cultural conspiracy; this "feminine mystique" led women to believe that their happiness lay only in the kitchen and nursery.[32] Friedan's analyses were part of the new feminist resurgence of the 1960s. In the years that followed, Friedan's analysis was criticized for neglecting the central concerns of working-class women and women of color, especially those who had long worked outside the home. Eventually, the concerns of many women became part of a complex women's liberation movement. The concept of social oppression, as it has been used in social movements since the 1960s, generally designates inhibitions people suffer "in their ability to develop and exercise their capacities and express their needs, thoughts, and feelings."[33]

Here we underscore the institutional and embedded character of contemporary societal oppression. In one sense, the term "oppression" covers the tyranny that a despot or ruling group exercises over others.[34] For example, in twentieth-century Europe numerous fascist and communist regimes oppressed their peoples in political terms. Yet there are other forms of contemporary oppression that do not involve this overt tyranny by force but rather are embedded, structural, well-institutionalized, and more or less hidden—in social norms and beliefs extending over long periods of time. Another term for this is "hegemony," or domination with "a velvet glove."[35] In today's forms of societal oppression, many individuals that contribute to maintaining and reproducing the various oppressions see themselves as merely doing their jobs and living out normal lives. If asked, they would strongly reject the view that they could be agents of oppression. Our emphasis on broad social processes and long-term institutions allows us to understand the apparent paradoxes of the oppressed sometimes contributing to their own victimization, and even turning into oppressors of others.

In the United States and other countries around the world, there are privileged groups and oppressed groups that differ in the goods, resources, and opportunities these countries make available to their members and in the degree to which they participate in societal decisionmaking that greatly affects daily lives. These differences are hard to deny, even though some might choose not to see their continuing reality and group nature. Indeed, as W.E.B. Du Bois noted, some groups are privileged because others are oppressed. For example, for long decades in the nineteenth and twentieth centuries the extreme poverty and degradation in the African colonies of European nations was "a main cause of wealth and luxury in Europe. The results of this poverty were disease, ignorance, and crime. Yet these had to be represented as natural characteristics of backward peoples."[36] Centuries of colonial exploitation of African labor and land have long been omitted from numerous historical reviews of European prosperity and development. A similar situation exists for the prosperity of generations of white Americans, whose prosperity is very deeply rooted in four centuries of exploitation of the labor and land of African Americans, Native Americans, and other people of color in North American history. A similar argument could be made for the privileges of men in regard to the conditions of women. This historical background of the United States is too often ignored or downplayed in contemporary accounts of racial discrimination and other oppression, especially in the mass media.

The heterogeneous society that is the United States is clearly differentiated in terms of oppressed and privileged peoples. Thus, we wish to gain some distance from arguments built upon the assumption of a homogeneous "American public," as found in much Western sociology of culture. Too often the term "Americans" in the media and in scholarly writings means "white Americans," and little thought is given by the commentators to the fact that a large proportion of the population may not share the view or behavior attributed to those "Americans."[37] Political and academic viewpoints that attempt to pass themselves off as neutral, or that claim a national consensus, are more often than not the viewpoints of the privileged.

The particular meanings attached to social differences—which make them seem natural, traditional, or necessary—are deeply embedded in our stock of tacit understandings and knowledge. As a result, we come to think nothing of them and often consider them as features of the social contexts that should go without questioning. A sociology of liberation often questions and uncovers the hidden aspects of these concrete, historically given social arrangements so that they can be better understood—and perhaps acted upon so that their oppression is undercut.

HUMANIZATION AND CRITICAL CONSCIOUSNESS

Increasing Humanization

One conceptual starting point for our endeavor is the human vocation, the calling to be fully human. Seldom stated in conventional social science, the initial assumptions of the researcher need to be made explicit, for they shape research much more than just in its methodological principles. The statement of underlying domain assumptions is an important means for preserving the integrity of research, a topic we will examine in detail later.[38]

Brazilian educator, Paulo Freire, once wrote that while human beings have the potential for humanization and dehumanization, their true vocation is only humanization. Injustice, exploitation, the violence of oppressors—and their denial and dissimulation in euphemisms and ideologies—generate and undergird dehumanization. Our humanity is affirmed in struggles to achieve freedom and social justice. Dehumanization marks and defines the oppressor as much as it torments the oppressed. For Freire, the struggle to recover humanity is a struggle of the oppressed "to liberate themselves and their oppressors as well."[39] Oppressors who exploit and exclude by virtue of their power ordinarily cannot find the strength to liberate anyone. At best, they may soften their grip and may become gentler in exercise of power. And the unjust social order, which makes generosity difficult, usually remains in place and continues to nourish "death, despair, and poverty." Liberation sociology struggles to understand society well and then to disrupt the realities of oppression, the taken-for-granted, "natural" order that supports it and makes it possible.

Facing Challenges in Communities

In the United States, sociology originated as a field whose early practitioners and thinkers were substantially committed to research for major social change. Among these were Jane Addams and W.E.B. Du Bois, whose work we examine in Chapters 3 and 4. Addams and Du Bois were what Antonio Gramsci has called "organic intellectuals,"[40] those from (or representing well) the oppressed sectors of society whose lived experience frequently gives them superior understandings to those intellectuals representing the highly advantaged sectors of society. Organic intellectuals work consciously for the liberation of their own oppressed groups, often in local communities. Sociologists like Addams and Du Bois brought into social science, for the first time, the actual experiences, history, and culture of formerly excluded peoples. Not surprisingly, their early research was aimed at improving the lives of the poor, the working class, immigrants, women, and Americans of color. Here sociology was to better the lives of the less powerful Americans, not to advance their careers or create a people-distancing social science discipline.

In later chapters we will see that there is much interesting social science research linking community activists and sociologists in common efforts to understand various types of oppression and to bring about social change. Some of this research is mainly evaluative; it attempts to assess the effectiveness of existing remedial programs. Another approach is broader and tries to collectively spell out community needs and how they might be addressed in new and innovative ways, and then works to help people deal with serious social problems. Such research is usually linked to community-defined goals.

Take the example of an organization called Project South: Institute for the Elimination of Poverty and Genocide, based in Atlanta, Georgia. This organization incorporates sociological research and theory into education and organizing projects. An activist organization headed and shaped by sociologists, it engages in workshops, action-research projects, and popular education projects across the country, but mostly in the South. Workshops are organized by and for community activists and activist scholars and are designed to help them better comprehend problems such as health care and the criminal "injustice" system. Project South's action-research efforts pull together teams of grassroots activists and social scientists to develop materials for popular education and community organizing. For example, one project has gathered oral histories and statistical data to describe socioeconomic conditions in Georgia communities and to discover what impact political campaign funds have had on these areas. To this point in time, low-income neighborhoods in several cities have been part of the project, and in each case the findings have been put into videos and pamphlets to use in workshops and for community organizing. Project South researchers begin the process of community discussion by conducting at least one local workshop to examine the research findings and often work with community leaders. Project South has also developed other projects, such as the Grassroots Popular Education Project, which is a resource-building program for grassroots organizations, and the Leadership Development Initiative, a development program for low-income grassroots leaders in Georgia.[41]

In 2007 the first ever U.S. "Social Forum" took place in Atlanta under Project South auspices. Project South organized this forum over two years of intense efforts. In late June and early July 2007, some 15,000 people, young and old, men and women, participated in nearly 1,000 workshops spread over the city. The forum's major themes included Gulf Coast reconstruction in the post-Katrina era; persisting U.S. imperialism, invasions, militarism, and oppressive prison systems; indigenous people's issues; immigrant rights; liberating people from gender and sexuality discrimination; and workers rights in a global economy.

Significantly, several sociologists have been active in this organization, two of whom we mention briefly here. One is Jerome W. Scott, who has served as the Director of Project South. Growing up in working-class Detroit, Scott "lived the reality of its poverty-stricken neighborhoods."[42] He is thus an organic intellectual whose sociological ideas have been honed by hard experience. After serving in Vietnam, Scott took courses at Lawrence Technical College but soon left for a job in an auto plant. There he participated in the League of Revolutionary Black Workers, a workers' group that pressed unions and management for more racial integration in auto plants. He also became part of groups of workers and scholars studying sociopolitical theory, including that of Karl Marx, W.E.B. Du Bois, and Malcolm X, in the context of building movements for social change. This provided an important part of his broad sociological and political education. As he has noted to us, "From both my lived experience and theory I developed an understanding of society rooted in class analysis and social struggle, as the larger historical and institutional context of white supremacy, male privilege, and U.S. global domination."[43] Subsequently working as a journalist, he traveled to Africa to do field reports. After moving to Atlanta in the 1970s, he began work on social justice issues. Soon he was working with community activists and activist sociologists and helped to found Project South. He also became involved in the American Sociological Association and the Association of Black Sociologists.[44]

An activist sociologist, Scott has coauthored articles and book chapters on U.S. history, globalization and the electronic revolution, race and class issues, and people's movements for social change. He has noted well current challenges facing sociologists: "Today, as globalization in the electronic age sweeps the world, liberation sociology is being transformed; and those of us who are engaged are building bridges to the emerging bottom-up movement for global justice and equality. For me, liberation sociology is an essential part of the larger project of human liberation."[45]

Another sociologist active in Project South is Walda Katz-Fishman, who has served as chair of the board of Project South. In a communication to us, she noted that her activism is rooted in her family background. Growing up in the South, she saw her parents active in the civil rights movement, in civic and Jewish organizations, and in the Democratic Party. At an early age, she became aware of racial, class, and gender inequalities, "but did not have a framework for truly understanding the world, a clear vision, or a strategy for how to change it."[46] After graduation from college, she attended graduate school in sociology at Wayne State

University, where she became educated in a working-class perspective and in Marxist interpretations of society. "From that point on," she reported, "I was always developing my historical materialist world-view and participating in many activist arenas—from scholar activism among professional groups to anticapitalist movements building in multiracial and multiclass organizations, often with women in the leadership."[47]

Moving to Washington, D.C., in 1970, Katz-Fishman took a teaching position at Howard University. She continued developing her liberation sociology ideas and has taught many students about ideas and strategies of societal transformation. Like Scott, she has worked as a scholar and educator who uses her research work on class, race, and gender inequality to help grassroots organizations working for social justice. Katz-Fishman views her sociological education and research work as a crucial background and constant resource for her community activism. As she noted to us, "To me sociology is a key to understanding social history and society—its past, its present, and its future, that is, what it is becoming. It offers me the tools for theoretically understanding the world and for practically transforming the world. But I have done and continue to do this within the collective process of study and movement building."[48]

Listening to the People

At its best, social action research involves a willingness of both community participants and social science researchers to listen carefully and democratically to each other. Historically, some community-based research has involved sociologists who were not seriously interested in listening to community residents. For example, one group of experienced action researchers, sociologists at Loyola University in Chicago, has noted that too often social science researchers have come in, gathered data, and left without giving anything back to the community.[49] In such settings, one problem is getting both social science researchers and local community activists to listen well to each other and to communicate better without jargon.

Although it may be seen by some mainstream social scientists as "too subjective," good collaborative research with community residents can be as carefully done and as meaningful as any other social science research (see Chapter 4). From the community point of view, good social science research provides people with ideas about the depth of their problems and about how local change strategies can be more effective. All social science research is pervaded by the perspectives of the researchers and of those funding or supporting the research. No research is conducted without underlying assumptions or without linkages to the structures of power and inequality in the society. Francis Moore Lappe has noted that "each of us carries within us a worldview, a set of assumptions about how the world works—what some call a paradigm—that forms the very questions we allow ourselves to ask and determines our views of future possibilities."[50]

TEACHING LIBERATION SOCIOLOGY

In the United States and other parts of the world, sociology is an academic discipline, with its teachings being part of the mainstream curriculum in institutions of higher education and sometimes in high schools. Much of what is published and read within the disciplinary boundaries of these institutions is written by academicians. We should pay particular attention to the teaching of sociology because the sociology taught in high schools, colleges, and universities is, or can be, practiced in everyday life—as a way for individuals and small groups to examine the societal conditions in which they live and the social consequences of individual and collective actions.

Teaching the sociology of liberation typically involves a process of creation of awareness, what Paulo Freire has called *conscientization*—a pedagogy of how oppressed people struggling for liberation can actually free themselves. The sociology of liberation is not just a sociology that discusses liberation; it is a sociology that can show or facilitate the way to it. Conscientization refers to "learning to perceive social, political, and economic contradictions, and to take action against the oppressive elements of reality."[51] A famous educator of adults, Freire discovered that his pupils learned how to read and write better when learning language details was associated with acquisition of a critical consciousness. Learning how to read and the process of education in general were thus projects of human liberation.

Freire contrasts radicalization, the aim of his pedagogical method, with political sectarianism. Whereas radicalization nourished by a critical spirit is creative, "sectarianism, fed by fanaticism, is always castrating."[52] Radicalization literally means going to the *root* of things, a process that in Freire's experience involves "ever greater engagement in the effort to transform concrete, objective reality." Political sectarianism of the right or the left, because it is usually "mythicizing and irrational," can create a wrongheaded image of social reality and a sense of futility in changing that reality.[53] This distinction between radicalization and sectarianism is vital to a viable sociology of liberation. As we see it, the goal of liberation sociology is not to replace one dominant mythology with another but to contribute substantially to the freedom of human beings to think critically about society and to liberate themselves from dominant reality-distorting mythologies.

Karl Marx once wrote that he did not seek to anticipate the world for all time to come but to engage in relentless criticism of existing reality. This does not mean hurling distorted and undocumented critiques at the way other people act or think. In our view liberation sociologists should stay deeply connected to empirical reality, with what they can discover about the daily experience of the members of a society, including global society. A full empirical understanding of a society like the United States leads to the knowledge that it and especially its social hierarchies are systematically structured in the *wrong* way for full human self-realization. In the nineteenth century, Marx studied the concrete realities of capitalism and came to the conclusion that the logic of modern capitalistic societies "made injustice, alienation, and exploitation inevitabilities rather than contingencies."[54]

Without this empirical connection to everyday life and its constraints, there is no viable sociology. For liberation sociology, this connection between the empirical reality that sociologists study and sociologists' subjectivity—personal commitments, social biases, and existential coefficients of all sorts—is part of an ongoing dialectical and reflective process. Indeed, subjectivity usually provides the impetus to explore the social world.

Liberation sociology does not seek to establish certainty for all time, as nineteenth-century sociologists sometimes tried to do. Practitioners of liberation sociology study current societal realities so they and others can better transform them. Thus, much new knowledge ("truth") is tied to the transformations that such sociological study and research bring about, to the remedial practices that are paired to what field researchers find in their work. They are not afraid of ordinary people or of participating with others in the search for knowledge. The liberation sociologist is not afraid of becoming an activist-researcher committed to an oppressed people's history or to fight on their side of human history. Liberation sociologists are the antitheses of the liberal intellectuals who believe they are liberators of the oppressed because of their copyright on some progressive ideas. The critical consciousness at the heart of liberation sociology is self-reflective and part of an interactive learning process. Reflective decisions about studying a societal problem and about methods for its analysis are acts of judgment and are made possible only by previous experience listening to and communicating well with other human beings.[55]

WHAT TYPE OF SOCIETY WILL WE HAVE?

Taking Sides with the Oppressed

If sociology is to become a stronger intellectual framework for people struggling for liberation from the structures and mystiques of domination, then sociologists need to decide on the type of sociology they will practice and whose interests they will serve. All sociologists, like all other social scientists, make personal choices as to the problems they are going to devote their energies to, the terms in which they will cast research questions, and the research methods they will utilize. They do not make such choices in a social vacuum but typically as they struggle to provide for themselves and their families, achieve financial security, and earn tenure and other personal career goals.

A decision to practice liberation sociology is a decision to take sides with the oppressed. Liberation sociology is committed to the causes of the oppressed, exploited, and dominated—and thus to the eradication of oppressions and the creation of better societies for all people. Mainstream sociology is often committed, albeit frequently in disguised ways, to vested interests in the established societal hierarchies. The noncommittal attitude of much sociology today—usually formulated as scientific detachment, objectivity, or value freedom—is too often a cover-up for the accommodation the research has made with dominant group interests. Mainstream sociology, like other intellectual endeavors, is part of the political, social, and psychological status quo. To ignore or deny the political, social, and psychological standpoints of our own sociological thinking and discipline is to make sure that the latter will stay rooted in a deeply troubled status quo. An eloquent examination of the social forces at play in the decision to take sides with the oppressed was provided by W.E.B. Du Bois: "The educated and cultured of the world, the well born and well bred, and even the deeply pious and philanthropic" cannot escape the contradiction that they "receive their training and comfort and luxury, the ministrations of delicate beauty and sensibility, on condition that they neither inquire [too closely] into the real source of their income and the methods of distribution nor interfere with the legal props which rest on a pitiful human foundation of writhing white and yellow and brown and black bodies."[56]

In our view all social science researchers should make every effort to do honest and open research work and to minimize as best they can the intrusion of unstated assumptions and inclinations that can distort that research work. We support "objectivity" in this sense, although we also recognize that this task is not necessarily an easy one since the

mainstream accent on "objectivity" is often part of an argument to co-
erce research into a certain mode. Indeed, it is often the countersystem
sociologists who have the greatest ability to be objective and socially
truthful because they critically analyze and demystify established interpretations of oppressive social arrangements. As Sandra Harding
has noted, the democratic values that legitimate critical analysis of
established structures from the viewpoint of the dispossessed "tend
to increase the objectivity of the results of research."[57] As the social
sciences become more diverse in terms of who does social science, the
field embraces a broader array of perspectives and knowledges, and
more critical questions are raised about traditional perspectives and
hidden societal realities. In addition, by regularly bringing in the social
and historical contexts of social science, one can increase its objectivity by reducing its parochialism. Democracy-enhancing practices can
only improve science, whereas democracy-retarding practices—the
traditional practices of much natural and social science—can only
limit and handicap science.

One of sociology's great contributions to modern thought is
that at its best it encourages us to think critically about the socially
patterned nature of the world around us. Early European sociologists like Max Weber and Emile Durkheim researched, and wrote
insightfully about, broad societal forces such as industrialization,
bureaucratization, and urbanization. Yet these are not the only processes that characterize the modern period in Western societies; the
differentiating processes of exploitation, social discrimination, and
oppression also distinguish the period.

These latter realities were perhaps best understood by other early,
though less well-known, sociologists such as Jane Addams, W.E.B.
Du Bois, and Anna Julia Cooper. All of the latter analyzed issues of
discrimination and exploitation in their efforts to understand U.S.
society.[58] Experiencing social oppression firsthand, the white women
and black men and women sociologists saw what most white men
at the time could not; that "social difference is the first consequence
of modern society and, thus, the more reasonable first principle of
sociology."[59] A relevant sociology must be grounded in the studied
realization of the extent to which U.S. society, as well as other societies,
are founded in social differentiation, inequality, and oppression.

Taking an Overt Moral Stance

As we see it, the flight from serious discussion of issues of morality and
ethics in social science must be ended. Beyond a desire for a deeper
understanding of exploitation and oppression, liberation sociology

takes an overt moral stance, which includes identification and empathy with the victims of oppression and a calling for and working toward their liberation from misery and inequality. Sociology can liberate when it applies its humanistic concern and empathetic reasoning to solving the everyday problems afflicting human beings. In this book we openly adopt a broad human rights standard for social research, affirm the value of humanization, and call for maximizing human self-realization and achievement. A start for a broad human rights standard, which has international resonance, is the United Nations' Universal Declaration of Human Rights. This international agreement stipulates in Article 1 that "all human beings are born free and equal in dignity and rights" and in Article 7 that "all are equal before the law and are entitled without any discrimination to equal protection of the law." Article 8 further asserts: "Everyone has the right to an effective remedy ... for acts violating the fundamental rights," and Article 25 states that these rights extend to everyday life: "Everyone has the right to a standard of living adequate for the health and well-being of himself and his family, including food, clothing, hous-ing."[60] From this increasingly influential international human rights perspective, no one can be expected to take care of their family and civic responsibilities without adequate daily sustenance and freedom from intrusive discriminations and oppressions (see Chapter 9). We believe that this commitment to basic and broad human rights and freedoms should be the starting point for much sociological research and analysis. Interestingly, the American Sociological Association has recently added a new research section explicitly on human rights, one in which both social science specialists and interested practitioners can exchange ideas about research and practice.

An important example of an interweaving of sociological analysis and moral concerns is *liberation theology,* a powerful tradition among Catholic activists in numerous postcolonial countries, especially in South and Central America. For some time now, liberation theology has drawn in part on sociological writings, and, in turn, liberation theology has influenced the thinking of sociologists, including our-selves. Stan Bailey, a former priest and sociologist, made this cogent comment on a early draft of this book:

> I am an ex-priest trained in liberation theology in Córdoba, Ar-gentina, where I spent nearly a decade working with oppressed communities. As a priest, what kept me going was the perspective of solidarity with the poor, and doing theology from the bottom up—being a voice for those denied a voice. Now, to hear the same terms being used to indicate a certain type of sociological praxis

is gratifying. ... It never ceases to amaze me the narrowness into which we can fall through our specialized knowledge. We reduce the world to our disciplines with their internal rules and regulations, and their authorities who determine the true path. Don't we realize the futility of our intellectual conclusions for most of the world's population living in subhuman conditions? Our "ivory towers" distort our visions and move us along in the justification of the powerful.[61]

Liberation theology emerged in Latin America in response to the inadequacy of doctrinaire European theology for Catholic priests doing pastoral work among the poor and politically disenfranchised. In 1968 liberation theology came to the world's attention as a result of the second meeting of the Latin American Bishops' Council in Colombia. At that meeting Father Gustavo Gutierrez and others called for new church initiatives to meet the economic and social justice needs of the poor in Latin America. As a result, these Catholic bishops declared that the Catholic Church should have a "preferential option for the poor," the liberation theology phrase for taking sides with the oppressed. The concern with what must be done in pastoral work when one is committed to the poor and disenfranchised is a central trait of liberation theology around the world.

Looking Beneath the Surface

In ancient Roman myth, the giant Cacus lived in a cave and once stole some oxen from Hercules, then dragged them backward into his cave. When Hercules came seeking his cattle, he saw tracks that appeared to indicate that the cattle had gone out of the cave, and he was initially deceived. All too often modern social science analysts are like the puzzled Hercules. They note the shape of the cave and count the number and direction of the footprints, but do not dig deeper into the social realities that their observations often represent.[62] Indeed, several social science commentators have noted that if social life were only what it seemed to be on its surface, there would be no need for social science.

Too much mainstream analysis of U.S. society, economy, and politics reflects a status-quo ideology that denies or hides this society's "distorting contradictions."[63] One of the tragedies of any society is the failure of its people and leaders to understand the real social problems confronting them. For example, today modern capitalism seems to be riding high, with many mainstream analysts, pundits, business leaders, and academics still singing its praises. Indeed, there is a general denial of the very serious social and economic troubles created for millions of Americans, and billions of the other residents of planet earth, by modern capitalism. In Chapter 9 we report on an early 2000s survey of the world's top newspapers. In a database of fifty major national newspapers, we found not one serious article probing in depth the fundamental problems and deep-lying crises of contemporary U.S. capitalism.

The United States appears to be on a path of continuing social conflicts, of accentuated economic and other inequalities, and of environmental degradation shaped by such trends as global warming and the deterioration of air and water. The social contradictions of capitalism are becoming ever more evident to those who attend to the empirical data. Clearly, there is no historical reason to expect the social system of capitalism to last forever. The failures of other societal systems, such as the demise of state communism in Eastern Europe in the 1980s and 1990s, have received far more academic and media attention than the continuing crises of U.S. and global capitalism. Political debates over cutting social programs, over terminating affirmative action, over job losses, and over trends in Social Security and Medicare have been conducted with little reference to the growing income and wealth inequalities underlying capitalistic societies like the United States. Today, many large U.S. corporations are part of a global market system and are directing more of their profit-making activities to low-wage areas overseas, as they close U.S. plants and eliminate many decent-paying jobs. Although many corporations have made very good profits, their economic "advances" have come at great cost to U.S. workers and their families. In the United States the real wages of a majority of ordinary workers are lower today than they were a few decades ago, a situation that has forced many to take on extra jobs or put more family members to work.[64] The so-called free market is celebrated by many mainstream analysts as the solution for social and economic problems overseas at the same time that it is creating recurring economic problems and severe environmental problems for the entire planet.

The increasing inequalities of income and wealth have been rationalized by many politicians, media commentators, and intellectuals—often with attacks on the principles of equality and justice that ostensibly underlie the officially democratic institutions of the United States. Human societies are controlled substantially by elites who take overt and covert actions to shape society in terms of their group interests. Oppressing classes and the bureaucratic organizations they control hide many of their exploitative operations from the public and do not wish for social scientists to do research on the systems of oppression they create or uphold. In analyzing society, liberation sociologists try to dig beneath these overt rationalizations and everyday fictions. Major tasks for critical social scientists are to ascertain the larger social framework around such elite actions, and how the actions arose or developed. Indeed, one liberating aspect of most sociology is its observational curiosity. At its best, sociology provides a useful collection of interpretive concepts and methods, and it relies on actual field observations, interviews, experimentation, and comparison to reach critical conclusions about conditions in society. Sociologists can thereby help liberate societies because they can provide a deeper understanding of their oppressive realities.

Empirical Social Science

Our defense of empirical science here may appear to fly in the face of much postmodernist questioning of science. Early in the history of social science the application of observation and reason through the scientific method was thought to bring societal progress. Scientific reasoning would make us free once we rid ourselves of ancient prejudices, but this promise was never delivered. Thus, a critical questioning of the physical and social sciences is certainly justified. Although reasoning in science can be used to liberate, it has also been used to exploit, to oppress, and even to exterminate.

However, some of the sociological methods used to buttress systems of oppression, as we show later in this book, can also be used to liberate human beings. For example, sociological methods in the hands of many corporate advertisers reduce human awareness and hide the business interest in manipulating human needs and generating unnecessary consumption. An example is the use of focus groups, an old sociological research method, to find out how to manipulate people into buying consumer products they do not need. Social science research clearly can have a repressive potential, as in the marketing research designed to get people to behave against their own interests. The tobacco industry, for example, availed itself of social science research techniques to produce some advertisement campaigns, such as those targeting younger people and those living in low-income neighborhoods in the United States and overseas. Nonetheless, the same sociological methods can be used to help human beings be more conscious of, and better equipped to fight, advertisers and related corporate interests that try to ensnare them.

Many sociologists and other social scientists who go into the field are often dramatically enlightened if not radicalized. Field research has radicalizing potential because it frequently reveals what researchers do not expect, or do not wish, to see. Thus, field sociologists have been among the first to bring to public attention the issues of youth culture, bureaucratic structure, racial discrimination, changing roles for women in society, the problems of individualism, divorce's impact on society, and the regulation of the poor by government agencies in the interests of capitalism. An example of the latter is a book by sociologists Richard Cloward and Frances Fox Piven, the latter a recent president of the American Sociological Association. In their influential book, *Regulating the Poor* (1971), they showed how some government programs for the poor have regularly expanded or contracted in direct relationship to the needs of the employers for low-wage labor.[65] Sociologists have also been at the forefront of those documenting the oppressive conditions faced by Americans of color, including African, Native American, Latino, and Asian Americans. Examples of this are the classical field study of African Americans under legal segregation by Gunnar Myrdal and his sociological associates, *An America Dilemma* (1944), and the more recent field study of Mexican American conditions by sociologists Leo Grebler, Joan Moore, and Ralph Guzman, *The Mexican-American People* (1970).[66] Field sociologists have often given the best pictures of poverty, juvenile delinquency, drug cultures, the homeless, and working-class lives.[67] It is in much of this exciting and often pathbreaking field research that we see the liberation potential of contemporary sociology.

Probing the Underlying Assumptions

Whether it is acknowledged or not, all social research has an underlying perspective and moral stance. Examining critically the problems of powerful nation states and corporations requires a bold and reinvigorated moral position that asserts the rights of all human beings as world citizens. As we noted previously, those researchers who work for or are significantly supported by a nation state are less likely to collect data or develop analyses subversive to that state, including such phenomena as overseas colonialism and imperialism.

Alvin Gouldner noted the ways in which the social sciences have been shaped by their sociocultural environments. Thus, major social theories such as the structural-functionalist theory of Talcott Parsons provide an "anxiety-reducing reorientation" to the world for those who more or less prefer the status quo.[68] Historian Dorothy Ross has suggested that in the United States the various social sciences have often been shaped by a shallow historical perspective, a practical outlook, and a confidence in technical methods. U.S. social scientists have often shared the optimistic views of ordinary citizens that the United States was different from the nations of Europe and could more easily solve the problems of class conflict and poverty.[69] By arguing for an American exceptionalism, U.S. social scientists have too often embraced "a scientism that proceeds in dangerous ignorance of historical differences and societal complexity."[70]

In social science research, various types of bias appear in many places, not the least in the choice of research topic and agenda. Too often those who do conventional social science research become hired hands selling their research skills to those who have the power to command them. In such cases, "objectivity" has too often meant the use of statistical methods that are operationalized so narrowly that the choice of research topic is not considered to be an area of possible bias. Sandra Harding has noted that "many critics of the natural sciences argue that racist and Eurocentric political concerns shaped the questions the sciences have asked and this is why the results of such research have been racist and Eurocentric."[71] Similarly, the choice of research topics in the social sciences is not independent of the values of the researchers. Indeed, the blind eye given by many social scientists to the way that compliance with elite interests impedes the growth of societal knowledge is in itself a major bias in the contemporary social sciences.

Questioning an Instrumental-Positivistic Social Science

As we show in the next chapters, an instrumental-positivistic perspective has come to dominate numerous areas of social science research in the United States and numerous other countries. Clearly, the phrase "positivistic science" has had a number of different meanings since August Comte accented the idea early in the nineteenth century (see Chapter 2). For example, some analysts have used the phrase for any social science approach that seeks to develop empirical data and to develop laws of human social behavior.

However, in this book we define contemporary positivistic social science as having at least these key elements: (1) attempting to delineate enduring laws of social life with little consideration of historical contexts; (2) accenting a conventional quantitative processing of data on social life as the main or only legitimate way to gain knowledge; (3) not researching those aspects of human life that cannot be measured by conventional quantitative methods, such as human imagination and the holistic complexity of phenomena; (4) conceiving of knowledge as something generated by certain instrumental methodologies—and downplaying other types of human knowledge; and (5) accenting a "value-free" (neutral) research and downplaying the underlying assumptions of those doing scientific research, including assumptions that the current political-economic status quo is legitimate.[72]

This contemporary positivistic social science is distinctively North American in its origins. It has been termed by some an "abstracted empiricism" or perhaps more accurately, "instrumental positivism." It is "instrumental" in that it limits social research to only those questions that certain research instruments and techniques will allow, and it is "positivism" in that it commits social scientists to research approaches attempting to mimic those of the natural sciences.[73] One of the early founders of U.S. sociology, Franklin H. Giddings, put the matter succinctly, and in gendered language, in a definitive and influential 1909 *American Journal of Sociology* commentary: "We need men not afraid to work; who will get busy with the adding machine and the logarithms, and give us exact studies, such as we get in the psychological laboratories, not to speak of the biological and physical laboratories. Sociology *can be made an exact, quantitative science,* if we can get *industrious* men interested in it."[74]

In the chapters that follow we will use the terms "quantitative positivism" or "instrumental positivism" for the social science research that more or less encompasses these several assumptions and inclinations. However, we should emphasize a broader point here: The practice of social science in the United States is generally permeated by what might be termed a "positivistic culture." This larger positivistic culture is so powerful that some who practice a social science that is often considered antipositivistic—such as phenomenologists, ethnomethodologists, and discourse analysts—can adopt in their qualitative research procedures some of the traits and trappings of positivism. Abigail Fuller notes that in our positivistic culture much "knowledge is fragmented, specialized, and divorced from its historical and social context, and as such, is robbed of its critical functions."[75]

Since World War II, many leading sociologists have emphasized the need for sociology to standardize and develop methodological "rigor" by using statistical techniques, survey methods, and the hypothetico-deductive framing of social analyses. As conventionally stated, this instrumental positivism involves developing formal hypotheses, using specified falsification procedures, basing theories only on statistical measurements, and being "value free," whatever that may mean.[76] The value-free position asserts that sociological research should be done in a technical and neutral way that allows it to be used by anyone who wishes to do so. However, the "idea of sociology for sale to all-comers also loses sight of the economics of truth. Empirical social research is expensive and therefore only available to those who can afford it."[77]

The repeated emphasis on certain types of traditional quantitative or survey research methods as the *only* way to do serious social science, and the teaching of narrowly defined social research techniques to young undergraduate and graduate students, has far-reaching societal consequences. Sheldon Wolin has noted that a heavy accent on traditional positivistic research techniques in social science "affects the way in which the initiates will look upon the world and especially the political portion of it. 'Methodism' is ultimately a proposal for shaping the mind.... [Its] assumptions are such as to reinforce an uncritical view of existing political structures and all they imply."[78] Furthermore, Thomas Kuhn, in his influential *The Structure of Scientific Revolutions,* is critical of much scientific education for being as narrow as orthodox theology. For that reason, this type of education produces relatively few researchers who ask new boundary-breaking questions and discover new paradigms and pathbreaking approaches.[79]

Countersystem sociologists are often interested in looking critically at their own field—engaging in a self-reflective sociology that looks closely at their academic settings. Gouldner commented on the dilemma of academic sociologists: "For tenured faculty, the university is a realm of congenial and leisured servitude. It is a realm in which the academician is esteemed for his learning but castrated as a political figure." That is, the professor can be a "tiger in the classroom" while being a "pussycat in the Dean's office" and, too often, in the outside society.[80] All social scientists have to accept the existing system some of the time, but many rarely or never make attempts to question or change the oppressive system around them. In contrast, the liberation impulse in sociology teaches us that we must resist the blatant and subtle internal oppressions in our own circumstances, as well as elsewhere in society.

"PUBLIC SOCIOLOGY": A LIBERATION SOCIOLOGY PERSPECTIVE?

Since the first edition of this book, an extensive discussion of what is termed "public sociology" has emerged within the field of sociology. The first to dramatically emphasize this approach was Ben Agger, whose book *Public Sociology* (2000) preceded the publication of our book by some months.[81] Soon after Agger's book was published, in 2002, sociologist Herbert Gans articulated the need for a public sociology in *Footnotes,* the newsletter of the American Sociological Association (ASA). And in 2004 the new ASA president, Michael Burawoy, made the plural of this phrase, "public sociologies," the theme for the national sociology meetings. In his presidential address, Burawoy spoke of the complexity of contemporary sociology and distinguished four legitimate types of sociology, all part of a "sociological division of labor": professional sociology, policy sociology, public sociology, and critical sociology. Although Burawoy's own research has often articulated a critical neo-Marxist perspective, in his address he portrayed a vision of contemporary sociology as a broad tent that includes these four legitimate forms of sociology. By policy sociology he means sociological research done for a specific client such as the State Department (for example, on issues of terrorism). By public sociology he means research whose sociological practitioners engage directly in interactive dialogue about that research with some public, though they do not necessarily accept that public's views. By professional sociology Burawoy means the "true and tested methods, accumulated bodies of knowledge, orienting questions, and conceptual frameworks" of contemporary sociology, which he sees as undergirding both policy and public sociology. By critical sociology he means sociology that is critical of the established research programs of professional sociology.[82]

Significantly, the corrosive character of the instrumental-positivistic "true and tested methods" within professional sociology is nowhere assessed in Burawoy's address. As we suggested above, a central problem in contemporary sociology is this instrumental positivism and the associated methodological dogmatism that sees the only way to gain legitimate social science knowledge of the world as being through certain quantitative methods and that accepts the assumptions or interests of the surrounding status quo. By accepting instrumental positivism as one of the four important types of sociology under his big tent, Burawoy provides support for the undeserved power of those sociologists who are dominant in the major journals and in numerous graduate departments of sociology, those who do generally not seek to challenge the oppressive status quo. And at no point does he offer a critical analysis of the linkage of much government-and foundation-funded sociology to the often oppressive needs of the nation state. Although he cites earlier sociologists who raised important questions of sociology "for whom" and "for what," his discussion of these matters never discusses the issues of sociology for "the oppressed" or sociology "to reduce that oppression" in society. In his view both traditional positivistic sociology and a critical non-positivistic sociology can make for a viable public sociology. Even so, he does briefly note that both public sociology and critical sociology, as he has named them, are in some danger because the professional and policy sociologies have greater control over career positions in sociology and over government funding. He does not analyze this admitted domination in his address, but rather expresses the hope that in the long run instrumental-professional sociology cannot thrive without the reflexive public and critical sociologies.[83]

Nowhere in his presidential address does Burawoy acknowledge the earlier pioneering work of Ben Agger. This may be because Agger's public sociology is centrally a critical liberation sociology like that we assess in this book. We agree with Agger's view that in this process Burawoy "watered down" the concept of a public sociology committed to progressive societal change, the view of public sociology articulated by many sociologists since Jane Addams and W. E. B. Du Bois, including Agger and the authors of this book. Interestingly, since Burawoy's presidential address, the American Sociological Association has set up a committee on public sociology and periodically accented the concept of public sociology on its website and in its newsletters. Yet there is little evidence yet of a significant shift away from instrumental positivism in mainstream sociology journals. Thus, in Agger's recent review of those journals since 2000, he found that instrumental positivism and its accent on a selected range of conventional quantitative methods still predominates.[84]

Still, Burawoy has brought important questions again to the forefront of contemporary sociology and helped to inaugurate important debates in the field. In the concluding section of his presidential address, he distinguishes the discipline of sociology as different from the disciplines of economics and political science, which focus on issues of the market and the nation state, respectively. He views the special standpoint of sociology as defending the interests of "civil society," by which he means the array of civic organizations, such as trade unions and community groups, lying beyond market corporations and the nation state. He also notes, very briefly, that numerous sociologists are critically aware of the "segregations, dominations, and exploitations" of society, and that sociology has sometimes been invaded by government and market concerns.[85]

Significantly, Burawoy explicitly notes that in most other countries sociology is not focused on professional sociology as he has defined it. In those countries the practice of sociology is often critical and liberation oriented. In South Africa, for example, there has been a very strong connection between sociological research and teaching and the antiapartheid struggles. A similar connection between progressive social struggles can be seen in numerous European countries, a point we accent in later chapters. In his conclusion to the presidential address, Burawoy expresses the hope that a progressive public sociology will eventually come to the United States, but not from above, rather from below, from civil society organizations and movements: "It will come when public sociology captures the imagination of sociologists, when sociologists recognize public sociology as important in its own right with its own rewards, and when sociologists then carry it forward as a social movement beyond the academy."[86]

CONCLUSION

Throughout this book, we have asked those hard questions, "Social science for what purpose?" and "Social science for whom?" In proposing a liberation sociology, we give a strong humanistic, democratic, and activist answer to these questions. Liberation sociology can be a tool to increase the human ability to understand deep social realities, to engage in dialogue with others, and to increase democratic participation in the production and use of knowledge. Making oppression more visible and forcing public discussions of it are essential tasks. Mills put it this way: "It is the political task of the social scientist ... continually to translate personal troubles into public issues, and public issues into the terms of their human meaning for a variety of individuals."[87] A critical, committed sociology can help those who are powerless to become more powerful. It can give voice to those who are oppressed and voiceless. For example, it can help women and people of color to understand better where and how sexism and racism operate and suggest useful countermeasures. Or it can also help white male workers who join right-wing supremacist groups like the militias to understand why they feel alienated and why reactionary ideologies play into the hands of their own class oppressors.

Well-established research methodologies, such as face-to-face interviews and social surveys, can be coupled with newer approaches such as Dorothy E. Smith's institutional ethnographies of schools.[88] For Smith, such a field ethnography means more than observation and interviewing; it means a commitment to finding out how a social entity really works in its actual practices and everyday relationships. Discovering social facts can thus involve a diversity of social science methods. For example, some researchers have made good use of the diaries and other materials left by the victims of the Nazi Holocaust to get at the everyday realities of this extreme oppression and genocide. In South Africa, new methods were pioneered by the Truth and Reconciliation Commission, which has looked into the atrocities of the old apartheid system. They have sought out the voices of the survivors of this often violent oppression in order to air the truth about the horrors of that apartheid and thus to allow the nation to face its future with its eyes wide open. Similarly in Chile, after the Pinochet dictatorship, a special national committee investigated and assembled data on the civil rights abuses of that brutal regime with the hope of bringing about societal openness and eventual reconciliation.

The ultimate measure of the value of social science knowledge is not some type of propositional theory building but whether it sharpens our understanding of society and helps to build a more just and democratic society. Liberation sociology seeks to stimulate debate in the field of sociology and in the larger society over what humane societal arrangements would look like and how they could be implemented. To bring change, powerless human beings must be empowered. Liberation sociology can provide probing research that supports the struggles of the oppressed against classist, racist, sexist, heterosexist, and other authoritarian types of oppression. Liberation sociology is oriented toward people acting to change oppressive conditions that restrict human lives. Marx once wrote that people "make their own history, but they do not make it just as they please; they do not make it under circumstances chosen by themselves, but under circumstances directly encountered, given and transmitted from the past."[89] C. Wright Mills noted a qualification to this point: "Men are free to make history, but some men are much freer than others. Such freedom requires access to the means of decisions and of power by which history may now be made."[90] Both Marx and Mills recognize that people are acting agents and can make or remake their history. A former secretary general of the United Nations, Dag Hammarskjöld, once put it this way: "We are not permitted to choose the frame of our destiny. But what we put in it is ours."[91] Each member of this society is a part of the systems of oppression, for no one can escape, and all are part of the struggle to maintain or remove these systems. But we can choose which side to be on.

CHAPTER 2

Improving Human Societies: Reassessing the Classical Theorists

Let us now turn to the theoretical background of modern sociology and examine several sociologists of different epochs and political persuasions, all of whom have emphasized a sociological concern with life improvement and societal betterment. We accent views that shed light on sociologists' early commitment to social justice or to building a better world. We want to dispel the idea that to practice sociology one must, or could, be "neutral" and somehow devoid of values and commitments. We argue that the pure-science, objectivist ideal of social science is a relatively new invention, mostly emerging in the 1930s and 1940s. Numerous early sociologists in Europe and the United States, as we will see, viewed sociology as generating new knowledge and as being directly applicable to building a better society. One central argument here is that the scientific discipline of sociology, in its inception, was mostly conceived as a way to *improve the human condition.*

Many contemporary sociologists have reinterpreted the perspectives of key "classical" sociologists, such as Emile Durkheim and Max Weber, to support instrumental positivist trends and certain other mainstream commitments. Recent advocates of professionalism in sociology have often tried to denigrate or downplay the activist and change-oriented aspects of the sociological tradition and accent instead a mechanical and instrumental positivism. They frequently appeal to a tradition of "pure science" and "value-free" social science.

To do this they must ignore, if not greatly distort, the actual history of sociological theory and research. In order to fully understand the perspectives of any sociological theorists, we need to understand the social and intellectual climates in which they lived. We should examine the historical events that shaped their lives and social contexts. Most important perhaps, we need to understand the theorists' social positions and their commitments to values and change. What follows in this chapter is an examination of some sociological theorists as a way of showing how their construction as "classical" often reflects a distortion of sociology's emancipatory vocation.

EARLY ROOTS OF SOCIOLOGY

A good case can be made that both Auguste Comte (1798–1857) and Harriet Martineau (1802–1876) were the original founders of sociology. In the early 1800s, Comte, a French philosopher, gave "sociology" its composite name, one constructed from Greek and Latin linguistic roots. However, the idea that human relations should be studied empirically predates Comte's idea of sociology by about a century. When the possibility of a realistic study of society was first proposed in the 1700s, it was a revolutionary idea. "In the eighteenth century," writes historian Peter Gay, "for the first time in history, confidence was the companion of realism rather than a symptom of the Utopian imagination."[1] During the Enlightenment, the intellectual movement that took place mostly in the eighteenth century, many intellectuals reacted against the dominant ideas and methods of Christian theology. In countries across Europe, these intellectuals included "religious skeptics, political reformers, cultural critics, historians, and social theorists."[2] The empirical study of human relations was viewed as replacing the dominance of knowledge by religious authorities.

Scottish philosopher David Hume (1711–1776), an influential Enlightenment thinker, repeatedly reminded his readers that ignorance is the mother of religious devotion. At the same time that Enlightenment analysts like Hume rejected the irrational in religion, they also rejected what they saw as the excessive rationalism of some earlier philosophers such as Rene Descartes (1596–1650). Thus, Hume understood that reason was limited by the power of emotions: "Reason is, and ought only to be the slave of the passions, and can never pretend to any other office than to serve and obey them."[3] Hume also understood that ideas like "causality" were only conventional and constructed ideas. Immanuel Kant (1724–1804), a German professor and perhaps the leading philosopher in the Western tradition, also broke new ground that paved the way for the rise of the social sciences. In contrast to England's influential social philosopher, John Locke (1632–1704), who viewed the human mind as passive and mirror-like, Kant viewed the human mind as creative and active in interpreting empirical experience. For Kant, both scientific and nonscientific knowledge are derived from experience, and thus both are valid ways of understanding nature and society.[4] Hume and Kant both had an impact on key sociological thinkers like Karl Marx, Max and Marianne Weber, and Emile Durkheim.

The American and French Revolutions took place near the end of the Enlightenment period, in the late 1700s. They inspired other liberation movements. Soon thereafter, for example, enslaved people of African descent in Haiti rebelled against the French colonial government that had persuaded the French National Assembly to grant political rights to free blacks but not to abolish slavery. In 1791 those enslaved rose up against their masters in a successful revolution. Haiti became an independent republic on January 1, 1804, thereby becoming the second independent country in the Americas. (This was the only successful slave rebellion in the history of the world.) After 1808, Latin American countries, one after the other, declared their independence from the European colonial powers. To one extent or another, these movements were inspired by the writings of Enlightenment intellectuals in Europe and the Americas. Numerous Enlightenment intellectuals had pressed for the liberation of human beings from fear and oppression and for their establishing sovereignty over their own lives.[5] Many European and American intellectuals viewed the American Revolution as a confirmation that their ideas could be applied—that human beings had a "capacity for self-improvement and self-government, that progress might be a reality instead of a fantasy, and that reason and humanity might become governing rather than merely critical principles."[6]

Auguste Comte

Reflecting the Enlightenment idea of human capacity for societal improvement, Auguste Comte initially sketched his ideas in the 1820s, in articles that caught the eye of England's theorist of liberty, John Stuart Mill (1806–1873). Mill agreed with Comte in, among other ideas, his attack on the subjugation of women.[7] Mill enthusiastically recommended to colleagues the series of private lectures Comte offered between 1826 and 1829 in Paris on "positive philosophy." This positive philosophy described Comte's systematic view on scientific knowledge. The word "positive" was chosen to indicate that the philosophy being proposed was a reaction against the highly critical (considered "negative") philosophy of the German Hegelian system.[8] Hegel started from the errors made by philosophers before him. Comte believed one should start not with the errors of the past but with a positive statement of what is discovered through observation and comparison. Comte believed that he had discovered a fundamental law of the stages "through which the human mind has to pass, in every kind of speculation."[9] The laws of human behavior could be discovered in the same way that Isaac Newton had discovered laws in physics.

Comte sought to set in place a natural science that would lay bare the reality of a society and thus help to transform it. The sciences had grown and developed from an understanding of simple abstract principles to the understanding of complex concrete phenomena. In this schema, mathematics was the initial science and the more complicated sciences were, in order, astronomy, physics, chemistry, and biology. Sociology was the queen of sciences at the top, the last science and the one that would discover laws governing social facts and synthesize the whole of human knowledge. Sociology would thus be equipped to assist in the reconstruction of society. In spite of his rejection of numerous Enlightenment ideas, Comte was a child of the Enlightenment who believed in the power of reason to make sense of the way the world works.

Thus, sociology has resulted from a blending of many perspectives and theories, including "natural law, science, materialism, determinism and inevitability, the romantic emphasis on organic wholes and on conflict, ideas of progress and evolution."[10] The concept of social order, so important in the history of sociological theory and analysis, is a legacy of sociology's historical roots in nineteenth-century conservatism in Europe.[11] Comte wrote in the period following the French Revolution, a social explosion that had destroyed the fabric of society in France. Although Comte was a political conservative opposed to democracy and supportive of social hierarchy, he was *not* for a return to the old French monarchy destroyed by the Revolution.[12] Comte's broad goals can be seen in his phrase "Order and Progress," which today appears on the Brazilian flag. Comte saw European society as advancing through stages, from a theological stage to a modern, *positive* stage where business and political leaders would rule with the help of sociologists. In this last phase, there would be reliable knowledge, rational government, and a human-oriented religion. The ideal government would be composed of an intellectual elite.[13]

Thus, sociology began as a grand science of reform and social harmony. Comte suggested that if people learned about the real laws of society—determined by sociologists through empirical investigation—and how to accommodate to them, then social harmony would follow. However, he turned his back on the Enlightenment's idea that society should be changed to allow for the continuous perfection of individuals. Instead, he stressed human adjustment to natural social laws. He saw individualism as a disease of Western civilization. Social order rested on moral consensus. Comte's ideas were shaped by his strong desire to contribute to restoration of the stability of French society, which was radically disturbed after the French Revolution, without giving up the goal of societal progress.

Interestingly, Comte viewed positivism as the "secular religion of humanity devoted to the worship of society."[14] Over time a positivistic movement became popular in many countries, in which circles and foundations were created to promote positivistic ideas. For others, however, a positive religion of humanity was an aberration that seemed to violate some ideas that Comte himself had proposed. Thus, John Stuart Mill, the British philosopher originally impressed with Comte's ideas on scientific study of society, eventually became a staunch critic.

Harriet Martineau

Without the efforts of the English sociologist and social activist Harriet Martineau, the ideas of Auguste Comte would likely not have become widely known outside of France, at least during the nineteenth century. Martineau translated and condensed Comte's work into a popular one-volume English edition, with which Comte was so impressed that he had it translated back into French. This volume is still the most accessible introduction to Comte's work.[15]

More importantly, although she remains little known today, Martineau was the *first* social scientist to see herself *as a sociologist* and to do systematic empirical research *in the field.* Over her lifetime, Martineau traveled extensively in Ireland, the United States, and the Middle East and kept detailed sociological accounts of what she observed. Her first major sociological analysis was of her careful observations during her visit to the United States, which were published in an important three-volume set called *Society in America* (1837).[16] In this pioneering assessment of U.S. society, this British sociologist developed sociological insights at least as original as those of her more celebrated male counterpart, Alexis de Tocqueville. The young Martineau, at this very early point in the history of sociology, helped to create a new social research approach using empirical data to assess theory and public policy. Indeed, she wrote the first book on sociological methods, in which she argued—preceding Emile

Durkheim by a half century—that research on social life is centrally about studying social "things" accurately and should involve research on "institutions and records, in which the action of a nation is embodied and perpetuated."[17] In addition, Martineau used her sociological insights in her activism, which in turn helped to hone her numerous sociological insights. She was also an abolitionist and a feminist and wrote extensively for the popular press about the important issues of her day. It is time to recover Harriet Martineau as one of the two early founders of Western sociology and as the first publicly visible and influential sociological analyst in Western history.

THE DISTORTION OF MAX WEBER'S THOUGHT

Western sociology has long had competing social perspectives. Many sociologists and other social scientists have offered theory or engaged in research that supports the established order. Typically, in these social science analyses they have emphasized the harmonious working of established institutions, and when they consider change, they have preferred slow rates of evolutionary change. In contrast, another sizeable group of sociologists has viewed the discipline of sociology as an enterprise that can help liberate human beings from their misery and social troubles through accurate sociological research on oppressive institutions and the introduction of societal reforms or more revolutionary changes based on that research.

The ideas of a value-free sociology and of the ideal type method are considered by many to be cornerstones of the work of the prominent German sociologist Max Weber (1864–1920). His cautions about values in social science are generally interpreted as proposing a sociological understanding not shaped by the researcher's social position, one free of the sociological researcher's values. Talcott Parsons introduced much of the work of Max Weber to North American social scientists, and this was generally his interpretation of Weber. Such an interpretation portrays Weber as a father of mainstream instrumental positivism, which often portrays itself as value-free, objective, and detached.[18] This view of Weber is too simplistic, for he was a sophisticated sociologist who struggled throughout his career with sociology's need to be socially useful but *politically* neutral. An in-depth discussion of Weber's ideas is necessary to gain an understanding of the complexities involved in claiming neutrality or objectivity in the practice of social science— as well as to understand the ways in which the evolving discipline of sociology has often constructed itself.

An early controversy over value-free social science flared up at a 1909 Vienna conference. At a session there, Weber himself was upset by a colleague's narrow use of the concept of productivity to judge agriculture in one region of Germany. Weber suggested that three different problems had to be recognized: (1) productivity in the sense of maximum grain production for a given area; (2) the interest or the welfare of the people in an area; and (3) the sociopolitical interest of an even distribution of property among the people of the area. As Weber saw it, these different concerns and interests compete with each other. Equating productivity with a certain profitability, as his colleague did, was objectionable because several economic interests were at stake in the situation studied. Weber objected to the use of concepts that represented a premature "value judgment." He accented and analyzed explicitly the role of value judgments and the interests then in conflict.[19]

More generally, Weber's advocacy of value freedom was not a call for a social science devoid of values but rather a call for a social science that not only is protected from intrusion by established *political authorities* and their values but also takes social values seriously and is careful not to transform questions of values into purely technical questions. Weber abhorred the unquestioned acceptance of conventional definitions of social phenomena. At the Vienna conference, Weber was eloquent on the need for values and ideals in social science: "I cannot bear it when problems of global proportions, with consequences that concern great ideals, in a certain sense the utmost problems that move the heart, are here turned into technoeconomical questions of 'productivity,' and are made a matter of discussion of a specialized discipline, as is the national economy."[20]

Weber was clear about the impossibility of social science unshaped by values. In an essay for the new social science journal *Archiv,* Weber was unequivocal: "There is no absolutely 'objective' scientific analysis of culture—or put perhaps more narrowly but certainly not essentially differently for our purposes—of 'social phenomena' independent of special and 'one-sided' viewpoints according to which—expressly or tacitly, consciously or unconsciously—they are selected, analyzed and organized for expository purposes."[21]

Nonetheless, since Weber's time, many instrumental positivists in social science circles have argued for a "value-free" social science. This value-free social science is supposed to be achieved through the application of certain scientific methods said to be independent of the researcher, of the problem at hand, and of the object studied (see Chapter 3). These instrumental methods are said to be generic and exist before a societal problem is actually tackled. Weber rejected this notion. He certainly saw linkages between observers, the observed, and the methods used: "Methodology can only be a reflection on the means which have been demonstrated in practice."[22]

A look at Weber's famous conception of "ideal types" makes it clear how far his sociology is from the instrumental positivism of much contemporary social science. These ideal types are stylized images designed as "standards of value by reference to which empirical existence can be evaluated."[23] Weber's ideal types are culturally specific ways of classification. A researcher's interests determine the significance attributed to events in the past. The simplification involved in the strategy of ideal types reflects those elements the researcher sees as significant—to the exclusion of other elements because of the researcher's particular interests. Weber does not claim that the facts that sociologists include in an ideal type are more essential than those excluded but rather that they are regarded as being more significant by the researcher. In this way, the ideal type that a social scientist constructs to organize data is not an arbitrary simplification but one that reflects the concerns, history, and values of the researcher. Ahmad Sadri notes that Weber "recognized that 'our' history inevitably bears the imprint of our particular interest in it. Thus, he liberated sociologists as well as other social scientists and particularly historians from the burdensome pretension of German idealism, which required them to be selfless oracles of reason (or revolution)."[24]

Ideal types are thus bound to the values of the researcher at a particular point in history. They have a liberating effect because the social scientists who use them are forced to make explicit their mental models and to examine those models for adequacy, keeping in mind that this conceptual tool is affected by their values and existential circumstances. The use of ideal types makes it possible to accept, rather than deny, the fact that "we confront our society and history as finite human beings whose interests define the past as much as they are defined by it."[25] In Weber's terminology, the measure of meaningfulness of an ideal type is its "subjective adequacy," that is, its agreement with "our habitual modes of thoughts and feelings."[26] It should be in agreement with our common sense, not in conformity with some abstract principles of logic. Social researchers determine the empirical validity of the ideal types by estimating their "causal adequacy," the odds of their actual occurrence.

For Weber, social researchers can look at history and societies *only* from the point of view of their own values and interests. Age, gender, class, racial group, religion, education, urban-rural location, occupation, and nationality are among the social factors that shape one's vision. These limitations, however, can be turned into a leverage for understanding. It is not necessary to claim that one has reproduced the worldview of the other or that one has transcended one's own culture. When social scientists erect the logically consistent structures called ideal types to accent certain aspects of the societal problems studied, they thereby submit their values and interests to examination. A self-righteous affirmation of cultural or methodological superiority only highlights the blissful unawareness of one's standpoint.[27]

Clearly, Weber did not call for a sociology devoid of human interests and values. In his strongest statements on values and social research, Weber was reacting against political intrusions into the German academy and against the transformation of social life into supposedly value-free technical questions. In fact, the ideal type method furnishes sociologists a practical way to examine the values and interests they incorporate into their research.

In the next two chapters, we will examine in some detail how many mainstream sociologists came to accent their view of sociology as rather devoid of human interests and values, as detached and as distancing of the subjects studied. This view did not develop without opposition, however. In an appendix to his 1944 pathbreaking book on U.S. racism, called *An American Dilemma,* Gunnar Myrdal, one of the few sociologists to win a Nobel Prize, took a Weberian position on values. Myrdal specifically criticized the detached positivism of prominent U.S. sociologists: "The specific logical error is that of inferring from the facts that men can and should make no effort to change the 'natural' outcome of the specific forces observed. This is the old do-nothing *(laissez-faire)* bias of 'realistic' social science."[28] He added as well: "Scientific facts do not exist per se, waiting for scientists to discover them. A scientific fact is a construction abstracted out of a complex and interwoven reality by means of arbitrary definitions and classifications. The processes of selecting a problem and a basic hypothesis, of limiting the scope of study, and of defining and classifying data relevant to such a setting of the problem, involve a choice on the part of the investigator."[29] Value neutrality in social science is impossible, for in choices about how to assess society there is always something of value at stake.

In the 1960s Myrdal expanded his view of how social scientists can provide a maximum of objectivity only by being candid about their values and biases. In a book titled *Objectivity in Social Research,* he argued:

> The logical means available for protecting ourselves from biases are broadly these: to raise the valuations actually determining our theoretical as well as our practical research to full awareness, to

scrutinize them from the point of view of relevance, significance, and feasibility in the society under study, to transform them into specific value premises for research, and to determine approach and define concepts in terms of a set of value premises which have been explicitly stated.[30]

One lesson here for contemporary social scientists is that we should not abandon the idea of objectivity to the instrumental positivists. Instead, as social scientists we should watch carefully how concealed biases and assumptions, both our own and those of other researchers, affect the sociological craft, and we should try generally to minimize the possible distortions from these influences. Indeed, it is often the critical sociologists who are most objective in this sense, for they are likely to recognize and question the hidden societal assumptions in which they, like other researchers, have generally been raised and socialized.

THE COMMITMENTS OF EMILE DURKHEIM

We need to demystify certain others among the classical "founding fathers" as well. Emile Durkheim (1858–1917), the pioneering French sociologist, has often been portrayed in relatively conservative terms as principally concerned with social order. However, the transformation of Durkheim into a sociologist of value-free instrumental positivism by some contemporary sociologists ignores his deep concern with morality, social justice, and societal change. He often saw his sociological analysis as a type of moral philosophy. The center of his thought system was the concept of the *"conscience collectif."* However, the common translation of this French word *conscience* with the English word *consciousness* obscures the fact that *conscience* in French also means "conscience" in the English sense of an ability to make moral *judgments.* It is quite clear, if one reads Durkheim in the original French versions of his books, that he was centrally concerned with the moral dimensions of society.[31]

In his important book, *The Elementary Forms of the Religious Life,* Durkheim offered seminal ideas about religion and thought that were much more than an abstract discussion when he first proposed them. His central ideas were that religion involves a view dividing the world into the sacred and the profane and that the sacred is the social par excellence. Moreover, as Durkheim saw it, his perspective had concrete political implications. At the time, the French government was expropriating the property of the Catholic Church. Catholic parishioners and their clergy, who were for the most part monarchists opposed to the French republic, vigorously opposed this taking on the grounds that the Church's riches were "sacred" and that the "profane" authority of the government had no right to intervene.[32]

Rather than dismissing this division of the world into sacred and secular as a sign of backward thinking, as many scholars did in his time, Durkheim viewed it as a characteristic of the religious way of thinking. Durkheim wrote of "religious facts," and not just of "religion," in order to emphasize that religious expression in a given society did not have to be part of organized religious systems.[33] In his analysis, Durkheim showed that organized religions like the Catholic Church did not have a monopoly over religious rituals and sentiments. He also argued that the sense of God and of moral control that all believers feel, whatever their form of religion, stems ultimately from the surrounding society: "The forces before which the believer bows are not simple physical energies, as they are given to the senses and imagination; these are *social forces.*"[34] Religious and moral forces are actually social forces.

Rather than segregating sacred things as beyond the reach of society, Durkheim declared them to be at least as social as other important phenomena:

> Sacred things are those in which society itself has elaborated the representation; in it enter all sorts of collective states, of traditions and common emotions, of sentiments that relate to objects of general interest, etc., and all these elements are combined following laws of social mentality. Profane things, on the contrary, are those that each of us constructs with the given of our senses and our experience; these notions concern all new individual impressions, and this is why they do not have, in our eyes, the same prestige than the precedent.[35]

The sacred takes precedence because it symbolizes collective images and reflects collective forces and pressures. Durkheim did not come to this fertile sociological idea from neutral and detached reflection on a random topic. On the contrary, it was the application of Durkheim's sociological reason to the historical turmoil burgeoning around the wealth of the Catholic Church in this era of France's history.

Although Durkheim did not extensively analyze the role of major oppressive structures such as imperialism and patriarchy in his day, he did underscore in his writings the critical importance of social justice and the move to equality. Indeed, he wrote eloquently about the need for justice. For Durkheim, a *forced* division of labor, like that found in a capitalistic society, was pathological: "The lower classes not being ... satisfied with the role which has devolved upon them from custom or by law aspire to functions which are closed to them and seek to dispossess those who are exercising these functions."[36] He was critical of any social inequalities generated by such mechanisms as inheritance over family generations. Inheritance "compromises organic solidarity."[37]

Durkheim used the term "organic solidarity" for a healthy society. In his view, "justice" (his term) required the elimination of social inequalities that are not generated by variations in personal merit and abilities: "If one class of society is obliged, in order to live, to take any price for its services, while another can abstain from such action thanks to the resources at its disposal which, however, are not necessarily due to any social superiority, the second has an unjust advantage over the first at law."[38] Moreover, he makes it clear that "the task of the most advanced societies is, then, a work of justice.... [O]ur ideal is to make social relations always more equitable, so as to assure the free development of all our socially useful forces." The trend to ever more complex and organic societies requires ever more social justice and equality. "Just as ancient peoples needed, above all, a common faith to live by, so we need justice, and we can be sure that this need will become ever more exacting if, as every fact presages, the conditions dominating social evolution remain the same."[39]

Clearly, the sections of the classical founders accenting issues and concerns of social justice have been neglected, probably because they do not fit in well with conventional perspectives or sociological theories. For example, in putting his influential structural-functionalist theory in place, beginning with his famous *The Structure of Social Action,* Talcott Parsons not only drew on a sanitized Max Weber but also relied heavily on the work of Durkheim, whom he positioned as a premier theorist dealing with Hobbesian problems of social order and stability.[40] There is no mention of Durkheim's concern with and recognition of issues of equality and social justice. Parsons was but one of a number of major sociologists who have developed and perpetuated one-sided distortions or misinterpretations of Weber and Durkheim in contemporary sociology.

CHALLENGES OUTSIDE ACADEMIA: KARL MARX

Unlike Durkheim and Weber, Karl Marx (1818–1883) was not an academic and wrote frequently for a nonacademic audience. He attempted to write for workers and about the political-economic sources of their suffering and tribulations. His aim was not just to understand the world but to change it. In fact, his influential ideas have changed— and continue to change—the modern world in major ways.

In U.S. sociology, Marx has often been ignored or treated as "insignificant." For example, in one 1960s theory textbook that taught social theory to a generation of sociologists, the author deals with Marx in just two and a half pages in a catchall chapter devoted to "other pioneers."[41] Marx is erroneously labeled as an economic determinist. Another popular theory textbook of the 1960s devoted seven pages to the seldom read idealist philosopher G.W.F. Hegel, but only six to the still-influential materialist thinker Karl Marx.[42]

In many textbooks and other social science discussions, Marx's dialectical approach is misunderstood or dismissed as mysticism. Much mainstream discussion inside and outside academic circles views this "dialectics" as describing a rigid social cycle: a thesis, opposed by an antithesis, which is resolved in a synthesis. This is alleged to be the central Marxist approach to analyzing history and society. Yet, Marx's dialectics entails an approach quite different from this simplistic portrait. For Marx a dialectical approach involves asking whether things really are what they seem to be. Through dialectics, Marx dug beneath the surface realities and tensions of socioeconomic life under capitalism and found that the apparently fair exchanges of labor and commodities hid an economic structure that dominated not only workers but also the development of various institutional structures of a capitalist society. A dialectical approach also recognizes that in the social world there is an ongoing tension and reciprocity among different social phenomena; one set of social arrangements can be in contention with another set of social arrangements, even to the point of replacing the latter. Capitalism is not just a social system but an unjust way of living in a society, and it is a system that is periodically challenged and thus ever changing.

Marx contrasted his research method, later called "dialectical materialism" or "historical materialism," with Hegel's idealism and spiritualism and argued that dialectical movements are part of the material world. Marx's idea is that human experience can be understood only as a complex and living whole, a dialectical whole with contending social realities—one always moving and in process. Marx does *not* reduce social phenomena to economic phenomena, as has often been claimed. Instead, Marx placed economic life in the context of society, of the whole that is human experience. An important contribution of Marx was to show how capitalism, apparently a purely economic system, actually shapes, interacts with, and often dominates the larger cultures and societies of which it is an integral part.

In recent decades, one of the better-known sociological proponents of the dialectical method has been French sociologist Georges Gurvitch. In his view, Marx's dialectics focuses on the dynamic character of everyday life. The nature of human social reality is fundamentally dialectical. Dialectics is a way to affirm "the complexities, sinuosities, flexibilities, and constantly renewing tensions, along with the unexpected turns of events of social reality."[43]

As we see it, liberation sociology should be contextual, historical, and dialectical in assessing the movement to a more just society. It should assess carefully the context around and processes behind current social observations. Particular social phenomena have histories and web-like relations to other, often less obvious, social phenomena. This approach examines contradictions and complexities within the whole, and also across space and time. In sociology this approach can be liberating and revolutionary "because it helps us to see the present as a moment through which our society is passing, because it forces us to examine where it has come from and where it is heading ... and because ... we have the power to affect it."[44]

Using this dialectical perspective, liberation sociologists view social reality as filled with tension, movement, backtracking, and renewal. No oppressive system lasts forever, and during its life it is periodically, if not constantly, challenged. Thus, social life is dynamic not static—with much counterpoint. Human societies are not only riddled with social contradictions but are shaped by people who make errors in arrangements, beliefs, and choices. Often these errors are covered over with rationalizations and myths. In analyzing society, sociologists working in a critical dialectical tradition dig behind these rationalizations and fictions. Recall the Roman myth of the giant Cacus, who stole Hercules's cattle and then made them walk backward into his cave to deceive Hercules into thinking they had walked out of the cave and vanished. Too often social scientists count the number of footprints but do not see where they come from or where they are going. A liberation approach attends to the larger social framework around observations, to how observed phenomena arise and develop, and to how they fit into the larger environment.

Too much contemporary social theory, such as exchange theory or rational choice theory, leaves out the flow of history and the deeper layers of social reality. In Marx's view, when we apply the standard logic of modern capitalistic societies, injustice and exploitation falsely appear to be inevitable. Yet, a particular injustice is *not* a static thing found at one point in time or place but ordinarily has a long history of social reproduction. Oppression at one place is part of a process that contains both the history of that oppression and its possible futures, including futures of resistance. A dialectical approach emphasizes that the aspects of oppression are but segments of a larger whole, which includes not only the present, past, and future of oppression but also the agents and individuals involved, including the researchers. The perspectival element, accenting the standpoint from which one views reality, is a critical element of the dialectical approach.[45]

Dialectical methods reject static truths. Everything in the social world, including our ideas of it, is in tension or contradiction with something else. There is nothing permanent; the apparent stability that human beings give to their affairs, through the creation of institutions for example, is temporary at best and the result of continuing negotiation and struggle. By using a dialectical method, we avoid the idea that social arrangements are stable, unchanging environments for our lives.

A sociological method that produces statements about social realities as if they were crystallized and immobile contradicts the fact that human beings and their groups are alive. To affirm the dynamic nature of social life, we need instead a method that concentrates our attention on that dynamism. At its best, a dialectical approach also has the advantage of making the changing humanity of the researchers themselves part of its investigation. The practice of research is a human experience. The claim to be "value-free," seen from this dialectical approach, is just a social construction of certain mainstream social scientists. C. Wright Mills criticized the "abstracted empiricism" of mainstream sociology in the late 1950s and early 1960s. The practitioners of abstracted empiricism, then and now, claim objectivity and detachment, a freedom from conceptual presuppositions, when in fact what they do "is to embrace one philosophy of science which they now suppose to be the scientific method."[46]

For many social scientists, past and present, physics has been the model for those who want to discover scientific laws that determine human behavior. From this viewpoint one proposes coherent hypotheses that, when tested correctly through certain limited types of empirical observation and experimentation in regard to research objects, become scientific laws. Thus, only the quality of the quantitative methods used to observe and experiment can protect scientists from error. It is a question of finding facts through instrumental-positivistic observation and experimentation in order to generalize. However, we should place in quotation marks conventional social science research terms like "subject," "object," "discover," and "determine" to call attention to how problematic these terms are. In reality, many of the "objects" studied by social scientists are as much "subjects" as the researchers who are supposed to discover relations among the "objects." Use of this type of distancing language makes it seem that the social research endeavor is not itself a type of *human social relationship.* It is as if the human beings studied by social researchers were no different from rocks, bugs, or any other thing studied by the natural sciences. Yet, they are quite different, for they are sentient beings that can "bite back," and they are ever changing.

THE PROGRESSIVISM OF GEORGE HERBERT MEAD AND LESTER FRANK WARD

Durkheim and Weber are not the only major sociological theorists whose ideas and proclivities have been distorted to fit contemporary interests and concerns. We should, thus, note the important work of the great U.S. social theorist and founder of the symbolic interactionist tradition, George Herbert Mead. Mead is usually considered a major member of the Chicago School of sociology, though in fact he taught in the areas of philosophy and social psychology. However, Mead had many sociology graduate students and interacted regularly with members of the University of Chicago sociology department and the sociologists at Chicago's Hull House (see Chapter 3). His ideas about symbolic interaction have greatly influenced subsequent generations of sociologists and social psychologists. Mead is best known for the posthumous book constructed from his classroom notes, called *Mind, Self, and Society.* The cover of the paperback edition of that book claims that Mead published little in his lifetime. Yet, Mead actually published more than eighty articles, most of which have since been forgotten. One likely reason for this amnesia about Mead's work is that over half of these articles are concerned with progressive reform issues, such as the conditions of workers and immigrants, war and peace, democracy, and public education.[47] Indeed, George Herbert Mead was an activist intellectual who participated in numerous local and national reform movements.

Contributing to the distinctive U.S. philosophical tradition of pragmatism, Mead took a dialectical approach to the human self. He rejected the dualistic division of "mind" and "body" common in Western thought, as well as the division of person and environment. Instead, as he saw it, the individual "constitutes society as genuinely as society constitutes the individual."[48] Human beings interact with each other substantially in terms of symbols such as language, and thinking in the human mind is an internal conversation involving social symbols, much like the conversations carried on with other people. Linguistic and other symbols have meaning because they are developed in the social interaction of human beings.[49] Social conflict arises when there is a breakdown in this symbolic communication and people are not able to understand the positions or roles of important others.

Moreover, while past experience certainly shapes symbolic meanings and communication, the acts of human beings are not strictly determined but have major aspects of creativity and spontaneity. All human beings are active thinking creatures working to shape and manipulate their surrounding environments. Thinking involves problem solving in order to take practical action in the social and physical environments.[50]

Central to Mead's perspective is the idea that human beings think critically about their environment, as well as about the thinking process itself. In this they are reflexive (reflective) and can act in a proactive manner. The reflective mind is a social mind and thus is shaped by the milieu in which people find themselves. As Ted Vaughan and Gideon Sjoberg note, human beings spend much effort in "justifying their moral beliefs and their normative order" and have the ability to "take the roles of others and to recognize another's humanity and commonality with oneself."[51] This ability, though in many settings seldom used, can be a critical step on the way to developing respect for the human rights of others.

Democratic rights and freedoms, especially the freedom of communication, were critical for Mead. Mead accented the advance toward human equality as essential for the development of healthy societies. His approach to both sociological research and social reform was humanistic; people and their ideas had to be respected. This was in contrast to the social scientific analysts (for example, the behaviorists) of his day who studied human subjects solely as "objects." Human beings had critical minds and intelligence and could change both themselves and their surroundings, and thus they were different from the usual objects of the physical sciences. Not surprisingly, Mead gave great weight to progressive and critical education, which he saw as encouraging a scientific method of inquiry that was self-reflective and integrated the social milieu into self-understanding.[52] Such education was essential to progress in equality and democracy, especially education for the poor, immigrants, and others who had been marginalized in society.

Although Mead has often been portrayed as an ivory tower scholar interested only in abstract ideas about self and mind, he was in fact a community activist and progressive reformer who worked with Jane Addams and other sociologist-activists in Chicago (see Chapter 3). Mead worked in the city settlement houses and played a role in the educational committee of the Chicago City Club. He was an editor of a publication of the Chicago Laboratory School, which was set up to experiment with progressive ideas in education. He actively worked on behalf of workers and unions in an era when this stance was considered radical, and he was a vice president of an organization committed to supporting immigrants' rights. He spoke at meetings on behalf of women's right to vote and generally supported the movement for women's suffrage.[53]

Another important progressive theorist and scholar among the early male sociologists was Lester F. Ward, the first president of the American Sociological Society. In contrast to most early male sociologists, who viewed women as naturally subordinate to men, Ward was egalitarian and feminist in his research and writing. In the first decades of his career, he did research and publishing in the areas of biology, geology, and anthropology, but later came to do sociological research, becoming a professor at Brown University in 1906. In his famous book, *Pure Sociology,* which was eventually translated into four other languages, Ward lays out a view of sociology as contributing significantly in its research and analysis to human achievement and societal reform. Perhaps most pathbreaking in Ward's research work is his conceptual analysis of gender and the subordination of women, work so important that women sociologists of his time, such as Charlotte Perkins Gilman, regularly cited his research as influencing them. Ward coined the now common term "androcentric" to describe the contemporary popular and social science theories that put men as biologically primary and the center of all important aspects of society and that played down the role of women as key societal actors outside the area of procreation. Indeed Ward countered the prevailing view with a *gynaecocentric* theory that viewed women as primary in the biological order and argued that the natural superiority of women had long ago been reversed by men who used their size and force to create androcentric and patriarchal societies.[54] In his view, modern marriage typically became a way of institutionalizing the dominance of women by men in patriarchal societies, a male dominance that has not taken into serious consideration the desires of women themselves. Gender subordination of women, Ward further argued, was rationalized extensively with "epithets, slurs, flings, and open condemnation of women as being in some manner vile and hateful, often malicious and evil disposed."[55]

Thus, Ward argued assertively for an egalitarian society in which men and women would have equal access to virtually all political and economic positions. He advocated openly for such a society and for women's rights in an era when this was considered "radical." In this regard Ward's views and activism were very much in line with the views and work of the early women sociologists whom we previously discussed.[56]

Clearly, Mead and Ward were early contributors to the liberation sociology tradition. They are yet more early sociologists whose role in activism and reform has been eradicated from the collective memory of contemporary sociologists.

INSIGHTS FROM THE PHYSICAL SCIENCES

In our century the natural sciences have changed dramatically. In his influential work on paradigm shifts in science, Thomas Kuhn rejects the idea that physical science has developed only in a gradual and accumulating fashion.[57] Instead, he accents the important revolutionary breaks that define much of the history of science. What he calls "normal science" is a period during which a dominant paradigm is gradually reinforced by accumulating knowledge. However, as scientific findings develop that cannot be explained by the dominant paradigm, pressures build and lead to a scientific revolution and a new paradigm. George Ritzer has clarified what Kuhn means by paradigm: "It serves to define what should be studied, what questions should be asked, how they should be asked, and what rules should be followed in interpreting the answers obtained. The paradigm is the broadest unit of consensus."[58] Kuhn also criticized education in the physical sciences for being too "narrow and rigid" and for not producing students "who will easily discover a fresh approach."[59]

Niels Bohr, a Nobel Prize–winning physicist, explained the old Newtonian way of thinking in a 1958 essay: "In Newtonian mechanics, where the state of a system of material bodies is defined by their instantaneous positions and velocities, it proved possible, by the well-known simple principles, to derive solely from the knowledge of the state of the system at a given time and of the forces acting upon the bodies, the state of the system at any other time."[60] However, at the end of the nineteenth and beginning of the twentieth century, a series of new ideas suddenly revolutionized the paradigm central to physical science. Physical scientists increasingly looked at the universe in more than just the mechanical terms of Newtonian science. The new idea of relativity—that the "description of physical phenomena depends on the reference frame chosen by the observer"—was indeed revolutionary for the physical sciences.[61]

A new era for atomic physics began with the discovery of subatomic particles and the complexity of matter and radiation—what came to be called "quantum" physics. What were once seen as only particles could now also be viewed as waves, and vice versa. The new physics showed that there was a holism to atomic phenomena. In this new era, Bohr explains:

> It became clear that the pictorial description of classical physical theories represents an idealization valid only for phenomena in the analysis of which all actions involved are sufficiently large to permit the neglect of the quantum. Although this condition is amply justified in phenomena on the ordinary scale, we meet in experimental evidence concerning atomic particles with regularities of a novel type, incompatible with deterministic analysis.[62]

The end of determinism was not the only radical change brought by quantum physics. There was also a major challenge to the distinction between the measuring apparatus, the person doing the measuring, and the objects being studied. According to the "uncertainty principle," the interaction between the instruments of observation and the observed particles is critical in the research process. Viewed broadly, one cannot be said to be measuring something exactly, if one cannot tell whether the changes recorded on instruments are the result of what is being observed, of something going on inside the instrument, or both.

Similarly, in the social sciences, the instruments of observation and the observers are also inseparable parts of a whole reality with the researched subjects. Indeed, Bohr even noted that the methodological situation in twentieth-century social science and biology reminded him of what quantum physics had gone through.[63] A rigid and neat distinction between the researcher, the method, and the object studied is no longer tenable in either the physical sciences or the social sciences.

CONCLUSION

Sociological dialectics is a method that allows sociologists—to use the same terminology that Bohr uses for physics—to "include a description of all the relevant features of the experimental arrangement."[64] Science is defined by the application of a method to the production of knowledge. Yet the method is to a large extent determined by what is to be observed. The use of a microscope allows scientists to observe realms that are hidden from the naked eye. But no matter how wonderful the method of using a microscope is, it is not appropriate for observing planets and stars. A different method needs to be used. And it is the human researcher who decides which method to use and why it is appropriate to use it.

In the social sciences, the researchers observing human beings are, of course, as human as those under observation, and a social research project would seem to have the greatest potential only if the researchers establish a human relationship with the people being studied. However, in recent years, government survey and demographic data sets have been made available to social science researchers who did not participate in their collection. There are two sets of potential problems here. First, it is often the case that these governmental statistics are produced by human beings whose careers depend on their turning out numbers that are acceptable to their bureaucratic superiors, whether they be in the executive or legislative branches.

Second, social scientists using the data collected by government agencies or other researchers may work under the illusion that their job as social scientists is only one of reporting statistical distributions or coefficients rather than understanding the human relations that those data usually represent. Typically, these social researchers do not meet or talk with the people they study or even with the people who participated in the original generation of the data. And they often do not inquire into the biases of the data collectors.

Those studying human relations in this fashion—and they include numerous social scientists in key research areas—are producing unduly limited, if not distorted, images of those human relations. The study of disembodied numbers from survey data can manufacture human beings who, like billiard balls touching each other in a game of pool, have only isolated or individualistic existences and random encounters. Yet this is not the social world in reality. Whether or not they realize it, social scientists study behavior more or less actively willed by their fellow human beings, who are interacting in situations meaningful to them and which they often define or redefine.

As we have seen, all the "classical" sociological theorists examined in this chapter were concerned with the moral and ethical issues of their immediate social contexts. They were in no sense detached scientists trying to be value-free, instrumental-positivistic researchers. All were actively involved not only in studying societal trends and structures sociologically but also in trying to effect positive change in their own societies. It is clear that in order to understand any social science theory, we must examine the social settings and intellectual climates in which that theory emerges and is utilized. All these sociological theorists accepted, in one form or another, an emancipatory or social-change goal for sociological research and analysis.

CHAPTER 3

U.S. Sociology from the 1890s to the 1970s: Instrumental Positivism and Its Challengers

Like other academic disciplines, sociology has long been molded by its national and international context, central to which is the economic system of modern capitalism. For more than a century, capitalism and its ruling elites have shaped the dominant assumptions underlying sociology and the other social sciences—both in Europe and in the United States.

In the late nineteenth and early twentieth centuries, the new discipline of sociology had a number of prominent and articulate advocates. Some of the early sociologists, such as Herbert Spencer in England and William Graham Sumner in the United States, strongly supported free-market capitalism and were opposed to government intervention in the capitalistic economy. Spencer generated the concept of "social Darwinism," with its idea of the survival of the fittest in society. Sumner picked up on Spencer's ideas, arguing, for example, that the rich were rich because natural selection sees to it that the "best" people rise to the top.

However, with the rise of progressive movements in the decades just before and after 1900, many of the new sociologists and other social scientists came to see this as an untenable position. This was a period of growing labor conflict and progressive ferment in the United States, and many leading academics, including some sociologists, supported moderate reform and some government intervention in the operation of capitalism—what has been termed a "corporate liberal" approach. Indeed, the U.S. university has long been a center of this moderate-reform approach. Such corporate-liberal social scientists have argued that without some "political regulation of economic life, capitalism would be destroyed by class conflicts involving militant labor unions and socialist movements on the one hand, and gigantic monopolies or monopoly trusts on the other."[1] Viewing capitalists and corporations as necessary and productive, corporate liberals have traditionally backed some government intervention in the economy— plus substantial government aid to support corporations when the market fails and some modest government aid to working people, especially if they protest. For decades, many mainstream sociologists have adopted some version of the corporate-liberal, moderate-reform perspective.

CAPITALISM AND THE FOUNDERS OF SOCIOLOGY

The "founding fathers" of U.S. sociology are sometimes said to be Lester Ward (1841–1913), William Graham Sumner (1840–1910), Franklin H. Giddings (1855–1931), and Albion Small (1854–1926). Not surprisingly, given the lack of early academic programs in sociology, not one was actually educated as a sociologist. Ward worked for the federal government as a clerk and paleobotanist; Giddings was a journalist, and Small and Sumner were educated in theology.[2] Note that these commonly listed sociologists were all white and male. All were aware of the major social and political issues of their period, and Ward, Giddings, and Small were committed to using sociology to bring some reform and thereby make a better society. Thus, in 1900 Albion Small gave a paper at the first meeting of the American Sociological Society in which he argued vigorously that sociological study and research were not ends in themselves but should serve to improve and advance society.[3]

Some of the early male sociologists had been ministers, including Small, while Franklin Giddings and Lester Ward had fathers or grandfathers who were ministers. Their backgrounds tended to be urban or rural Protestant. Not surprisingly, perhaps, they were often concerned with the negative effects of urbanization and industrialization. The "social pathology" and "social disorganization" of cities became early topics in their research.[4]

A few of the prominent male sociologists were moderately critical of capitalistic enterprises. For example, Small and E. A. Ross

(1866–1951) occasionally went beyond the conventional wisdom espoused by the dominant intellectual and business elites to argue that workers should have greater power in enterprises and the right to organize. Indeed, at the turn of the twentieth century, Ross was fired from Stanford University for his critical views on exploitation of Chinese laborers by capitalists. Nevertheless, even sociologists like Ross were unabashedly racist in their views of people of color, and they were by no means sympathetic to the views of more radical social reformers who sought to substantially remake capitalist society or replace it with a more just political-economic system.[5] Among these early white male sociologists there was some criticism of the existing society, but mostly from the corporate-liberal perspective. Very few took issue with the use of government force and related actions to expand the interests of the capitalist elite, and they rarely took the perspectives of working people, immigrants, women, or black Americans in either their research or public actions. A more assertive liberalism among sociology's founders can be seen in the statements of Lester F. Ward, the first president of the American Sociological Society (now the American Sociological Association). Ward believed that there should be a practical use for sociology. He argued that "the true guide, the Moses that is to lead man out of the wilderness, is science" and that "the real object of science is to benefit man."[6] Ward, writing in the early 1900s, viewed sociology as divided into "pure" and "applied" areas. Pure sociology ignores what ought to be and aims at "truth for its own sake." Applied sociologists should apply sociological intelligence to everyday life. Applied sociologists should deal only in broad generalizations to guide action. An applied sociologist should not "abandon his science."[7] As we saw in Chapter 2, Ward made intensive scientific efforts to examine gender issues, and concluded that a highly patriarchal society was not a healthy society. On the basis of his gender research, he advocated for a more egalitarian society.

A SOCIOLOGY FOR THE PEOPLE: EARLY WHITE FEMALE AND BLACK SOCIOLOGISTS

The Early Women Sociologists

From the beginning, U.S. sociology has had a strong countersystem tradition, one that often aggressively sides with the oppressed against social injustice and calls for an involved sociology. Scholar-activists like Jane Addams and W. E. B. Du Bois were "organic intellectuals" who emerged out of the aggrieved sectors of society to articulate the experiences of the oppressed. Addams and Du Bois sought the liberation of women and African Americans from the deep-lying oppressive structures of U.S. society. To a significant degree, their sociological sensitivity and sophistication stemmed from their experiences in dealing with such oppression in their own lives, as well as in those of friends and relatives. They were sociologists whose interpretive, epistemological, and theoretical insights grew, in part, out of concrete encounters with societal oppression.

In the late nineteenth and early twentieth centuries, numerous women sociologists took strong positions on behalf of women, children, the poor, and immigrants. Among these were Jane Addams, Emily G. Balch, Florence Kelley, Julia Lathrop, Lucy Salmon, Ann G. Spencer, Mary Eliza McDowell, Charlotte Perkins Gilman, and Marian Talbot. These women were practicing sociologists and early members of the American Sociological Society (ASS), founded in 1905. Some gave presentations at Society meetings. Numerous female sociologists were committed to bringing real societal changes that would stem from alliances between sociologists and communities of the poor, immigrants, and African Americans.[8]

Between the 1890s and the 1910s, many of these female sociologists were linked to Hull House in Chicago, a major settlement house and intellectual center of the day. The settlement house movement was part of a large progressive movement to better conditions and opportunities of the poor and immigrants in U.S. cities. Out of the group of female sociologists, and a few associated male sociologists, came a major humanistic perspective termed *feminist pragmatism*. Pragmatism was a U.S. intellectual movement of the late nineteenth and early twentieth century whose central idea was that the real test of a concept lay in its observability and practical significance in the real world of everyday experiences. Pie-in-the-sky philosophizing was unsatisfactory. A developed variant of the prevailing pragmatist perspective, feminist pragmatism emphasized a strongly cooperative and nurturing humanist ethic. It accented the values of liberal education and democracy as essential to progressive development in the everyday world.[9]

As the pioneering scholar of U.S. sociology's history, Mary Jo Deegan, has underscored in extensive research on Jane Addams and her numerous colleagues inside and outside sociology, these efforts were part of a decades-long successful attempt to bring a "feminist pragmatist welfare state" to Chicago, Illinois, the United States, and ultimately the world. Deegan has described these activist-intellectuals as the "most powerful network of women" in U.S. history, a network that aggressively articulated an activist framing of society that was

much more democratic, feminist, and antiracist than the dominant interpretive frame, which was strongly patriarchal, corporate-capitalistic,
and white-racist. The women and a few male colleagues developed
an important counter frame to the dominant frame of the white
male elites, and then pressed hard to bring major changes in societal
support and social welfare programs. Although the credit is often
given to male politicians in the 1930s and 1940s in Europe and the
United States, to a very substantial degree the basic ideas lying behind
the *modern welfare state* come from these early feminist pragmatists
and their aggressive efforts to provide major socioeconomic support
programs for people in U.S. society.[10]

Significantly, the first graduate department of sociology was
created in the 1890s at the University of Chicago, not far from
Hull House. There, in the early days of U.S. sociology, white men
dominated the development of academic sociology. Even before this
department was founded, and as it was growing, women sociologists
at Chicago's Hull House (a community facility) were pioneers in
empirical field research in U.S. sociology. These women sociologists—
including Jane Addams, Florence Kelley, and Julia Lathrop—worked
and did research from the feminist-pragmatist point of view at their
Hull House facility. Clearly, these women should be listed among the
early founders of sociology.

The Chicago sociology department was a male bastion, and numerous white men there saw themselves as intellectually superior; they
often saw women as data collectors who could implement the ideas
of the male sociologists. The latter viewed Hull House, and indeed
the city of Chicago, as a "sociological laboratory."[11] Albion Small, a
founder of the department at the University of Chicago, first used the
term "sociological laboratory" in the 1890s but did not view it then as
suggesting a specific research strategy. Later, the men in the Chicago
department who did what became the most famous urban research
in sociology came to view the city as such a sociological laboratory.[12]
However, this conception of Hull House and of the people of Chicago
was rejected by Addams and other women sociologists at Hull House.
Instead, they viewed the needs of the working people in the area as
more important than the needs of researchers. The people were not
primarily "specimens" to be studied and objectified.

These women sociologists were—and perceived themselves to
be—scholars, researchers, and intellectuals, and some were faculty
members or students at the University of Chicago. Indeed, at the
University of Chicago, a group of female sociologists, including
Marion Talbot, Ella Flagg Young, and Sophonisba Breckenridge
(all in a subordinate division of the sociology department), worked

with the more progressive men there such as George H. Mead and W. I. Thomas to educate Chicago students, often in the ideas of the feminist pragmatists.[13]

By the 1920s, most of the leading male sociologists saw sociology as having moved from the early rudimentary stage, in which female sociologists at community settlement houses facilitated sociology's development, to a more "mature" stage of academic research, which was increasingly done with support from corporate foundations. Sociology students from the department at the University of Chicago came to Hull House, yet the men who controlled the department had increasingly negative views of Addams's "uplift" sociology.[14] Indeed, by 1920 all the women affiliated with the department of sociology at the University of Chicago had moved out of the sociology department and into the new school of social work. Whereas in the first two decades of U.S. sociology, leading white male sociologists spoke of both disinterested knowledge gained for its own sake and the need for justifying knowledge on the basis of its societal utility, by the 1920s and 1930s, these leading sociologists were dropping this accent on the social and policy utility of knowledge.[15]

WOMEN AND THE ORGANIZED PROFESSION

In the early 1900s, the American Sociological Society was established by several sociologists who were members of the American Economics Association. Significantly, during the earliest (1905–1931) period of its existence, not one woman was elected to its four highest offices, and only a few were included at professional meetings. Even moderately progressive male sociologists, such as the influential Albion Small, saw the spheres of women and men as different and *separate* and openly stereotyped women. As the chair of the first graduate-level department, and an early ASS president, Small hired women sociologists only for such specialized areas as household administration, social settlements, and sanitary science. Indeed, the ASS began in old-boy networks and was viewed as an association for (white) men. A few women were allowed as presenters or discussants at association meetings, if they engaged in a certain type of women's sociology viewed as acceptable by male sociologists.[16]

The Influential Jane Addams

Despite their marginalization or exclusion, some women and black sociologists were influential, if more outside the academy than inside.

Between 1892 and 1930, Jane Addams was one of the country's leading sociologists and policy intellectuals. She was cofounder and head resident at Hull House and a leader of the community settlement movement across the United States. She had a major impact on the political and intellectual life of her era. At first taking a Christian humanist approach, she soon came to accent strong ideas about expanded democracy, arguing that all people should have a voice in decisions affecting their lives. She advocated participatory democracy and social equality and pressed for reforms to improve the lives of black Americans, the poor, immigrants, and young people. In facilitating people working together, she felt that gathering scientific facts was important to convince all people of the correct type of action needed. Addams wrote effectively on important sociological issues of the day—including immigration, poverty, women's issues, delinquency, and aging.[17] An early social science analyst of the problems of cities, she was advanced in her sense of justice. Her perspective on democracy saw it as more than fairness and legal equality: "We are brought to a conception of Democracy not merely as a sentiment which desires the well-being of all men, nor yet as a creed which believes in the essential dignity and equality of all men, but as that which affords a rule of living as well as a test of faith."[18] As she viewed U.S. society, for there to be participatory democracy, working-class Americans had to actively take part in major decisions affecting their lives.

Clearly, Addams saw herself as a sociologist, and she was at the center of a network of important sociologists and activists. Yet, over subsequent decades, numerous mainstream scholars have tended to view her as "only" a reformer or social worker, and as a person with a moralistic and status-quo view of the world. Even C. Wright Mills, one of the few later sociologists to recognize her importance in sociology, viewed her in this light. This view of her is highly inaccurate, for Addams, who was often attacked as a "radical" in her day, had a critical, emancipatory view of society, in contrast to many of the men of the Chicago School, most of whom had a more moderate, corporate-liberal, and technocratic view.[19]

This was especially true of the later men in the powerful Chicago department, who viewed sociologically informed action as not involving real "science" and thus distanced themselves from it. The science of sociology, which had begun as a commitment to the betterment of society, now increasingly became a science that was more distant, abstract, and based on a natural science model. "These later men therefore condemned political action for sociologists, while the ideas of the elite, in fact, permeated their work.... Rather than condemn the exploitation and oppression of daily life, the later Chicago men described it. They justified it through their acceptance of it."[20] Most were allied with the moderate corporate-liberal wing of the controlling elite and rejected a more critical and emancipatory perspective. Most were oriented toward building an academic, generally elitist sociology. In contrast, Addams and a number of other white women—as well as some black men and women sociologists—stayed involved in aggressive social change organizations, such as the antiwar movement, the women's movement, and militant labor unions, and most were committed to building a new societal order for an oppressive United States.[21]

The First Empirical Sociology

Conventionally, the department of sociology at the University of Chicago has been given credit for inventing empirical field sociology, particularly the social-demographic mapping of urban areas. *Yet it was the women sociologists at Chicago's Hull House who first developed this major research technique.* In their book, *Hull House Maps and Papers* (1895), they collected extensive data on the urban areas of Chicago and analyzed it using detailed maps two decades before it became important in the work of the male sociologists at the University of Chicago. Engaging in the first collaborative research in the field done by U.S. sociologists, they used this technique for some years as a way of gathering and interpreting information on income, occupation, nationality, family size, and housing conditions. These data were often used to help local residents understand community patterns in order to make better decisions, not to provide abstract data just for published sociological analysis. Addams worked to get women of all class levels, rich and working class, involved in meetings and community organizing. She sought their advice and brought them onto the stage at gatherings, breaking down both class and gender lines.[22]

The quality and importance of the research done by Hull House researchers is evident in the *more than fifty* articles published between 1895 and 1935 in what was then the leading journal of sociology, the *American Journal of Sociology.* Some *twenty-seven books* by the Hull House researchers were also reviewed in the journal.[23]

The fact that the women sociologists were indeed the pioneers in empirical sociology was occasionally noted in the 1910s and early 1920s by the men in the University of Chicago department of sociology, but later these men criticized the early work as little more than social work or ignored it. Subsequently, methods textbooks rewrote the history of sociology and cited the technique of demographic mapping as the invention of male sociologists at the University of Chicago![24]

During World War I, a strong new wave of political repression was aimed at U.S. political radicals and liberal reformers. This government and private-sector repression forced a reduction in the involvement of social scientists and social workers in reform activities. Some of this attack continued into the 1920s and 1930s. Addams, who won a Nobel Prize in 1931 for her antiwar activities (one of two, and the first ever won by a sociologist), noted that "any proposed change was suspect" and that social researchers and social workers "exhibited many symptoms of this panic and with a protective instinct carefully avoided any phraseology of social reform."[25] This extensive political attack by repressive governmental and private authorities on progressive dissent played an important role in generating and supporting the move to a more detached, academic, and distancing social science. Even urban settlement houses were seen as "radical" by local and national elites obsessed with any challenges to the corporate-capitalist system. Moreover, from this period to the present day, "any attempt of [sociologically oriented] community organizers to become involved in the development of militant grass-roots movements has been seen as a blatant disregard of *professionally* defined functions."[26]

A Leading Black Sociologist: The Pioneering W. E. B. Du Bois

One of the most important of the early sociologists, W.E.B. Du Bois, taught sociology in U.S. colleges and universities from 1894 to 1910. He had close ties to the settlement house movement, which had spread to Philadelphia by the 1890s with its accent on community-based research. In 1896 Du Bois became an "assistant in sociology" at the University of Pennsylvania and conducted a major study of black conditions in that city using the "best available methods of sociological research." The book resulting from this research, *The Philadelphia Negro,* was the first systematic sociological field study of life in an urban black community.[27] Du Bois drew on the earlier studies and demographic mapping of immigrants by the settlement house researchers (see Chapter 4). Du Bois's book and the *Hull House Maps and Papers* were the first community studies in U.S. sociology. These origins of urban sociology have been generally ignored by later scholars. For example, in their otherwise useful historical account, sociologists Stephen P. Turner and Jonathan H. Turner locate the origins of empirical research in sociology in the labor statistics movement after the Civil War. Showing an unawareness of the actual history of U.S. sociology, they ignore both the Hull House studies in urban sociology and the pioneering sociological work of Du Bois.[28]

In his urban monograph, Du Bois gave recognition to a community of poor city dwellers, analyzing their conditions and exploring the impact of racial discrimination. His book received some good reviews by historians, but little support from white male sociologists. In spite of his stellar qualifications—major field research, a Ph.D. from Harvard, and study abroad with major European social scientists like Max Weber—no white-dominated sociology department made him an offer to be a regular colleague. In contrast, some white female sociologists in the settlement house movement strongly supported him, and he had rich intellectual exchanges with them.[29] Indeed, one white female sociologist, Isabel Eaton, worked with him and authored a chapter in the book on a Philadelphia black community. Du Bois, like early women sociologists, should be given credit as one of the significant founders of the new U.S. discipline of sociology.

In the mid-1890s, Du Bois was invited to come to the historically black institution, Atlanta University, to teach sociology and develop a research program and conferences on issues affecting black Americans. He hoped to build a "center of sociological research" there and developed plans to study many aspects of black life, from mortality and urbanization to religion and crime. In his field work in Philadelphia and increasingly in other areas, Du Bois saw himself as contributing to a social science "that studies the actions of human beings and seeks laws and regularities among those actions."[30] Du Bois sought the scientific data on the conditions of African Americans in the North and South. As with some other early social scientists like Addams, however, Du Bois did not see social science as an end in itself or isolated from the world of policy and action for change, but rather saw it as working to better society, particularly for African Americans. Surveying his work in sociology, Adolph Reed summarizes this way: "Rather, it is that for Du Bois scholarly pursuit always was linked directly and consciously with some purpose of societal reform."[31]

In his pioneering research work at Atlanta University, Du Bois envisioned close ties to the major sociology departments at Harvard, Columbia, Johns Hopkins, and the University of Pennsylvania.[32] However, Du Bois's opposition to views of the leading black educator of this time, Booker T. Washington, created serious difficulties for him. Washington had the backing of powerful corporate capitalists, who liked Washington's approach to change in U.S. racial relations. (Washington proposed gradualism and an orientation to vocational education and manual labor for African Americans.) Not surprisingly, thus, Du Bois had trouble getting research funds from corporate foundations for a variety of important projects. Nonetheless, at Atlanta University, Du Bois did engage in an ambitious and successful research program of study of African American issues, resulting in major conferences and more than two thousand pages of publications. By 1910, however, opposition to him from certain corporate officials associated with Washington led him to leave Atlanta University to begin new activist work, principally as director of publications and research of the new civil rights organization, the National Association for the Advancement of Colored People (NAACP).[33]

Du Bois did not abandon his ties with the women sociologists. Significantly, between the late 1890s and the 1930s, he had nearly twenty professional contacts with Jane Addams alone. For example, in 1907 Addams invited him to speak at Hull House, where he gave an address on Abraham Lincoln. Moreover, several sociologists linked to Hull House, including Addams, Du Bois, Florence Kelley, Ida B. Wells-Barnett, Mary McDowell, Anna Garlan Spencer, W. I. Thomas, and Charles Zeublin, signed the initial call for the NAACP, which was established in 1909.

The Sociological Ideas of Du Bois

In his books and as editor of the new NAACP journal, *The Crisis,* Du Bois was an early articulator of the intellectual foundations of the movement for social justice for African Americans. He spoke for those who were racially oppressed. In his work on the Philadelphia black community, Du Bois had gone beyond a documentation of realities of poverty and racial discrimination to make clear his moral position and the central role of whites: "Such discrimination is morally wrong, politically dangerous, industrially wasteful, and socially silly. It is the duty of whites to stop it, and to do so primarily for their own sakes."[34]

Later on in the 1930s, drawing on Marxist class analysis, Du Bois was perhaps the first major sociological theorist to emphasize the link between racial oppression and class exploitation. For him the interplay of institutional racism and capitalism explained why there had never been real democracy in the United States. Both white capitalists *and* white laborers maintained the system of racism: "The resulting color caste founded and retained by capitalism was adopted, forwarded and approved by white labor, and resulted in subordination of colored labor to white profits the world over. Thus, the majority of the world's laborers, by the insistence of white labor, became the basis of a system of industry which ruined democracy and showed perfect fruit in World War and Depression."[35] White capitalists and workers were more or less united in their whiteness—with its array of material and psychological privileges. Du Bois asserted that white workers accepted lower than necessary money wages in return for a "public and psychological wage" of whiteness. White workers were allowed by white elites to participate in the dominant racial hierarchy; they were admitted to certain public areas (for example, segregated parks) and functions entirely off limits to people of darker color. Yet by not organizing with workers of color, these privileged white workers paid a heavy economic price (for example, lower wages) for their bequeathed sense of "superior white selves."

In a chapter in *Darkwater* (1920), the first extended analysis of whiteness in the social science literature, Du Bois noted that "the discovery of personal whiteness among the world's people is a very modern thing.... The ancient world would have laughed at such a distinction.... We have changed all that, and the [white] world in a sudden, emotional conversion has discovered that it is white and by that token, wonderful!"[36] Indeed, Du Bois was perhaps the first sociologist to deal with the sociology of racial emotions. As he noted, color barriers are created not only by maliciousness but also by "unconscious acts and irrational reactions unpierced by reason."[37]

Du Bois also offered some of the first sociological analyses of a globalizing capitalism and imperialism. Writing of the years around 1900, he argued, "White supremacy was all but world-wide. Africa was dead, India conquered, Japan isolated, and China prostrate.... The using of men for the benefit of masters is no new invention of modern Europe.... But Europe proposed to apply it on a scale and with an elaborateness of detail of which no former world ever dreamed."[38] Analyzing Europe's colonization of Africa, Du Bois demonstrated that extreme poverty and degradation in the African colonies were "a main cause of wealth and luxury in Europe. The results of this poverty were disease, ignorance, and crime. Yet these had to be represented as natural characteristics of backward peoples."[39] He summed up European imperialism and the damage it did to peoples of color around the globe: "There was no Nazi atrocity—concentration camps, wholesale maiming and murder, defilement of women and ghastly blasphemy of childhood—which the Christian civilization of Europe had not long been practicing against colored folk in all parts of the world in the name of and for the defense of a Superior Race born to rule the world."[40] Few social science analyses of more recent racialized atrocities have examined the deep roots of racial oppression here well noted by Du Bois.

Du Bois was the first U.S. sociologist to analyze racial oppression in the Americas as thoroughgoing systems of white racism. In the Americas, the European-origin peoples applied slavery "on a scale and with an elaborateness of detail of which no former world ever dreamed. The imperial width of the thing—the heaven-defying audacity—makes its modern newness."[41] An essential feature of North American slavery was the denial of most human liberties. Slaves "could own nothing; they could make no contracts; they could hold no property; nor traffic in property; they could not hire out; they could not legally marry ... they could not appeal from their master; they could be punished at will."[42]

Du Bois was a pioneer as well in regard to an activism that was both sociologically informed and oriented to expanding human rights. He was a leading thinker and activist in regard to Pan-Africanism. As he saw it, Pan-African nationalism was a partial solution for the conditions in which people of African descent found themselves across the globe. Against major objections by the U.S. State Department, Du Bois put together the first Pan-African Congress in 1919, which was attended by delegates from fifteen countries. The Congress called for the abolition of all forms of slavery and curtailment of colonial exploitation.[43]

Early Black Women Sociologists

Among the early sociologists were a number of black women, perhaps the most visible of whom were Ida B. Wells-Barnett and Anna Julia Cooper. Wells-Barnett, together with Fannie Barrier Williams and Mary Church Terrell, was active in the Hull House group of sociologists. The important sociological work of Wells-Barnett and Cooper is finally being rediscovered by contemporary sociologists.[44] Both were practicing sociologists and very penetrating theorists of society.

Ida B. Wells-Barnett was born in 1862 to enslaved parents in Mississippi. Once freed, her parents put her into Rust College. However, when her parents died from yellow fever, she dropped out and became a teacher to keep the rest of her family together. She spent her life writing about, and fighting against, the often violent discrimination faced by African Americans at the hands of whites. She researched and wrote tirelessly about white lynchings of African Americans, using accounts from white newspapers to build a database. She approached such data with a profound understanding of U.S. racism: "The purpose of the pages which follow shall be to give the record which has been made, not by colored men, but that which is the result of the compilations made by white men, of reports sent over the civilized world by white men in the South. Out of their own mouths shall the murderers be condemned."[45] She wrote in detail of the myth of the black male rapist, who allegedly desired to rape white women, and she herself barely escaped being killed for suggesting that white men's desire for black women might be related to this rapist mythology. At this early point in the history of U.S. sociology,

Wells-Barnett developed deep empirical and theoretical understandings of the connections of racial and gender stratification.

Anna Julia Cooper was born a slave in 1858 in North Carolina.
Her father was likely the white slaveholder. She learned to read at
an early age, later attended Oberlin College, and became a teacher,
school principal, and gifted social theorist. In a major 1892 book,
A Voice from the South, Cooper developed a sociological analysis and
articulated the idea that black women have a distinctive standpoint
because of the double oppression they face. Like Wells-Barnett, she was
very critical of distorted representations of African American history
and contemporary conditions in the often aggressively racist white
media and academic scholarship.[46] Wells-Barnett and Cooper created
a sociology from the viewpoint of the oppressed and one dedicated
to full social justice in the United States. They were among the first
social scientists to analyze data on the social situations of both black
Americans and women in terms of such critical concepts as social
"domination," "subordination," and "repression."[47]

ESTABLISHMENT SOCIOLOGY: THE CHICAGO SCHOOL

Numerous textbook writers and other social science writers regularly
assert that the first well-developed sociological research program at a
university, the first research-oriented "school of sociology," was set up
at the University of Chicago in the 1910s or 1920s. This program is
usually termed the "Chicago school" of sociology. However, several
researchers have demonstrated that the first major sociological research
program at a university, one named as such, was the one developed in the
1895–1917 era at Atlanta University (now Clark Atlanta University), a
historically black institution established right after the Civil War. There
the Atlanta Sociological Laboratory played a critical and early role in
developing the "discipline of sociology, including the establishment of
the first American school of sociology, institutionalization of method
triangulation, institutionalization of the insider researcher, and institutionalization of the public acknowledgment of one's research."[48] In
1895 this laboratory was established by the Atlanta University president
and trustees to do extensive research on the socioeconomic conditions
faced by African Americans, especially as they moved from slavery to
freedom in the decades after the Civil War. As noted previously, after
his graduation from Harvard University and research in Philadelphia,
W. E. B. Du Bois became the head of this research laboratory in 1896.
There he developed an extensive and important research program, one
that accented one research problem for each year over a substantial

period of time. In addition, Du Bois instituted a series of important research conferences on this research on African Americans during the years between 1896 and the 1920s. Liberation-oriented researchers like sociologists Jane Addams and Monroe Work, anthropologist Franz Boaz, and educator Booker T. Washington came to these conferences, at which the field research was presented, and the research reports were published on an annual basis.[49] This was in fact the first research-oriented "school of sociology," yet because it was headed up mostly by African Americans it has somehow been ignored in the mainstream history of sociology. Moreover, we should underscore the point that similar sociological field research had already been done at Chicago's settlement facility called Hull House, as we noted above. Jane Addams and other women sociologists had not only pioneered in sociological field research there but also been the teachers and supporters of Du Bois in his own involvement in a research program on African Americans, including the field research program at Atlanta University.

By the decade of the 1910s there were at least four hundred colleges and other institutions of higher education offering at least one sociology course. A 1909 *American Journal* of *Sociology* report on courses in sociology based its calculations on questionnaires from 173 colleges, universities, and theology schools. A few institutions reported having a sociology course by the 1880s (Yale reported the first, in 1873), but most did not offer such courses until the 1890s and early 1900s. In the academic year 1907–1908, only 35 of these higher-education institutions had at least one professor devoting full time to teaching sociology; most institutions had only part-time teachers at this early stage in sociology's history. Only the University of Chicago had as many as six full-time sociology professors. In addition, just 20 institutions had full-fledged departments of sociology under that name, and only 6 universities reported offering ten or more courses in sociology: Brown University (10); Columbia University (26); Indiana University (12); Syracuse University (11); University of Chicago (100); and the University of Missouri (19). Chicago was the leading department in 1907–1908, at least in terms of having the most developed program of sociology courses. That department then had the largest number of undergraduate student registrations and by far the largest number of graduate student registrations of any U.S. college or university for the academic year 1907–1908.[50]

A Key Figure at Chicago: Robert E. Park

During the 1920s and 1930s, sociology did blossom at the University of Chicago, and many sociology students there focused on field research on urban problems. In field studies in the city of Chicago, Robert E. Park, his students, and his associates often accented the idea of urban "disorganization." Urban phenomena such as prostitution, "slum" communities, and the homeless were primary topics for this new sociological research. Although there was some demographic and ethnographic work on the communities of the black and immigrant residents of the city, the deeper dynamics of gender, racial, and class oppression were rarely examined.

Dozens of dissertations, theses, and books were written by students and junior faculty during Park's years at Chicago, and they collectively influenced the shape of U.S. sociology in this period. They included books like that by Nels Anderson on hobos, by Paul Cressey on taxi-dancers, by Edwin Thrasher on gangs, and by Louis Wirth on the Jewish "ghetto."[51] Park had a major impact at the University of Chicago; he taught there for nearly two decades and became ASS president in 1925. Interestingly, he himself was *not* educated in the discipline of sociology. As an undergraduate at the University of Michigan, Park had specialized in philology and philosophy. Then, after a decade of work outside academia as a journalist, he went to Harvard, where he took a master's degree in philosophy. Then he migrated to Friedrich-Wilhelm University in Berlin; there he took mostly history, philosophy, and political economy courses—and his only sociology course ever, with Georg Simmel. He would later note, "I never had any systematic instruction in sociology. . . . I got most of my knowledge about society and human nature from my own observations."[52] Park then followed one of his professors to the university at Heidelberg, where he did much work on his doctoral dissertation, titled "Crowd and Public." His first academic position was as an assistant in the department of philosophy (not sociology) at Harvard, where he finished his dissertation.

In 1905, Park went to the Tuskegee Normal and Industrial Institute, where he became a publicist and fund-raiser for the histori-cally black college created by Booker T. Washington. "Having spent four years in universities, he was eager for action. . . . He yearned to do something worthwhile."[53] During the Tuskegee years, Park traveled and interviewed many black residents in the South. The impact of his seven years there was such that he once commented, "I became for all intents and purposes, a Negro myself."[54] He was a student learning about the "curious and intricate system" that defined the black southerner's rela-tions with white southerners.[55] In his mind there was some distancing of his black subjects. He reported that in studying black people in the South, he remained "sufficiently detached to see it in more general social and sociological significance," and he argued that the "Negro in his American environment is a social laboratory," using the subject-distancing language that the early women sociologists had rejected in their work.[56] In 1910 Park toured Europe with Washington and began a coauthored book, *The Man Fartherest Down,* with Washington.

Though relatively liberal for his time, Park reflected the white-racist thinking of the era, as did numerous other white male sociologists of the time. Thus, in his writings Park suggested that racial characteristics, seen as "innate biological interests," determine characteristic features of groups, including their "racial temperaments": "The Negro is, by natural disposition, neither an intellectual nor an idealist, like the Jew; nor a brooding introspective, like the East Indian; nor a pioneer and frontiersman, like the Anglo Saxon.... His *metier* is expression rather than action." Park, like his white colleagues, generally saw the social world from a white racial frame.[57]

In April 1912 an International Conference on the Negro was held at Tuskegee Institute. The conference—with its theme "The Education of Primitive Man"—was the brainchild of Park, who saw education in racialized terms as helping the primitive "younger races" (blacks) relate better to the civilized "older races" (whites). Park invited William I. Thomas, a professor at the University of Chicago, to give a talk at the conference. This led to Park's being offered a position in sociology at the University of Chicago, where he gave his first course in 1914 on "The Negro in America." This was one of the first such courses ever given at a historically white university. There in Chicago, at a time when the NAACP and the Urban League were growing, Park chose to work with the less militant Urban League. Nevertheless, he was opposed to discrimination and saw black Americans as eventually becoming socially integrated into mainstream white institutions.[58]

One incident suggests that both Park and his young associate Ernest W. Burgess were reluctant to take overt action against racial discrimination. At the 1923 meeting of the ASS in Washington, D.C., E. Franklin Frazier—who would later be the first black president of the association in 1949—engaged in a protracted battle with hotel management and staff over discrimination. The hotel had a policy of not letting blacks use the regular elevator, insisting instead that they ride the freight elevator. Thus, one white elevator operator insisted that Frazier could not ride the elevator. Two white men on it pushed him out, commenting, "Why don't you go back to the jungles of Africa where you belong?" Holding his ground, Frazier replied, "No, thank you, I prefer to remain in the jungles of America with you white savages."[59] A police officer was called and tried to put Frazier on the freight elevator. Frazier sought out the assistance of Burgess, who was then ASS secretary. Burgess went to the manager and reported back to Frazier that the manager was adamant in refusing to let black sociologists use the regular elevator. Frazier was later harassed by hotel police officers when he was in the lobby of the hotel. At the time Burgess took no further action to challenge the color line. Park had also witnessed one of the discriminatory incidents and offered to ride the elevator with Frazier, but did not intervene further. In this case, "liberal" Chicago School racial relations experts meekly reacted to the brutal exclusion of a black colleague. There is no record of any individual or ASS organizational protest against the racial harassment of Frazier, and the association met in the same hotel the following year.[60] Later, in the early 1950s, Frazier would even face discrimination at the University of Chicago, where he had earlier done his graduate work. The "liberal" university turned him down for a faculty position because "the wives of white professors would object."[61]

The Chicago Department Becomes Dominant

In 1916 the young Ernest W. Burgess was hired as an instructor at the University of Chicago, and Robert Park helped him organize readings for an introductory sociology course. This course led to the development of a very influential textbook, *Introduction to the Science of Sociology,* by Park and Burgess.[62] This is a large textbook, with 1,000 pages and nearly 200 readings with interspersed commentary. Georg Simmel, Charles Darwin, Herbert Spencer, Emile Durkheim, Gabriel Tarde, Gustave Le Bon, William Graham Sumner, Charles Cooley, William I. Thomas, and Park himself are the ten most excerpted scholars. There is *no* mention of Karl Marx and no serious discussion of the work of sociologists like Jane Addams or W.E.B. Du Bois. Park and Burgess considered the book to be a major and comprehensive treatise on world sociology.

In the view of Park and Burgess, the permanence and solidarity of social groups rested on common traditions and voluntary consensus. Their general theory of social conflict, competition, assimilation, and accommodation had social Darwinist assumptions and was taken to be universal and applicable to all social interaction. Yet their analysis was actually grounded in assumptions about a stable society centered in modern capitalism. This was a corporate-liberal view like that of other early sociologists, who also did not deal seriously with systems of class, racial, and gender oppression and coerced social order all around them.[63] The Park and Burgess textbook was widely used, and subsequent sociologists have considered the book one of the most influential sociology textbooks ever written. The book helped set the direction of sociology in the United States for decades thereafter.

When it came to issues of social class, Park, Burgess, and most of their sociological associates took a moderate corporate-liberal approach that viewed capitalism as basically a good system, but requiring some technocratic reform and regulation. From the 1920s to the 1940s, numerous sociology textbooks took an approach accepting, more or less uncritically, the central features of the capitalist framework yet sometimes calling for moderate reforms. For example, in one textbook, *Social Pathology* (1925), Stuart Queen and Delbert Mann argued that sociological interpretations of societal problems should include ideas of maladjustment, demoralization, and disorganization.[64] In most textbooks like this one, there is a preoccupation with the failure of individual Americans to fit in with the established norms and roles, but sometimes attention is given to modest reforms that might be implemented by government. Some structural problems may be considered, but little attention is given to their deeper roots in the class-riven capitalistic system.

Criticizing Activists in Sociology

Not surprisingly, thus, by the 1920s, Park and some of his influential associates were opposed to the more activist and emancipatory sociology of the white female and black sociologists. In the sociology department at the University of Chicago and elsewhere many graduate students were interested in reform-centered careers and organizations, and there was much student demand for courses on social problems. Over time, Albion Small himself had moved away from his strong commitment to social reform, but it was Park who played a major role at Chicago in shifting the emphasis from a sociology concerned with studying *and* eradicating serious social problems to an "objective science." Using grant money from the new Rockefeller (corporate) foundations channeled through the University of Chicago, Park headed up the Local Community Research Committee, which had control over new research projects. He shaped these projects and the graduate program at Chicago away from the reform-oriented concerns of the incoming graduate students. From this perspective, the urban reform movements had too much concern for "unwholesome" activities such as dance halls and alcohol. Park moved sociological research in the direction of looking at urban issues without what he saw as the earlier puritanical "do-goodism," of which he often made fun.[65] Some of the graduate students in sociology at Chicago came by way of the settlement houses, and Park clearly pressed them hard to change their aggressively reformist orientations.

In addition, and in contrast to more progressive male sociologists there like W. I. Thomas and George H. Mead, Park did not develop close relationships with women sociologists, such as Sophonisba Breckenridge and Jane Addams. The latter were at Hull House or were members of a subdepartment in the sociology department. Although he did admire a few research studies done by the women sociologists, he even argued that the women reformers had done more damage to Chicago than corrupt politicians.[66]

Park was complex and contradictory. He had in his earlier life been involved in doing muckraking journalism supportive of reform movements, and into the 1920s he sometimes got involved in reform activities, such as his presidency of the National Community Center Association (1922–1924). He clearly wanted to see the lives of the urban poor become less trying and more democratic, yet at the same time he pressed his university colleagues and students to move away from the emancipatory sociology of those like Addams and Du Bois. He supported a multifaceted approach to research. He and his urban sociology colleagues at Chicago were broad in methodological understanding and used a range of methods. One scholar who visited Park's sociology classes commented that the latter emphasized the importance of "life history cases, the value of contemporary newspaper accounts, the place of the participant observer, the need for defining fundamental concepts, and the proper role of statistics. He had an unearthly horror of the use of statistics for trivial or unproductive purposes."[67] In his letters, Park suggested that good social science requires not only accuracy and precision but also wide experience, and he pressed for the naturalistic study of human beings and their lives within particular groups and social settings. As Chicago sociologist Andrew Abbott has put it, the Chicago School "thought—and thinks—that one cannot understand social life without understanding the arrangements of social actors in particular social times and places."[68] All social facts are situated in space and time, and the Chicago School studies of gangs, prostitutes, poverty, and delinquency were set constantly in their immediate settings and at specific times in a city's urban history. This approach to accenting the spatial and temporal contexts of social life was to be gradually lost as U.S. sociology developed ever more in the instrumental-positivistic direction in the ensuing decades.

Oliver C. Cox: A Dissident in the Chicago Tradition

An early power-conflict analyst who drew on Du Bois and on a critical class analysis was Oliver C. Cox. Like Addams and Du Bois, Cox was an organic intellectual concerned with the impact of social oppression on working-class Americans and on Americans of color. He clearly was motivated by the experiences of Americans of color, their history of exclusion and oppression, and wanted to bring these issues to the forefront of sociological analysis. An African American, he himself came from the ranks of the aggrieved. Although Cox is not familiar to many sociologists today, he engaged in pathbreaking work on issues of racial and class stratification in U.S. society, and his work has greatly influenced our thinking on institutional racism in the United States.[69]

Though educated at the University of Chicago, Cox rejected the new objectifying and "value-free" sociology often found there. Recall that instrumental positivism views "good" sociological research as being more or less limited to those research questions that certain research instruments and statistical techniques will allow. Often mimicking natural scientists, the positivistic sociologists have usually sought to serve established authorities. Cox's work shows that this turn to instrumental positivism did not take place without resistance. He argued that human beings can design a better social order, and he took sides with the socially oppressed. He practiced sociology from their standpoint. For black Americans, "the very process of living in America as citizens implicates them in an interminable struggle for social equality."[70] As a good sociologist of knowledge, Cox noted how a scholar's social position shaped the production of scientific data and ideas. He was an early pioneer in what has come to be called "standpoint" analysis.

Consider Cox's analysis of Robert Park's work: "Park's theory of race relations is weak, vacillating, and misleading; and to the extent that it lends a 'scientific' confirmation to the Southern rationalizations of racial exploitation, it is insidious."[71] This is a strong indictment of the use of sociology as a political weapon by the ruling elite. His quotation marks around the term "scientific" suggest a questioning of the nature of Park's new sociology. In the preface to the book in which this passage appears, Cox wrote: "If social science has any claim at all to be science, it should at least refrain from distilling social data through a context of designedly developed, popular prejudices."[72] Cox impeaches Park's new sociology for not being a self-reflective science and for using a scientific cloak to support, if often indirectly, racial prejudices and other notions. Cox was also one of the first social scientists to examine the role of the ruling class in shaping U.S. and world history. Indeed, the deliberate designer of the racial "others" in society is this white ruling class—the "powerful, elite interest group which also orients the society in all significant questions."[73]

Committed to a sociology that would assist in bringing major change, Cox defined his own sociology as a reaction against a detached eclecticism or "tradition of tentative expression," the perspective that he attributes to Park and other mainstream sociologists. Much mainstream sociological work was thus irrelevant. "To be sure, it is well to keep our heads while the world is in convulsions, yet we may become inane if we discuss them as if we were describing an Egyptian mummy."[74] Sociologists must do relevant research and assess society critically and forcefully when the lives of people are at stake.

Taking a sophisticated and nuanced position on the role of values in sociological practice, he proposed that although accuracy and objectivity are very important for the sociological craft, one could not remain neutral: "Clearly the social scientist should be accurate and objective, but not neutral; he should be passionately partisan in favor of the welfare of the people and against the interest of the few when they seem to submerge that welfare. In a word, the reason for the existence of the social scientist is that his scientific findings contribute to the betterment of the people's well-being."[75] A sociologist should be *partisan* in favor of the welfare of the people. The contribution to the people's well-being is not just another trait of the sociological craft; it should be the reason even for the existence of sociological practitioners.

This was not a sociology just for those "immediately engaged in research," but for a broader audience.[76] Cox's work is replete with tactical advice for those struggling against oppression. For example, he insisted that ideas of racial superiority are rooted in the social system, and not the other way around: "We cannot defeat race prejudice by proving that it is wrong. The reason for this is that race prejudice is only a symptom of a materialistic social fact. . . . The articulate white man's ideas about his racial superiority are rooted deeply in the social system, and it can be corrected only by changing the system itself."[77] Here the practical advice seems to be not to focus on proving racial superiority framing wrong but rather to concentrate on changing the racist system in which that framing is found.

Moreover, Western capitalism's subordination of non-Western societies and its transformation of cultures around the globe are crucial for the explanation of systemic racism, because in the process of capitalist transformation the "other peoples became convinced that their way of life was relatively static and impotent."[78] Cox is not ignoring the physical violence responsible for the expansion of capitalism but is anticipating here the idea of domination by seduction of the oppressed, well captured today by the concept of "hegemony." The international hegemony linked closely to racial oppression is that of the world capitalist system. Cox thus did pioneering work on what we now call "world systems theory." The capitalist system's expansive nature is a form of societal organization that tends "to systematize the world in a hierarchy of interdependent, economically centered communities," which cannot easily remove themselves from this all-encompassing international system.[79]

Working alone as a black sociologist dissenting from the University of Chicago tradition, from which he had learned the craft of sociology, Cox and his work received little attention from the sociologists of his time. It is only recently that his brilliant and critical work has been rediscovered—work very much in the liberation sociology tradition.

THE GROWTH OF INSTRUMENTAL POSITIVISM

East Coast Departments: Social Surveys

During the 1930s and 1940s, several East Coast departments of sociology, particularly those at Columbia University and Harvard University, gradually became influential in U.S. sociology. During the 1920s and 1930s, the roots of a more statistically oriented sociology were established at Columbia University. A key figure was Franklin H. Giddings, a major force in Columbia University's sociology program from 1894 to the late 1920s. Giddings was one of the first to insist that the use of statistics should become the central method of social science. Recall his comments from an earlier chapter: *"Sociology can be made an exact, quantitative science,* if we can get *industrious* men interested in it."[80] At Columbia University, the idea of a rational social science came to be linked to statistical surveys and quantitative methods.

By the 1940s and 1950s, opinion polling had become a common research technique used in the fields of market and consumer research, advertising, and political campaigns. One of the key figures at Columbia was Paul Lazarsfeld, who was very interested in survey research on consumer issues. Indeed, Lazarsfeld became known for his view that the study of the buying of consumer goods could lead to the development of a paradigm for studying and theorizing human action more generally.[81]

Leaders in the survey research movement, which remains central in social science today, included not only Lazarsfeld but also the prominent Harvard University sociologist, Samuel Stouffer (see below). Stouffer saw survey research and analysis as the only way to effectively build the discipline of sociology. As Andrew Abbott has noted, decontextualization was central in this opinion-survey approach to sociology:

The necessary decontextualization of particular social attributes was then accomplished through the rapidly advancing discipline of [statistical] sampling, which not only separated individuals from their social context of friends, acquaintances, and so on but also deliberately ignored an individual *variable's* context of other variables.... This would later enable a whole generation of sociologists to act as if interaction were a methodological nuisance rather than the way social reality happens.[82]

Relying on public opinion surveys meant in practice that the social researcher emphasized only a limited number of (often superficial) survey items, or variables, and considered them statistically in relation to a modest number of other variables. Typically, the analysis assessed these variables in isolation from their rich social contexts. In an article in an influential 1955 book, *The Language of Social Research,* Paul Lazarsfeld and Morris Rosenberg codified this focus on "variables," noting that the term is borrowed from mathematics. They describe how one moves from "vague concepts" to a "battery of indicators," with explicit and implicit reference to examples from survey and census research.[83] Indeed, they go so far as to say that the end result of this "indicators" stage of research is "always the same":

> The investigator will have transferred a piece of social reality into a set of objects which are given a place in a variety of conceptual dimensions which the investigator considered pertinent to his purpose. The symbol and the complete formal equivalent of such a representation is the IBM card. To each dimension corresponds a column; the position along the dimension is given by the punched square.[84]

Lazarsfeld and Rosenberg refer here, of course, to the early computerization of social science research, in which punched computer cards were used to enter data on survey variables into the computer for statistical analysis. For these instrumental-positivist social scientists, "any subject matter under investigation has to be translated into IBM language."[85]

The richness of social life can thus be reduced to numerous columns on punch cards; the new language of statistical analysis and computers therefore becomes the "language of social research." Unquestionably, we have here a clear break not only with the work of activist sociologists like Addams and Du Bois, but also with the central methodological commitments of the earlier "Chicago School." Most of the earlier sociologists believed one could understand particular phenomena only by situating them in their social and ecological contexts.

Instrumental Positivism and New Sources of Funding

This new survey-variables approach got substantial financial support from major foundations, such as the Russell Sage Foundation and the Rockefeller Foundation, which sometimes channeled funds through organizations such as the Social Science Research Council (SSRC). As early as the 1920s, considerable money from the several Rockefeller foundations had flowed into the SSRC, where the goal was now to create a social science relevant to public policy—but one that accented quantitative and business-oriented research. Under the leadership of sociologists like Giddings at Columbia, an active effort was made to make survey research the central sociological method and to link sociologists' research to funding by foundations and government. Giddings's students, particularly William F. Ogburn, spread the doctrine of quantitative and/or survey-based sociology as the best sociology. Ogburn served on the new SSRC, and from that position he worked aggressively to promote the quantitative-positivistic approach to sociology and identified it as the way to unify the social sciences.[86]

During the decade before World War II, sociology gradually became a common element in the curricula of colleges and universities, and the focus on survey and quantitative techniques became more commonplace. President Herbert Hoover set up a Research Committee on Social Trends, and many of the thirty studies of that committee were conducted by sociological researchers trained by Giddings. This was one of the few times before the war that this type of quantitative (survey) methodology was used in studies for federal government policy. The final report of this committee called for an integration of social science efforts to provide new knowledge of social problems, knowledge on the basis of which the industrial and government elites could then make social and political policy.[87]

Ogburn brought his strong instrumental-positivist perspective to the University of Chicago when he was appointed senior professor there in the late 1920s. Between the 1930s and the 1960s, the Ph.D. dissertations and other research work conducted in that department of sociology became increasingly quantitative in their methodology.[88] In his presidential address to the American Sociological Society in 1929, Ogburn called for a rigorous sociology emphasizing quantitative methods and statistics. He also underscored the point that sociologists as professionals should not be interested in improving society but should focus only on discovering new knowledge.[89]

In 1935 a group of statistically oriented sociologists set up a new journal, the *American Sociological Review,* to propagate the new quantitative version of instrumental positivism. In the 1940s, two advocates of this quantitative positivism, Read Bain and F. Stuart Chapin, served as its editors. During World War II, a growing number of sociologists moved into positions in government agencies or were the beneficiaries of government funding largesse. Harvard's Samuel Stouffer became director of research for an office of the War Department. With several dozen social scientists, this office conducted many (later influential) survey studies of the U.S. Army and its soldiers. Sociologists also worked as researchers in numerous other capacities for the federal government.[90]

At Vermont's Bennington College, and after 1945 at the University of Washington, the prominent sociologist George Lundberg was one of the most visible promoters of instrumental positivism. Lundberg served as American Sociological Society president in 1943 and wrote books that carried his influence beyond academic settings. Lundberg emphasized a separation of fact and value in sociology. Writing in his 1947 book *Can Science Save Us?* Lundberg argued that, if social scientists had as developed a body of knowledge as physical scientists, then their "knowledge would be equally above the reach of political upheaval. The services of real social scientists would be as indispensable to Fascists, as to Communists and Democrats."[91] One analyst has suggested that in his presidential address of that year, Lundberg "seemed to some to verge on open anti-Semitism, while his other public statements appeared to repudiate democracy."[92]

During the 1930s and 1940s, remarkably few of the country's leading sociologists researched, or spoke out publicly against, the numerous fascist movements and governments of the time, including major fascist organizations in the United States. One reason for this was perhaps the new accent on a detached social science of quantitative methods. As Roger Bannister has put it,

> As sociology professionalized, a rising cult of scientific objectivity inhibited public statements on public issues while at the same time marginalizing those most inclined to speak out against developments in Europe. Intellectually, the treatment of fascism during the 1930s and 1940s revealed the continuing isolation of American sociology from European social theorists (Marx, Weber, and Freud, among others), an isolation that grew more marked as a second and third generation of American sociologists, unlike their founders, sought their training at home [in the United States].[93]

More Critics of Instrumental Positivism

By the late 1930s and 1940s, sociology and other social sciences had reached the point where the "tail" of the new technical methods was

beginning to wag the social science "dog." As early as 1938, a prominent social scientist, Gardner Murphy, warned of this in a presidential
address to the Society for Psychological Study of Social Issues:

> Undoubtedly a large part of our trouble has been an over rapid
> development of research techniques which can be applied to the
> surface aspects of almost any social response and are reasonably
> sure to give a publishable numerical answer to almost any casual
> question.... Woe to that science whose methods are developed in
> advance of its problems, so that the experimenter can see only those
> phases of a problem for which a method is already at hand.[94]

As Robert Lynd put it in 1939, in a book dealing centrally with
the problematical character of trends in social science, the modern
social scientist is "deeply committed, by training and by the need
for security and advancement, to the official concepts, problems,
and theoretical structure of his science. Quantification and refined
measurement carry heavy prestige, in part related to the reliance upon
them by the authoritative natural sciences."[95] Lynd noted the way in
which social scientists become organization men and women. When
social scientists were asked to "experiment in the manifestly safe enterprise of quantifying their familiar problems and to engage in the
more hazardous venture of faring forth into unfamiliar problem-areas,"
they usually opted for the first choice.[96] Lynd saw a strong reluctance
to get involved in innovation and intervention: "So one observes
these grave young scientists hiding behind their precocious beards
of 'dispassionate research' and 'scientific objectivity.' They observe,
record, and analyze, but they shun prediction. And, above all else,
they avoid having any commerce with 'values.'"[97]

Lynd argued that sociology and the other social sciences should
target crucial problems and dilemmas that involve the pain and frus-
trations of large numbers of people. He called for an expansion of
democracy in U.S. government, industry, and other areas that was
informed by sociological research. If this could not be done, he saw
democracy being abandoned by the country.[98] A second deep-seated
crisis lay in the "disorganizing confusions" of modern capitalism:
"Private capitalism does not now operate, and probably cannot be
made to operate, to assure the amount of general welfare to which the
present stage of our technological skill and intelligence entitle us; and
other ways of managing our economy need therefore to be explored."
From Lynd's perspective, social science should be a *holistic* enterprise,
with each social scientist linking her or his problems to an "inclusive
totality."[99] In effect, he called on social scientists to examine what

kind of world would exist if we used our social science knowledge and resources to maximize the "quantity, quality, and useful variety of daily living" for all Americans.[100] Social science should help to define and to spur the development of a society that would be more humane and livable for all.

Lynd was joined in his criticism of value-free sociology by perhaps the most distinguished non-American sociologist (and economist) of the day, Gunnar Myrdal. Recall from Chapter 2 that in the early 1940s Myrdal specifically criticized the move by Park and Ogburn to a detached academic sociology: "The specific logical error is that of inferring from the facts that men can and should make no effort to change the 'natural' outcome of the specific forces observed. This is the old do-nothing *(laissez-faire)* bias of 'realistic' social science."[101] He early rejected the faddish accent on a "value-free" social science: "Scientific facts do not exist per se. ... The processes of selecting a problem and a basic hypothesis, of limiting the scope of study, and of defining and classifying data relevant to such a setting of the problem, involve a choice on the part of the investigator."[102]

THE GROWTH AND BUREAUCRATIZATION OF SOCIOLOGY

Anticommunism and Expanded Funding for Sociology

Before the 1930s, most sociologists had conducted relatively small-scale research projects, and most used qualitative or descriptive-statistics research methods. Indeed, there was a significant diversity of qualitative and descriptive-statistics research in the early period of U.S. sociology. There were few grant-awarding agencies or large grants from any source. During and after World War II, however, the funding for sociology and other social science research increased dramatically. Still, during the 1940s and early 1950s, there was tolerance for methodological diversity in numerous established sociology departments. "Case study" researchers often coexisted with quantitatively oriented researchers. However, in the mid-1950s, the prominent Chicago department reportedly purged some of the qualitative researchers in its move toward more quantitative research. There was also a dramatic expansion of funding for survey research by governments and private foundations.[103]

From the 1940s to 1960s, the growth in the scale and influence of the U.S. government, especially in the form of new social welfare and military programs, provided new positions for sociologists. Numerous sociologists were employed during World War II on a variety of survey and quantitative research projects. Moreover, the Soviet Union's achievement in launching the first satellite, Sputnik, in 1957 created serious concern in the U.S. government over a technological lag. Such events helped to spur increased spending for the Defense Department and natural science research, with the social sciences also benefiting from this concern.[104]

Since World War II, sociology has been reshaped into a discipline in which many of its most prestigious members are linked to government agencies, foundations, and other bureaucracies that supply much of the money for conventional social research. After 1950, there was a great expansion of federally funded research in the physical sciences, and some sociologists pushed for a share of the new federal money for sociology. Indeed, in the late 1950s, fifteen prominent social scientists, including Robert Merton and Samuel Stouffer, signed a statement, "National Support for Behavioral Science," which pressed the federal government for more funds for social science, in part to help with the Cold War. These scholars commented on trends in social science: "We assume the probability of a breakthrough in the control of the attitudes and beliefs of human beings.... This could be a weapon of great power in Communist hands, unless comparable advances in the West produce effective counter-measures."[105] This openly expressed anticommunist orientation of the statement led Robert Friedrichs to describe it as an "essentially evangelical tract" put out by sociologists who had previously argued for "value neutrality" in social science.[106] Clearly, there was no value neutrality here. This was a period of great anticommunist fervor and of McCarthyism, with loyalty oaths being imposed on many college faculty members. Being critical of established institutions was often all it took to be labeled a political subversive and get on a government surveillance list.

In 1960 the National Science Foundation established a Division of Social Sciences and appropriated $3.5 million to fund social science research projects. Also in 1960, the American Sociological Association (ASA) moved to Washington, D.C., with a full-time congressional lobbyist. Funding from corporate foundations was also growing.[107] Between 1956 and 1980, private research money flowing to the social sciences increased from $21 to $41 million, while federal grants increased from $30 million to $424 million. Outside the universities there was new demand as well for contract research projects from private agencies and all levels of government. Graduate enrollments and degrees increased dramatically.[108]

Large bureaucracies developed under the auspices of private foundations and at the federal government level to fund social science research, and these agencies helped develop large research institutes at selected universities. This governmental underwriting of research fed the growing emphasis on advanced quantitative methods and on social scientists as research entrepreneurs. To facilitate this funding, many sociologists put on the protective clothing of "hard scientists" who, like natural scientists, accented quantitative and statistical methods of research. It seems that a majority of the sociologists who sought funding from government agencies or private foundations made a conscious attempt not to do research on controversial social issues. The instrumental-positivism tradition became dominant, with its emphasis on advanced statistical methods, on "variables," on demographic and survey techniques, and on the unimportance of assessing domain assumptions or using critical social theories.[109]

By the 1960s, numerous sociology departments at large universities, such as those at the University of Michigan and the University of Wisconsin, became influential as sociological research was increasingly sought out by the private and public sectors. For example, one well-funded tradition began at the University of Wisconsin (Madison), where opinion surveys have been used to examine "status attainment" in U.S. society. Researchers at other universities have also participated in this particular tradition, which has generated many articles and some books. One underlying assumption of this research is an optimistic image of U.S. society as relatively fair and open. The researchers have contended that their data show that the United States has an open mobility system.[110] However, numerous sociological researchers in this tradition have generally ignored the class-stratified (in the Marxist sense), sexist, and racist dimensions of U.S. society and the consequent major restrictions on upward social and economic mobility for many Americans.[111]

By the late 1960s sociology departments were growing in colleges and universities across the country. Large-scale federal and corporate funding brought major Ph.D.-granting departments into prominence. Today, these powerful research departments often disproportionately control major sociological publication sources such as the *American Sociological Review,* and thus can often act as gatekeepers for much sociological research and debate.

On occasion, sociologists have used their government or private research grants to develop very critical and probing approaches to significant problems in society, but not many have done so. And those who have made this attempt have usually had difficulty getting additional state or foundation funding. In addition, periodically sociological grant projects do uncover data that the country's governing elites would prefer to keep hidden. Indeed, this is a major problem for sociologists who are researchers for the nation state—they often become aware in their research of the oppressiveness and pain of state-generated conditions and programs and thus must make difficult decisions about how to write up and present their findings.

State Bureaucratic Expansion and Sociology

During and after the 1960s, the major increase in U.S. welfare-state operations—such as new educational programs at all levels, new hospitals, and new public health programs—was very important for the development of the social sciences, including sociology. In the decades since the 1960s, government solutions to the painful problems of such groups as poor Americans have varied but have regularly taken the form of piecemeal measures, such as the poorly funded War on Poverty programs of the 1960s and the underfunded housing programs of the past few decades. When the 1960s' War on Poverty started involving sociologists, many who got the call from government for contracts were the social statisticians who utilized opinion surveys or government-generated statistics in their analyses. Since that time there has been a tendency for sociologists and other social scientists to study social problems in terms of opinion surveys or government-generated (indeed, official) statistics. As sociology has become ever more linked to the federal governmental apparatus, it has lost some of its progressive reform roots. As C. Wright Mills put it, "Liberalism has become less a reform movement than the administration of social services in a welfare state; sociology has lost its reforming push; its tendencies toward fragmentary problems and scattered causation have been conservatively turned to the use of corporations, army, and state."[112]

With the rise of the United States to global dominance and influence, sociology and the other social sciences have been shaped into disciplines whose most prestigious members are often closely linked to major research university social science departments and to the large government agencies that put significant federal dollars into social science research. "Being closely tied to American capital and the U.S. state for both funds and jobs, American sociologists bought and sold a very liberal [corporate-liberal] analysis. Stratification was good and necessary; mobility was based on merit. ... The state played a beneficent role; social problems were tractable and sociology would help the state manage them."[113] Not surprisingly, these government and corporate links have meant that relatively few social scientists in elite colleges and universities have done critical research on the most privileged racial, gender, and class groups and their role in maintaining a hierarchical and oppressive society.

Sociology courses and programs benefited greatly from the expansion of the federal government after World War II. The number of graduate students and sociology professors grew dramatically. In the 1950s and 1960s, as a result of popular books by sociologists and because of growing social unrest, sociology came ever more to the attention of college students, the general public, and government policymakers. Contemporary sociology, in the United States and Europe, was reinvigorated by social protest movements of the 1960s and 1970s, including protests on college campuses. By the 1960s, hundreds of thousands of college students were taking sociology courses, thousands of sociology books were being sold, and thousands of credentialed sociologists were teaching and doing research. Sociology degrees at all levels increased significantly in the 1960s and 1970s.[114] Sociology was not alone in this regard, for most of the social sciences experienced much growth during this period.

In the period of the 1960s and 1970s, sociology was not all of one piece. The era brought a new concern with serious social problems, and many sociological research studies were at least oriented toward some greater government intervention to repair these problems. This period also saw a reinvigoration of more critical and radical sociologies. Critical social theories, such as Marxist, feminist, and black nationalist theories, developed and expanded, as we noted in Chapter 1. Some sociologists were directly involved in research associated with important student or civil rights movements or in the movements themselves. During the 1960s, many of the activist students, including student leaders, in protest movements in France, Germany, and the United States were undergraduate students, graduate students, or younger faculty members in sociology.

For example, in the late 1960s Dick Flacks (who later became a member of the American Sociological Association's governing council) was an untenured faculty member in the department of sociology at the University of Chicago. In the spring of 1968 he was involved in organizing the New University Conference (NUC), which sought to bring together radical faculty and students to support the student protest movements of the period. NUC sociologists and graduate students at Columbia University soon joined together to form the Sociology Liberation Movement. Flacks supported student protests at universities, and at one point was brutally assaulted by a man opposed to his activism. Senior members of the sociology department and other departments at the University of Chicago verbally attacked those college students who were protesting the Vietnam War. Sometimes, the senior faculty members at Chicago and other major universities even took the position that the nonviolent student demonstrations were "Communist led," thereby often radicalizing yet more college students.[115] Across the country, mainstream sociologists attacked the counterestablishment ideas of the many activist students and faculty members and called for more ties between sociological research and the making of conventional government policy. Clearly, sociology was to some degree at war with itself.

The dominance of instrumental positivism in U.S. sociology was not unique. In the first few decades after World War II, many other disciplines in the physical and social sciences experienced a similar trend. In many cases there was a certain arrogance exaggerating the authority and importance of mainstream social science, what Friedrichs has called the idea of the "scientist as priest."[116] Writing in the 1950s, Reinhard Bendix described how mainstream social scientists were trying to become priestly interpreters of truth for lay people. He noted that contemporary social scientists

> no longer believe that men can rid their minds of . . . impediments to lucid thought: *only scientists can.* . . . They assert that there is only one escape from the consequences of irrationality: that is by application of the scientific method. And this method can be used effectively only by the expert few. . . . Instead of attempting to make people more rational, contemporary social scientists often content themselves with asking of them that they place their trust in social science and accept its findings.[117]

THEORIES OF SOCIAL ORDER AND CONSENSUS

From the mid-1940s to the late 1970s, the U.S. economic system absolutely dominated the world economy. In addition, the United States was one of the world's two great military powers. For the first time in its history, the United States substantially dominated the globe. At home, meanwhile, economic prosperity enabled the United States to provide many ordinary workers and their families with an ever improving standard of living.

Writing sociological theory in this buoyant environment, Talcott Parsons, a leading theorist and Harvard sociologist, and his associates accented a renewed concern with issues of social order and consensus. From World War II to the mid-1960s, their structural-functional perspective was dominant in English-language social theory, and to some degree, portions of it can still be found even today. One reason for its popularity was that structural functionalism claimed to be able to embrace all societal phenomena.

This structural functionalism was generally compatible with the mode of operation and the writings of most instrumental-positivist researchers in sociology, in that it provided a theoretical framework with little questioning of the status quo. Most social science positivists used data generated by government agencies or by research grants, and many wrote up their data with little theoretical analysis. Those who did make use of theory often did so in a perfunctory or uncritical way, providing citations to theorists like Talcott Parsons, Emile Durkheim, or Max Weber (but usually *not* Karl Marx), yet they clearly viewed theory as subsidiary to their main purpose of presenting "hard data." When one reads the empirical research of the two decades after World War II in journals such as the *American Sociological Review,* the *American Journal of Sociology,* and *Social Forces,* one finds that many of the theoretical concepts used in these research reports stem from the then-dominant structural-functionalist tradition.[118]

Social science often draws on underlying models of social reality, and these models usually elaborate iconic metaphors. In social science there seem to be several basic metaphors that are used as broad images of the societal world: society as organism, machine, market of exchange, drama, game, conversation, and war. One of the oldest overarching metaphors is that of society as biological organism. Drawing on the metaphor of a living organism, structural functionalists explain the parts of a given society in terms of how they function in the larger social system. Just as the human body has certain requirements, such as food digestion, it has interrelated parts, such as the digestive system, which function to meet the requirements.

However, research by cognitive scientists in recent decades on such use of metaphors suggests that metaphors are not simply figures of speech that map one domain of life onto another but rather are critical to the structuring of the understandings themselves. As linguistics researcher George Lakoff notes, metaphors give rise to a "rich system of metaphorical entailments."[119] That is, ideas from the source domain of a metaphor, such as the digestive system of the human body, suggest new ideas in the target domain, such as the economy being like a digestive system in certain adaptive ways. These entailments can stimulate thinking in the target domain in new ways. Yet, as Naomi Quinn has cautioned, particular metaphors do not underlie thinking as much as they are *chosen* by speakers "because they provide satisfying mappings onto already existing cultural understandings."[120]

Structural functionalists such as Talcott Parsons are, to be more accurate, "system functionalists." British sociologist Ian Craib has noted, "The idea of a system gives us the crucial analogy or metaphor in Parsons's theory: that of the biological organism or living system...

He does not stop at saying that social life is *like* a living system, he says that it *is* a living system of a particular type."[121] These system functionalists typically accent the importance of social consensus and stability and view a major aim of theorizing as explaining social order. In his 1959 presidential address to the American Sociological Association, for example, Kingsley Davis argued that the structural-functional approach was so pervasive that it was no longer a distinctive school of sociology; whatever was valid in functional analysis was to be found in one form or another in most sociological analysis.[122] As of 1964, thus, a large survey of sociologists found that 80 percent were favorably disposed toward structural-functional theories.[123]

Structural-functional analysis has played a more or less conservative role in U.S. sociology because of its strong emphasis on assessing the status quo and deviations therefrom. Working in the golden age of U.S. global hegemony (1944–1970), and with the federal government moving to bring modest welfare and civil rights reforms, Parsons-type sociology reflected a relatively optimistic approach to societal change. This optimistic functionalism provided "an anxiety-reducing reorientation" to the social world.[124]

Parsons rejected critical power-conflict theories, such as black-nationalist and neo-Marxist theories, that were skeptical about the long-term survival of capitalist societies and that forecast substantial resistance by society's oppressed groups. Significantly, in his influential theoretical book, *The Structure of Social Action,* Parsons makes no reference to earlier U.S. sociological theorists and analysts of social domination and oppression such as Jane Addams or W.E.B. Du Bois.[125] In this important sociological book, he does not include a theoretical analysis of social oppression that would likely have come from a serious reading of the early women and black sociologists. As an establishment intellectual, Parsons was committed to moderate reform and orderly change and was optimistic about agreement on values between groups often in conflict, such as privileged whites and oppressed blacks, and about a forthcoming decline in social injustice in capitalistic societies. Parsons and the many sociologists influenced by structural-functional thinking tended to downplay the serious problems of social class, racial, and gender discrimination and conflict within societies like the United States.[126]

For example, in writing about racial issues and conflicts of the 1950s and 1960s, Parsons accented the traditional U.S. values of equality and justice, which were seen as pressuring whites to eradicate racial prejudices rapidly during the period of the 1960s. In a mid-1960s article, "Full Citizenship for the Negro American?" Parsons argued that full participation in U.S. society for black Americans was part of a broad "egalitarian" trend that was well underway, a trend that would eventually resolve U.S. racial tensions. "Today ... we are witnessing an acceleration in the emancipation of individuals of all categories from these diffuse particularistic solidarities."[127]

Parsons accented symbolic ideals and generally ignored deeplying material interests—such as the historically derived racial privileges and unjustly gained wealth of white Americans and the unjust impoverishment of black Americans that resulted from more than three centuries of slavery and legal segregation. He ignored, as well, the local and national political and governmental interests that supported the system of antiblack racism before and after the 1960s. For centuries, white Americans have garnered their economic prosperity partially at the expense of African Americans. For example, during the Civil War, the U.S. Congress passed a major Homestead Act, which provided access to productive land to many U.S. families from the 1860s to the 1930s. An estimated 246 million acres of federal lands were provided by the U.S. government to about 1.5 million homesteading families.[128] For the most part, African Americans were excluded from this program by racially discriminatory barriers, including white violence. Some scholarly estimates by social scientist Trina Williams suggest that about 46 million adult Americans, almost all of them white, are today the likely beneficiaries of this government wealth-generating program.[129] There is more to U.S. racism than racial prejudices or stereotypes. Material inequality along racial lines underlies the U.S. racial hierarchy, and it has largely been unchallenged since the 1960s. One of the major weaknesses in structural-functional thought is the failure to recognize and assess the central importance of strong and conflicting socioeconomic interests in the foundational institutions of a society like the United States, interests that generate or link to the inegalitarian norms that are routinely acted upon in this society—as opposed to those norms that are asserted in societal rhetoric as being central (such as "liberty and justice for all"). Certain groups have distinctively different material interests and life chances than do others because the society has long been basically structured to benefit some members much more than others.[130]

Open and assertive support for structural-functional theories had begun to decline by the late 1960s. Indeed, today, few sociologists explicitly make use of this theoretical perspective. In his classic book, *The Coming Crisis of Western Sociology*, Alvin Gouldner described the crisis in sociology as involving the alienation of most sociologists from this structural-functional theory and a movement toward alternative theories, such as those of Erving Goffman, which encouraged a middle-range, social-problems approach that was more oriented to freedom and equality than to order.[131] To some degree, Gouldner was right, although his predicted professional consensus on a more liberation and equality-oriented sociology has not yet developed.

Organized Challenges to Establishment Sociology

By the 1950s, the expanding social science research for U.S. military agencies and other mainline government agencies was being challenged by groups of sociologists who emphasized the importance of a more critical perspective on U.S. society and global society. For example, in the early 1950s the Society for the Study of Social Problems (SSSP) was created by Alfred M. Lee, Elizabeth Lee, and other activist sociologists—as well as some social workers and other concerned professionals and students. This group was concerned with giving legitimacy to progressive activism and research among social scientists, especially in regard to major social problems. They also were concerned about protecting freedom of teaching and research in an era of political McCarthyism and other societal censorship. The SSSP is still influential in sociology today, with many progressive members committed to a sociology of change, although it has in recent years succumbed, to some degree, to the mainstream professionalization trends.

One significant source of the critical sociology of recent decades has come from the aggrieved sectors of U.S. society, those sectors from which earlier countersystem sociologists had emerged—women and Americans of color. Other countersystem sociologists have come from the white middle-class sectors of the society, yet have sincerely taken up the concerns of those who are oppressed. In the late 1960s, the Women's Caucus and the aforementioned Sociology Liberation Movement (SLM) were formed. At the 1969 and 1970 American Sociological Association (ASA) national conventions, the SLM openly confronted the sociology establishment. It began the publication of *The Insurgent Sociologist* (now *Critical Sociology*).[132] The Women's Caucus, which became Sociologists for Women in Society (SWS) in 1970, pressed the ASA to take action to rid itself and its member departments of discrimination against women. Also important in the 1960s was the Black Caucus, which became the Association of Black Sociologists (ABS).

Another group with restructuring goals is the Association for Humanist Sociology, which was created in 1976, again with the involvement of Alfred McClung Lee. Lee once argued that this organization is "one of several alternative sociological societies that are keeping the discipline alive, relevant, and exciting for faculties and students and useful for socially constructive efforts in our communities."[133] Moreover, elected in an important write-in campaign, Lee was an outspoken and progressive president of the American Sociological Association in the mid-1970s.

CONCLUSION

In an important 1978 book, Alfred McClung Lee noted that between 1905 and the late 1970s the American Sociological Association as a national association had "never represented the needs and interests of American society generally or even many of the concerns of those working in the discipline."[134] He argued that the "ASA and its journals and other projects are still largely in the hands of entrepreneurs or 'research' institutes preoccupied with grants and contracts."[135] Even with pressures from women sociologists, gay and lesbian sociologists, African American sociologists, Latino/a sociologists, Native American sociologists, Asian American sociologists, Marxist sociologists, and other progressive sociology groups, this is still substantially the case in the 2000s. A case in point is the 1999 rejection by the national ASA Council of a proposal for change by the elected ASA Publications Committee. The committee wanted the ASA Council to designate the committee's choice for an editorial team for the association's official journal, the *American Sociological Review,* a very diverse editorial team that they felt would dramatically signal a new openness to the many different research orientations of sociologists now within the discipline. In rejecting the committee's progressive proposal, the council seemed to signal to those sociologists who have traditionally been excluded from the *American Sociological Review* and other mainstream journals that Lee's 1978 assessment was still correct.

CHAPTER 4

Sociology Today: Instrumental Positivism and Continuing Challenges

A Crisis in Sociology?

Periodically, social scientists have argued that their disciplines are in "crisis." This is true for fields as diverse as economics, history, political science, and sociology. The recurring crises in the social sciences have been explained in a number of different ways. Some have criticized and bemoaned the breakup of their disciplines into too many uncoordinated specialties, whose diverse adherents often do not understand scholars in other areas.[1] In the case of sociology, the critics have often argued that sociology is too much of a catchall discipline with no common consensus or integrating conceptual paradigm. Certainly, sociology has been the social science where, from time to time, issues not researched in other fields have been housed. This has created significant and continuing intellectual diversity. Still, some suggest that without more integration and a consensus on core ideas, there will likely be a decline in sociology as a discipline.[2]

Degrees in Sociology

In the case of U.S. sociology, some observers saw declines in undergraduate enrollments, Ph.D.'s awarded, and academic jobs in the 1980s era as signs of crisis in the field. The number of master's degrees in sociology hit its peak in the mid-1970s, at just over 2,000 a year, then dropped to about 1,200 a year by the late 1980s. The number of Ph.D. degrees peaked at a little more than 700 a year in the late 1970s and decreased to about 500 a year by the late 1980s. The number of undergraduate degrees showed the same pattern, peaking at a bit more than 35,000 in the mid-1970s and dropping to just 15,000 a year by the late 1980s. Numerous analysts in the United States took these declines as suggesting something more or less *permanent* about the declining status of sociology. However, by the early 2000s, the data no longer supported this sense of crisis in regard to degrees and jobs. The number of college sociology courses recently taught each year has approached 50,000 annually. During the 1990s and early 2000s, the number of college students awarded B.A. degrees in sociology again increased significantly—from 15,993 in 1990 to 27,020 in 2004. Interestingly, this trend is opposite that for the field of economics, the social science often said to have the greatest national prestige. Over the 1990s, the number of B.A. degrees in economics actually decreased. Paralleling this significant increase in sociology B.A.'s, moreover, has come an increase in M.A. and Ph.D. degrees awarded in sociology—to 1,700–2,000 M.A. degrees and 550–600 Ph.D. degrees each a year from the late 1990s to the mid-2000s.[3] In the late 2000s the underemployment rate for sociologists was very low (1.3 percent), and membership in the American Sociological Association reached record highs, as did attendance at some national meetings. By the late 2000s sociology seemed to be becoming very popular yet again.

Because sociologists as a group have a less prestigious professional identity and have less intimate ties to powerful business and government interests than economists and political scientists, the field of sociology has sometimes been said to have a tenuous position within colleges and universities. In fact, a major bulwark undergirding the development and institutionalization of U.S. sociology since the 1960s has been undergraduate demand for college and university courses in sociology and for majors in sociology. Undergraduate students are mostly attracted by the relevance of, and problems content of, sociology courses, such as those dealing with crime, delinquency, family problems, racial matters, and poverty. Without this student demand, there would likely be much less support for sociology departments in colleges and universities. Much sociology teaching is at the lower-division level, where the courses meet general education requirements or the need for service courses for other professional programs. Moreover, many of the Ph.D.'s from graduate sociology programs become teachers in sociology departments with relatively heavy undergraduate teaching loads. Without the substantial undergraduate demand for courses at all levels of colleges and universities, there would be no large graduate sociology programs.[4] However, one should be careful not to exaggerate the situation for sociology in this regard, as undergraduate student enrollments are also very important in maintaining the viability of other university departments in the social sciences.

The decline in students seeking sociology degrees during the 1980s did reflect a rational response to declining job opportunities for sociologists. There was good cause for crisis talk among graduate-trained sociologists in the 1980s. Beginning in the late 1970s, sociologists and other social scientists faced a decline in the number of good jobs, especially in college settings, as the corporate disinvestment in parts of the U.S. economy began to have an impact on the public sector where most social scientists are located. This disinvestment was part of a larger societal trend. After World War II, U.S. dominance among the world's economic powers brought national prosperity, but by the 1960s the reinvigorated European and Japanese economies had begun to challenge this position, and by the 1970s and 1980s the U.S. economy was feeling major negative effects from this competition. In response, many large companies disinvested in U.S. plants and workers and sought lower wages and other incentives for enhanced profitability overseas. Increasingly, many corporations abandoned U.S. workers, a trend that continues in numerous sectors of the U.S. economy today. This disinvestment spread to state and federal government employment as well.

For a time there was a reduction in academic positions in the humanities and social sciences, including positions for sociologists. Although this employment situation has improved since the 1990s, there have been long-term effects. Thus, in many areas the character of numerous college teaching and research positions has changed. Since the 1970s there has been an increase in part-time and untenured faculty positions in many colleges and universities. The phenomenon of part-time work and temporary workers that has long been central in many areas of the U.S. economy has now penetrated college and university employment.

In addition to the general economic shifts, other explanations for the periodic "crises" in employment in sociology and some other social sciences have been cited. One change is the decreased funding for social science research. Funding for sociological research peaked in the early 1970s. Cutbacks in research funds reduced the number of certain types of academic jobs, such as for graduate students and researchers on temporary research grants. Yet other analysts have argued that periodic difficulties in sociology and other social sciences are in part the result of a reduction in government policymakers' deference to social scientists for data on which to make public policy decisions.[5]

A Changing Philosophical Climate?

Among the analysts who have contended that there is a disciplinary crisis in sociology, a few allege a change in the philosophical climate within U.S. and other Western sociology—toward more radical ideas and a more subjective approach to social science. For example, the sociologist and publisher Irving Horowitz, who developed the social science magazine *Society*, has contended that in recent decades there has been "a huge shift from 'scientific' sociology to 'liberation' sociology. In this world, survey research, empirical verification, and so-called data-rich theory yield to a sociology in which lifestyle issues prevail and decisions about how to present the self come to prevail."[6]

Pursuing his own eccentric analysis, Horowitz further argues that these supposedly dominant liberation sociologists are much too critical of the status quo: "The entire weight is not only on presumed displeasure with the way things are but with unrelieved blaming of the system for all ills—past and present. The approach is enshrined by the constant repetition of phrases such as 'institutional sexism' and 'institutional racism.'"[7] Horowitz is here putting his own distinctive interpretation on the growth of more critical perspectives within U.S. sociology since the 1960s. From marginal movements that challenged scattered professional sociology meetings in the late 1960s and early 1970s, critical sociology groups and organizations have blossomed with a range of perspectives that have increasingly achieved scientific maturity and intellectual relevance. Interestingly, Horowitz does not indicate clearly what traits lead him to consider sociological projects that are unconcerned with justice and equality as "scientific" and to consider the new critical sociologies as "unscientific." The opposite case can be made, for the new critical sociologies are often more scientific in that they break new ground in challenging biases and assumptions and add much data and knowledge about social worlds that have long been ignored by conventional social science.

Most conspicuously, politically conservative analysts such as Horowitz greatly exaggerate the influence within mainstream sociology today of those who accent inequality ideas and conduct research on such important matters as institutional racism and sexism. We can speak to the marginalization of research on these matters within mainstream sociology from our own and our acquaintances' experience with leading sociology journals, which are more often than not unreceptive to any form of countersystem research seeking to explore class, race, and gender issues. The most prestigious journals in U.S. sociology, such as the *American Sociological Review,* rarely incorporate these critical concerns in *major* ways in appointments to their editorial boards. Moreover, Horowitz seems to suggest the notion of many conventional analysts, including those in the country's mostly white and male governing elites, that problems of institutional racism and sexism are no longer fundamental to the country's daily realities. The extant data strongly suggest that this view is rather misinformed.[8]

The tension between so-called committed and scientific sociology is not new for the field of sociology. We saw in earlier chapters how Robert E. Park and other leading sociologists made a determined and successful effort to move away from the committed, activist sociology of early sociologists like Jane Addams and W.E.B. Du Bois to the "more scientific" approach, which developed into the detached instrumental positivism of much modern sociology. To take a more recent example, in 1975 the prominent sociologist Peter Blau wrote, "I have been concerned with the antisystematic, antitheoretical and antiquantitative biases that seem to characterize many members of SSSP."[9] He was referring to the Society for the Study of Social Problems (SSSP), which, as noted in Chapter 3, was an association created to resist the turn away from concern with social problems and social policy. Actually, the SSSP was founded to promote "a significant move toward scientific realism and away from the traditional scientific image sociologists once constructed for themselves in order to obtain legitimacy for their profession in university and in intellectual, political, and business circles."[10]

Who Are Sociologists Today?

What underlies the recurring complaints of too little concern with "rationality," too much accent on "subjectivity," and too much analysis of inequality issues in sociology? One reason for this view among some critics may lie in the changing makeup of those who actually do sociology in the United States. Over the past three decades, there has been a growth in the number of sociologists who are women and people of color. These sociologists often raise new research issues and theoretical concerns.

Terms like "rationality" and "value free" are used as part of the methods talk in much mainstream social science, yet this language is itself reflective of group bias, in that it is often an ideological cover for the perspective held by the traditional interests long dominant in the social sciences. Interestingly, when white men were the only social scientists engaged in research on women and people of color, their science was usually considered to be objective, value free, and detached. Now that women and people of color, once "objects" of detached research, are active researchers, they are often accused of doing "subjective" or "biased" sociology. The transformation of these previously marginalized objects of research into active practitioners of research has been central to the liberation trend in sociology that the critics lament. Thus, among many traditional social scientists there is great concern over the increasing research interest in a broad array of relatively new issues, such as institutional racism and sexism, class exploitation, heterosexism, patterns of methodological and theoretical bias, and a variety of cultural issues. Moreover, the growing numbers of women and people of color coming into sociology and the other social sciences, which has accelerated since the 1960s, have forced white men, who formerly faced little or no such competition, to have to compete for academic and other employment positions with those formerly excluded.

In the 1960s, white men made up most of the sociology Ph.D.'s being graduated across the country; some 85 percent of the Ph.D. degrees given in 1966 went to men, the overwhelming majority of whom were white. The percentage of women Ph.D.'s grew relatively fast over the 1970s, and since then has continued to grow. Since the late 1980s, half or more of the Ph.D.'s in sociology have been earned by women; by 2004 the figure had reached 60 percent and was growing. Interestingly, the 2000–2004 figure of 59 percent for sociology was much higher than comparable figures for most other social sciences (for example, 28 percent in economics and 38 percent in political science) and for the physical and life sciences (27 percent and 51 percent, respectively).[11]

Over this period there has also been a significant increase in sociologists of color. In the 1960s the percentage of Ph.D.'s, and also of sociologists generally, who were not white was quite small. By 1976, the year the number of Ph.D. degrees in sociology reached its high point, whites still received most of the degrees, with scholars of color receiving just 13 percent. Two decades later, this latter proportion had increased to more than one-fifth. Between 1976 and the 2000–2004 period, the proportion of sociology Ph.D.'s awarded to black candidates grew significantly from 5.1 percent to 9.1 percent. This percentage was significantly higher than in economics, psychology, and political science.[12]

In addition, the proportion of Latino/as in the total group of sociology Ph.D.'s increased from 0.9 percent in 1976 to 6.6 percent in the 2000–2004 period. Over these recent decades, the greatest increase in Ph.D.'s earned was for Asian and Pacific Islander Americans. Their share of the total Ph.D.s increased from just 1.8 percent in 1976 to 11.5 percent in 2000–2004 (44), the largest percentage and absolute number among these groups of color. The number of Native Americans awarded Ph.D.'s is not available for 1976, but the percentage increased from about 1 percent in 1986 to 1.7 percent in 1996. Most recently, the percentage has declined to the point that the National Science Foundation only reports a group number for all the social sciences together (only 13 doctorates reported for 2004). The Ph.D. numbers for sociology students of color are better than those for some other social science fields, and they do have the potential to increase more in the near future, for the recruitment pool has grown in recent years. Moreover, between 1985 and 1995, the number of students of color who earned B.A. degrees in the social sciences doubled, from about 15,000 to about 30,000. The degree numbers have remained substantial since then. In addition, women have received a substantial majority of sociology B.A. and B.S. degrees since the late 1970s. [13] It is likely that there will be even more female, African American, Latino/a, and Asian American sociologists in the future.

However, increasing just the entry numbers is not enough. In her 2006 SSSP presidential address, Claire Renzetti noted the serious mismatch between the percentage of SSSP members who were people of color and the fact that in that year, "as in many years past, all of the Society's officers were white. The Society's journal, *Social Problems,* has never been edited by a person of color."[14] The American Sociological Association has faced similar problems, even to the point of its governing council rejecting in the late 1990s the first editor of color (and an editorial board of women scholars and scholars of color) ever to be nominated by the association's nominations committee to edit the *American Sociological Review.* Significantly, in her forthright address Renzetti next called on the SSSP membership to immediately "develop strategies for making SSSP a more welcoming professional home for sociologists of color, one in which white sociologists acknowledge their whiteness and the privileges that have historically accompanied it, but do not use it to dominate, dismiss, or disparage colleagues of color." Diversity of membership has not yet meant a similar diversity in positions of power and influence in key sociological organizations.

If these demographic changes in graduate sociology degrees do finally become translated into major structural and institutional changes, it is also likely that there will be more women scholars and scholars of color not only in associational leadership positions but also in chair, dean, and other administrative positions within academic institutions and managerial positions within private organizations. In this case, there will likely be ever more social science research on areas of interest to the communities from which these sociologists come. There is already evidence for this latter contention, though it is by no means at the dominant level suggested by some fearful white male commentators. Thus, in the year 2007, the Section on Sex and Gender, the Section on Race, Gender, and Class, and the Section on Racial and Ethnic Minorities were among the largest of the various research groups among sociologists (both regular and student members) in the American Sociological Association. To a significant, if varying, degree all research reflects the social origins and positions of those who implement and articulate it. Clearly, one would not expect these incoming scholars to celebrate the social science "rationality" that formerly defined them as backward, culturally impaired, less intelligent, or too emotional.

This new diversity in education will probably bring substantial benefits to all people, not just to the new entrants. In the United States, straight white male scholars and administrators have long controlled the processes and institutions that develop academic learning, information, and knowledge. Yet, creative new ideas and data on long neglected issues of social import often come from those traditionally excluded from mainstream processes and institutions. We have seen this in past eras, such as when Jewish American scholars and researchers were finally allowed substantial participation in U.S. and European universities. Today, women scholars, gay/lesbian scholars, and scholars of color, the new "outsiders within," have introduced much intellectual ferment into the study of traditional research topics, such as families, gender, and crime, and have opened up, in innovative ways, a range of newer issues such as institutional sexism, homophobia, and systemic racism. For example, in her pathbreaking book, *Black Feminist Thought,* African American sociologist and American Sociological Association President Patricia Hill Collins has argued that a black-feminist theoretical framework is essential to developing a meaningful sociological understanding of women in U.S. society, particularly African American women. Thus, she critically analyzes traditional stereotypes of blacks, such as the white notion of the docile mammy or the irresponsible welfare mother; and she demonstrates how such severely negative images (sometimes part of older social science as well) arise out of and undergird the system of institutional racism and white privilege in the United States.[15] The black-feminist perspective, pioneered by early sociologists like Anna Julia Cooper and Ida Wells-Barnett (see Chapter 3), is hereby reinvigorated for contemporary sociology. For its long-term intellectual health, the field of sociology needs a regular infusion of new ideas and inventive research that expands its intellectual reach and depth.

INSTRUMENTAL POSITIVISM IN CONTEMPORARY SOCIOLOGY

Mainstream Positivism Today

In Chapter 3 we noted that before and during World War II there was a trend in the direction of a sociology less concerned with progressive change and reform and that was increasingly accenting the statistical and survey methods. The anticommunist crusades of the 1940s and 1950s placed sociology and indeed all intellectual activity under a repressive umbrella of self-censorship. Alfred McClung Lee, a founder of the SSSP, wrote that "McCarthyism's red-baiting excesses stimulated a nervous dread of the socially critical and controversial, of any basic or radical approach to human affairs."[16]

In the decades since the 1950s, many sociologists have worked to shape contemporary sociology into a field whose prestigious departments have often emphasized survey research, demographic methods, and quantitative analytical approaches, usually to the detriment of other research procedures. This type of instrumental positivism typically involves the aggregation of survey data, the development of formal hypotheses, the adoption of specified falsification procedures, and the grounding of theories in statistical measurement and data. Indeed, for many sociologists, the idea of "scientific methodology" has become largely equated with the application of statistical techniques to government census data or other survey data. We should make it clear here that we do not oppose the use of quantitative methods in social science, a point to which we will return below. Our concern about contemporary versions of instrumental positivism is the way in which quantitative research methods have come to be seen by many social scientists as the only, or the most acceptable, way of doing "proper" social science—an approach to social science that is too often ahistorical and atheoretical and which downplays other important ways of generating significant social knowledge.

Qualitative research and analysis, such as focus group interviewing or ethnographic research in the field, have often been relegated by powerful elites in various social science fields to the unscientific or "softer scientific" category. In a conventional positivistic approach, propositional statements are accepted or rejected solely on the basis of a statistical evaluation of the evidence; subjective factors in this (and all) research, such as the underlying assumptions and implicit biases of the researchers, are not ordinarily foregrounded or analyzed. By the 1970s, most major, and many other, sociology graduate programs had accepted this establishment quest for a quantitatively oriented, instrumental-positivistic sociology.

There are, of course, numerous knowledge-producing systems in social science, and quantitative positivism is but one of them. As with other such methodological systems, this approach to sociology is based on assumptions about how we know what we know and involves a set of metascientific underpinnings, a methodology, and some theory—all factors that are webbed together.[17] However, the mainstream tradition of instrumental positivism has often displayed a general lack of self-critical reflection on its underlying assumptions and other metascientific ingredients. Thus, even a quick look at the articles published in the American Sociological Association journal, *Sociological Methodology,* will show that only rarely have there been serious discussions of the social research process within a holistic and critical framework—of the interrelationships between mainstream methods, theory, and the role of underlying background assumptions and values in the research process.[18]

All research methods have their own languages. In the case of quantitative positivism, the language of research and presentation "pervasively reflects the foundational presumption of an objective world of concrete components that can be represented in terms of 'hard data.'"[19] The methods talk of quantitative positivism makes the social phenomena studied appear very substantial and coherent. Yet this substantiality and coherence is, at least in part, achieved through the use of conventional language and the interpretive framework of this type of research: "Method talk in the quantitative workplace conveys a deep commitment to systematically and rigorously representing a separate and distinct order of things without disturbing that order in the process."[20] Whatever the methodological approach, the language used involves at base more than spoken or written words, because it entails categories of thought and the speaker's or writer's underlying assumptions. These underlying assumptions are often deeply embedded not only in cognitive processes but also in individual feelings or group-related emotions. This methods language has little to do with the truth or falseness of the facts being created in the research process. Indeed, all academic research disciplines are constituted by their errors as well as their truths.[21] But the language of a discipline does have a lot to do with being "in the truth." As a rule, those wanting to do the "most acceptable" sociology must use the discipline's mainstream vocabulary and place their ideas and findings within the conceptual horizons enforced by the discipline's principal gatekeepers, such as the mainstream editors, editorial boards, and peer reviewers of certain major journals.

Nonetheless, the real social world is not neat, and since research is done by fallible human beings, many extra-scientific factors necessarily intrude into research on that world. From research on how hypotheses and theories are made, we know that they are often accepted before the evidence is in because they are in line with the researcher's background assumptions. All social science hypotheses and theories are shaped by the social contexts of their creators. Social science theories, methods of data collection, and the actual data collected are shaped by many of the same forces that mainstream social scientists study, yet these scientists are often unwilling to closely examine these forces as they pervade their endeavors. By its nature the generation of ideas and theory is historical and social and riddled with underlying moral assumptions and collective values. "Every social theory has both political and personal relevance, which, according to the technical canons of social theory, it is not supposed to have."[22] All too often the instrumental-positivist tradition has sought to portray researchers as "value-free" outsiders, yet all social science has involved the routine intrusion of researchers' values, including choices about what to study and not study.

Funding Agencies and Instrumental Positivism

We noted in Chapter 3 the great increase in grant and contract money that became available to sociologists and other social scientists in the decades following World War II. The increase in social-welfare-state operations during the 1960s and 1970s was also important for social science research. The new social-welfare orientation of the 1960s involved many social scientists in research studies for federal and state government programs, such as War on Poverty programs. Some of these projects did come up with exciting new information and ideas for social understanding and social change, though elite policymakers often ignored them. Over time this social science research for government agencies, with some notable exceptions, has generally became less reformist and/or more bureaucratized.

Over the decades since World War II, the increase in social science grants has created significant umbilical linkages to government agencies and private foundations. Generally speaking, these enticing research grants have provided not only equipment and data materials but also research assistance—and thereby have supported many graduate students, particularly at the larger "research 1" universities.

Sometimes, the grants have also provided salary support for faculty members. Most of these major research grants in sociology and many other social sciences have been oriented to a quantitative positivism, which often makes use of opinion surveys and census data. Why is this the case? One reason is that since World War II social scientists seeking research grants have typically found that the "hard science" methods of quantitative positivism are most acceptable to government and other funding agencies that are used to dealing with physical scientists and with a mathematical or statistical framing of scientific research (see Chapter 3).

Another probable reason for this situation is that much quantitative work in the social sciences has been in the form of a relatively atheoretical or hired-hand empiricism, which allows elite policymakers to more easily manipulate it as they see fit. Such instrumental-positivist projects more easily serve administrative ends.[23] Much sociological research done under government and foundation grants and under auspices of businesses and corporations has provided the knowledge that officials and policymakers need to pursue the undemocratic interests of elite social groups. This is clear in the case of market surveys done for corporations to ascertain consumer preferences and in the case of workplace surveys done for employers to enhance profitability at the expense of workers. In many research projects, sociologists and other social scientists have knowingly or unwittingly played a role in legitimating the problematic perspectives and actions of the U.S. government and business interests.

It is mainly those research projects viewed as fundable by government and private granting agencies—and not screened out by the professional reviewers, the mainstream social science scholars who generally function as gatekeepers—that can get significant research support. To get substantial funding for social research, one must usually do the type of research that is acceptable to government agencies and corporate-funded institutes and foundations, which are typically oriented to the status quo or, at most, to modest reforms thereof. Many social scientists' research goals have been shaped, often intentionally, to coincide with the establishment-oriented interests of the conventional bureaucratic benefactors. In seeking this attractive funding, many sociologists and other social scientists have fashioned themselves into grant-seeking entrepreneurs with the narrow scholarly goals and identifiable niches of inquiry that enable them to get research grants. Thus, in major areas of sociological research, the accommodation to funding sources has resulted in only a limited array of acceptable research topics being studied.

For several decades now, we have had a situation of significant de facto restrictions on the types of social research that will be funded by private and public agencies. To take just one critical area of research, in recent years very few major studies primarily involving qualitative methods (field studies) have been funded by conventional agencies to study the everyday practice of racial and gender discrimination within workplaces, educational settings, and public accommodations—areas with major and continuing problems of such serious discrimination. Since 1990, the first author has done numerous field studies (most resulting in major books) on how racial discrimination works in everyday practice but has been unable to secure funding from the conventional governmental and foundation sources of funding for social science. Similarly, our recent review of the literature on gender discrimination has revealed no major field studies using in-depth interviewing or other qualitative research methods to study the range and character of everyday discrimination faced by women in the United States. Studies of such discrimination issues, other than a few involving demographic analyses and opinion surveys, are rarely funded by government agencies. In recent decades numerous important qualitative research studies in sociology have been self-funded or funded by small grants from college faculty programs or a few progressive foundations.[24]

The larger academic context has been shaped by an intrusive government and corporate framework of contracts and grant procurement. Not only individual researchers but also college and university settings have become closely tied to government funding and grants, which often carry lucrative overhead allocations to academic institutions where grant-supported researchers are located. This quest for outside funding has increased as many colleges and universities have periodically suffered budget cutbacks at the hands of state legislators or their boards of regents or trustees. Coveting the prestige and the overhead money—what universities charge to administer the grant— higher level administrators at public universities from the University of Georgia to the University of California and private universities from Harvard University to the University of Southern California pressure their faculties to devote much time and energy to seeking outside research grants. Indeed, some administrators go so far as to disproportionately hire those who are likely to bring in large research grants, often regardless of their teaching skills, field of specialty, scholarly promise, or experience. U.S. colleges and universities are far from being the independent, pluralistic, unattached, and free-thinking organizations they often proclaim themselves to be. Increasingly, we see U.S. colleges and universities run and managed as profit-seeking businesses. (Another example recently in the media is the tilt at many colleges and universities toward athletic programs run with an accent on securing million-dollar profits.)

Relying on Nation-State Data

We have noted several impacts from this commitment in sociology and the other social sciences to an instrumental positivism and to working closely with governmental agencies and corporate foundations. Also noteworthy is the impact that the great social science reliance on data sources generated by official or establishment sources has on social scientific findings and development. (One alternative is independent collection of data by social scientists in the field.) In fact, the data used for much mainstream social science analysis usually come directly from government sources, such as the Census Bureau, or from opinion surveys generated out of conventional research grants vetted and made by government agencies and corporate foundations. Much sociological research involves extensive statistical analysis of these survey and demographic data sets, both new and old.

Interestingly, U.S. social scientists have often been critical of biases in government-generated data in other countries, such as those of the former Soviet Union or of contemporary Communist China. Yet they much less often raise substantial questions about the political and economic biases in comparable data created by U.S. government agencies—at least not in a fundamental and ongoing way. Various bureaucratic agencies collect data on such items as military casualties (such as in Vietnam and Iraq), urban crime, family income, family wealth, education, and migration. Several studies have shown that some bureaucratic agencies do not collect data that might put them in a bad light or that might be controversial. Some key officials in local, state, and federal government agencies "cook" their data to fit their own bureaucratic and political ends.[25] It is often in the interest of the generators of data to shape the data to fit the needs of the bureaucratic setting in which they work, if only to preserve their careers.

A heavy reliance on government grants and data can foster a general acceptance of the existing organization of, and data from, the government, yet such government data can be very problematical. For example, one study of local police data on gangs and gang activities found that most of the criminal activities the police said were done by real gangs were only a small portion of the crimes included in the official "gang statistics." The researcher, Albert Meehan, concluded that social scientists tend to ignore the police and other governmental manipulation of such crime data: "Statistics generated by organizational personnel, for their own 'good' organizational reasons ..., should never be treated as an indicator of events as they would appear to be to an observer."[26]

A leading criminologist, William Chambliss, has shown that many FBI and other police officials have periodically exaggerated the number of major crimes in the United States, including murders and assaults. He summarizes his analysis this way:

> In an effort to take a bite out of the budgets of other governmental agencies, the Department of Justice and its law enforcement bureaucracies, especially the FBI and the National Institutes of Justice, consistently inflate or bias reports of data on crime. These same federal agencies hand out lucrative research grants to criminologists who uncritically accept the Department of Justice's crime control perspective.[27]

All too often, establishment officials and politicians have played up these manipulated and exaggerated statistics for their own political purposes, yet only a few social scientists have regularly spoken out against these distortions and political uses of governmental data. Indeed, by accepting the data without serious and recurring questioning, mainstream social scientists make a moral commitment to the U.S. government and to the persistence of certain types of corruption, whether or not they consciously recognize that commitment. They choose to reject the alternatives, which can include going into the field without large grants, collecting research data on neglected aspects of society, working locally with communities on research relevant to progressive goals, and doing countersystem research analyses significantly critical of the nation state.

PROFESSIONALIZATION AND INSTRUMENTAL POSITIVISM

A Straitjacket for New Social Scientists

The professionalization of sociology over the past few decades has taken a distinctive turn. As with other social sciences, this direction is often characterized by sociology careers built around the methods and language of quantitative positivism, associated grant procurement, and research and teaching based on conventional statistical methods, usually with little consideration of qualitative research alternatives. This narrow professionalization has shaped the education and careers of many new recruits coming into the sphere of the social sciences. Over the past few decades, much graduate student training in sociology has stressed the importance of instrumental positivism, including a heavy accent on advanced statistical analyses. In fact, new graduate students are usually required to take several quantitative methods and statistics courses, while comparable in-depth training in qualitative research techniques—such as in-depth interviews, focus groups, and participant observation—is less likely to be required. A graduate or undergraduate education oriented to quantitative positivism is conventionally thought to help students, once they are graduated, to get good jobs and to teach mainstream sociology—as well as, in many cases, to compete for grants and publish in conventional outlets such as mainstream journals.

In this process, the education of new social scientists is often corrupted. The methodological critic Paul Feyerabend has castigated modern physical-science education as

> simplifying its participants: first a domain of research is defined. The domain is separated from the rest of history ... and given a "logic" of its own. A thorough training in such a "logic" then conditions those working in the domain; it makes their actions more uniform and it freezes large parts of the historical process as well.... An essential part of the training that makes such facts appear consists in the attempt to inhibit intuitions that might lead to a blurring of boundaries.[28]

All too frequently, the education of new social scientists restricts their research efforts and interests by "simplifying" them as scientists, by narrowing the focus of their research imaginations. Needless to say, such an education can also reduce their ability to contribute to the research necessary for building a more just and sustainable society.

Journals and Careers

Since the 1960s, quantitative analysis of survey data, census data, and similar materials has become dominant in the most prestigious sociology journals, usually to the point of minimizing other research styles and innovative data. New sociologists, as well as other new social scientists, are often pressured by their professors to adopt instrumental positivism as their main research style and to aim for presentations and publications that embed that conventional approach. If this commitment is made early in a career, it may put the neophyte social scientist onto a research track that is unimaginative or narrow. The prestige of presenting or publishing instrumental-positivist research is typically high in the circles of those doing such research. Indeed, just a few such publications in mainstream journals like the *American Sociological Review* (the profession's flagship and indeed *official* journal) can substantially boost one's career in academia, even many years after their publication.

A few mainstream journal publications can elevate a scholar greatly in prestige in comparison to other researchers who may be more (or much more) imaginative and prolific in other venues of publication. This is especially true for those who publish in specialty journals that deal with issues of great interest to formerly excluded groups, such as the journals dealing with gender, gay/lesbian, racial, and class issues, in which female sociologists, gay/lesbian sociologists, and sociologists of color often publish. Ironically, some of these specialty journals have a high rejection rate for research papers submitted to them, yet they do not confer the privileges granted by the *American Sociological Review (ASR)*. Moreover, a lack of publications in "mainstream refereed journals" can have often serious consequences when a faculty member comes up for promotion or when salary raises are distributed at many colleges or universities, especially at educational institutions that accent funded research. Collegewide evaluation committees too often just accept the conventional rankings of mainstream journals as a substitute for a responsible judgment of the quality of a scholar's work when faculty records are evaluated for promotion, tenure, and salary raises.

Given the importance of prestigious mainstream journals to publication performance and professional evaluation, it is not surprising that there have been a number of controversies over the editorial makeup of the most prestigious journal, the *ASR*, since the 1970s. Periodically, numerous sociologists have protested the dominance of quantitative positivism in that and other major sociology journals. This dominance did not develop by chance. One factor has been the increasing linkage of sociologists at major research-oriented universities to government and private granting agencies. In order to demonstrate success from such grants, there is a constant need for prestigious outlets in which to publish the results of the funded research. Thus, many of the sociologists who do this type of funded research have had a vested interest in making certain mainstream journals remain very accessible to them and their research, even if this has meant a significant restriction or marginalization of other important types of sociological research.

It is also interesting to note that although the *ASR* has had articles with an instrumental-positivist cast since its earliest days, the prose of the more quantitative articles was mostly essay-like and readable until the 1960s. Some accent therein was on method, but it was usually a secondary concern. By the 1970s, quantitative-positivist methods, especially advanced statistical methods, became ever more central, and the articles became less accessible to the general sociological reader. Furthermore, before the 1970s, most *ASR* articles were single-authored, but since that time many have been multiple-authored—probably a sign of the development of research by teams of sociologists working on grant-funded projects.[29]

Viewed narrowly, debates on the character of leading journals like the *ASR* seem to focus on what type of research should be featured in the journal and which editors should be at its helm. Yet, these controversies also reflect long-simmering tensions within the field over what theories and which research methods will be given full respect and attention. The prestige and dominance of a "value-free" positivism in the journals and elsewhere within the field of sociology create continuing problems for those who opt for unconventional qualitative research or for a liberation-oriented interpretive framework.

There is yet another problem created by this journal dominance: If qualitative researchers do not use at least some of the talk (such as the language of hypotheses) or the apparatus (tables with numbers) of instrumental positivism, they may find it very difficult to get published in the prestigious sociology journals or to get a hearing with a large audience of conventional quantitative sociologists. As a result, qualitative researchers seeking publication in mainstream journals are often forced to make some concessions to the quantitative-positivist framework.[30] Perhaps, even to be an employed sociologist in the United States, one must accept, at least implicitly, some of the framework of instrumental positivism. To be heard by sociologists trained in this positivism, one often has to meet them at least partway, by using some of their methods talk and apparatus.

Article and Book Sociologies

One ironic effect of the bias and censorship operating in some of the mainstream sociology journals is the development of a "mainstream-journal sociology" and a "book sociology," often with important differences in style, methods, and subject matter. The texts and data of the two are to a significant degree nonoverlapping. Since perhaps the 1960s, articles in the prestigious mainstream journals have increasingly focused on advanced statistical methods and mimicking the apparatus of natural science.[31] Significantly, words capture the nuances of human experiences better than numbers, yet the analytic or literary-quality essay seems to be dead as a genre in many mainstream sociology and other social science journals. As a result, the readership of these usually statistically oriented journals outside a narrow group of specialized researchers is limited. Because advanced quantitative research usually does not sell well in book form, commercial publishers look for alternatives—often a readable book using more qualitative research techniques.

Thus, in recent years, one of the best-selling introductory sociology textbooks—titled *Sociology* and authored by John Macionis—draws heavily on book sociology and on nonsociological book sources, the majority of which do not use the advanced statistical techniques favored in the prestigious sociology journals.[32] This and other major introductory textbooks infrequently cite articles in the mainstream sociology journals. In fact, they could easily have been written with almost no citations to research presented in the mainstream *ASR*-type journals. One reason for this pattern is that the mainstream journals usually do not provide a significant in-depth analysis of major societal events, developments, or crises, a point to which we will return below. Not surprisingly, book-type social science often provides a more accessible and contextualized source of data and interpretation for summary writing in sociology textbooks about the modern social world.

Sociology Is Not a Physical Science

One mistake of those who take the instrumental-positivist perspective too seriously is the assumption that the social sciences should be much like the physical sciences. Recall from earlier chapters the point that numerous positivistic social scientists have modeled themselves on the physical sciences, or at least a traditional image of these sciences, and thus have spoken of "the scientific method" as something separate from themselves and their assumptions. They assume that researchers can separate themselves from the method used and the object studied. These social scientists frequently use an approach and logic that distances those studied from themselves. However, in reality, the "objects" studied are as much "subjects" as the researchers who are supposed to discover relations among the "objects." The research endeavor is itself a very human relation.

Not surprisingly, those whom sociology usually studies, the "distanced" human beings, often have strong opinions about their lives and are able to routinely alter the social matrices in which they live. Sociological research is different from natural science research in that sociologists study those who act to change the conditions being studied. As we have noted, there is a long tradition in sociology—going back to Addams, Du Bois, and Mead—that recognizes the important differences between a positivistic social science modeled on physical sciences and a social science sensitive to the distinctive character of human beings who are its subjects. Human beings develop intersubjective meanings and act on meanings they attribute to physical and social phenomena. They are interpreting subjects in interaction with one another—with individual and collective memories retaining and utilizing the accruing meanings over time. Thus, qualitative-humanistic social science may on occasion use some of the same methods as the quantitative-positivist social scientists, but the orientation toward the subjects and their understandings, and an awareness of broader social issues, usually make the former approach quite different in its everyday practice from the latter.

Moreover, it is not humanly possible to be neutral in the human sciences because there is "a moral relationship between the human beings studied and those who study them."[33] Edward Shils has underscored the point that a certain empathetic sensitivity appears to be important to the development of much insightful sociology. The central thrust of this sociology lies in the view that "all human beings possess a quality which entitles them to the respect and consideration of their fellows."[34] Social scientists are, of course, human beings and cannot escape being part of the human world they study. This research situation is much different from a scientist whose study of stars, minerals, or plants is much less intertwined with her or his own life. No amount of empathy will add to understanding a planet or ancient rock, whereas such empathy indispensably adds to a deeper understanding of human beings and their societies.

The professionalization of sociology over the past several decades has frequently included a distinctive distancing of those studied. Ivan Illich argued that the mainline "professions" often become machines to extract money from those they study and serve without enabling them to act for themselves.[35] Reviewing the professionalization of social science research, Robert Blauner and David Wellman note some of its consequences: "According to this view, only the social scientist can define a suitable problem for research because he or she alone knows enough about the theories of the field and the methods by which theories are tested. In this model of science there is no place for the community-of-those-studied to share in the determination of research objectives."[36] Thereby, professional sociologists often disable those whom they research. Those preoccupied with being social science professionals may not listen carefully to—or provide an outlet in their research reports for—the ideas and deeper concerns of those human beings they study, especially those who are subjugated and dehumanized.

CONVENTIONAL SURVEY RESEARCH: SOME LIMITATIONS

A positivistic theory agenda often attempts to "test" or "falsify" theories with "neutrally" collected data. This approach is highly suspect because *all* data collected by social scientists are theoretically channeled and situated from the beginning of the data collection process. Counter-system sociologists reject a narrow instrumental positivism because "knowledge is not simply a reflection of an inert world 'out there' but is an active construction by scientists and theorists who necessarily make certain assumptions about the worlds they study."[37]

Underlying Assumptions and Methodological Individualism

Nevertheless, the fact-finding procedures of countersystem sociologists and conventional quantitative-positivistic sociologists may sometimes appear to be the same, for they both may use census and other official data or social surveys. Yet, viewed broadly, these procedures are not likely to be the same in practice, because the social scientists who use them have different perspectives and theoretical outlooks. To exemplify the way in which apparently similar procedures can become different methods when applied from divergent theoretical standpoints, let us briefly review the example of the measurement of "class conscious-ness," which has been a dynamic reality in Western societies since the Industrial Revolution.

Survey researchers have periodically tried to discern how class conscious North Americans are. In the 1940s, one opinion survey found that more than 80 percent of respondents identified themselves as "middle class." The conclusion drawn was that class was not a sub-jectively meaningful concept for describing the U.S. social structure. Then social psychologist Richard Centers conducted another survey allowing the respondents to choose from "working class" and "middle class" and found that half chose the "working class" label for them-selves.[38] Since Centers's study, data on the subjective dimensions and distribution of social class have been collected using interviews, phone surveys, and voting data. As one review noted, methods "that yield large data sets, utilize precise sampling techniques, and provide op-portunities for statistical manipulation of the data have been strongly favored in the study of class consciousness in the United States."[39]

Using the typical quantitative survey methods, contemporary social scientists have tried to study class identification, as well as class-linked attitudes and political preferences. The result from this body of mostly survey research is anything but the objective and neutral set of findings proclaimed by many advocates of quantitative-positivistic research. Measured this way, some researchers have found the presence of class consciousness among U.S. individuals, whereas others have not. Furthermore, others have found class consciousness in their data but have actually denied it. As Rich Fantasia has put it, "Such differences have tended to reveal more about the preconceptions of the researchers than they have about any collective consciousness of class in the society."[40] In practice, those who use survey research methods often do not acknowledge that their data collection procedures and analyses have certain built-in biases.

One common assumption of survey research can be seen in the typical focus on individuals responding in isolation. This "methodological individualism" involves an excessive emphasis on the isolated individual as the subject studied. Methodological individualism remains dominant in the social sciences because of the heavy use of survey and census data based on the interrogation of individuals. The image of the human being here is of the individual respondent, the person giving views in isolation from family and community. As Gideon Sjoberg has put it, "Many social scientists, including economists, psychologists, and sociologists, perceive the individual to be the proper unit of analysis. ... The primacy given to the individual as an isolated entity becomes the foundation for social scientists who, utilizing experimentation and social surveys, champion a natural science mode of analysis."[41]

This methodological individualism tends to ignore or downplay the omnipresent collective contexts of the creation of meaning. Taken alone, public opinion and demographic surveys cannot give an adequate portrait of important social phenomena because they typically do not provide much information about the broader contexts and interrelationships in which those surveyed arrive at their views and live their lives. Thus, in class consciousness research, the collection of individual data is insufficient to assess the character and development of a collective class consciousness. The way in which class consciousness and other human meanings are constructed in interrelationships involving two, three, or more individuals—or within the multiple social groups (for example, families) to which individuals allocate their energies—is generally lost when using this survey research method.[42]

A second limitation of much survey research is that it is conducted at one point in time, and responses to the survey questions are typically recorded "as fixed, static entities, minimizing any denotation of process, change, maturation, or ambivalence in consciousness."[43] This can be a problem because people may change the way they think or feel, often over short periods of time.

Yet another problem with survey research is that the realities being probed may be far enough below the surface that rather brief (often 10–60 second) answers to brief questions cannot tap respondents' often complex and nuanced views. Much of what we think we know as social scientists comes from these brief answers to brief questions, often relatively superficial queries framed from the viewpoint of (white) middle-class researchers in relatively isolated university or corporate offices. The deeper realities of human thought, opinions, attitudes, and emotions usually cannot be probed by such brief questioning. Thus, the deeper reality of class consciousness may not be tapped by quick responses to simple poll questions. This consciousness is more than cognitive, for it typically involves emotions, interests, and often suffering. Class consciousness may be well hidden beneath a rationalizing surface frame. Additionally, survey research is limited in that it ordinarily assumes that important attitudes, conceptions, feelings, and consciousness can be easily elicited in verbal or written responses to survey questions.

Survey questions on class issues are "artificially decontextualized because they are abstracted from the class practices and social relations that give them meaning."[44] For example, even an apparently simple survey item, such as "income," can be problematical. When a survey researcher uncovers a positive statistical relationship between income and attitudes toward, say, the privatization of prisons (the higher the income of a respondent, the more support for privatization), the variable "income" measures social status. However, when the same researcher reports that "income" is negatively correlated with age (the higher the age, the lower the income), the variable "income" here also measures financial solvency and life support. In actual research reports, a measured variable (such as "income") may be ambiguous and problematical; it thus can be an indicator of different social realities that need deeper probing to understand.

Social surveys need not be decontextualized, and they can be used for emancipatory purposes. We can go back more than a century to see an early example. Even Karl Marx once tried survey research and drew up an early social questionnaire, which was published in April 1880 in a French journal, *Revue Socialiste*. Many copies were distributed to French workers' societies, socialist and social democratic groups, and newspapers. The questionnaire's preface asked workers to reply because only they could describe "with full knowledge" the problems of the workplace and "only they … can energetically administer the remedies for the social ills from which they suffer."[45] Marx's questionnaire did not ask for workers beliefs, attitudes, and opinions, but instead requested ordinary workers to describe in some detail their working conditions, including wages, work hours, and safety. It also used valuable open-ended questions, which today are usually considered to be too expensive (in time and, thus, money) to be included in most opinion surveys. Consider a few of his one hundred questions: "If you are employed in a chemical works, in a factory, in the metal working industry, or in any other industry which is particularly dangerous, enumerate the safety measures introduced by your employer"; "Are there shifts of children and young persons which replace each other during the hours of work?"; "When work continues day and night, how are the shifts organized?"; and "Do you know any instances in which the Government has misused the forces of the State, in order to place them at the disposal of employers against their employees?"[46]

The open-ended questions were not designed just for research reporting, but rather to raise class consciousness and promote discussion among workers responding, and to draw "an electoral program for the workers in connection with a coming election."[47] Marx was not just interested in workers' subjective appraisals of conditions but in promoting group discussions about conditions as a way to inspire action. Workers' opinions did matter, but not divorced from meaningful action.[48] Here a survey that was used for liberation goals—to promote critical conversations and discussions, taking advantage of different individual levels of awareness and interest in working conditions. Such research-generated conversations are an important tool for change. Clearly, the aims of fact-finding procedures, what their results mean, and what kinds of understanding they bring about are dramatically different for social scientists depending on their theoretical orientations and underlying assumptions.

Missing the Big Questions

Another problem with a too heavy focus in the various social sciences on opinion and census survey data, and on the advanced-statistical analysis thereof, is the restriction of much research to questions of relatively limited consequence for human societies. In many social science circles there is a serious neglect of a range of important issues that cannot be well studied with survey techniques or that are not likely to be funded by established agencies. For example, data on top corporate executives' attitudes and actions on critical social matters— such as on racial and gender discrimination in employment—or data on large landlords' discrimination against single women with children seeking rental housing have not been systematically gathered by mainstream social scientists. Much survey-oriented research focuses on relatively small-scale questions, often in isolation from broader societal issues.

Thus, too many sociologists "have tended to scatter their attention."[49] Of course, this approach is not limited only to those committed to variations on quantitative positivism. There is a more general problem of decontextualization in the social sciences. Many other social scientists, who may use an array of research methods, tend to study issues and problems in isolation from one another, from their historical context, or from the larger frameworks of class, racial, and gender stratification.

Official presentations of sociology in major handbooks frequently emphasize the need for standardization in the discipline and recommend more quantitative-methodological rigor as a way of dealing with sociology's allegedly low prestige in the academy and in society. Yet the real problem is quite the opposite. Ted Vaughan has shown that several sociology handbook editors and commentators misunderstand the basis for the current marginality of much mainstream sociology to larger intellectual concerns.[50] The reason is not a lack of rigor but the fact that much sociological research has little relevance to major human and societal issues and needs. Yale sociologist Kai Erikson has asserted that a review of the issues discussed in leading sociology journals published over a period of several decades would reveal that "many of the truly decisive happenings of our own time have passed with little or no comment from the sociological community.... [A future] historian would learn almost nothing about the pivotal events around which the flow of modern history turned."[51] Moreover, one empirical study of more than two thousand *American Sociological Review* articles published between 1936 and 1984 examined numerous major social and political events for five periods within this time frame—such as the Great Depression and McCarthyism. The study discovered that overall *only one in twenty* of the articles dealt with the major societal events of the particular periods examined.[52]

Walter Powell, former editor of the book review journal of the American Sociological Association, has noted the substantial difficulty he had in finding sociologists able to think and write about broader societal issues to review for the journal.[53] This may be, at least in part, a result of the more or less exclusive training many sociologists have received in instrumental positivism. A too-technical education may prevent social researchers from seeing the broad changes going on around them and from envisioning possible social futures. Such an ivory tower education creates what Thorstein Veblen, an early U.S. social scientist, once termed a "trained incapacity" to see beyond a very limited area of immediate concern.

The Narrowness of Sociological Perspectives

In addition to methodological narrowness in much modern social science, including sociology, there is a certain topical narrowness in many mainstream analyses. This narrowness can be seen in introductory textbooks in sociology, textbooks the content and format of which are usually dictated by editors seeking to sell large numbers of books. Editors at textbook publishers often know little about the conceptual richness or diversity of sociology, but they are usually influenced by the early reviews of textbook manuscripts that come from teachers of sociology at various colleges and universities. The reviewers' comments persuade the textbook editors that there is an established canon in sociology, such as the three major theoretical paradigms noted below. As a result, the editors insist that these perspectives be featured in order for the textbook to be credible and commercially competitive.[54]

For example, for some years, in numerous introductory sociology textbooks, one found an accent on three basic conceptual perspectives in sociological analysis, usually termed the "structural-functional (order)," the "conflict," and the "symbolic interaction" approaches. Until rather recently, most introductory textbooks provided a "balanced" approach focusing on these three perspectives.

For example, one best-selling introductory sociology textbook has for some time been the aforementioned textbook by John Macionis, which in its 2001 edition emphasized these three theoretical paradigms. Discussed first, the structural-functional (order) paradigm was said to have explanatory power for understanding how societies are socially integrated and to have had a significant influence on the recent development of sociology. A brief critique of this paradigm noted that it neglects "class, race, ethnicity, and gender, which can generate considerable tension and conflict."[55] This is an understatement. The domination of the structural-functional and related status-quo perspectives was so strong in U.S. sociology from the late 1930s to the mid-1960s that there was little serious use of the extensive conceptual tradition of Karl Marx among U.S. sociologists. Indeed, Marx's probing analyses of capitalism as fundamental and oppressive in modern Western societies was long considered too radical for U.S. academics, including most sociologists. Social theorists and analysts who pressed similar arguments about the fundamental character of gender and racial oppression were similarly ignored or marginalized during this period.

After discussing structural functionalism, introductory textbooks often note a second and more recent conceptual paradigm, usually termed the "social-conflict" framework. Traditionally, this contemporary approach is said to have developed in response to the structural-functionalist approach. Viewed as influenced by Karl Marx, it is said to help students to understand social divisions and inequality. In his 2001 textbook Macionis, like other textbook authors, suggested that this perspective has been criticized because it allegedly "ignores how shared values and interdependence can generate unity among members of a society." He noted that some sociological critics see the social-conflict approach as often advocating explicitly political goals, thereby giving up the "claim to scientific objectivity."[56] Macionis did then note that those who support the social-conflict approach counter this criticism with the argument that all social theories have political consequences.

However, something important is omitted here: The social-conflict tradition actually arose *much earlier* than the structural-functionalist perspective in North American and European theorizing about society. Moreover, in its influential U.S. form the structural-functionalist perspective was developed, in part, as a response to intellectual challenges coming from Marxist thinkers inside and outside (in unions, for example) the major U.S. colleges and universities in the 1930s. Marxist thought probed and criticized the reality and impact of modern capitalism, whereas structural functionalism "did not so much justify capitalism (although it often did) as offer an explanation and understanding of its difficulties without condemning it."[57] Thus, the social-conflict perspective should be discussed as a serious conceptual perspective that emerged in Europe and the United States well *before* the structural-functionalist perspective evolved in U.S. sociology.

A third paradigm, usually called the symbolic-interaction paradigm, is discussed by numerous textbook authors as different from the other two in that it gives much more attention to the details of everyday life than to the larger structures of society. It is often argued too that this perspective places too little emphasis on the structural factors in society. Such a commentary, however, ignores the fact that much symbolic interactionist research focuses on how social inequalities are created. Indeed, George Herbert Mead, one of the founders of symbolic interactionism, was a progressive activist and recognized the great importance of social inequality in his writings on U.S. society. Important, too, in the symbolic interactionist tradition is the emphasis on social relations among individuals; an important corollary to this emphasis is the rejection of a methodological individualism. After presenting these three perspectives in his 2001 edition of this textbook, Macionis concludes that the three conceptual paradigms offer different sociological insights but that none is more correct than the others. As he sees it, "each paradigm is helpful in answering particular kinds of questions."[58]

The emphasis on just three conceptual perspectives is a major error in describing the state of the diverse theoretical and empirical field that is now sociology. Recently, this has been recognized by Macionis, and in the 2008 edition of his textbook he does tuck in a gender-conflict approach and a race-conflict approach as subdivisions of a broad social-conflict approach. Still, numerous sociology textbooks contain no substantial discussion of the important critical-theory, feminist, antiracist, or humanistic conceptual traditions in sociology. We should note too that these critical perspectives cannot simply be subsumed under a general "social-conflict" perspective because they raise fundamental issues about social science as well as about society, including questions about the very nature of social science theory and methods. Even textbook writers who give more attention to issues of social oppression in U.S. society are generally pressed by textbook reviewers and publishers to emphasize the "three basic perspectives," whether they wish to do so or not.[59] Although textbook publishers doubtless see themselves as following the desires of the teachers of sociology, their actions nonetheless restrict the knowledge available to students of sociology and the other social sciences.

THE ALTERNATIVE TRADITION:
SOCIOLOGY ORIENTED TO CHANGE

Since the 1960s, U.S. social movements such as the feminist movement, gay rights movement, and the civil rights movement have underscored the reality that heterosexual white male social scientists have in their research and writings often left out or distorted the everyday realities of women, gay/lesbian Americans, and people of color. Across the globe, anticolonial movements have demonstrated that Western social scientists have historically misrepresented the lives of non-Western peoples. And the union movements seeking to organize ordinary workers in many countries have regularly made it clear how such workers are categorized, "othered," and oppressed by the machinations of modern capitalism. Thus, as Sjoberg reminds us, "we must take great care to continually weed out the distortions and downright errors that social scientists have constructed about other peoples." This is particularly true for establishment-funded projects that are constructed "for administrative purposes (i.e., for social control), not to understand the other's definition."[60]

The social movements of oppressed peoples have provided a recurring infusion of new insights and support for a progressive and liberating social science. In this book, we have stressed the liberation tradition in U.S. sociology that emphasizes social research and analysis for expanding justice and democracy. As we have seen previously, and will see again in the next few chapters, an array of qualitative research methods are frequently central to this progressive approach to sociology.

Qualitative Approaches and Liberation Sociology

An underlying assumption of all critical analysis in social science is that one must look beneath the overt surface realities to understand well the often hidden realities of hierarchy and oppression. This probing for the hidden reality of power relations was a lesson taught well by Karl Marx, one of the first social scientists to analyze Western capitalist societies critically and in depth. In an 1843 letter, Marx suggested that the goal must be the "reform of consciousness not through dogmas but by analyzing mystical consciousness obscure to itself, whether it appear in religious or political form." Then he noted that the task for social scientists was the clarification of the "struggles and wishes of the age."[61] In his major writings, Marx showed how numerous surface realities of capitalism, such as market-oriented trade in commodities and the money wage, disguised the important underlying realities of worker exploitation and class oppression.

Since the time of the early social scientists Harriet Martineau and Karl Marx, the liberation social science tradition has been sensitive to the omnipresent realities of hierarchy and power. Thus, aware social researchers realize that their research and methods are affected by the power hierarchies of the society within which they work. As those power relations change, so do questions about the collection of data on and interpretations of shifting societal realities.

Within the social sciences, significantly, the various dimensions and assumptions of qualitative research methods have been more systematically scrutinized than quantitative research methods. For example, most qualitative researchers have been aware, for some time now, of the Eurocentric bias of much traditional anthropological research done in colonized societies across the globe. Hidden biases and domain assumptions in most areas of qualitative research have for some time been targeted, debated, and analyzed. Qualitative researchers have also pointed out problems in mainstream quantitative positivism. Most have recognized that the instrumental-positivist triad of detached observer, distanced object, and "objective" scientific method remains highly problematical.

Recall from Chapter 2 that even in the physical sciences, to which social scientists have frequently looked for methodological models, the mechanistic Newtonian views of the physical world have given way to the idea of relativity—the idea that the character and description (and thus the reality) of physical phenomena depend on the reference frame of the scientific observer. In addition, physical scientists such as Werner Heisenberg and Niels Bohr have made it very clear that the scientist's measuring apparatus, the person doing the measuring, and the objects studied are closely interrelated and not independent of each other. Similarly, in social science, the instruments of observation, the observed, and the observers are inseparable and intertwined parts of a larger holistic reality. The instrumental-positivist distinctions made among these are no longer tenable in the natural or the social sciences.

Using a variety of qualitative methods, social scientists can do research in everyday social worlds and make visible how people operating "in everyday life constitute, reproduce, redesign, or specify locally, what the institutional and cultural contexts of their actions make available to them."[62] There are different approaches in regard to field methods and theorizing in qualitative research. The array of field methods include, among other approaches, participant observation, life histories using in-depth interviews, and case studies using multiple methodologies, including social histories. Theorizing and interpretation can involve ethnomethodology, grounded theory, the interpretive case method, and the extended case method. The interpretive case method, often used by anthropologists, views microevents as expressions of the macrodimensions of a particular society. The grounded theory approach attempts to build new theories inductively from assessing several qualitative case studies. And the extended case method extends and reconstructs existing social theory by constantly examining its utility in explaining new qualitative research cases. In this latter approach, the current theory is laid out in advance and, if contradicted by data, is rejected or reconstructed for yet another testing with more field data.[63]

Qualitative Research and Countersystem Sociology

Although qualitative research methods and interpretive techniques need not be oriented toward the goals of a progressive or liberation sociology, they are so oriented more often than quantitative methods and techniques. Indeed, most progressive and critical sociology researchers have often made use of various types of qualitative research methods, in addition to some quantitative methods.

Why is there frequently a connection between qualitative research methods and progressive sociology? From the beginning of the field, many sociologists have viewed their vocation as one of improving the world through field research. Though relatively conservative politically, Auguste Comte thought a positive investigation of the world could liberate human beings from the shackles that prior metaphysical and military thinking had imposed on them. Others linked a commitment to progressive social change to qualitative methods for observing and analyzing the social world. Harriet Martineau not only translated Comte's work but also in the 1830s did the first qualitative field work in Western sociology. She was strongly committed to the abolition of slavery and the improvement of conditions for women and the poor in both Britain and the United States. Committed to improving French society, Emile Durkheim proposed the idea of studying social phenomena according to their consequences for human beings. For Durkheim, sociology was a moral enterprise and not a sterile exercise in data collection. Max Weber accented the need to study meaningful social action with regard to societal change. To varying degrees, most of the founders of European sociology thought that sociology was a discipline to improve the world. They accepted the necessary intertwining of a critically assessed moral theory with critically assessed social theories.

As sociology developed in North and South America, many early sociologists had a similar interest in changing oppressive societies for the better and in keeping a critical moral perspective intertwined with their social research and analysis. For example, sociology was apparently the first academic discipline in which researchers, albeit just a few, undertook serious studies of racial and gender inequality. It was one of the first where social researchers conducted serious research on class inequality. From the beginning, U.S. sociologists in the liberation tradition have been among the sharpest analysts of society, as can be seen in early commentaries on racism by W.E.B. Du Bois, in the early analyses of class and gender inequality and of democracy by Jane Addams and her female colleagues at Hull House and the University of Chicago, and in the early analyses of gender relations and sexism by analysts such as Charlotte Perkins Gilman.[64] Although these analysts and their research were later marginalized within U.S. sociology, the field of sociology provided some early support for their research and writings. Interestingly, these early sociologists combined various types of qualitative and quantitative (usually descriptive statistics) methodologies with a progressive and emancipatory approach to U.S. society. However, they often used qualitative research methods, as most in this sociological tradition do today.

One explanation for this reliance on qualitative research methods today, some might suggest, is the high cost of quantitative research methods. Large-scale survey research, large-scale demographic research, and experimental research are typically intensively quantitative and relatively expensive. For several decades now, most of the social science researchers who have received significant amounts of research money from government agencies and large corporate foundations have been those committed to some type of quantitative positivism and, usually but not always, to the status quo or modest reform therein. Researchers oriented toward a more progressive sociology have often had trouble getting significant grants for their research, so they may make use of less expensive qualitative methods. But the explanation lies deeper than costs. More important than access to money for research are the theoretical and ideological assumptions (such as an acceptance of the status quo) underlying much instrumental-positivist research.

Another explanation lies in the character of the data gathering itself. Quantitatively oriented survey research, to take one major example, often entails a certain restrictive instrumentalism in the way that the interview questions are framed and the data are gathered and statistically analyzed. The respondents are typically given preformatted questions and answers to choose from. In contrast, much qualitative field research, such as participant observation or unstructured in-depth interviews, allows those being studied to generate or shape many of the issues and questions raised in the research—and, often, the direction in which the research proceeds. In this way, qualitative research frequently entails understanding how people think, act, and react. Qualitative researchers can garner new ideas and theories from listening carefully to their subjects' questions and interpretations, some of which cannot be anticipated in advance of the field research.[65]

Although there is no guarantee that qualitative researchers will listen carefully to the developed ideas and interpretations of those whom they research, at least that opportunity is there, which it is not in typical survey, demographic, or experimental research. If one does qualitative fieldwork with those who are oppressed, listens carefully, and examines candidly their experiences and views, it is often the case that a more nuanced, perceptive, and critical perspective on society will emanate from that research—a perspective that may well be unacceptable to the contemporary elites of the society. Of course, as we have noted, some qualitative researchers do share substantially in the positivistic culture and, to varying degrees, constrain their observations and drape their discoveries and analyses in the terminology and assumptions of that conventional research culture.

Finally, to draw on a medical metaphor, most qualitative research is interested in discovering, identifying, and describing social "syndromes." A social syndrome is an interrelated pattern of numerous social "symptoms," and one well-studied case can be sufficient for understanding it. Quantitative research, in contrast, serves to map out the distribution of selected symptoms, usually called "variables." In quantitative work, assessing causal inference generally proceeds from findings of concomitant variation in individual traits. This abstracted process of causal inference conventionally follows a mechanistic Newtonian model of characterizing discrete objects moving in relation to each other according to their individual traits. For example, when some quantitatively oriented social scientists find a statistical relationship between "race" and "wealth" (inequality) variables for a country like the United States, they may draw the inference that "race is highly correlated with, or causes, wealth inequality." However, such researchers will have to go well beyond their quantitative data into speculation—or, preferably, significant qualitative research—in order to discover the dynamics of this relationship, its roots and history, or what it means to have to "live it" in everyday life.

Qualitative researchers are not encumbered by such rules governing quantitative methods, and they can more easily research the many and nuanced ways in which racial histories are closely linked to wealth inequality—and how wealth inequality causes racial inequality, or vice versa. They can explore how "race" is socially invented and examine its historical and contemporary ramifications in many directions, and they can better understand its textures and enfoldings. They can also probe and examine race's component parts—which encompass a large investment of energy and resources in maintaining white privilege, including great and continuing wealth inequality.

It is often the case that researchers using qualitative methods have opened up an area of research and understanding first, thereby allowing the possible use of selected quantitative methods to assist in the analysis. Moreover, even the best quantitative analysis usually requires outside insights—perhaps from qualitative research—to gain penetrating and cutting-edge understandings of the social life of human beings.

Research Techniques, Social Interpretation, and Moral Theory

A major consideration in adopting a particular research method to study social questions and issues should be choosing the method appropriate for the questions and issues at hand, rather than sacramental compliance with formulaic procedures. In fact, a major scientific rule is that the methods chosen should be appropriate to the object of study. Clearly, much survey research has contributed to our knowledge of the social world, and statistical analysis of various kinds has had its important place in contributing to this knowledge. There are, of course, quantitative researchers who use survey data in quite reflective and critical ways. Thus, we clearly recognize that the problem is not quantification per se but the too-frequently unreflective use of quantitative methods, including advanced statistical techniques, without consideration of the research's social context, societal relevance, hidden assumptions, probable uses, moral and ethical implications, and limitations in regard to probing deeper social realities of a given society.

How one collects and interprets research data is important. For example, recall the first empirical field study of black Americans, the 1890s field study by Du Bois published as *The Philadelphia Negro.* This pioneering study combined survey methods and descriptive statistical analysis with qualitative data and historical analysis of the community. Du Bois also joined social-theoretical interpretations of his data with a moral (human rights) reading.

In the research process, Du Bois made use of survey questionnaires to gather data to map out the conditions faced by working-class and poor Philadelphians, yet he was significantly limited by the institutional context for this research. The white men who commissioned his study were openly worried that "native stock" whites would be overwhelmed eventually by the "plague" of the urban black poor, whom they stereotyped as immoral and criminal. Du Bois was to conduct a sociological study of the black Philadelphians who were predefined by the funders as a "social problem." The charge they gave to Du Bois was as follows: "We want to know precisely how this class of people live ... and to ascertain every fact which will throw light on this social problem."[66]

Working within these significant limitations, Du Bois ignored this paternalistic mandate to some degree. He spent many hours in the field interviewing some 2,500 households. Although he knew that his research manuscript had to be acceptable to the whites in charge, he worked into the final analysis sociological and moral interpretations that subverted the racist thinking of his day. He worked inductively, drawing generalizations from field data, and historically, profiling the background of Philadelphia's black population and its flight from the South. Webbing an antiracist analysis into his important monograph, Du Bois compared the black population with white immigrant groups just coming into the city—noting how the latter got the better societal deal. Du Bois did not do much with the qualitative data he had at hand, such as the quotes from his interviews. However, he did detail the poverty of many black Philadelphians—and condemned their actions occasionally in moralistic terms—and offered what is likely the first racial and class analysis of poverty and crime among black urbanites. His analysis was historically contextualized and sociologically nuanced.[67]

Although most reviewers of Du Bois's pioneering work have missed it, then and now, his concluding chapter used his survey and other social data to provide damning indictments of white racism as an underlying cause of the distressed black condition in the city. Du Bois closes his 520-page analysis of empirical data with a final section bluntly headed "The Duty of Whites." There he notes that whites may have "a right to object to a race so poor and ignorant and inefficient as the mass of Negroes; but if their policy in the past is parent of much of this condition, and if today by shutting black boys and girls out of most avenues of decent employment they are increasing pauperism and vice, then they must hold themselves *largely responsible* for the deplorable results."[68] Then he added an additional comment on the ethical responsibilities of white Americans: Racial discrimination is "morally wrong, politically dangerous, industrially wasteful, and socially silly. It is the *duty of whites* to *stop it,* and to do so primarily for their own sakes."[69] Writing in the first decade of empirical sociology in the United States, Du Bois combined survey and qualitative data with a sociohistorical analysis that was unafraid to combine social theory with moral assessments of the need for social change. Unlike many contemporary social scientists, moreover, Du Bois was unafraid to assert from his data that *white* discriminators were the actors directly responsible for generating urban contexts that created the black poverty and other "problems" he had researched.

Du Bois was a contemporary of the pioneering European sociologists such as Emile Durkheim, who also viewed moral interests as part of sociological research. A long line of sociologists from the nineteenth century to the present day have maintained a similar position. Indeed, over the past two decades or so a variety of sociologists have argued that moral issues are and should be part of sociological research and analysis. These include communitarians, such as Amitai Etzioni, who mix ideas from the conservative and progressive traditions, as well as critical feminists such as Dorothy Smith and world-system Marxists like Immanuel Wallerstein.[70]

Those working in the liberation sociology tradition today often accent moral and ethical concerns. They argue that social scientists have ethical obligations not only in regard to the rights of their research subjects but also in regard to all those who may be helped or hurt by the impact of their research.[71] They often note the impact of *not* doing certain kinds of much needed research as well. And they are the most likely social scientists to note the hidden moral assumptions underlying much traditional social science research, such as the utilitarian (for example, cost-benefit) assumptions lying behind much evaluation research done by social scientists for government agencies.[72]

CONCLUSION

Liberation sociology assertively orients the decision on which methods, qualitative or quantitative, are to be used to the decision about what data are needed to build a better society and increase social justice. Social life is too complex for researchers to accept a methodological monolith, a reliance on only one type of social science method. We are certainly *not* arguing here that there is no room for mainstream quantitative research in understanding societal worlds or in developing strategies for liberating the oppressed majorities in many such societal worlds. There is, of course, much room for diversity of thought and methods.

Nevertheless, we must recognize that, over the course of the history of sociology, instrumental positivism has seized many centers of influence and far too much of the important resources within the field. This dominance must be challenged if sociology is to help build better societal worlds. As we have reiterated, central to the liberation sociology tradition is a constant looking for the hidden social realities usually missed by conventional researchers. As we envisage the future of social science, instrumental positivism must be replaced by research methods and interpretive procedures that provide deeper and more holistic pictures of important social realities, especially the continuing realities of human oppression. From our considered viewpoint, liberation sociology should draw on the tradition of such social researchers as Karl Marx and Harriet Martineau in their concern with not trusting the surface readings of a society.

Liberation sociology not only tries to find methods that voice the voiceless but also seeks to reveal how oppressive systems create voicelessness—and how governing elites create, maintain, and enhance such exploitative and despotic systems. Doing and publicizing research on the ruling class and the powerful bureaucratic structures it controls is of great importance for ongoing social science research, and such research requires more than conventional opinion surveys. For example, using multiple research techniques and sources, University of California sociologist Bill Domhoff has published numerous pioneering and nuanced research reports since the 1960s detailing what the ruling class is and how it rules. Combining an individual-level analysis with a class-oriented viewpoint, Domhoff has demonstrated that individual capitalists and their close subordinates do in fact rule in the United States, in part, by serving in top government positions. Accenting social and organizational networks, Domhoff has also shown the close linkage between land-interested businesspeople operating at the local level and those at the helm of major corporations.[73]

At its best, liberation sociology, like the political sociology of Domhoff, often must develop adversarial methods to get at the procedures and secrets of top social elites and the onerous worlds they often maintain and to suggest ways of fighting back against this misery and subjugation. The countersystem tradition in sociology assumes that all social worlds are changeable—and that ordinary people, often with the aid of liberation sociology, have the capability to change the world around them for the human ends of liberty, freedom, and social justice.

CHAPTER 5

Sociology in Action

Sometimes working with community activists, liberation-oriented sociologists have interactively developed concepts, methods, and practices to assist people in their struggles as well as to better understand and improve their everyday lives. In this and the next chapter we examine specific examples of sociological projects that are in this praxis tradition, most with a progressive or countersystem orientation. The examples are not exhaustive but illustrate the range of ways in which a type of liberation sociology has had its impact on communities, as well as the ways in which community activism has shaped liberation sociology in thought and practice. The first case we turn to is an example of the interaction between progressive community practice and a perspective that is essentially sociological.

MAKING LOCAL REVOLUTIONS:
SAUL ALINSKY AND URBAN ALLIANCES

During the change-driven 1960s, as University of California sociologists Bob Blauner and David Wellman have noted, "many of the assumptions of the academic world were challenged by events both external and internal to campuses. There was a growing tendency for powerless and excluded groups to view academics and their activities politically, to criticize their relation to, and responsibility for, existing economic, social and ideological commitments of social science."[1] Social action by ordinary Americans was a major source of the pressure on social scientists to face the exploitative and inhumane realities of contemporary U.S. society.

These 1960s movements were preceded by numerous social movements in earlier decades, efforts that often laid the basis for the successful movements of the 1960s. We now turn to one of the principal community organizers and intellectuals in the recent history of urban activism and community struggle, activist and practicing sociologist Saul Alinsky (1909–1972). An intellectual activist who worked for and tried to understand the experiences of the oppressed, Alinsky founded the Industrial Areas Foundation (IAF) in 1940.

Alinsky's IAF evolved over time and has fostered much community organization across the United States. Indeed, the IAF currently has 57 affiliates that operate in more than twenty U.S. states, as well as in Canada, the United Kingdom, and Germany. With some 150 field organizers, the IAF serves numerous coalition organizations linking hundreds of local groups and at least a million families. A recent IAF statement summarizes the organization's current goals and efforts:

"IAF leaders and organizers first create independent organizations, made up of people from all races and all classes, focused on productive improvements in the public arena. IAF members then use those new political realities to invent and establish new social realities." The statement continues with a clear example of their contemporary efforts: "One new reality is the living wage movement in the United States. The first living wage bill was conceived, designed, and implemented by the IAF affiliate in Baltimore in 1994. The second bill was the work of the IAF affiliates in New York City in 1996. Since then, IAF affiliates in Texas, Arizona, and elsewhere have passed living wage legislation.[2]

Over several decades of building up the IAF organization, Saul Alinsky took some ideas from the sociological tradition and honed them as he became one of the more successful community activists in the Western world. From the beginning, a "thoroughly sociological perspective" underlay Alinsky's community organization.[3] Between the 1930s and 1970s, Alinsky created opportunities and procedures for local communities of the poor to do action research on social problems and act on that research to improve their communities. This community activism has, in turn, helped to stimulate a more activist social science.

Saul Alinsky's ideas on community, organization, power, racial groups and crime, the poor, welfare programs, and social movements deserve an important place in the annals of sociological theory, analysis, and practice. As we will see later, Alinsky articulated these ideas in his books and speeches on community organizing, as well as in papers that he gave at the meetings of professional associations and charitable organizations.

Building New Organizations

Born in 1909 in a poverty-stricken area of Chicago, Alinsky was the son of Russian immigrants. He graduated from the University of Chicago in archaeology and applied for graduate work in criminology, where he encountered the classes and ideas of urban sociologists. Soon thereafter, appalled by urban poverty and the growth of fascist and other reactionary movements of the 1930s, Alinsky abandoned the academic setting and began to organize poor immigrants in the community known as Back of the Yards, located behind the Chicago stockyards. The grassroots organizing transformed the Back of the Yards community into a national model of effective organization against many types of economic and political exploitation and discrimination. Alinsky and his allies pulled together a diverse array of local groups, including union locals, bowling leagues, and ethnic clubs. The movement established better services in housing, public health, and welfare for poor residents. Alinsky's efforts focused on the development of community institutions and building community-based power, which enabled poor residents to act more effectively in the political arena and bring social change.[4]

Later on, Saul Alinsky's organizing work and ideas brought him to the attention of other progressive activists and analysts in the United States and overseas. For example, Jacques Maritain, a prominent French philosopher, was impressed with this work and argued that the achievements of the Back of the Yards movement "opened a new road to real democracy."[5] Maritain identified Alinsky as one of two major social revolutionaries in recent times. His other choice was Eduardo Frei, the president of Chile from 1964 to 1970, a man whose administration claimed to implement a program of far-reaching reform. Indeed, communicated through progressive Catholic sources, Alinsky's ideas were influential in politics in South American countries like Chile.[6]

Using Creative Tactics

In pursuing community change, Alinsky's tactics were creative and sometimes irreverent. He sometimes said that revolutionaries should enjoy revolutions—and that such an approach expands participation. For example, in a Rochester campaign to improve the conditions in poor communities, Alinsky came up with some irreverent proposals.

"One suggested tactic was to buy one hundred tickets to the opening performance of the Rochester Symphony Orchestra, a cultural jewel highly prized in the city." These tickets were to be given to residents of poor communities, who would be hosted at a dinner party where the sole food item would be baked beans. "In the end Alinsky never carried through on the tactic, but the threat alone accomplished much."[7]

From the 1940s to the present, the Alinsky tradition of community organization and citizen participation has had a significant impact on the United States. Over time, organizations similar to the Back of the Yards organization have been created in other U.S. cities. Moreover, in the late 1960s, the U.S. Conference of Catholic Bishops initiated the Catholic Campaign for Human Development (CCHD), "a crusade to organize associations of poor Americans to exert economic and political power on behalf of their communities." The CCHD has become an official arm of the U.S. Conference of Catholic Bishops. By 2008 the Catholic Church had spent several hundred million dollars on the campaign. Among its efforts on behalf of low-income Americans has been pressing for more than one hundred living wage ordinances, which have so far generated three quarters of a billion dollars in new wages for workers in various cities and counties. The CCHD has helped fund a dozen of these local wage efforts.[8] Overall, the CCHD was greatly influenced by the ideas and work of Alinsky and his urban organizations for community change.

Other local and national movements for change have been linked to the ideas and work of Alinsky. The late Cesar Chavez, longtime leader of the U.S. farmworkers movement, was hired by Alinsky as a staff member of the Community Service Organization (CSO) in 1953, an action that initiated Chavez's important career as a community organizer.[9] Founded in the late 1940s, the CSO was an organization devoted to the expansion of the political rights and economic opportunities of Mexican Americans. In 1962 Chavez left the CSO and moved to Delano, California, to begin his efforts to organize a farmworkers' union, which was eventually successful in improving conditions for farmworkers. In a 1984 interview, Chavez noted, "We took the growers as a union but it was really a community organization.... The foundation for the union was laid by the CSO through Alinsky's perception of power and how to strategize for power and Fred Ross's [an Alinsky ally] organizing techniques on how to put people together and make them work together."[10] The union's most successful tactic, one that farmworkers still use, was to launch food boycotts to supplement strikes, slowdowns, and picket lines.

The best-known umbrella organization associated with Alinsky is the IAF, the national organization that he founded. Over the decades, the IAF has trained many organizers, and as we noted above it currently serves hundreds of local groups and hundreds of thousands of families in numerous states and overseas. Today, the IAF is "the center of a national network of broad based, multiethnic, interfaith organizations in primarily poor and moderate income communities."[11] Typically, these organizations are broad coalitions, which include an array of local churches, synagogues, mosques, unions, schools, and environmental, health, and civic organizations. These coalitions get local organizations to listen to, and learn from, each other—and then work to develop coordinated strategies to get local decisionmakers to sit down with them to make meaningful changes in community conditions and services. IAF groups work to establish and renew local democracy by empowering citizens through participation and political action.

One IAF organization is the South Bronx Churches (SBC). Founded in the 1980s, the SBC has built a coalition of several dozen churches and politicized many citizens to challenge the local political leadership. The group has petitioned for better schools and affordable housing and won improvements in hospital services. In the state of Texas, the IAF has helped build several successful organizations, including Communities Organized for Public Service (COPS) in San Antonio—one of the more successful such community organizations in the United States. In the 1970s, Ernesto Cortés, an organizer trained by the IAF, was invited to help the Mexican American community inventory its needs and plan action. Using the parishes of the local Catholic church as organizing units and securing aid from the national CCHD, the Alinsky-shaped organization adopted both electoral and confrontation tactics. It thereby secured concessions from the city's traditional white leaders and elected a more representative city council, one with more Mexican Americans on it. Today COPS continues to develop job training programs and to seek significant improvements in local educational systems in San Antonio.[12]

COPS and similar Texas organizations constitute a statewide network and have brought together Mexican American Catholics, African American Protestants, and white Protestants to work on issues of common interest. Across the country, various multiracial coalitions work for political candidates, yet they are often temporary formations with cooperation restricted to those at the top. The Texas IAF organizations, in contrast, bring together groups that include more than just organizational representatives—such as grassroots people—and unite all participants around a common agenda and commitment. "IAF organizations are consequently more broadly participatory, and their leadership more united than a typical coalition."[13]

Mark Warren, a sociologist who has studied the work of the IAF in Texas, has attributed the success of this interracial cooperation to three factors. The first is that, while Latino, black, and white leaders are united in a single organization, considerable autonomy is allowed to the different groups and neighborhoods. A second factor is that the IAF organizations "follow a consensual issues strategy that avoids divisive campaigns and frames issues in a nonracial manner."[14] The third factor is that IAF "taps the religious culture of its social capital base to provide trust for the initial establishment of multiracial organizations and a common identity to sustain cooperation."[15] This has allowed IAF organizations to frame issues in terms of religious and family values. Stanley Ziemba has noted that Alinsky's social-analytical and activist "principles and tactics continue to be employed by community groups across the country, and scores of community organizers he trained personally or inspired continue to strive to make his dream a reality."[16]

THE THINKING OF SAUL ALINSKY: LIBERATION SOCIOLOGY IN ACTION

A Practicing Sociologist

Although trained as an archaeologist and a criminologist, Alinsky was often called a sociologist in the media when he was actively involved in bringing changes to communities, and he did not reject that appellation. Various scholarly commentaries, then and more recently, have noted the importance of sociological ideas in his thinking, including those that guided his organizing. He understood how social problems were commonly rooted in the deep-seated structural realities of racial discrimination and impoverishment under a capitalistic economic system. Not surprisingly, Alinsky's success as a community organizer was based on an insightful understanding of local communities, which was based in part on sociological concepts drawn from his work in the University of Chicago's department of sociology and in the Institute for Juvenile Research there. Alinsky took sociology courses at the university in the 1920s and 1930s when the sociology department there was the country's most influential and a national center for urban sociological research and theorizing.[17]

In the 1920s Robert Park and his associates at the University of Chicago asserted their view of the city as a laboratory for sociological research. Drawing on urban fieldwork and ideas of earlier women sociologists—though rarely acknowledging the fact—the sociologists at the University of Chicago developed a distinctive approach for studying urban communities and problems, an approach that Alinsky drew from in building his own ideas. For the Chicago sociologists, and for Alinsky, the city was not only a geographic entity made of streets and buildings but also a state of mind—a matter of customs, organized attitudes, and sentiments.[18] From this perspective, neighborhoods were "natural areas," the organic living units of a metropolis. In such neighborhoods, individuals and families developed long-term attachments. The neighborhoods had distinctive formal and informal organizations according to the particular social, economic, and political needs of their populations. A crucial idea in this vision of the city is that neighborhoods are not detached but are parts of a larger social structure of the metropolis and are thus affected by social forces at play in that larger context. Urban residents are members of two major and interconnected frameworks: both the neighborhood and the larger city.

Parting Company with the Chicago Sociologists

In his thinking and sociological practice, Alinsky parted company with the Chicago sociologists of the 1920s on at least one key assumption. Unlike many of them, he wanted to bring major social change in urban communities by sociologically informed activism. By the 1920s, most Chicago sociologists viewed these communities as evolutionary worlds that changed slowly through long-term effects of broad social forces. Most were moving away from the commitments of earlier sociologists to substantial reform and societal change. Recall the discussion in Chapter 3 on how the white male sociologists at the university ignored or downplayed not only the earlier field research of the women sociologists at Hull House but also their support and action for substantial reforms in urban areas and across the country.[19]

In contrast, Alinsky's conceptual world envisioned great community changes brought about by purposive human action. Although Alinsky sometimes criticized what he saw as the timidity of the urban social workers in the settlement houses, Alinsky's thought was much in line with the thinking of Chicago's earlier sociologist of the poor, Jane Addams. Although the full development of this liberation sociology, and certainly of major societal reformation, remains to be accomplished for the United States, Alinsky is one of the sociological pioneers who has pointed the way to such a framework. Indisputably, he sides with analyst-activists like Marx and Addams in the view that the point of social science disciplines is to change the world in the direction of expanded social justice.

Human Dignity and Social Activism

When Alinsky met Jacques Maritain, a leading French humanist and philosopher, in the 1940s, they both had developed a distinctive system of ideas about human nature. The Jewish leftist from Chicago and the Catholic philosopher from France became friends, and they shared the same views on the humanity of ordinary people. From the 1930s forward, Maritain broke with conservative thought within the Catholic Church and called on Catholics to develop a stronger social conscience. During the 1930s, when the Church was supporting reactionary monarchies and fascist regimes, Maritain took a progressive position within the Church.[20] Thus, in some ways he was an early forerunner of what would later be termed "liberation theology." As a humanist, Maritain pressed for the recognition of the dignity and rights of ordinary workers, of the common people. He was against just doing charity for people and proposed instead that "we must first choose to exist with them and to suffer with them, to make their pain and destiny our own."[21]

At home among social philosophers, Alinsky shared his friend's faith in the dignity of the common people. He developed his own ideal type of the "radical" with this orientation in mind. At the most general level, such a radical is a person who has a deep feeling for other people—in contrast to most liberals and conservatives whom Alinsky thought feared, distrusted, or merely tolerated the poor. Yet he did not idealize the oppressed:

> I do not do what a lot a liberals and a lot of civil-rights crusaders do. I do not think that people are specially just or charitable or noble because they're unemployed and live in crummy housing and see their kids without any kind of future and feel the weight of every indignity that society can throw at them, sophisticated or nakedly. Too often I've seen the have-nots turn into haves and become just as crummy as the haves they used to envy.[22]

Alinsky's sociological acumen comes through clearly in such penetrating social analyses.

The Idea of Democracy in Action

In his classic book, *Reveille for Radicals,* Alinsky develops a historically informed sociological analysis. He explains that in all political systems one finds both "aristocrats and democrats." In early American history, the term "democrat" was often a synonym for "radical." About these early democrats, Alinsky writes: "They fought for the right of men to govern themselves, for the right of men to walk erect as free men and not grovel before kings, for the Bill of Rights, for the abolition of slavery, for public education, and for everything decent and worthwhile."[23] As he sees it, activist radicals can be found throughout U.S. history. Unlike many other commentators on early U.S. history, Alinsky recognizes and singles out perhaps the most radical democrat among the founders, Thomas Paine, who fought to abolish not only monarchical oppression but also African slavery. Reviewing later history, he notes the many Americans who ran the Underground Railroad and the numerous labor radicals who secured the workers' right to organize. Radicals "are to be found wherever and whenever America moves close to the fulfillment of its democratic dream."[24]

Alinsky anchored his ideas and methods explicitly in democratic ideals:

> Democracy is a way of life and not a formula to be "preserved" like jelly. It is a process—a vibrant, living sweep of hope and progress which constantly strives for the fulfillment of its objective in life—the search for truth, justice and dignity of man. There can be no democracy unless it is dynamic democracy. When our people cease to participate—to have a place in the sun—then all of us will wither in the darkness of decadence. All of us will become mute, demoralized, lost souls.[25]

Democracy, seen as active citizen participation, is a means to change society. To achieve it, Alinsky argues that radicals must work at "the awakening of our people from the abysmal apathy which has resulted in the decay and breaking down of a large part of those few ideals which mankind has desperately clung to."[26] Community-based organizations of people participating democratically are a way to emancipation. They are the way to move from a monotonous existence into "a brilliantly lit, highly exciting, avenue of hope, drama, conflict."[27] By means of this democratic participation, the people "become informed, educated, and above all develop faith in themselves, their fellow men, and their future. The key is for them, the people, to have the opportunity and power to implement their decisions. No clique, or caste, power group or benevolent administration can have the people's interest at heart as much as the people themselves."[28]

For Alinsky democracy is not just an end in itself. As he put it in his famous book, *Rules for Radicals*, "It is the best political means available toward the achievement of these values."[29] By these values he meant freedom, equality, and justice. Alinsky was constantly concerned with the moral and ethical character of human life, and especially with showing the have-nots how to take illegitimate power away from the haves. Indeed, the original title for this book was *The Morality of Power*.[30]

Activist Organizations: The Broad View

Alinsky reacted against conceptual approaches that isolated problems from their social contexts to understand them. In this manner, he thought along the holistic lines of earlier activist sociologists like Addams and Du Bois. Alinsky argued that problems such as those of delinquency and crime should *not* be understood or studied as separate social problems; they are both facets of the larger problem of social inequality. He began his sociological and community-oriented writing in the 1930s. In 1934 Alinsky published his first article, titled "A Sociological Technique in Clinical Criminology." There he argued that to communicate with and research those in trouble with the law, one should use the "vocabularies characteristic of the inmate's community."[31] Moreover, in 1937 he presented an important paper at the American Prison Association in which he showed the close relationship between the capitalistic system and the individualistic approaches common in mainstream criminology. He sent the paper to the young C. Wright Mills, who thought it was a fine paper and congratulated Alinsky on his sociological "radicalism," radicalism here in the sense of going to the "roots" of societal problems.[32]

In Alinsky's view, unemployment, disease, undernourishment, demoralization, and crime are parts of a larger societal picture, and are not separable social problems.[33] This holistic view of social problems led Alinsky to develop broad activist organizations that were not organized just to deal with one community problem such as troubled youth. As he saw it, citizens narrowly organized to deal with one local issue will often abstain from other controversial efforts when those efforts are needed to meet squarely larger social issues and to courageously rebuild local communities. The purpose of organizations of the poor is to battle all social forces that create poverty and inequality in cities.[34] In addition, Alinsky insisted that local change-oriented organizations should be "completely cognizant of the place of their community in the general mosaic of communities which make up their nation," as he put it in writing about the Back of the Yards movement.[35] Alinsky criticized some trade unions for not adopting this broader view of organizational position and goals. Radicals have traditionally seen the labor movement as the way to bring economic justice and human betterment, but when he examined the labor movement, he found it often wanting. Unions and other local organizations should look at the world through the lens of what some sociologists have called the "total social phenomenon."[36]

Alinsky's argument for local organizations having a citywide vision and for unions developing a broad set of social goals is similar to the view of the social world of leading European sociologists. Consider, for example, Marcel Mauss, Emile Durkheim's socialist nephew. Mauss argued that social phenomena are not just economic, religious, familial, political, and the like, but that all these dimensions are aspects of the same *social whole.* Social life does not take place divided into these neat categories but rather all at one time and all together. Recall our discussion of Marx's dialectical perspective. He, too, insisted that social phenomena come with many dimensions embedded into one comprehensive whole. For Alinsky, as for Mauss and Marx, social life is always a holistic phenomenon.

Respect for Racial and Ethnic Diversity

One of the harshest criticisms made by Alinsky in regard to labor unions was his disapproval of the white-male-led labor movement's attitudes and practices toward workers of color. Like corporations, most labor unions practiced racial discrimination and reflected the racist prejudices of the general white population. Some unions excluded African Americans by explicit provisions, whereas others did so informally. Alinsky condemned these practices as destroying the possibility for effective coalitions across key social groups.[37]

In his astute organizing book, *Reveille for Radicals,* Alinsky develops the idea that the people of the United States are as socially diverse as any people on the planet. He adopts a broad sociological view of the country's diversity: U.S. residents represent a bridge between the narrow nationalism of the past and a new humankind, a people of the world. Yet, although many people claim to fight against racial and ethnic prejudices, they are often rather prejudiced themselves. Assessing the perspectives of a broad range of Americans—from Irish Catholics and white Protestants to Jewish Americans, black Americans, and Mexican Americans—he draws on historical data to argue that they all have their prejudices and inconsistencies in regard to other groups. From this standpoint, he then calls on all groups to join a coalition against intergroup hostility, inequality of opportunity, economic insecurity, and educational inequality. Once again, a holistic sociological view is aggressively asserted.

Capitalism and Left Analysis

Although Alinsky repeatedly declared that he was not a Marxist, he did agree with Marx that capitalism had failed and that economic control in a capitalist country is usually associated with substantial political power. To achieve full human emancipation and realization, modern capitalism has to be effectively overcome. Like Marx, Alinsky suggested that this would not happen through evolutionary change but rather through collective and purposive action. Generally, Marx wrote about and worked for a proletarian revolution, but Alinsky took a broader view. He wrote about and worked to accumulate significant power in the hands of the community organizations of common people—not just workers but much larger groups of ordinary people.

Alinsky, and the many community activists his organization has trained, see much left-wing analysis, both that of social scientists and that of general commentators, as too abstract and removed from the everyday life of ordinary people. Traditional leftists look too much to the male workers in the working class for change. Supported by activist theorists like Alinsky, community activists often argue that successful social movements must cross traditional class lines.[38] In contrast, critics on the left have often viewed the IAF-inspired community and other populist movements as too grounded in religion and ethnicity and as too localized and parochial; community movements are viewed too focused on individual and family consumption and not enough on the worker-capitalist struggle.[39]

Alinsky and the Settlement House Approach

Alinsky had a critical view of traditional social work and settlement house approaches to the poor, even to the point of some harsh attacks on women activists who had helped spread the settlement movement in Chicago and other cities.[40] Indeed, reflecting the sexist thinking of his day, Alinsky was skeptical about women doing field organizing.

Alinsky's organizing approach differed from the approach of many women activists, including those who had founded the settlement house movement (see Chapter 3). The most famous of these settlement houses was Chicago's Hull House, founded by Jane Addams and Ellen Gates Starr. These settlement house activists had pioneered in efforts to improve the lives of the poor of numerous cities, including Chicago. They pressed successfully for recreation facilities and social services for the poor and often worked for more radical reforms in regard to workplace and labor conditions, the protection of children, immigrant's rights, and women's rights. This settlement house work by the women activists was well developed in Chicago when Alinsky started his Back of the Yards organizing. He and his fellow male organizers tended to overlook this history and to view the women as do-gooders mostly doing charity work, rather than the type of adversarial activists whose activism could accomplish real social or political change.[41]

Alinsky also accepted the idea of political power being a zero-sum game. As Randy Stoecker and Susan Stall have noted, he believed that "you either have more of it or less of it, and if you have less the only way to get more is to take it from someone else. Alinsky was adamant that real power could not be given, but only taken."[42] As a result, Alinsky directed his organizing of the poor toward singling out a few elite targets and isolating them from other parts of the elite. In contrast, the women settlement workers and sociologists did not accept the idea of the zero-sum game in organizing the poor. They saw power as more or less unlimited and accented the creation of "co-active power," which was "based on human interdependence and the development of all within the group or the community through collaboration."[43] From the women's holistic perspective on organizing, the empowerment of the poor entails developing their self-confidence, building up their individual and collective skills and resources, and enabling them to develop a critical view of their social and political environments. Cooperative organizing builds lasting communities and is more effective than an in-your-face adversarial approach.[44]

As Stoecker and Stall see it, the Alinsky approach emphasizes conflict, opposition, and winning, which tends to be the traditional masculine-role approach. Many men are taught to be aggressive and competitive and to deal with confrontations head-on, while women are more likely to be taught connectedness and relationship building. From the women's perspective, sensitivity to others and to building relationships is centrally important in organizing and coalition building. Clearly, in particular local situations the two approaches can be complementary and can be combined for more effective local efforts to bring social and political changes.

Alinsky and Organized Labor

In his sociological perspective, Alinsky had a critical view of organized capitalists and organized labor. Both are groups that accumulate economic power ordinarily used for their own ends, not those of the larger community. A successful change strategy requires a move away from the "jungle of laissez faire capitalism" to one where broader human values are relished.[45] The control of production facilities by a small capitalist class is injurious for the masses of people because it brings about a concentration of social and economic power that prevents a democratic and egalitarian way of life. Alinsky developed a critical analysis of the labor movement as being too dependent on capitalism. Organized labor is not the likely vehicle to achieve a more democratic society because it too fully participates in that capitalistic system. Because it is predicated upon bargaining between employers and employees, the union movement envisions only, or mainly, an employer-employee type of society. Indeed, labor leaders often think and act like business leaders, and labor has often become the partner of business. Ever the sociologist, Alinsky used empirical instances from the history of labor and business to support his critical view that organized labor has often sought "to secure its own interests at the expense of both technological progress and the general public."[46]

However, the capitalistic system is basically responsible for much pain and oppression. There is too much accent on money, profits, and wages. In contrast, true radicals "want to do away with economic injustice, insecurity, unequal opportunity, prejudice, bigotry, imperialism, all chauvinistic barriers of isolationism and other nationalistic neuroses. They want a world where life for man will be guided by a morality which is meaningful—and where the values of good and evil will be measured not in terms of money morals but in social morals."[47] Alinsky strongly suggests here an outline of a healthy society. Clearly, this moral community cannot be fully accomplished under modern capitalism with its heavy accent on individual or corporate profit.

Yet, in spite of his stinging sociological critique, Alinsky was in favor of unions, because many radicals could be found there. Even with their weaknesses, many unions have more democratic participation than most other organizations. The problem was not that radicals had made their beds in the union movement, but that they were often "asleep in it."[48] Radicals, he contended, must work to change the philosophy of the labor movement into one "whereby it will clearly recognize that the welfare of its constituents does not depend solely upon an improvement in economic earnings but upon a general improvement of all of the standards in the life of the worker."[49] Thereby, Alinsky proposed that the labor movement help build a broad people's organization that could bargain aggressively and effectively beyond the factory gate.

Gaining Power by Conscious Action

For Alinsky, and most of his followers today, a major aim of people's organizations is to become powerful so that they can sit at the same political table with established decisionmakers and achieve their community goals. Goals are defined in a commonly agreed upon program of principles and action. This is the opposite of welfare-state programs, which are usually designed to fit people into their oppressive situations. People should not be "adjusted," Alinsky wrote, "so they will live in hell and like it too." He adds that many "apparently local problems are in reality malignant microcosms of vast conflicts, pressures, stresses, and strains of the entire social order."[50]

In Alinsky's often sociologically informed perspective, communities do not develop a strong political identity as a result of unintentional actions, but rather as result of a conscious response to common political-economic enemies. This is why Alinsky developed strategies to use the often negative responses of city officials and the local media to build community identity and action. The identification of common enemies, who in their turn responded negatively, enabled local communities to overcome to some degree their own racial, ethnic, class, and religious differences in seeking to better social conditions in their communities.

Summing Up

Saul Alinsky put his education in urban sociology to good use for community change. Over his lifetime he was a practicing sociologist with connections to the sociology discipline. He had contacts with numerous progressive sociologists, such as C. Wright Mills and Robert Lynd, with the latter serving on the IAF board when he was a sociology professor at Columbia University. Robert Lynd's son, Yale professor and antiwar activist Staughton Lynd, was for a time a faculty member at Alinsky's IAF training institute, set up in the late 1960s.[51] Indeed, in the 1950s, Alinsky was asked to teach a course on social disorganization at Catholic University in Washington, D.C.

Alinsky was active as both a community organizer and a sociological theorist of citizen action. He viewed cities from a strong sociological perspective and constantly encouraged community leaders to set their local struggles within a broader conceptual and action framework accenting a range of social justice goals. This broader view not only fostered a better vision of community futures but also facilitated successful coalitions for community improvement across otherwise divisive lines of race, ethnicity, and religion. Some groups used the sociologically informed perspective of Alinsky to develop action research projects supporting relatively radical political agendas, and in this fashion, sociologically oriented research has helped to change the social or political face of numerous U.S. communities.

Beyond his impact on community organization and movements, Alinsky has had a significant impact on social science research and thinking. We did a computerized search of the Social Science Citation Index database for the years between 1977 and 2000 and found more than 500 citations to Saul Alinsky's books and other publications.

(These are citations in articles in social science journals only and do not include citations in progressive magazines or in social science books.) Alinsky's ideas and actions are cited in research and commentary articles in journals as diverse as the *Journal of Social Issues, Human Relations, Human Organization, Crime and Delinquency, Theological Studies, Urban Life, Social Science Quarterly, Social Science and Medicine, Community Theory, Journal of Urban History*, and the *Sociology of Sport*.[52] Clearly, Saul Alinsky's action-oriented ideas continue to inspire many social scientists, as well as other researchers and community activists. Alinsky's ideas have been consequential for those working in the liberation sociology tradition. Indeed, we both read Alinsky's books early on in our careers and were influenced by Alinsky's efforts to dovetail sociological ideas and research with efforts to bring progressive change. Several other social scientists have noted the influence of Alinsky's writings or of participation in IAF organizations in their own personal development toward community activism or toward a liberation sociology perspective.[53]

Nonetheless, the fact that the creative sociological analyses in Alinsky's articles, addresses, and books are not included in most sociology textbooks—either in the theory or in practice discussions—yet again suggests an ingrained resistance to sociologically oriented activism within most mainstream traditions of sociology.

ACTIVIST SOCIOLOGY: A COLLEGE SETTING

Sometimes high school or college students, convinced of the need to build a more just and egalitarian United States, seem a bit overwhelmed and ask, "But what can one person really do to bring change?" Unquestionably, Saul Alinsky, like his activist-sociology predecessors Addams and Du Bois, made a difference as an individual, a person committed to progressive and positive changes in the conditions faced by the poor and oppressed. Let us now briefly examine the example of another bold sociologist who has more recently made a real difference in the direction of building a more just and egalitarian society.

Fighting Racism: Making a Difference

In the mid-1990s, Noel Cazenave, a sociology professor at the University of Connecticut, decided to teach a course specifically on "White Racism," for which one of our new books was to be a textbook.[54] Because he felt it might not be easy to get the White Racism course put into the curriculum as a regular course at his New England university, Cazenave proposed it first as an experimental course.[55] The sociology department there approved it, but from the beginning, Cazenave had difficulty in securing approval from his college's Committee on Curricula and Courses. In October 1995, he was told by the chair of the college committee that his course proposal was tabled and that some white faculty members were "jumping up and down about the course title."[56] At a meeting two weeks later, the course was again tabled. There were long discussions in the meetings about this course proposal. Such debate was unusual, since most experimental courses were routinely approved. According to reports from committee members, some on the committee wanted the title to be watered down, and in the second meeting "questions were raised about the appropriate subject matter of sociology and about the legitimacy of sociology as a discipline." One member of the committee was quoted as saying the title was a "derogatory term."[57] Of relevance in understanding these events is doubtless the fact that Professor Cazenave is African American and that the committee had *no* African American (or Latino) members.

Before the third meeting of the college committee, the chair received numerous letters and messages from the campus and from around the country in support of the course. This time the experimental course was approved by voice vote, with some expressed opposition. Interestingly, the local mass media now got involved, yet did not focus so much on the academic freedom issue as on the fact that the course had been approved. Some university committee members were cited in a local newspaper as having negative views of the course. They said "the course is itself racist" and "offensive to whites because it implies that whites are morally defective."[58] The next step was for the course to be approved by a faculty meeting of the College of Arts and Sciences, ordinarily a routine matter. Again, there was strong vocal opposition from some white faculty, and the vote was close, but in favor of allowing the course.[59]

Even though this was just one experimental course, it got considerable political and mass media attention. On and off campus, whites tried to end the course. One white professor, for example, argued that "Cazenave clearly has an agenda that has no place in a university that should be a house of dispassionate inquiry."[60] Another professor, who voted against the course in the committee, was quoted as saying that any course with a racially inflammatory title would have stirred debate. Not surprisingly, local politicians weighed in on the matter. The course's "title alone is an example of racism and discrimination," fumed Connecticut State Senator Louis De Luca in a letter to the university's president requesting that the course be eliminated.[61]

Campus and state newspapers gave the issue considerable attention. A commentary article in the *Hartford Courant* by Laurence

Cohen, the director of the Yankee Institute for Public Policy Studies, attacked the course as symptomatic of the "peculiar and ill-conceived" courses that "lurk in black studies, women's studies, and sociology departments across the land." After hearing Cazenave lecture on the controversy, Cohen wrote that his own sources at the university said Cazenave had a "racial agenda so strongly implanted in his psyche that you want to jump across the faculty lounge and strangle him."[62] National papers were more cautious. The *Chronicle* of *Higher Education,* the major national education weekly, featured what it called a "skirmish." The *Chronicle's* coverage opened with this sentence: "If Noel Cazenave had called his new course 'Racism in American Society,' it probably wouldn't have set off any alarms."[63]

Cazenave did not let this swirl of criticism deter him. He wrote carefully reasoned articles for the newspapers and gave local community lectures explaining why this type of sociology course was necessary to improve the social health of the United States. He also spoke at other universities and at professional social science meetings about the course and its opposition. In one lecture, he explained why he wished to teach this course: "Why do it? Why risk the danger? Because it's there! White racism exists. Only through breaking the yolk of denial of the existence of white racism can we begin to address the problem. As long as white racism remains an invisible and a forbidden topic, it is virtually impossible to ameliorate."[64] The hostile white reaction to the course, he noted, offered a case history "on the militant refusal to not only acknowledge the existence of white racism in this country, but to even allow the words 'white racism' to be spoken." One conclusion Cazenave drew from his experience is that "we should organize to have white racism courses taught in every school in America."[65]

Researching the Protests

In a later research paper on the course-related events, Cazenave and his colleague Darlene Alvarez-Maddern offered a deeper sociological analysis. They suggested that the course controversy was an instance of symbolic conflict that "occurs when groups compete over the language used in the discourse."[66] The struggle over the course showed how racial symbols are often linked to ideological power. The authors carefully examined statements that were critical or supportive of the course, statements in newspaper articles and commentaries, cartoon editorials, and letters to editors, as well as commentaries on the Internet, anonymous materials placed in Cazenave's department mailbox, and notes taken at the college's curriculum committee meetings. The data on those who opposed the course on the campus showed that opposition came exclusively from white male faculty members: "No published criticisms of the course were made by European-American female faculty or students, or by faculty or students of color of either sex."[67] Since the committee had more professors from the natural sciences than from the social sciences, one might speculate that opposition to the course came from "hard scientists" critical of social science methodology and concepts. However, as Cazenave and Alvarez-Maddern indicate, this was unlikely to have been the main source of opposition because other social science courses were routinely approved. In addition, some of the course's most vocal critics were not natural scientists. Interestingly, although there was no overt opposition by women students or faculty on campus to the course, off-campus opposition was about evenly divided by gender.

The largest categories of criticism of the course were (1) that it had a racially offensive title and (2) that it was inflammatory and racially divisive. The first type of criticism suggests the notion that the "White Racism" title is offensive to whites, while the second type of criticism contains a claim that the title would worsen "racial relations" among different groups. One letter from the president of a manufacturing company began with the words, "I am personally insulted." Interestingly, his letter about this alleged insult concluded with an insult of his own: The writer noted what he saw as the low "IQ" of the substantially black jury that acquitted O. J. Simpson of murder. Other whites attacked sociology professor Cazenave personally, for example, by calling him "nutty" or attributing the course to an agenda of leftist propaganda.[68]

Significant positive commentary also came from campus sources. One student responded that he did not feel offended because the course was about racial structures deeply rooted in this country. One professor who wrote to the curriculum committee noted: "Several weeks ago a U.S. president gave a speech in Texas calling for all Americans to work hard to combat—you guessed it—'white racism'. Perhaps the first step in combating it is to name it."[69] Other arguments in favor of the course addressed the educational benefits from teaching a subject that badly needs to be addressed, cited the appropriateness of the course for the sociology curriculum, and noted the course's carefully conceived format. Moreover, the department of sociology at the university passed a set of resolutions, one of which stated what should have been obvious: "Naming the problem of white racism is not equivalent to claiming that all white Americans are racists, nor does naming the problem express racism or animosity."[70]

In their research presentation, Cazenave and Alvarez-Maddern noted that their focus on racial discourse and commentary neglected the local context and power relations responsible for the course's eventual approval. In the end, the support of the students and the sociology department faculty was important. However, "the ultimate department consensus," wrote Cazenave and Alvarez-Maddern, "did not emerge quickly, easily, or naturally. In some instances, it was forged through intense internal conflict."[71] Also important was a carefully researched, positive article in the major local newspaper, the *Hartford Courant.* The article was written by Frances Grandy Taylor, a reporter who interviewed opponents of the course, attended class lectures, and talked with students enrolled in the course. After this detailed article appeared, opposition to the course dissipated. It was clear from the article that the sociology course was solid and scholarly.[72]

Action-oriented sociologists often take into account the larger contexts. Cazenave wisely took the issue outside the University of Connecticut, something that irritated some colleagues. "While there was more of an element of risk in taking the issue off-campus, it was feared that otherwise, the matter might be settled by a group of largely affluent, European-American male faculty members who were unlikely to have experienced white racism, or any other form of social oppression."[73]

Later Events

In February 1997, the White Racism course was approved as a permanent course without further conflict, and later, at the request of graduate students, Cazenave began teaching a graduate seminar on the topic. To meet the undergraduate demand for the course, in the spring of 2000 the class was offered as an interactive distance learning course televised to several regional campuses of the University of Connecticut. Clearly, there was demand for candid discussion about the problem of and solutions for white racism in the United States. Cazenave has continued effective teaching on the subject.

This success story in activist sociology required the courage and superior scholarship of a committed sociology professor. It required an educational strategy aimed at opening the debate on racism issues in the larger community. White racism is a "significant social phenomenon and a major social problem which has devastating consequences for many people in modern societies. Neither the structure nor the dynamics of these societies can be understood without understanding white racism."[74] In developing his course, Cazenave was aware that, although racial prejudice is a widely accepted field of inquiry, white racism and its many dimensions are not. He had reviewed the American Sociological Association's publication on teaching racial and ethnic relations and found that the only course among three dozen featured in this important teaching resource that had the words "white" and "racism" in its syllabus was his own.[75] The titles of the conventional sociology courses there revealed a strong tendency to focus on the victims of racial oppression rather than its white perpetrators.

As with all examples of liberation sociology, there was a significant personal cost. In proposing the course, Cazenave became the target of strong personal attacks and intense scrutiny by his colleagues and administrators. His teaching was publicly commented upon and criticized by a broad array of students, colleagues, and journalists. In many ways, he became the messenger that was blamed for the message. Like W. E. B. Du Bois long before him, Cazenave was operating as an "organic intellectual," a scholar-activist representing the interests and concerns of those directly oppressed by racism in the United States.

We should also underscore the point that cases like those of Professor Noel Cazenave raise the issue of certain personal and career risks that scholar-teachers take in doing liberation sociology and other emancipatory social science. From one point of view, these risks may seem rather daunting, thereby discouraging some younger or newer teachers and scholars from doing this important teaching and research. However, in the Cazenave case, as in many others like it, a major and necessary way to counter such risks emerged: Finding an important local or national network of experienced scholar-teachers and other colleagues who can provide significant support and mentoring to assist in these campus and disciplinary struggles. Most liberation scholar-teachers need to find colleagues across disciplines in their own college settings, or in departments in other colleges and universities, with whom they can talk about their problems and from whom they can get moral support and significant ideas for strategies to counter those who are trying to limit their academic freedom, such as racially reactionary activists and politicians (like some in the Cazenave case) who have tried to stifle discussion and debate in U.S. colleges and universities. Indeed, we predict that in the future the creation of these critical mentoring networks will be a topic of much more general discussion within the social sciences, especially as more teachers and scholars who are not white and male enter the ranks of college teachers and researchers.

MAKING A DIFFERENCE: A COMMUNITY SETTING

Working with Immigrant Activists

Let us now consider a sociologist working for liberation sociology goals outside an academic setting. Operating in a rural area near San Jose in

California, the organization called ¡Vote! is nonprofit, nonpartisan, and community based. Its members have included many Mexican women who are immigrants to the United States and their family members. Among other goals, the organization works for expanded citizenship and better job opportunities. Their headquarters are in Salinas, California, but they also work in other areas of California. Founded in the 1990s in response to California's Proposition 187, which tried to restrict immigrants' use of social services, this citizenship project was created by Mexican American farm and cannery workers active in the movement for union democracy and racial justice. The movement initially focused on union members and their families, but the activists soon realized that recent immigrants needed assistance, for they were facing exclusionary welfare and immigration laws. Thus, !Vote! expanded to organize and serve the larger Latino/a communities.[76]

Also known as the Citizenship Project, ¡Vote! has been affiliated with the Community Studies Program at the University of California–Santa Cruz. Paul Johnston, a practicing sociologist, was brought in as a researcher and executive director for the group and developed a staff of Mexican American organizers.[77] With this staff, ¡Vote! has run a number of important community service projects, including a naturalization campaign helping thousands apply for citizenship and a Freedom School where citizens-to-be can learn English and study for citizenship and participation in public life. ¡Vote!, the name of the project, refers to campaigns to educate and mobilize voters. In addition, a strike-support program has helped the labor movement fight for a better economic future for local communities.[78]

Sociological Reflections

Johnston's extensive involvement in this type of sociological practice is yet another example of how one sociologist can make a difference. He has provided us with some autobiographical details. "This experience," Johnston noted, "has convinced me of the viability of this model of sociological practice, and has led me to begin envisioning a form of training and a model collegial organization (an alternative to the pre–information age university department) which would support and promote it. I hope someday to help build such an institution."[79] In our interview with him, Johnston reported that he began to study social theory intensely "through reading and practical work, at the same time that I dropped out of Stanford as a freshman at the height of the Vietnam War (on the occasion of the invasion of Cambodia, the Kent and Jackson State shootings, my moral revulsion [in regard to] student deferments for kids like myself, a particularly distasteful experience with my advisor and teacher William Shockley, and an interest in working for the United Farm Workers)."[80]

Some years later, Johnston returned to college and enrolled at the University of California–Berkeley. His intention was "to return to practical work, better informed or at least more confident of my understanding. It didn't sink in for several years that I was being trained to be a professor."[81] Johnston took a job at Yale University, but after being promoted to associate professor he grew restless. He returned to California right after the passage of Proposition 187 and the Republican "Contract with America" to start "a mode of scholarly practice in which research and writing would be combined with participation, rather than with teaching."[82] Like Alinsky and Cazenave, Paul Johnston's research and activism are grounded in an understanding of the importance of social justice. He has described his general view in this way:

> I learn best about a phenomenon (usually, because of the nature of my research, an organization or a social movement) by participating in it, working on it, acquiring an almost tactile feel for it in the same sense that we know our clothes by wearing them.... I am well aware of the dangers that involvement poses to scholarship; I understand, however, that we are all always participants in the settings we study even when we imagine that we are not, and that an essential avenue to insight is analysis of the effects of our participation on the questions we ask and neglect to ask and the things we see and fail to see. I believe that the best empirical research and theoretical work can come from engaged researchers who struggle with their own bias. But I confess that though I am fascinated, obsessed, addicted to that purely scientific challenge of understanding social processes, my main motive for doing sociology—both scholarly and practical—is a commitment to social *change*.[83]

CONCLUSION

In Chicago, and eventually in many other cities, Saul Alinsky made a major difference in the progressive cause as an individual activist committed to change—progressive and democratic change for all Americans, especially those Americans who are poor and oppressed. Using sociological ideas tested thoroughly in activist practice, and working with other organizers and the poor themselves, he succeeded in significantly improving the lives of many in numerous poverty-burdened communities across the country. Alinsky was strongly committed to a society where people's class, racial, and ethnic backgrounds do not bring social oppression. Today, he remains an example of how one individual committed to sociologically informed activism can make a major difference in expanding democracy and social justice.

Yet, as we have seen, Alinsky's example is not unique. In a savvy book on participatory action research, titled *Building Community: Social Science in Action,* the social science editors note how Alinsky's sharp critique of general academic relevance can be a starting point for discussing the alternative route for the growing numbers of social scientists concerned with working with local activists to create healthier communities. One can see the inspiration of Alinsky in their stated perspective:

> Traditional academic-based research does not always have the betterment of a particular community in mind, nor is it consistently concerned with finding ways to improve the quality of life for those in society who do not have a fair share of their nation's wealth.... The purpose of this book is to present an alternative route to gaining a better understanding of the world around us.[84]

At the University of Connecticut, Professor Noel Cazenave's efforts to expand academic discussion beyond the narrow limits of a European/American–oriented curriculum represent an important type of liberation-oriented sociology, one that can be carried out by individuals who generate change with the cooperation of key others. As individuals and as groups, liberation social scientists can take effective actions to challenge established ways of thinking about society and established ways of oppressing others. Here a young sociologist was willing to take some risk in order to assert his right of freedom of thought and to choose a course's subject matter. There should not have been extensive debate among the faculty or in the community over such a scholarly course, one dealing with the everyday realities of white racism in the United States, which are all too evident to African Americans and other people of color and are documented in numerous research studies. Although the well-crafted sociology course was finally approved, this type of faculty debate signals a continuing and serious problem with academic freedom within U.S. colleges and universities. Sometimes academics are seen as isolated from the real world in their ivy-covered towers. Yet, the real world is ever present there, and some sociologists have had to make very significant sacrifices to bring the practice of liberation sociology to their own institutions.

Similarly, Paul Johnston left a secure life at Yale University and put his concern with making sociological understandings relevant into practice by directing an organization devoted to the expansion of the rights and the improvement of living conditions for some of the poorest of Americans. Like other activist researchers, Johnston did not give up the principles of good sociological research. He has continued his sociological research and has published in both scholarly and popular outlets. As we see in his comments, he is well aware of the dangers that community involvement imposes on scholarship, but he is even more concerned that all social researchers recognize that they are indeed participants in the settings they study. To imagine that as social scientists we are not participants is naive. And the desire to change the world for the better as a sociologically informed activist only changes the character of that participation. Especially important in Johnston's autobiographical comments is his view of the importance of researchers' settings on the questions they ask, and neglect to ask, and on the things they see and fail to see.

CHAPTER 6

Doing Liberation Social Science: Participatory Action Research Strategies

The social science research strategies variously called action research, community action research, participatory research, and participatory action research (PAR) commonly engage social scientists with people in local communities. These social researchers usually take issue with the main tenets of a detached instrumental social science and work directly for the betterment of human society. Today, there is a great diversity in this type of applied social research, which has spread dramatically across the globe. In this chapter we explore some of these research strategies.

Dimensions of Action Research

Conceptually, one can distinguish between three dimensions of participatory research—its goals, its sources, and its trajectory over time. There is a significant range of goals in what is called participatory or action research. One can visualize the goals on a continuum. At one end, the conservative end, there are large corporations, corporate foundations, and governmental bureaucracies that sometimes use participatory research as a device to get people at the grassroots to comply with the profit-making or other establishment goals of these organizations. Examples of this are the agricultural "research" projects in various postcolonial nations that are set up by chemical or petrochemical companies, or their related foundations, in order to get peasant farmers to use agricultural chemicals such as pesticides and fertilizers in local farming. In these cases, the participatory aspect, such as bringing in peasant farmers for feedback, participation, and education, is often a *ruse* to make more profits off expanded sales of petrochemicals. There is little interest in helping local people determine what their problems—and local solutions—might be, and in their significant participation in the decision-making.

As one moves from the conservative end of the continuum to the more progressive end, one finds an increasing level of concern with democratic and liberation goals. Participatory research aimed at expanding the participation of people in research directed at their self-defined needs is booming and growing across the globe—with a lot of diversity in its application. Sociologists and other social scientists are making much use of participatory action research to serve and learn from an array of grassroots people's organizations. These researchers are often re-creating sociology in new and innovative ways.

Another aspect of participatory action research is the point of origin or source for the research. In our review of the literature, we have found several major sources of participatory research projects. These include local community activists, an activist social scientist coming from the outside, progressive organizations outside local communities, and a corporation with a limited economic interest.

In many cases, action research undertakings are generated by activist leaders or community organizers who come to social scientists seeking their help in researching local community problems and their possible solutions. We will examine several examples of this type later in the chapter. Yet another source for these participatory projects is an activist sociologist coming to a community with ideas for localized research that will be of use to the community in defining its problems and their solutions. We see an example of this in the work of a leading South American sociologist, Orlando Fals-Borda, in a later section. A third source for participatory research projects is when a progressive organization comes to a local community and to social scientists seeking to get them both to join in efforts to deal with local community problems. In some cases, the progressive organization doing this stimulation of research is new and has emerged in connection with recent movements for democracy, women's rights, or indigenous people's rights across the globe. In other cases, older nongovernmental organizations (NGOs) have moved in a more progressive direction and are currently working to stimulate research oriented to local community needs. A fourth source of participatory research occurs when more conservative organizations, such as the aforementioned petrochemical companies, seek to use participatory research to pursue their own political or economic goals, such as expanded profits.

Another dimension of participatory research projects encompasses the varying trajectories of community projects once they are underway. The point of origin clearly affects the trajectory. Some participatory action research projects seeking corporate goals are successful, whereas others fail because they are not seeking the self-defined interests of the communities involved. However, even those projects seeking corporate goals by involving local people, such as peasant farmers, in some type of participatory research sometimes manage to generate radical protest movements down the line. Once local people are organized for a limited purpose, they have often used their new community organization to seek more radical goals. This is an example of the social science concept of "unintended consequences." Even conservatively conceived research can unintentionally generate movements for progressive social change at later points in time.

Historical Precedents for Participatory Research

William F. Whyte edited a much-cited volume reviewing a number of different participatory projects. Those projects range across the aforementioned continuum, with the degree of community input into the research projects varying significantly. In an opening article to this volume, Whyte and his colleagues note that it is possible to achieve good scientific knowledge and provide action-oriented solutions to concrete problems at the same time: "Science is not achieved by distancing oneself from the world; as generations of scientists know, the greatest conceptual and methodological challenges come from engagement with the world."[1]

Whyte and his colleagues trace the origins of participatory research to three historical influences. The first is the traditional methodology of social anthropologists and sociologists who have involved insightful local informants as active participants in their field research projects in particular communities. These researchers have often discussed with their informants the interpretation of the societal processes being observed.

A second cited influence on the development of participatory action research is the corporation-fostered study of workers' participation in workplace decisions, such as Quality of Work Life (QWL) programs. These QWL programs have often focused on humanizing some aspects of the workplace, on the assumption that a better quality of work life increases productivity and loyalty to a company. In the area of agriculture, the recognition that new high-yield varieties of crops developed by scientists were predominantly benefiting large farmers led to an interest on the part of some governmental agencies in incorporating small farmers into research and development projects. A third line of influence in the development of participatory research is the emergence of the systems-theory framework that since the 1950s has been applied in organizational research, such as that attempting to understand how workplaces can better integrate social and technological factors. In this sphere, social scientists have worked to better understand technological factors by inviting those workers who use the technology to be part of the research process.[2]

In Whyte's edited book there is some discussion of applied research with community cooperatives, but most of the book's examples focus on establishment organizations. The emphasis is on enhancement of the applied use of social science for existing private and public organizations.[3] There is relatively little discussion of participatory research projects that try to empower communities of the oppressed that are unorganized or just beginning to organize in nontraditional ways. Thus, the emancipatory potential of participatory action research projects for the people involved varies greatly and needs to be determined for each such case.

EMPOWERING THE POOR

Participatory action research with a strong emancipatory cast has other historical and regional roots, which the authors in the Whyte collection generally neglect. Indeed, one needs to go back to the beginnings of U.S. sociology to find the ultimate roots of participatory action research. As we described earlier, activist sociology was pioneered in the 1890s by the mostly female sociologists working out of Hull House in Chicago. These female sociologists did the *first* extensive sociological research in local communities, and as activist researchers they provided their field and demographic research studies to local residents for their information and input. These sociologists saw progressive reform of society as essential and used sociological research to further that goal.

Moreover, since the 1950s, renewed efforts directed at participatory action research on behalf of the poor have been generated in postcolonial countries, especially in Latin America, where a growing number of important links have been established between researchers and grassroots movements. In this research tradition, people in local communities define many research questions, control much of the research process, have substantial access to research results, and decide on much of the use of research results. The generation of knowledge in this action research usually becomes a source of group and individual empowerment. Knowledge ceases to be the private turf of professional experts and political elites.[4]

A crucial impetus for participatory projects is the provocative perspective of the late Brazilian educator Paulo Freire (see Chapter 1). His seminal ideas have now reached a broad international audience of educators, social scientists, and other scholars and community leaders. Freire pressed the idea of establishing a two-way dialogue between the researcher and the people researched, thereby overcoming the traditional subject-object dichotomy in social science research. The accent in the Freire tradition is on close ties between researchers and community members, with no necessary tie to the academic setting. These participatory research sociologists work with an awareness that there are many sources of knowledge and that knowledge is indeed power. People's empowerment and what Freire called "conscientization" are the major goals of participatory action research. Recall from our earlier discussion of Freire that *conscientization* means the creation of an awareness among people—a pedagogy of how oppressed people can liberate themselves.[5]

This empowering social science research often contrasts significantly with traditional social science research. In one traditional "professional" model of social science, "there is no place for the community-of-those-studied to share in the determination of research objectives."[6] As sociologists Blauner and Wellman have noted, academically oriented social scientists tend to respond to the interests of fellow social scientists: "The theories, the interests, and the very concepts with which we work respond to the dynamics of increasing knowledge within our individual disciplines and professions, as well as to fashions and status concerns. The life problems and needs of the communities-under-study affect the scholar only indirectly; they are rarely the starting point for theory and research."[7]

The empowerment perspective attempts to involve ordinary residents in the local community, who not only have needs that should matter to social scientists but who also can do important social theorizing. Not surprisingly, one impetus for this type of action research is the realization that the usual armamentarium—theoretical, epistemological, and methodological—provided by academic training in social science generally does not well equip one to participate in active societal transformation. Ideas, theories, and methodologies of social improvement are not ordinarily part of the frame of reference of mainstream social science, and they must be added to that frame of reference if social scientists are to assist in creating a better world.

ACTION RESEARCH: THE WORK OF
ORLANDO FALS-BORDA

We will now turn to some major examples of participatory action research (PAR) in the empowerment tradition. Orlando Fals-Borda, a leading Latin American sociologist educated in the United States, was one of the first to engage in participatory action research on behalf of the poor. He pioneered several action research strategies. His methods have sometimes been criticized by mainstream sociologists, and for a time his research alliances with peasant movements in Colombia even led the U.S. State Department to refuse him entry visas to the United States.[8]

In 1955 Fals-Borda published a pioneering book, *Peasant Society in the Colombian Andes,* a study he completed without institutional sponsorship, and which was the first major empirical sociological research done in Colombia.[9] Over the next few decades, he honed new participatory research strategies working with Colombian peasants. For example, in a study of Andean peasants, Fals-Borda and his research team examined the development of a rural peasant community. At the time, he was chair of a university sociology department and also head of Colombia's Ministry of Agriculture. This project involved community action in a rural Andean community of seventy poor families, a community whose younger generations were leaving. In the 1950s, the local school was in a dilapidated building with few windows. Since the municipal authorities did not respond to calls for repairs, the local people organized bazaars and gave the money collected to the authorities, who still did little. At the same time, new urban growth and technologies were creating some new values and often undermining such traditional cooperative practices as "brazo prestado" (the borrowed arm), in which labor contributed to a neighbor's project was repaid later. In his report on the research project, Fals-Borda commented, "The new values being adopted seemed to destroy the old social structure without offering any apparent compensation or alternatives to a new integration."[10] Under these conditions, the apparent apathy of the local people made it seem impossible to solve the problems of the community without outside agency.

After doing some research in this rural community in the late 1950s, three change agents—a rural sociologist, a social worker, and an architect—decided to help the community meet its own defined goals. By providing the community with the results of the sociological research—which included a demonstration of the people's concern for a better school—these researchers were able to spur a local community meeting. All local residents attended, and the social worker and the sociologist helped to facilitate discussion. When the mayor came to understand the strong concerns of the people for a school, he offered to provide building materials if residents supplied the labor. A newly created community organization elected its own board of directors to represent the community and defend its interests. An important step was the appointment of a treasurer, who would keep the money collected within the community and thereby increase the confidence of the people. After the new school was completed, numerous community activities and organizations were developed, thereby strengthening the local community.[11]

A striking difference between Fals-Borda's research report on the project and more traditional sociological reports is that it contains a large section of photographs of local people and of places in the community. It also includes the inaugural minutes of the community's organization and a report from the treasurer. This type of research publication is not only a contribution to sociological knowledge but an important historical record for use by people in the community.

In his monograph on the community project, Fals-Borda reflects on his research experience and discusses sociological theories of group dynamics. Successful community action, he notes, is the result of a community taking charge of its problems and organizing to solve them through the development of local and external resources. One principle here is "social catalysis," the process of change that develops because of the presence of action agents who ensure that the new democratic approach proceeds, certain mistakes are avoided, and latent community needs become explicit. Social-catalytic agents can facilitate community stability. In this case, a sociologist was one catalytic agent. The stimulus for community action initially came from outside, and the outsiders gradually received recognition from local church and municipal leaders. More importantly, they gained the trust of the local residents. Contact with agents of change, who became trusted, was important in launching a process of community change. Local groups without active change agents like Fals-Borda or Saul Alinsky often fail. However, the catalytic agents cannot be effective if they become permanent advisors and "the experts." The programs initiated by the change agents are successful only because they help train new leaders for the local community. These new leaders then "become the yeast that rises the whole dough, adopting the catalytic qualities that the external change agent had so that they can continue the work and take initiative and responsibility."[12]

Recent Research and Activism

In recent decades, Fals-Borda has continued to pursue PAR methods and strategies in innovative ways. Indeed, in 1985 Siglo Veintiuno,

Editores, perhaps the most influential publisher of social science literature in Spanish, published a book by Fals-Borda on social knowledge and people's power. This is, in effect, a handbook for PAR in postcolonial countries.[13] In contrast to Whyte's handbook, noted above, Fals-Borda's is much more clearly about PAR as a methodology and strategy for actual popular empowerment.

Since the 1970s, Fals-Borda has been reaching broad audiences with his PAR ideas through his active presence at many meetings and conventions across the South American continent. In 1977 his presentations at the World Symposium on Participatory Action Research in Cartagena, Colombia, served to systematize his PAR methodology. His presence at the World Assembly of Adult Education resulted in a seventy-three-page book on participatory research that has been highly influential in Latin American countries.[14]

We should note that, in addition to his PAR work, Fals-Borda is an important sociologist of education with influence in many countries of Latin America and elsewhere. In Latin American countries, personal presentations at meetings, symposia, and conventions, as well as other forms of face-to-face scholarly communication, are far more important than in the United States and Europe, where written publications are generally regarded as more important. Indeed, one idea for liberation sociologists in the United States and Europe is to expand the strategies for research presentation to include many more interactional settings for ordinary people. In Chapter 1, we noted one U.S. example of such interactive work by Project South, the Atlanta-based organization committed to popular education for low-income communities.

Rethinking the Research Process

Fals-Borda's participant observation and action at the grassroots level came to shape his scholarly view of the research process. For him, "the results of participatory research are open to validation and judgment like in any other discipline, not only by fellow scholars and bureaucrats—who are now in a rampage to co-opt it—but also by the opinion of the subject peoples themselves."[15] Here the ultimate validation of the research instruments and process lies in its value to those researched.

Similarly, Fals-Borda's presentation of his research has broken new ground. In the mid-1980s, he published four volumes of sociological and historical research on the coastal region of Colombia. He dedicated Volume 4 to "the resurgent grassroots movements struggling for life, democracy, and peace, because they will be able to save Colombia if they stick to their historical destiny: to replace the current ruling classes whose devastating and egoistic performance is once again laid bare in this volume."[16] In this study, he traces a Colombian region's social history, from pre-Columbian times to the 1980s. Significantly, the four volumes present research information in a different and innovative format. Thus, on the left-hand pages of the books, one finds historical accounts and empirical descriptions, while on the right-hand pages, one finds concepts, theoretical interpretations, sources, and methodological discussions of what is on the left-hand pages. For example, on one left-hand page, there is a brief story of how several Native American groups were exterminated or conquered by the Spanish and how their lands were occupied. On the right-hand page, we learn that the main workforce, which produced the wealth of the conquering Spaniards, was made up of enslaved Africans. The direct and indirect destruction of the Native American population was so complete that the Spanish exploiters could not use their labor by the late sixteenth century.[17]

"Commitment" and Participatory Action Research

Articulating his view of participatory action research in a major 1987 book, Fals-Borda reports that he initially used traditional academic techniques, such as participant observation, without being fully aware of their epistemological implications. In traditional academic research, "participant observation" has meant that sociological researchers observe but do not get fully involved in the processes observed.[18] In contrast, Fals-Borda began developing by the 1960s the concept of *commitment*, the idea that participatory social scientists should work to transform an intolerable society into a humane one. The practice of sociology should be explicitly focused on the needs of people who are victims of social exploitation. In thinking through the implications of his own action research, Fals-Borda did not find his Ph.D. training in sociology of much use—a frequent report of many sociologists doing participatory action research—and thus did not resort much to Western academic sources and techniques in developing his understandings of community research. Indeed, for new ideas he sought out Latin American and Native American thinkers, though few of the latter's perspectives have survived centuries of Western colonial onslaught.[19]

Very influential in the case of Fals-Borda and fellow sociologists were yet other intellectual stimuli from postcolonial sources. During the 1960s and 1970s, Latin American researchers linked to the United Nations Economic Commission for Latin America came up with what came to be called "dependency theory" to explain societal structures in South American countries. This was the first theory to break with the notion that the so-called backwardness of postcolonial countries was due to the social, economic, or cultural inferiority of the people in those countries. Instead, the realities of economic under-development across the globe were now set within the framework of the capitalistic world system—one in which the more industrialized countries at the center intentionally created economic dependency in less industrialized countries on the periphery. As Fals-Borda has noted, this was the "first cry of Latin American intellectual independence from the traditional colonialism that has characterized our elites."[20] As Latin American social scientists began to break with older patterns of European-influenced thinking, they joined a reworked Marxism, a dependency theory configured to their own political-economic conditions.

During the 1960s, Pablo Gonzalez Casanova, a Mexican politi-cal scientist, expanded the traditional Marxist concept of exploitation and made it applicable to the economic complexity of agriculturally oriented Latin American societies. Another current that influenced Fals-Borda and his colleagues was the work of Paulo Freire in popular education, whose impact on activist scholars was noted previously. Yet another critical influence was the action in the field of Camilo Torres, a Catholic priest and former academic social scientist who died with Colombian guerrillas fighting for social change in that country. Clearly, the Latin American perspective on participatory ac-tion research is rather different from that accented in the often more managerial, applied-research tradition accented in the edited volume by William F. Whyte.

In 1985 Fals-Borda gave an important keynote address at a Southern Sociological Society meeting in the United States. There he described how research for social justice by researchers in the North-ern and Southern Hemispheres is now beginning to converge. Latin American and other postcolonial researchers have had a twenty-year lead over U.S. sociologists, but the latter are beginning to catch up. "Participatory researchers in the Third World," Fals-Borda told his audience, "contributed to this merger with a version of 'commitment' which combined praxis and phronesis, that is, horizontal participation with peoples and wise judgment and prudence for the good life." He continued by noting that he, as an activist sociologist, had worked hard "in the service of peasants and workers' struggles, which meant a clear break with the Establishment, plus an active, sometimes dangerous search for social justice there."[21] Indeed, he was actually imprisoned several times with the peasants and workers he served.

In his U.S. address, Fals-Borda added this personal note about being an activist sociologist:

> But I could not consider myself a scientist, even less a human being, if I did not exercise the "commitment" and felt it in my heart and in my head as a life experience, *Erfahrung* or *Vivencia*. This methodology became an alternative philosophy of life for me and for many others. There is no need to make an apology for this type of committed research. Nearly everyone knows that PAR combines qualitative and quantitative techniques. It utilizes hermeneutics, literature, and art according to needs. And it joins with action simultaneously. There appears to be now ample agreement that PAR can serve to correct prevailing practices in our disciplines which have not been altogether satisfactory or useful for society at large.[22]

In the last decade or so many sociologists and anthropologists in the United States have finally recognized Orlando Fals-Borda for his pioneering efforts in participatory research. Indeed, in 2007 he was awarded the Malinowski award by the Society for Applied Anthropology.

Commitment to progressive change is central for Fals-Borda. Note too that he views participatory action research as usefully *combining* qualitative and quantitative research methods. By itself, quantitative research can rarely produce deep understandings of the social world. When quantitative data are found to be useful, this often means the introduction of sociological insights from other sources such as those gained from qualitative field research. Used well and together, qualitative and quantitative methods have the potential to lead to cutting-edge understandings of the social world.

The intellectual ferment and community from which Fals-Borda's participatory action research emerged are different from other forms of applied sociology. The main reason for this is the close connection between the researchers and communities of the aggrieved. Indeed, it is the pressures from the oppressed that, directly or indirectly, generate this type of participatory action research. Today, such research is spreading across the globe. It has increased because of the quality of findings that it produces, which often assist in community development for and by the poor.

Some observers have seen in the increasing funding of participatory research approaches—mainly by Western nongovernmental agencies and certain private foundations—a new form of northern "co-optation" of southern nations. Indeed, participatory development, sustainable development, human rights, feminist, antiracist, and other critical actions against the societal status quo "have been relentlessly subjected to efforts at co-optation and domestication."[23] Yet, this does not mean that this funded research is necessarily co-opted in all features by its corporate and bureaucratic funders, since participatory research, once inaugurated by means of extensive community participation, is hard to contain. Local people, once organized, may move their organization in the direction of more radical goals, such as expanded political democracy, than its funders ever conceived. Moreover, even at the heart of heavily industrialized societies, participatory action research can increase local organization and thereby increase pressures for democratization and greater participation in governance on the part of working-class communities.

PARTICIPATORY ACTION RESEARCH AROUND THE WORLD

Patients Shaping Research: A Chilean Project

In regard to action research, Chile is an important country to examine because of the extensive involvement of sociologists in such research with a variety of people's organizations. This participation has varied with the ebb and flow of the democratic institutions in that country. Ironically, in the mid-1960s, Chile was the location for one of the largest research projects ever involving sociologists, a multimillion-dollar research project called Project Camelot, which sought to study groups engaged in popular dissent against the country's sociopolitical structure. This reactionary research effort was designed in the United States to measure the potential for insurgency among the people and to reduce or eliminate these people's movements. The head of the project was a U.S. social scientist, and several other U.S. and Chilean social scientists, including sociologists, were heavily involved in the large-scale undertaking. During the "cold war" with the former Soviet Union and its allies, the U.S. government had an overt goal of destroying numerous popular movements across the globe, movements it fantasized were allies with the communist bloc in Europe. Fortunately, Chilean social scientists and university administrators were successful in the battle they waged against this misguided research project.

One of the authors of this book, Hernán Vera, has done participatory action research in Chile. He studied the quality of the performance of medical clinics providing important services to the poor. The inauguration of the project stemmed from the progressive managers of the medical clinics, who during the redemocratization of Chile in the late 1980s were running clinics with substantial input from those poor Chileans whom they served. Since the managers of the clinics had initially defined the project as a probing self-analysis, Vera decided to present the staff and the managers with the strategy of participant action research. In this research plan, the people served by the clinics and the medical staff would all participate directly, if in different ways. Initially, participatory procedures were difficult to implement because the physicians, nurses, and midwives expected the kind of scientific research that they had learned about in their own training. Early in the process, one of the clinics' physicians expressed the view of most of the medical staff that the sociologist should not involve the staff but should proceed with conventional questionnaires and methods of reporting: "I do not ask patients to make decisions," and "You should not ask us to make yours."

Gradually, the terms of this participatory research project were negotiated between the staff and the sociologist, with the staff voting on each aspect of the research. In weekly meetings, they were presented with concrete ideas for the research project, and they became a reservoir of innovative ideas that greatly improved the research instruments and procedures used by the sociologist. There were some immediate benefits for the clinics' personnel and operation. In organizations like these, frequent staff participation in research decisions—including participation in designing interview protocols, in selection of interviewers, and in commenting on drafts of the research report—served to allay fears among the medical personnel that the project was only a managerial effort aimed at greater control of them.

At this stage, the research was participatory for the staff, but not yet for the patients. Soon, however, Vera began to involve the poor Chileans served by the medical clinics as well. They were interviewed using a series of open-ended questions designed to allow them flexible input, and they also participated in focus groups—group interviews that allowed for interactive expression and creativity. Substantial benefits accrued from this part of the participatory action research. The medical practitioners now came to see how the patients themselves actually felt about the services provided. From this comprehensive participatory research process, the medical staff gained a better sense of what needed to be improved. Given this success, the innovative participatory methods spread to other medical clinics across the country. One physician who had witnessed the patient focus groups was so elated at the results of the research technique that he argued that this focus group technique should be *taught in medical school* as an essential communication tool for medical practitioners.[24] Interestingly, this is an important idea that has yet to be developed in the medical school settings of the "democratic" United States.

For the most part the clinics' patients were disenfranchised low-income women served by a weak health care system that never consulted them about their needs. The open-ended interviews and the opportunity to exchange ideas with other women in focus groups were actually liberating for these women. Indeed, the research-oriented focus groups were sometimes transformed into workshops and community action groups. For example, one focus group, consisting of a dozen low-income women, eventually became a local action group working to inform pregnant women in a neighborhood of the need for early medical checkups. Clearly, sociological research, conducted in an emancipatory mode, can help create more democratic social, economic, and political systems across the globe.

Community Action Research in Mexico

In 1973, sociologist Maria Sanchez began conducting research for her dissertation in Mexico's poverty-riddled Sierra Norte de Puebla region. Spending her first year learning about indigenous life, she studied kinship rituals, the power structure, and the economy. She gradually became friends with local families. In a later discussion of the research project, Sanchez noted that "her initial goal was to collect information for her dissertation, but her interactions with the villagers persuaded her to give her academic concerns secondary priority."[25] Soon she persuaded a group of urban friends, some social scientists and some members of religious groups, to join her as a live-in team working with the indigenous people in the town of San Miguel, which was in a mountainous region populated substantially by indigenous people. This was a poor region whose economy was centered in corn and coffee production.

From the start, Sanchez and her team were involved in a participatory action research project. The outside team of activists and researchers met interactively with the local villagers weekly to plan action, with Sanchez presenting research results and villagers and team members proposing community projects. The villagers proposed such programs as first-aid courses, vegetable gardens, and the creation of a handicraft group. Gradually, rural-urban, racial-ethnic, and class barriers between the researchers and the people were somewhat broken down. Working together, the team and the villagers gathered research data and significantly improved local living conditions. A coffee cooperative was established, and a processing plant was built with newly gained foundation support. A regional agriculture cooperative was formed, which built a farm and served as an agricultural experiment station. A Study and Educational Promotion Center was founded. Eventually, roughly half the community, about 120 families, were participating in the various projects and activities. Sanchez and Almeida have written about the results: "A remarkable infrastructure had been created in the community, including a coffee processing plant, the farm, the communal store, and other projects such as a small clinic, a preschool program, a research program, and an oral tradition program."[26]

However, some political authorities, some rural teachers, and the local oligarchy were opposed to this new type of participatory teamwork. Some officials in governmental agencies, political parties, and the Church tried to co-opt the community movement, but unsuccessfully. The activist research team was accused of being "foreigners" with no respect for established authority, but the community strongly defended them.

Over more than two decades, the participatory research project greatly benefited the local community. Three local peasant leaders put it this way: "We have seen that change has been taking place.. Critical thinking abilities have increased. We do not allow people to impose their ideas any more. We all have the right to express our own ideas. People are participating in San Miguel because they have seen more than promises."[27] In addition, the team of activist researchers felt important goals had been achieved, including much reciprocal learning:

> Through our twenty-year experience we, as team members, have witnessed the capacity of community members to question their own knowledge and to theoretically reconstruct it. We do not believe that the permanent role of the academician is to be the people's theoretician. At the same time the cause of good research was also served by knowing from below and knowing from inside. The idea of social science and the idea of development were born paternalistically. Academicians usually go to community, neighborhoods, and villages with unidirectional purposes: to teach, to do research, to provide service, to liberate. When academicians (scholars, students) experiment with PAR, the same unidirectional attitude comes through.... One of the most valuable things *we* have learned during these twenty years is the importance of reciprocity in research, learning, providing service, liberating.[28]

Over time, the activist sociologist Sanchez and her team members had developed a strong appreciation of local knowledge and folk wisdom and a respect for traditional community ways. As the researchers saw it, the university community could benefit greatly from the popular education of its researchers. In this participatory research modality, community changes are not imposed from above. This goal requires vigilance in regard to the ethics of the relationship between community members and researchers. Ideally, the purpose of participatory action research is to produce local relevant knowledge and mobilize people to end their misery.

Action Research in Tanzania

Another example of liberation sociology helping ordinary people is the project of social researchers Rakesh Rajani and Mustafa Kudrati, who researched the conditions of street children in Mwanza, Tanzania, that country's second largest city. Working with a small nongovernmental organization (Kuleana) and financed by UNICEF and the Population Council, these sociologically oriented researchers sought to develop reliable knowledge about the children of the streets, especially about their sexual activities and related health consequences. The goal was to devise social programs for the street children.[29]

Rajani and Kudrati approached this research with a human rights perspective and have noted that "building relations of mutual trust and respect with street children lies at the heart of conducting effective research and promoting healthy sexual behavior."[30] Their research priorities were driven substantially by the children's concerns. Two groups of boys and girls were chosen as consultants on gathering and using the information. The children participated in regular, candid, and in-depth discussions about sexual practices with researchers and the organization's staff. The researchers conducted in-depth interviews with many of the street children. When the research was launched, the risk factor in HIV infection among street children was derived mainly from the necessity of them selling sexual favors to exploitative adults. However, the research pointed to the importance of children's sexual expressions with each other as a risk factor. A baseline set of data on each child's past and present was collected, and the children's experiences and views about sex were shared in discussions in a variety of structured and informal contexts such as classrooms, theater performances, and impromptu interactions with the children.[31]

In their research report, Rajani and Kudrati note the difficulties in trying to help the street children develop healthy lifestyles. They argue that researchers and staff members should avoid autocratic and paternalistic programs, which are usually doomed to failure. They suggest that "children and adolescents are also sexual beings, with feelings of desire and connection, curiosity and lust. Sexuality and the license to deal with sexual feeling are rights and responsibilities for children as much as for anyone else. In denying this, adult-run

NGOs may be doing the greatest disservice to the children and young people they aim to serve."[32]

As a result of this consultative and participatory research, the children got better health and education programs, which were substantially designed based on knowledge gained in the research. The research also facilitated the establishment of training programs producing a more knowledgeable staff to run programs. Staff members who work with street children have received training to act in nonpatronizing ways. Critical in this training is learning to encourage open discussion of sex. The Kuleana programs are implemented in two related centers. One is a shelter that serves one hundred children a day, with programs that integrate health, education, and community consciousness-raising. The other is a center for sexual health that offers innovative sexual education, provides counseling, gives support to HIV/AIDS patients, and maintains a community resource center for children. Participatory research continues at both centers.

In this case the social researchers became human instruments at the service of poor and oppressed children. The decisions required to conduct the research were still made in the best social science terms, but with an explicit awareness that the interests and concerns of the oppressed should drive the research. The researchers did not forfeit their knowledge or training, just the academic elitism and social distance that too many social science researchers claim for themselves in such settings.

Participatory Research in Germany

European social scientists have made important use of participatory action research. For example, Peter Mettler and Thomas Baumgartner conducted a future-oriented participatory experiment that sought to make the shaping of ongoing technological developments more democratic. Financed by the Ministry of Labor, Health, and Social Affairs of North-Rhine-Westphalia in Germany, these sociologists persuaded ninety local residents from different parts of the region, different social classes, and several ethnic groups to attend several days of intensive group discussions. The aim of this experiment was to test a new framework—called the Participatory Delphi Procedure for Future-Oriented Interdisciplinary Policy Planning—aimed at developing new decisionmaking procedures that fully take into account the social and environmental consequences of scientific and technological advancements.[33]

The ninety citizens met in several groups and became the "experts" on daily life and work in regard to three possible scenarios that were presented to them. These scenarios were constructed by the researchers based on three different logics of societal development, each involving certain technologies and work arrangements. Participants were asked to imagine what their society would be like in the year 2020 and to describe it in detail. For example, work in Scenario A is seen as compensated activity in a dependent relation to the employer, much as it is today. But the Delphi participants were to envision a shorter (25–30 hour) workweek by the year 2020. In this scenario, housework and other modes of labor were regarded as less useful activities. They were asked to evaluate this futuristic scenario.

In Scenario B, a broader view of work in the future was asserted. Work was viewed as an important part of life, one that comprises all activities in the economy, society, and private household realm. The different work activities, including housework, were to be of equal value. Participants were asked how they would see such equality of work efforts.

Then, in Scenario C, the image of work was one of achievement entirely determined by the multinational corporate sphere: "The organization of labour is strictly hierarchical and work hours are strictly determined by production necessities with shifts and Sunday work."[34] In this scenario the present work arrangements would more or less persist, but all under the control of a multinational managerial elite. In this project, various research procedures were used, including the assessment of the future-oriented scenarios and role-playing exercises. For example, the social science researchers introduced the idea of a film studio in which the group participants imagined themselves as the stage managers and the research team as the actors that the former had to tell how to act in a particular scene.

Most research participants indicated that they had not thought much about the future of German society. Moreover, the participants, and by extension the citizens of North-Rhine-Westphalia, had not yet noticed the lack of future-oriented planning by their government. The citizen participants admitted that they themselves were not innovative with regard to new technologies and work arrangements and that although they were interested in new knowledge, they could likely assimilate a limited amount. Nevertheless, they wished to see improvements in the way scientific and technological knowledge about future work and economic arrangements are communicated and implemented.

This large-scale use of participatory research methods is emancipatory in that its investigations furthered large-scale participation by ordinary citizens in regard to critical decisions about their future. Without projects such as these, such decisions would likely be made only by a wealthy political-economic elite, and mostly outside of the democratic political arena. Needless to say, such important decisions can set the life conditions for people for generations. With the people's participation in these determinations, the environmental forces cease to be seen as obscure and determinant, but as socially invented life conditions. It is impossible to conduct a research project autocratically in order to improve democratic governance and participation. Like the projects in Colombia and Chile above, this participatory research project provided democratic ways of discovering and producing new sociological knowledge, which, in turn, could be used to bring both a better standard of living and a more democratic way of living.

Applied Research in Norway

We note next one example of a more conventional type of applied sociology, in this case an example that assisted corporations in profit development, but that also had a significant democratic impact. The case we consider is applied sociological research in the international shipping industry.[35] During the 1960s, the Norwegian shipping industry was undergoing major changes because of a shortage of seafarers, which was mainly due to competition from onshore jobs that offered a better quality of life. The idea of action research developed when social science consultants began to examine how to bring participatory research to bear on increasing workers' involvement in work planning and supervision in the shipping industry. In their conceptualization of the change process, these social scientists focused on what they termed the "action cycle": the series of steps one goes through once a problem and the factors that may influence its solution are identified. These action-cycle steps involve the formulation of proposed changes and a plan to implement them, the initiation of the changes, the assessment of changes and methods used, and the further diffusion of the changes.

Taking advantage of Norwegian legislation permitting smaller crews, a contact group was created including representatives from workers' unions, the shipowners' association, and government directorates. Researchers from the Norwegian Work Research Institute (WRI) participated in the numerous group meetings that took place over a period of several years. The meetings were "an open forum for exploring options, confronting differences, and clarifying—if not endorsing—organizational principles."[36]

The WRI researchers also assisted a shipping company whose ship *Mistral* had been chosen to conduct the first field trials of greater worker participation in everyday decisionmaking. The seafarers chosen as the crew visited work sites where experiments had been conducted in other industries to learn from workers, union officials, and managers about issues they were likely to face. On the *Mistral,* significant crew involvement in work planning and supervision was implemented. A common recreation room for officers and crew was established, together with a new personnel planning and salary system designed to enhance crew continuity. Democratic input was encouraged. After a year, the project was evaluated and found successful at the ship and the firm levels. The contact group approved the *Mistral* experiment and supported a second project. A third major experiment was launched aboard a ship of a different company. By 1976 the three experiments had shown that democratic crew arrangements were feasible and cost-effective. Eventually, the innovations introduced in these ships were diffused to other Norwegian ships, and active participation by crews and trade unions in decisionmaking was extended. By the 1980s, this tradition of group participation and experimentation within the Norwegian shipping industry was firmly established.[37]

Indeed, since then a number of the Norwegian innovations have spread to fleets of other countries. In this case, the participatory research projects were large-scale and involved private corporations, as well as unions and government agencies. Although corporate profitability was sought and enhanced in the process, the corporations were forced to consult directly with unions and thus to involve their workers more centrally in decisionmaking. Worker satisfaction with their work lives on these ships increased. The results in Norwegian shipping were liberating for the crews, which are now more directly involved in work planning, supervision, the development of recreation facilities, and the salary system. Although this project can be seen as a type of "corporate liberalism," by involving workers directly, this particular research project helped to make the lives of ordinary workers much better.

PARTICIPATORY ACTION RESEARCH IN THE UNITED STATES

In the United States much participatory action research has dealt with environmental issues, education, health care, racial and class diversity, and community control. Sociologists have been central participants in the expansion of PAR strategies across the United States.

Action Research in Housing: Milwaukee

In Milwaukee, for example, several sociologists have worked with the local Fair Lending Coalition in a participatory action research relationship. This coalition is a multiracial, inner-city organization with representatives from churches, unions, civil rights organizations, and community groups. Led by a racially diverse board, the coalition worked with Gregory D. Squires and other social scientists then at the University of Wisconsin–Milwaukee in order to bring change in local banks' investments in the central city of the Milwaukee metropolis.

Prior to this effort, the city of Milwaukee had experienced a high ratio of black-to-white rejection rates in home and small-business loans. Drawing on federal statutes requiring financial institutions to disclose local lending practices and to be responsive to needs of moderate-income communities in their areas, the coalition has negotiated numerous community investment agreements with local financial institutions, thereby securing commitments to make millions of dollars in new loans in formerly redlined neighborhoods. Working closely with the coalition groups, local PAR sociologists did research on lending practices, which showed high loan rejection rates for low- and moderate-income communities. The data also showed which lenders had a low number and percentage of their loans in areas with poor residents and residents of color. These data on income and racial barriers enabled the coalition to press lending institutions to provide commitments for new loans in these seriously underserved communities. Funding for the coalition began with a small grant from a local union, and office space was provided by a nonprofit organization. Later, the Milwaukee Foundation and the city government provided some funds for an executive director for the Fair Lending Coalition.[38]

Although it went out of business in the late 1990s, during its lifetime the coalition was effective because of its broad community representativeness and its close collaboration between housing activists in the community and the sociological researchers in the university. The Milwaukee Fair Lending Coalition thus got the accurate data that it needed to pursue aggressive challenges to racial and economic bias in local lending practices. As the researchers have noted, "research, in the absence of effective organizing, would become little more than an academic exercise. And the organizing, without a strong research foundation, would be far less effective."[39]

More Action Research: Chicago

In Chicago another group of sociologists and community activists, initially coordinated by Philip Nyden, a sociologist at Loyola University, and Josh Hoyt, then executive director of Organization of the Northeast (ONE), used sociological research to shape efforts to improve the lives of the moderate-income residents in two Chicago lakefront communities. The residents of these two large areas are very diverse in racial, ethnic, and class terms. ONE, the name of an umbrella group headed by an elected board drawn from about eighty local organizations, is dedicated to maintaining stable racial-ethnic diversity in housing in the areas and to improving the housing and socioeconomic conditions of local residents. Since the 1990s, ONE has organized strategy teams to work on local issues of education, housing, jobs, and economic development. In a series of field research reports, several local sociologists have assisted ONE activists and community residents to better understand what is happening in their area and to formulate progressive strategies for change.[40]

For example, in 1990 ONE began organizing tenants in ten apartment buildings constructed with major financial assistance from the U.S. Department of Housing and Urban Development (HUD) low-interest loans. The large apartment buildings, housing many of the area's tenants, were supposed to provide below-market-cost housing to low-income families. However, the owners used a loop-hole to convert some buildings to market-rate apartments, sharply reducing reasonably priced housing in the area and likely increasing owners' profits. Working with ONE, action-oriented sociologists conducted interviews and surveys with tenants and found that there was substantial racial-ethnic diversity in the buildings and that this affordable apartment housing was a key base on which families built stable and self-sufficient lives. Although the study did identify tensions between renters and homeowners, it found much satisfaction among the residents with a residential area where relations between diverse racial and ethnic groups had stabilized. The joint effort between community activists and social researchers was successful in keeping several of the buildings in the uptown area affordable for low-income residents. More recently, however, there have been renewed threats to the buildings, including a reduction in the availability of certificates used to subsidize rents and the expressed desire of new middle-class residents to force out the low-income residents. Nonetheless, ONE has continued pressing to improve the lives of people in this part of Chicago. In 2001, ONE work was recognized by several foundations, including the John D. and Catherine T. MacArthur Foundation, as the community organization of the year.[41]

In this case of participatory action research, the trust built up between the team of researchers and the community activists led to a longer-term collaborative research project, which resulted in research reports on the nature of business in the community, on tenant organizing, and on youth and family issues. These reports had some impact on local policymaking, for they showed not only community residents but also funding agencies, officials, and newspaper editors that these highly urban areas had relatively stable racial-ethnic relationships, with different groups actively cooperating to improve local conditions. The sociologists' reports showed that community organizational struggles were often effective in marshalling resources and bridging to progressive change. The research studies also provided knowledge and skills for staffs of the community organizations. Significantly, it was the trust and respect that the sociologists gained from community leaders and residents that made the collaborative relationship work. These field researchers had shown early on that they were not just doing research for journal articles of no use to the community. Instead, they shaped the project with the active involvement of local community residents and their organizations, empowering them to address their own concerns. These researchers have noted the significance of such collaborative sociological research: "Your research will not merely be catalogued and placed on the library shelf only to gather dust; it will be used by community organizations and other researchers."[42]

Given the sharp increase in predatory and exploitative lending by various banks and mortgage companies, and the resulting major housing crisis in what is called the subprime mortgage market, we should add a note on the growth in community groups and national organizations seeking major changes in this mortgage industry. Sometimes advised by sociologists and other social scientists, like those noted above, the Association of Community Organizations for Reform Now (ACORN), the National Community Reinvestment Coalition (NCRC), and the National Fair Housing Alliance (NFHA) have pressed for better mortgages and financing for moderate-income Americans who have faced much discrimination at the hands of the financial services industry, now over many decades. In a recent summary report, sociologist Gregory Squires has noted the following: "ACORN estimated that between 1995 and 2004 it generated more than $6 billion for low-income communities through its CRA organizing efforts and another $6 billion from its antipredatory lending campaigns. Combined with its work to encourage enactment of living wage ordinances, develop affordable housing, and reform various public services, ACORN pegs its return to low-income communities at more than $15 billion.... NCRC estimates that more than $4.7 trillion in new loans have been secured for low-income and minority markets, largely in response to community organizing efforts. ... The National Fair Housing Alliance estimates that nonprofit advocacy groups, under authority provided by the federal Fair Housing Act, have generated $225 million for plaintiffs since 1990." Still, the scale of the major crash in the mortgage and lending markets in recent years indicates that much stronger coalitions of such activist groups, perhaps with significant sociological research assistance, will be necessary to deal with the severe housing problems still faced by low- and moderate-income Americans.[43]

Action against Environmental Racism

Sociologists have worked on a variety of environmental issues with local community groups. For example, sociologist Robert Bullard and his associates have done much important, often pioneering, research assisting a number of local groups facing serious environmental hazards. As an "organic intellectual" representing excluded people of color, Bullard has worked hard to make their concerns about the environmental degradation of their communities public. In the 1970s he and his students at Texas Southern University examined the pattern of waste facility siting in Houston, Texas. They found that from the early 1920s through the 1970s, all city-owned landfills and most incinerators were located in black neighborhoods. A local community group, the Northeast Community Action Group, used the sociologists' findings of racial discrimination in their political efforts to bring changes. Although they were unable to block one landfill threatening their community, they did succeed in forcing a change in state permitting requirements for waste facilities and in getting the city council to restrict the location of future waste facilities.[44]

More recently, Bullard did research for a local Louisiana group, Citizens Against Nuclear Trash (CANT), which was trying to stop the location of a privately owned uranium enrichment plant in the middle of unincorporated rural black communities. This research showed discrimination in the choice of the final site for this hazardous plant— a working-class community that was 97 percent black. Community groups pressured the Nuclear Regulatory Commission (NRC) to look into environmental justice issues, but the final environmental impact statement only dealt briefly with these hard environmental questions.[45] Even the Environmental Protection Agency (EPA) criticized the NRC report as inadequate and recommended additional study of environmental impact. In 2007 Bullard was the Ware Distinguished Professor of Sociology and Director of the Environmental Justice Resource Center at Clark Atlanta University in Atlanta, Georgia, where he has continued his work on behalf of local community groups dealing with environmental problems. He has been instrumental in creating the concepts of "environmental racism" and "environmental justice," and has coauthored or coedited numerous recent books dealing with these policy issues. Bullard concludes from his research for community groups that "it is not enough to determine the existence of unjust conditions; the practices that caused the conditions must be eliminated.... Collaborative social research linked to action is an integral part of this movement to change environmental policy."[46]

Action Research on Violence against Women

In 1986 the Rainbow House, a center for battered women in south Chicago, began a violence prevention program. This included programs for high school students on the patterns of male violence in U.S. society. As they realized that children's attitudes toward violence were learned at a young age, they also developed programs for ever-younger children, including a plan to instruct the teachers of children in conflict resolution. A Rainbow House Institute for Choosing Non-Violence was established to facilitate programs teaching about the pervasiveness of societal violence and about nonviolent ways of countering that violence. Numerous Chicago organizations and agencies have made use of the nonviolence training programs of the institute to the present day. At one point in its development, the director of Rainbow House asked sociologist Nancy Matthews of Northeastern Illinois University to help design a research program to evaluate the training program at the institute.[47]

A key goal of the collaborative research project was to assess the effectiveness of nonviolence training programs at Rainbow House by means of qualitative social science methods. Other goals included building more ties between the bold new antiviolence program and key local leaders and funders, as well as the general public, and exploring the utility of a new site-intensive approach to nonviolence training. The research on this latter approach took place at another facility, Fellowship House, where a pilot program involved full nonviolence training for the staff of twelve and sessions for mothers served by the Fellowship House.

The sociological researcher, Matthews, "conducted observations of trainings followed by interviews with individuals and groups about the perceived effects of the training, and observations of interactions at the site."[48] In the research, many participants in the training programs reported that they had become desensitized to societal violence and that the programs resensitized them to the seriousness and pervasiveness of this societal crisis. The Rainbow House staff learned from this research about how people react to violence in their everyday lives, including how they cope with the stress and how they contribute to violence by becoming desensitized. The research also generated expanded discussion across racial, ethnic, and other community lines, thereby facilitating community building. In this case, the goal of reducing violence in urban communities was furthered by collaboration between a community group and an activist sociologist.

We should add that in recent years numerous female sociologists and other female social scientists, as well as some male social scientists, have developed a now significant body of field research on the violence faced by women in society, not just in the United States but now across the globe. Indeed, in the 1990s an important new international, interdisciplinary journal, *Violence Against Women,* was started, one that has explicitly encouraged not only traditional academic researchers but also clinicians, practitioners, poets, and activists to submit material for publication.[49]

CONCLUSION

We see a number of important lessons in the research projects in this chapter, as well as in the previous chapter. Community-oriented, collaborative research often takes time to develop fully. The sociologists involved must be flexible enough to fit into a dynamic and ongoing collaborative process. From the point of view of community residents and activists, participatory action research can demystify research and policymaking by academic "experts" and create an environment that welcomes new community participants to the research process. It provides a collaborative and more democratic way to develop social policy and has helped to build networks of community activists and projects in many cities. Participatory action research tends to use limited resources effectively and to build new research capacity in communities. Moreover, participatory action research has theoretical, empirical, and personal rewards for the researchers that come from assisting in positive community changes.[50] Clearly, this type of community action research involves researchers in everyday worlds, where they can see social life as it unfolds in all its complexity, raggedness, and richness.

Interestingly, as one can see in numerous examples in this book, much progressive sociological research now is conducted by researchers from the less elitist colleges and universities, where the pressures to do abstract-empirical, instrumental-positivistic research may not be as great. Some of the less elitist universities and nonuniversity think tanks appear to have developed much more extensive relationships with community activists and organizations. Increasingly, this has meant the creation of new networks of knowledge production. Indeed, these college and university settings have also generated some of the most important alternative and countersystem sociological thinking about U.S. society.[51]

In addition, much of the impetus for participatory action research has come from the efforts of scholar activists in postcolonial countries to reduce or end various forms of social oppression. Recall Orlando Fals-Borda's comment that he could not be a scientist, much less a human being, and remain uncommitted in sight of injustice and suffering. In participatory action research, the social scientist is still under the broad oversight of some of his disciplinary peers but must additionally submit his work to the review of the people she or he is trying to serve. Theories must survive practical tests.

Moreover, the method of participatory research varies greatly in its application. Sometimes, it refers only to the presence of a few open-ended questions in the research instrument being used. For example, one international health organization recently advertised a "woman-friendly" program that contained a participatory research component consisting only of a few open-ended questions. Much other participatory action research involves those researched in key decisions on what is researched, how it is researched, and how it is reported. Between these two examples, there is a range of research projects in which those being studied participate to varying degrees in the research process.

Today, participatory action research has extended throughout the world, though its use in the industrialized world has not always been faithful to a commitment to end social misery and oppression. Oppression is not just limited to the Southern Hemisphere. As Greenwood and Levin suggest, "the racially oppressed, the homeless, the drug addicted, the abused, and the illiterate in the north are oppressed, as are the workers in factories run by executives who use participation as a cover-up for speed-ups, downsizing, and union busting, as are middle managers who are being replaced with cheaper labor that is more easily manipulated. Oppression is oppression everywhere it is found, south or north."[52]

As we have seen, many participatory action researchers are concerned with finding progressive *solutions* for the problems of real people in everyday settings. This accent on solutions is an important virtue of participatory action research, including that in the United States. Oddly enough, in U.S. colleges and universities, we have numerous courses on social *problems* but very few on social *solutions:* "To map and analyze the dimensions of social problems—crime, inequities, racism, corporate control, and environmental hazards—is seen as scientific research. To discuss and describe alternative practices and develop solutions is seen as moving toward politics and advocacy—areas that are perceived as a threat to the objectivity of research."[53]

This skew in U.S. sociology is problematic and discourages many, including new or younger, social scientists from getting involved in community-related research with a clear solution focus. Fortunately, participatory action researchers are helping to change this view. In the coming century, solutions will be central to the social science research process, if only because of the many current threats to human civilization over the next century. As a rule, participatory action research involves the social researcher in the lives and activities of those people being researched. At its best, participatory action research involves those being researched in both the decisionmaking and the interpretation phases of the research project. Such an approach does not view the people studied as passive but helps to empower them to bring change in their own lives and communities.

CHAPTER 7

Liberation Theory and Liberating Action: The Contemporary Scene

Diversity is a key aspect of the theories and perspectives developed by countersystem sociologists. This is not surprising, given that this way of practicing social science aims to create a sociology for those who struggle for their liberation from various types of oppression. The methodological and conceptual needs of emancipation struggles are multiple and varied. In this chapter we turn our attention to some contemporary theorists engaged in critical social theory, those social scientists who choose to centrally elaborate theories that aid in action to build a better social world. We illustrate here how liberation sociologists have integrated social theory, research, and activism in their lives.

ABSTRACTIONS FOR WHAT?

Generally, the theorizing of liberation sociologists is different from much conventional theorizing that proposes abstractions to explain social relations as if these abstractions were neutrally and naturally generated ideas. Recall that the term "abstracted empiricism" was given by C. Wright Mills to designate a style of social theorizing (or lack thereof) that has been commonplace in the social sciences from at least the 1930s to the present. In the case of abstracted empiricism, theory becomes the collection of low-level generalizations—generally

189

"variables useful in interpretations of statistical findings."[1] As we saw in Chapter 3, those working in this social science style tend to view answers to opinion surveys and censuses as the best data, data to be manipulated statistically to seek relations among variables. This usually results in assertions of statistical proportions and relations—some simple, some complicated—that are considered to be empirical tests of abstract ideas and conceptions.

Another style criticized by Mills and others is the development of "grand theory," as exemplified in the work of Talcott Parsons and his associates. Such grand theory entails speculative attempts at constructing all-encompassing taxonomies of social phenomena. In the era after World War II, what Alfred McClung Lee called "Talcott-Parsonianism" was one of the clouds hanging over sociology. Parsons's teachings, according to Lee, "were dogmatic and elitist, useful both to the obscurantist and the managerial."[2] For example, in an important theoretical book, *Toward a General Theory of Action* (1965), Parsons and Edward Shils illustrated how they practiced grand theory. They wrote that "the theory of action is a conceptual scheme for the analysis of behavior of living organisms. It conceives of this behavior as oriented to the attainment of ends in situations, by means of the normatively regulated expenditure of energy."[3] For them, good social science theory has three functions. The first is to "aid in the codification of our existing concrete knowledge" understood as "unifying discrete observations under general concepts."[4] In addition, theory should be a guide for good research and should help control "the biases of observation." These seem reasonable goals, but in reality whose observations were Parsons and Shils seeking to codify? On reviewing the index of this influential book, one discovers that such leading and critical sociological theorists as Karl Marx, Jane Addams, Thorstein Veblen, W. E. B. Du Bois, Oliver C. Cox, and C. Wright Mills are *not* even cited.

By the time this book was published, Parsons and his associates had been shaping the then-dominant structural-functionalist framework in the direction of the ideas of Emile Durkheim and Max Weber, both of whom were constructed conservatively as forerunners of the sociological theory of social consensus and social system they were proposing. The more progressive or radical ideas and proclivities of Durkheim and Weber (see Chapter 2) were generally left out of the influential structural-functionalist analysis. From the 1930s to the 1960s, Parsons and his associates made little use of the ideas of such probing theorists as Karl Marx. Indeed, Alfred Marshall, Vilfredo Pareto, Emile Durkheim, and Max Weber were the key figures examined in detail in what is perhaps Parsons's most famous work, the 1937 book *The Structure of Social Action* (see Chapter 3). Parsons saw in the ideas of these scholars—each working in a different European country—a convergence in the direction of a new "voluntaristic theory of action."[5] This generalized social theory successfully accented the importance of traditional values and ritual in human societies as opposed to the older utilitarian, means-ends, economic interpretations of societies. Parsons's grand theory thus made some important contributions in bringing certain neglected aspects of social life back into the theoretical discussion, yet his attempts to develop social theory were usually at a very abstract level and made use of too much obscure jargon.

By not drawing significantly on the more critical theoretical and empirical analyses of Western capitalist societies, Parsons left out a serious consideration of hierarchy, oppression, and ongoing intergroup domination, such as that found in racist, sexist, heterosexist, and classist arrangements. By doing this, Parsons helped to shape the future of U.S. sociological theory in a direction more or less supportive of the oppressive status quo. As C. Wright Mills put the matter, "The ideological meaning of grand theory tends strongly to legitimate stable forms of domination."[6] A generation or two of graduate students were thereby shielded from the critical tradition in social science theory and analysis, including both of this book's authors.

As a point of contrast, consider how the black feminist scholar bell hooks has described her theorizing efforts in the area of contemporary feminism: "Writing progressive feminist theory was so compelling precisely because we knew that the work we were doing, if at all useful, would have a meaningful transformative impact on our lives and the lives of women and men both inside and outside the academy."[7] Compare the distancing vocabulary of "living organisms" and "expenditure of energy" that Parsons and Shils use to refer to human beings with the active "we," "useful," and "impact" language of bell hooks. Also compare the grandiose aim of abstract knowledge assembly on living organisms in Parsons and Shils's analysis with bell hooks's aim of theorizing in order to have a "transformative impact" on actual human lives.

Liberation theorizing aims at human emancipation through the development of "knowledge that helps persons locate their experiences, discontents, and troubles as aspects of processes that are subject to human intervention and transformation."[8] As Mills put it, this theorizing involves a sociological imagination that allows people "to grasp what is going on in the world, and to understand what is happening in themselves as minute points of the intersections of biography and history within society."[9] Liberation theorizing also means reflecting on the methodological and normative principles governing the contemporary practice of sociology.

IMPLICIT THEORY AND EVERYDAY EXPERIENCE: OPPRESSION IN BUREAUCRATIC SETTINGS

Emancipatory sociological theories are important to those engaged in transforming the world into a more just place for two principal reasons. First, theories are like looking glasses that allow us to read social reality. Theories can render important aspects of social reality, the "facts," visible while hiding other aspects of reality. We place "facts" in quotation marks here because what these facts are—and what they are called—will vary with the social science theory being used. Second, the decision that one solution and not another—or one result and not another—is what is needed to bring desired change typically depends on the social theory chosen. In this way, social theories can become linked to action; they are "ideas to think with" about troubled times and realities. Ultimately, most human interactions, whether orderly or conflict-riddled, are based on social theories, whether or not we are aware of them.

Although we are usually unaware of the intricacies of the thought processes that lead us to our choices of frames, perspectives, and strategies, few of us will claim that we act without thinking. Sociological theorizing is the systematic thinking behind what social scientists and others observe and discover, as well as behind the actions they take in application of discoveries. Systematic theorizing in social science is, typically, different from everyday thinking in that it ordinarily involves more detailed analysis, greater rigor, more reflection, and more attention to both current and historical contexts.

Nevertheless, there are some important similarities between systematic theorizing and everyday theories. Often the latter are the beginning of the former. To illustrate the process of everyday theorizing and the impact it has on our understanding and actions, consider this hypothetical case of a college professor whose salary is considerably lower than that of a male colleague who performs work identical in nature, effort, and responsibility to hers. Initially, she was shocked and angry to find this out, since this male colleague was hired some years after her, and she had actually trained him for his current job. And she has continued to help him on a regular basis. "Why is this happening to me?" she asked a group of coworkers over lunch. This type of question—why is this happening?—is one that usually initiates the search for a specific or generalized explanation in everyday life, as well as in the practice of social science.[10]

One of her colleagues advanced the idea that the disparity in her salary had to do with the sometimes biased ways in which her department "chairman"—the title often given to academic middle managers—made some salary decisions. Her colleague added that the explanation may be "in the evil in this man's heart." Expanding on this idea, her colleague added that "he often gives salary raises and other privileges to his friends instead of rewarding objective merit." On hearing this, a female colleague who was present in the group noted that not all the fault should be placed on this chair. The favored male colleague is well known for being obsequious, in a manner that has earned him a place in the chair's inner circle, an "ole boy" network that runs this particular department. A third colleague agreed, but argued that the critical thing to observe is that this network is composed exclusively of white men. The problem, in her view, was not in the ill will of the chair, but in the different way in which men and women are differentially allowed into decisionmaking networks in most college and corporate bureaucracies. Thus, she argued, the lower salary of the better-qualified female professor had to do with "institutional sexism." Moreover, since the latter person was a woman of color, it was proposed too that some racial bias was likely present, not just in the chair's discriminatory practice but also in the institutional (exclusionary) discrimination built into managerial inner circles at most historically white colleges and universities. "These are well-established ways of doing things, of thinking about people, and of feeling toward what they deserve because of what they are perceived to be able to do, and not do, well," this female colleague added.

This third explanation captured the imagination of the group around the table, whose members then came up with a number of other examples of similarly unfair situations affecting white women and people of color. Take some examples drawn loosely from several incidents of which we have heard: A woman faculty member was passed over for an appointment in spite of being better qualified, and another had spent many more years in a lower rank than men typically spent. Additionally, women faculty members in many departments have reported that they are asked to perform too many of the dead-end tasks that typically do not lead to significant salary rewards and career advancement.

Moreover, in the case we began with, yet another woman faculty member commented on the disproportionate burden that women, including women faculty, ordinarily bear in the U.S. family. The woman being discussed may have had less time for research and publication because she had the greater burden of child care in her family. Finally, someone called the group's attention to the possibility that the woman faculty member being discussed might not be an isolated case and that men in their college were probably paid more than the women there for the same work. Further study disclosed that, in fact, women were making on average only 70 cents for every dollar men made for the same teaching and research activities. Once again, institutional sexism was likely evident.

In this plausible example of a woman faculty member facing problems in a college department, it is clear that, although the various explanations contribute to understanding, some are more useful than others in probing beneath the surface to interpret what is going on—and to learn what might be done to correct the situation. The explanation that the situation is a result of the "evil in the manager's heart" is, of course, very difficult to verify. This explanation identifies the cause of the problem as one that is difficult to remedy. The next explanation—that part of the blame should be attributed to the active influence of the better paid male faculty member on the chair—can be verified through observation and comparison, yet it is not clear what corrective action could be exercised. The third explanation, or explanatory theory, does not contradict the previous ones and can be more easily verified with numerous empirical observations of similar cases. In numerous real-life situations like this, the recognition of an institutionalized pattern of discrimination against women faculty has led a female faculty member to consult a lawyer, sue her college or university, and perhaps see a jury declare her salary to be the result of willful discrimination. Those who are targets of discrimination can sue their employers based on a theory of recurring and institutionalized discrimination, although this action can mean much research work on an organization and can lead, regardless of its outcome, to further discrimination against them by their employers.

THEORY TO CHANGE THE WORLD

The Prophetic Tradition

A crucial element of much liberation sociology thinking is the ancient belief of numerous prophetic traditions that the world can be changed in fundamental ways through intentional human effort. This old ideal has some deep-lying religious roots. In the West some attribute its origin to early Judaism.[11] A number of analysts of U.S. social science have distinguished between what they call the prophetic and the priestly traditions of social science. Robert Friedrichs has noted that, although the biblical prophets testified to the alienation of human beings from God, the prophetical tradition in sociology speaks of a different alienation, that is, "from one's untapped creative resources and an estrangement from the bonds of community with one's fellows."[12] Prophetic sociology calls for freeing human beings from this human-imposed alienation. This belief in human change not only informs all liberation sociologies but also to varying degrees progressive thinking in other social science specialties and numerous professions. Such conceptions extend, of course, beyond Western traditions. Indeed, the liberation theologies or progressive worldviews of people in Latin America, Africa, and Asia, as well as of those of Jewish, Latino, Asian, Native American, and African Americans in the United States, usually share in this fundamental assumption about human change.

Critical Social Theories

In this chapter we cannot review the full range of social science theories that are currently in use. We will discuss instead some of the conceptual frameworks termed "critical social theories," those frameworks that involve theorizing that is particularly useful for human emancipation and liberation from oppression. Whereas some postmodern analysts have called for an end to social theory, especially broad theories such as those of Karl Marx, we see this view as out of touch with everyday human reality. Whether we like it or not, most human action is embedded in some type of explicit or tacit social theory. Indeed, there are still many social science analysts intent on developing useful and developed versions of critical social theories. One of the exciting developments in recent years has been the emergence of an array of critical theories in both the humanities and the social sciences. A recurring theme among these critical theorists is that of social domination, subjugation, and oppression. Most of these analysts seek the liberation of human beings from these oppressive circumstances.

Introductory sociology textbooks often designate the structural-functionalist, the social-conflict, and the symbolic-interactionist perspectives as *the* three distinctive sociological paradigms. However, this way of presenting theoretical orientations within sociology is misleading. These three paradigms do not capture the richness of contemporary theory in sociology and related social sciences. For the purpose of assessing a sociology of liberation, we will here distinguish between instrumental-positivistic approaches to theory and critical approaches to theory. These differences are fundamental. They distinguish among social scientists in terms of how they claim to know what they know—in terms of their fundamental assumptions, in regard to what they see as the scientific method, and in regard to their ultimate aims in doing social science.

Critical social theorists seek to bring about awareness in individuals and their groups so that they can overcome the social oppression in the world around them. To bring about this awareness, one needs to be involved in a recurring dialogue with the human subjects of research and not just in a distancing observation or experimental manipulation of observed objects. In contrast, instrumental-positivistic science seeks a neutral way of learning about the world, a way to produce knowledge that is not tied to any particular self. When transferred to social science, this attitude makes society into scattered, neutral pieces of information—into raw data to be observed from the outside.

Today, numerous contemporary theorists can be said to be critical social theorists. This explosion of social science theory has numerous branches, including feminist theory, queer theory, postmodern theories, antiracist theories, European critical theory, critical criminology, and critical legal studies. What these perspectives have in common is that they start from the belief that all human beings are "potentially active agents in the construction of their social world and social lives."[13]

THE CRITICAL THEORY OF THE FRANKFURT SCHOOL

One of the oldest critical theory traditions is that of the "Frankfurt School" in Germany. Sociologists and other social scientists associated with the University of Frankfurt have had a major impact on what is often termed "critical theory." Their work has been a major source of inspiration for liberation-oriented theorists since the 1920s, when the Institute for Social Research at the University of Frankfurt was founded. A group of Marxist intellectuals established the Institute as a privately financed research organization. Its critical and radical orientation, and the fact that most of its members were Jews, led to serious attacks by fascist forces in Germany, and the Institute was forced to relocate to the United States in 1934. In 1949 the institute and its members were able to return to Germany. Its members sought to synthesize a large number of social science and humanities disciplines, to integrate theory and empirical research, and to overcome the isolation of traditional social theory from practical uses and implications. They were critical of orthodox Marxism too, but did not reject its ambitious project, which was "the ultimate unity of critical theory and revolutionary practice."[14]

The scholars in the Frankfurt School developed major critiques of capitalistic ("bourgeois") ideology and culture for a growing audience of intellectuals and university students across the globe. The participation of the working class in European fascist movements before and during World War II led them to argue that "the struggle for socialism could not be carried on successfully unless the working class developed a 'conscious will' for a liberated and rational society. It was the responsibility of intellectuals to produce the critical and liberating ideas which might eventually shape the working class' conscious will."[15] The Frankfurt School's concentration on class-linked social exploitation and domination has made their writing inspiring to many liberation-oriented social scientists in many countries.

Theodor Adorno and Max Horkheimer

Among the best-known members of the Frankfurt School are Theodor Adorno and Max Horkheimer. In their important book, *Dialectic of Enlightenment,* they examined problematical ideas of eighteenth-century European Enlightenment thinkers. Although the ideas of thinkers such as Jean Jacques Rousseau did influence the French revolution for liberty, these same ideas also helped spur despotism in Europe, such as that of Napoleon, as well as the conservative apologetics of Auguste Comte's positivism.

The aims of the Enlightenment thinkers were mostly reformist and libertarian, not radical. Their intellectual program was not to launch a radical break with a reactionary past by fully enabling ideals such as freedom, liberty, and equality, but rather to achieve "the disenchantment of the world; the dissolution of myths and the substitution of knowledge for fancy."[16] Enlightenment thinkers thus often paved the way for some new forms of social domination and control under the newly emerging capitalist bourgeoisie, with its strong scientific and technological commitments. In theory, at least, scientific thought was supposed to improve the welfare of ordinary folk, but too often it created more effective ways of dominating them. (Indeed, this was the era of major developments in the overseas enslavement of Africans and indigenous peoples, to the profit of Europeans.) The major advantages of the late eighteenth-century political revolutions and of newly emerging capitalism usually accrued to European elites and upper-middle classes. Whether evolutionary or revolutionary, societal changes are not necessarily progressive.

Thus, in Germany, long considered one of the most civilized and advanced societies, a far-right totalitarian state developed in the 1930s out of the political turmoil provoked by economic depression and political oppression of Germany by the European victors of World War I. Interestingly, the world's most populous country, China, at the time one of the least developed societies economically, had become a communist totalitarian state by the late 1940s. As Adorno and Horkheimer remind us, the possibility of a rationally organized and free society lies not in faith in some natural force of progressive change but in the determined efforts of human intelligence guided by a critical and democratic vigilance.

The Current Generation: Jurgen Habermas

Jurgen Habermas is a key contemporary sociologist, one who wears the theoretical mantle of the Frankfurt School. Very productive, Habermas began to have an impact in the English-speaking world when his book, *Knowledge and Human Interests,* was translated into English in 1971.[17] Habermas's theorizing covers the social sciences as well as ethics, law, literary issues, and communications, and shows a recurring concern with the emancipatory ideas of Karl Marx, the need to overcome positivism in social science, and the need to create social theory relevant to modern societies. His main critique of traditional social science theory is its tendency to interpret the world narrowly within the confines of physical science and its accompanying technologies.

Habermas notes two alternative tendencies in contemporary social theory, what he terms the "empirical-analytical" (instrumental-positivistic) orientation and the "historical-hermeneutic" (dialectical-interpretive) orientation. This empirical-analytical orientation generally uses controlled observation of behavior, "which is set up in an isolated field under reproducible conditions by subjects reproducible at will." In contrast, those working from a dialectical-interpretive approach examine "the situational consciousness of acting individuals themselves" in their social life-worlds and explore sociologically the meanings articulated therein.[18]

Representatives of both orientations can make use of the idea of a larger social whole within which particular observed phenomena are situated. Yet, the instrumental-positivists may rely on the idea of a social system, an organic entity of mutually related elements. We see this idea in the work of sociology's structural functionalists, as previously discussed. The purpose of this type of research is to specify the manner in which system components, often viewed as certain operationally defined "variables," react or relate to each other. This social scientific research lends itself to use for established bureaucratic administration. Scientifically accurate predictions are supposed to be based on theories that deal with observed objects that have law-like patterns.

In Habermas's view, social systems are in reality *not* among neatly law-like repetitive systems because social systems of human beings always "stand in historical life-contexts." At best, the often useful findings of instrumental-positivistic research relate only to parts of real social systems, and conventional research techniques cannot demonstrate how a particular societal phenomenon relates to the societal totality.[19] Habermas is also critical of the positivistic notion of value-neutral research. As he sees it, this value-neutral claim is only a way to avoid openly discussing the problem of how, by whom, and for what purposes social research is actually conducted. In his view mainstream social scientists too often fail to take responsibility for the uses of their research.

Habermas is critical of much postmodernist thought, a tradition we discuss below. He sees today an implicit alliance of postmodernist conservatives with older premodernist conservatives and neoconservatives. The newer conservatives, among whom he places Georges Bataille, Michel Foucault, and Jacques Derrida, claim that they have discovered the idea of a "decentered subjectivity"; that is, individual agency is no longer a basic assumption necessary for analysis. This decentered subjectivity is "emancipated from the imperatives of work and usefulness, and with this experience they step outside the modern world. On the basis of modernistic attitudes, they justify an irreconcilable antimodernism."[20] Moreover, some conservatives and neoconservatives in U.S. social science have observed the "decline of substantive reason, the differentiation of science, morality and art, the modern worldview and its merely procedural rationality, with sadness and recommend a withdrawal to a position anterior to modernity."[21]

The neoconservatives, among whom Habermas places the sociologist Daniel Bell, "welcome the development of modern sciences, as long as this only goes beyond its sphere to carry forward technical progress, capitalist growth, and national administration."[22] As Bell sees it, late capitalism is a postindustrial society, one that is now moving beyond the old industrialization, such as that of steel and automobiles. Bell expresses the fear that what he sees as a democratic populism of the current era has a desire for "wholesale egalitarianism" that insists "on complete leveling," and that these egalitarians are seeking to get rid of the ideas of individual merit and rewards for personal achievement.[23] The development of a critical theory and science that deeply question the status quo is not seen as valuable by these neoconservatives, who seem wedded to the many social inequalities still created by contemporary elite decisionmaking.

The critical theories of Germany's Frankfurt School have roots in the Marxist tradition. The influence of Marxist thought in European and U.S. social science was greatly reduced between 1917 and the late 1950s, for two major reasons. One was the political dominance of

Soviet Marxism, "which pushed other versions into a marginal position ... with the result that they were, generally speaking, little known and largely ignored."[24] The second, and more important, reason was the fascism and anticommunism in many Western countries, including Nazism in Germany and protofascist movements such as political anticommunism and McCarthyism in the United States. Only a few brave intellectuals and community activists dared to work with Marxist or neo-Marxist ideas during this long period.

Since the late 1940s and 1950s, Marxist scholarship has been going through a process of renewal and reinterpretation, especially in Europe. Although theorists like Habermas and Herbert Marcuse have been consistently critical of Marx and have abandoned some of his important ideas, they nonetheless have accepted much in his dialectical and historical approach to understanding society. The dialectical and historical perspective generally accents the important idea of social totality. The idea of the social whole must be grasped, as they see it, by ordinary people if societal emancipation is to occur.[25] In Marx's thinking "totality" refers to the ways in which the social whole, such as a capitalist system, can be seen in each of its parts. The totality is always there, in this sense. There are no fixed boundaries, and the interconnectedness of the social world is central to Marx and to later interpretations of European critical theory.[26]

Communication and Liberation

Habermas is a strong advocate of the idea of societal progress and the critical use of human reason. His optimistic view includes the idea of an increased interactive dialogue among people across many different groups and societies. He calls this a theory of "communicative action."[27] To put it briefly, Habermas views the macroeconomic structures of bureaucratic capitalism as routinely burdensome for the worlds of human action. In a modern capitalist society, these macroeconomic structures crash in on the everyday worlds of people, thereby "colonizing" these life worlds.[28] They constantly create the everyday mechanisms of social exploitation faced by ordinary people as they live, work, and consume.

In U.S. sociology, "symbolic interactionism" is the common term for theories that call attention to the role that meaning and communication play in everyday life. However, symbolic interactionism is often concerned with situations in which actors negotiate to "mutually fit their interpretations in order to coordinate their actions."[29] Although there are aspects of symbolic negotiation in communication processes, the latter involve much more than symbolic negotiation. Habermas's theory of communicative action is founded on the distinction between instrumental action and emancipatory communicative action. We engage in instrumental actions to achieve anticipated goals under given conditions with available means. A commercial advertisement is a one-way communicative device, an instrument typically designed to achieve the goal of persuading people to consume.

Communicative action, in contrast, is more democratic and is about conveying messages to others who interpret the message and then *interact with* and *talk back to* the first actor. Success, in this case, consists of the actors mutually understanding each other and agreeing how the messages should be interpreted—and on how each should act. The primacy of the communicative mode is a major theoretical insight of Habermas's general framework. "Communicative rationality," Habermas writes, "carries with it connotations based ultimately on the central experience of the unconstrained, unifying, consensus-bringing force of argumentative speech, in which different participants overcome their merely subjective views and, owing to the mutuality of rationally motivated conviction, assure themselves of both the unity of the objective world and the intersubjectivity of their life world."[30]

These democratic communicative forms of discourse, language included, thus can be emancipatory. Habermas identifies elements of an emancipatory social theory, one that works as a "frame of reference for distinguishing between 'what appears to be' and 'what is,' so as to eliminate institutional domination."[31] His theory relates to George Herbert Mead's ideas about the social self and to Emile Durkheim's theory of the linkage of sacred rites to the realm of the secular. Amplifying their views helped Habermas "to provide a kind of double-edged theory of communicative behavior, evolutionary and procedural."[32] Moreover, for Habermas, the idea of communicative rationality serves as a basis for a theory of modernity, a theory of evolution, an ethics of discourse, and a theory of language.

A crucial aspect of communicative reason, suggests Habermas, is that it "does not simply encounter ready made subjects and systems; rather, it takes part in structuring what is to be preserved. The utopian perspective of reconciliation and freedom is ingrained in the conditions for the communicative sociation of individuals; it is built into the linguistic mechanism of the reproduction of the species."[33] Thus, in our terms, Habermas is proposing that communicative reason—interpersonal discourse in its most uncorrupted and democratic form—is intrinsically emancipatory. His theory allows for a moral reading of the world that accommodates the aim of changing the world, and it is flexible enough to use with various utopian democratic projects.

Nevertheless, one problem with his theory is that its principal level for analysis is the society taken as a whole. In trying to shed light on the relationship between social conditions and individual freedom, Habermas implicitly theorizes about an undifferentiated public, about individuals struggling to free themselves from the social and cultural constraints that compel their behavior. Some theorists of democracy have raised serious questions about this assumption of a homogeneous public in this theory of communicative action. Instead, they underscore the persisting divisions and diverse languages of class, race, heterosexuality, and gender that constantly interfere with goals of increased societal communication and democracy. Clearly, such limitations invite a thorough revision and extension of this theory of communicative rationality, which is certainly an innovative start toward conceptualizing a better social world.

Impact on the United States

The penetration of European critical theory into U.S. sociology has occurred, but rather slowly. During the 1960s and 1970s, the critical turn in U.S. sociology was only modestly influenced by these creative European sources. More important in challenging the dominance of a too-quantitative, instrumental positivism was the work of interpretive scholars and theorists like Erving Goffman. For example, the study of public place interaction was pioneered by Goffman and his students, who gave much attention to the meaning of microlevel interaction between strangers in public places. Goffman was perceptive in examining interactive rituals, such as deference rituals between people seen as superior and inferior. Obsequious words and gestures, such as the etiquette of racial relations in the South during legal segregation, were a type of deference ritual, which "functions as a symbolic means by which appreciation is regularly conveyed to a recipient."[34] With great innovativeness and much new sociological insight, Goffman described other subtle dimensions of social behavior, such as the distinction people make between their actions in the front stages and the back stages of their lives.[35] Goffman, and other interpretive scholars like Harold Garfinkel, helped U.S. social scientists see the importance of the everyday symbolic interaction and recurring interpersonal meanings. Although the latter too often ignored the larger structural realties around the everyday "micro" events, these U.S. innovators did help to stimulate more interest in the critical sociologies of European scholars like Habermas. Today we see an increasing use of European critical theory in U.S. social science, especially by those concerned with systems of social oppression.

CONTEMPORARY FEMINIST THOUGHT

Among the important critical social theories, contemporary feminist theories stand out for their dynamism and growing contributions to understanding society. Feminist theories generally assess the situations and experiences of women in male-dominated societies. They view women as central subjects in the investigative project—that is, they seek to see the world from the vantage point of women. In feminist analyses, there are well-developed conceptual frameworks targeting key aspects of gendered oppression and liberation. A feminist framework is often "critical and activist on behalf of women, seeking to produce a better world for women—and thus, it argues, for humankind."[36] Beginning with the intellectual and activist efforts of feminist pragmatists like Jane Addams, Charlotte Perkins Gilman, and their many female (and some male) colleagues in the late nineteenth and early twentieth centuries (see Chapter 3), feminist thinkers have brought to critical social theory a major concern not just for the cognitive underpinning of oppression but also for the negative emotions, feelings, and attitudes that underlie contemporary oppression—as well as for strategies of resistance that encompass counteremotions by means of consciousness-raising, a major resistance strategy. Consciousness-raising includes self-inquiry into one's own attitudes as well as dialogue with numerous others.

Feminist scholars and researchers in sociology and other disciplines work not only to broaden their academic disciplines but also to rework the fund of disciplinary knowledge in terms of the experiences of women. Within the discipline of sociology, feminist concepts and approaches are gradually beginning to have a general impact. Feminist sociologists Judith Stacey and Barrie Thorne have noted that today the fields of economics and political science are more masculinist than sociology, whereas anthropology and history have incorporated some feminist ideas into the mainstream of their disciplines. They view sociology as falling in between, with feminist ideas just beginning to have an important impact. Stacey and Thorne also accent the extent to which feminist ideas are having a transdisciplinary impact on academic life, such as in feminist critiques of androcentric social structures and of the Enlightenment concerns with separating mind and body, nature and nurture. They note that "many academic feminists are now involved with overlapping, interdisciplinary, interpretive communities, such as ethnic studies, queer theory, critical theory, and cultural studies."[37]

As we have seen in the work of the early feminist pragmatists, feminist theories have long been interdisciplinary and still make much use of perspectives as diverse as social psychology, psychoanalytic theory, Marxism, democratic socialism, postmodernism, and cultural studies in order to interpret and understand the realities and meanings of gendered structures in various societies. Significantly, scholars in many disciplines—including sociology, anthropology, biology, economy, history, law, literature, philosophy, political science, psychology, and theology—have contributed to the burgeoning and diversifying of contemporary feminist theories.

Much feminist work argues for a distinctive materialistic perspective, one that locates the heart of sexism and patriarchy in the tangible and material realities of everyday life. One approach is sometimes called "radical feminist theory." For example, legal scholar and social analyst Catharine MacKinnon has suggested that at the heart of a feminist analysis should be the material reality of reproduction and sexuality—the tangible reproductive and sexual relationships that exist between men and women. Analysis of the identities and symbols of gender must be grounded in these everyday realities. In the core of a sexist society like the United States is the very alienating reality of a dehumanized sexuality forced onto women. A woman's sexuality is that which should be most her own, but in fact is that which is most taken away from her in a highly sexist society. Who she is sexually is defined for a woman within the patriarchal system, which shapes men's treatment of and orientation toward women across many generations. Dehumanization for women is sexism's psychological dynamic, and the gendered roles of inferior women and superior men are its persisting social masks.[38]

One of the most influential sociological theorists is Dorothy E. Smith, who has helped to develop an important sociological perspective often known as "standpoint theory." Smith proposes a sociology done from the standpoint of women, a distinctive viewpoint not unlike that of the proletariat's perspective in Marxist theory. She writes, "At the line of fault along which women's experience breaks away from the discourses mediated by texts that are integral to the relations of ruling in contemporary society, a critical standpoint emerges."[39] For some time, Smith has critically explored and questioned the discipline of sociology, which she has described as a "means of knowing about the shape of my world beyond the immediately known."[40] However, she calls into question the very objectified ways of knowing in which the usual patriarchal "relations of ruling" become manifest. Taken-for-granted mainstream sociology, and its conventional methods and conceptual theories, are "built up within the male social universe, even when women have participated in its doing."[41] She discovered in her own life, especially at a dramatic moment in her graduate education, that there was a distinctive standpoint from which women often experience and thus know the world differently than those men who create the established knowledge of academia and much other public discourse. From this place, women can "speak to and of the society at large, moving into a terrain of public discourse that somewhere along the line had been appropriated by and ceded to men."[42]

In one biographical sketch, Smith explains that her critical social theory derives from her everyday life as a woman, especially as a woman living between the male-dominated academic world and the essentially female-centered life of a single mother.[43] From these experiences, she has drawn the concept of "bifurcation," or disjuncture, which plays an important part in her theorizing. This refers to the separation between social scientific descriptions and people's lived experiences, between women's lives and the often patriarchal ideal types used by mainstream social science to describe such everyday experience.

For liberation sociologists, Smith's work is important for several reasons, including her accent on the diversity of human experiences and standpoints. If they are to be sustainable in the long run, all human societies must be restructured to be much less oppressive and to be meaningfully democratic—in the sense of full participation by all in the society, including its female majority, in decisionmaking about all critical facets of social and personal lives. The diversity of people and views must be recognized structurally and culturally. Monocultures are not healthy, and they tend to deteriorate. In her contemporary feminist theory, Smith tracks the earlier insights of the feminist pragmatists and provides numerous important insights into the character of the social domination and oppression of women. As she sees it, oppressors are not simply individual actors making rational decisions based on self-interest. In making sense of societal oppression, she contextualizes it. She thereby integrates Marx's concerns with the structures of domination with insights into a variety of subjective and microsocial life worlds. As with Habermas, these everyday life worlds are shaped by the larger macrostructures, which are in turn shaped by specific historical demands.

Numerous feminist social scientists have accented these and other key elements of a feminist research methodology. These elements include not only a focus on gender and gender inequality with constant reflectivity, but also a goal of giving voice to the everyday experiences and realities of women. There is usually an accent too on the importance of social action being linked to feminist research. Moreover, central to the research effort is an accent on breaking down the traditional distancing relationship between the researcher and those researched. In one revealing account of this feminist methodology, Claire Renzetti, a recent president of the Society for the Study of Social Problems and editor of the important journal *Violence Against Women,* has discussed her shift from a positivistic approach to sociology to that of a "reformed positivist" doing pioneering qualitative research on domestic violence among lesbian women. Discussing the feminist participatory model used in this field project, she notes how social scientists have too often undertaken such field research as "outside experts" who make little effort to look at the world from the point of view of those they are studying or to listen carefully to their voices. In her view, feminist participatory research involves researchers being *learners* as well as teachers. She summarizes well the ways in which the participation of those researched in a project can sharply improve its quality: "[T]hey help to ensure that (a) the most significant issues—from the perspective not only of the researcher but also of the researched—get identified and studied; (b) meaningful (in terms of their lived experience) and nonalienating research instruments are developed; (c) the data collected are analyzed in the realistic context of their everyday lives; and (d) the project has a practical effect in terms of personal and social change."[44] In this way, she argues, research is much more than some academic exercise and can have a positive impact on societal change.

In recent years one of the most important contributions of some feminist thinking and research is its growing recognition of racial and ethnic diversity. For example, in pioneering analyses, bell hooks and Patricia Hill Collins have accented the importance of the thought and action of African American women in making feminist thought in the United States and elsewhere more nuanced, inclusive, and liberationist. Though technically a humanities scholar and activist, bell hooks is sociological in much of her savvy societal analysis. For example, she has examined the deep structures of racist imaging that portray black women as ugly, deviant, and criminal. The omnipresent standard of white-female beauty, seen in the mass media and many other places, is consistent with a continuing ideology of white superiority. As a result, African American women, who of necessity depart from the common white-beauty norm, suffer much painful humiliation and everyday discrimination. In addition, hooks has pointed out the numerous ways in which a white perspective on society constantly gets precedence in regard to a variety of views of women.[45] In one probing article, hooks discusses the omnipresent misogyny sometimes found in the rap music of certain black male musicians. Ironically, these negative views of women in much commercial rap music are often condemned by white commentators and politicians, even as white corporate executives are central to their propagation and as young whites purchase most of the CDs made by these rap artists. The black male misogyny seen in much commercial rap music is seen as a severe social malignancy by numerous white analysts, including white male analysts. Yet, the widespread misogyny of *white men,* such as that seen in many movies and other areas, gets no similar public commentary and assertive criticism. Indeed, hypermasculinity and misogyny are old creations of European Americans in U.S. society and are even glorified in the larger white-dominated culture, especially in times of overseas invasions and wars.[46] As a pioneering analyst in feminist thought, hooks constantly raises serious sociological questions about the fundamental patriarchal and racist structures of U.S. society.

Moreover, as we noted in Chapter 4, the influential feminist sociologist, Patricia Hill Collins, has argued that a black-feminist theoretical framework must critique the negative stereotypes of black women: "Portraying African-American women as stereotypical mammies, matriarchs, welfare recipients, and hot mommas has been essential to the political economy of domination fostering Black women's oppression."[47] These images are webbed deeply into the social fabric of the United States and—thanks to the U.S. mass media—many other societies, and they frequently precipitate and rationalize antiblack discrimination. Collins insists that one must also look at resistance to discrimination. Thus, she has shown how black women were a constant and integral part of the civil rights movement of the 1960s.

In her challenging book, *Fighting Words,* Collins has taken her arguments ever deeper in regard to the character of critical social theory and the condition of African Americans. "Social theory in particular can serve either to reproduce existing power relations or to foster social and economic justice." She adds that "elite groups routinely minimize the workings of their own power in what counts for theory.... As a result, prevailing definitions of theory portray it as an ahistorical, static system of abstract logic, reason, of science."[48] Elites do not produce more socially oriented thought than others, they simply have the ability—such as through the control of the mainstream media and major think tanks—to make their thought central and accepted as the only legitimate framework in society. Thus, given the white dominance of U.S. sociology from the 1890s to the 1960s, there is virtually no treatment of black women from an emancipatory viewpoint in any of the major sociology journals over this long period.[49] After developing a critique of sociology and of critical social theory, Collins moves to a level of analysis that accents the moral foundations of all social theory: "Because the search for justice has been central in African-American women's history, I emphasize an ethical framework grounded in notions of justice as specific cultural material for exploring this more general question of moral authority for struggle."[50] Once again, we see the centrality of ideas of freedom and justice for liberation theories.

The approaches of these and other feminist social theorists provide yet more theoretical support for social scientists doing research on oppression and domination in society, as well as for those pressing social change strategies. As feminist theories become more powerful in the social sciences, they will likely become ever more threatening to established male groups and their hierarchical interests.

QUESTIONING HETEROSEXUAL THEORIES

One of the areas of critical social theory that has expanded impressively in recent years is sometimes known as "queer theory." Much of this theorizing is located in the humanities and is influenced by both feminist and postmodern thinkers. Within sociology, this theoretical work has developed as a critique of the way in which this social science discipline has ignored the heterosexual assumptions often shaping its methods and knowledge accrual. The issues dealt with in queer theory have to do with how categories such as "gay," "lesbian," and "straight" are socially and culturally constructed and how these categories serve to define positive and negative identities and to include and exclude people within communities. Thus, the conventional heterosexual-homosexual boundary places some inside and some outside a given human community.[51]

Some critical sociologists have tackled the issue of the hegemony of heterosexuality and the part that it plays in distorting research on and analysis of gender and sexuality. Chrys Ingraham, for example, writes about an ideological construct, termed the "heterosexual imaginary," that "conceals the operation of heterosexuality in structuring gender and [closing off] any critical analysis of heterosexuality as an organizing institution."[52] She calls for a feminist sociology that develops a critique of the often hidden, fully institutionalized heterosexuality, a new sociology that does not participate in the heterosexual imaginary. A crucial step in developing such a liberated sociology is the reframing of gender as "heterogender" to emphasize the asymmetrical stratification of the sexes within the conventional system of patriarchal heterosexuality. This concept, Ingraham argues, "de-naturalizes the 'sexual' as the starting point for understanding heterosexuality with the gender division of labor and the patriarchal relations of production."[53]

In addition, Dorothy Smith's idea of bifurcation is applicable here since much mainstream sociology uses, however implicitly, many ideas developed within and exclusive to a heterosexual "male universe."[54] In this way, sociology is "heteronormative," inasmuch as heterosexuality is generally the conceptual starting point for analysis. One can see a related bias in most public opinion surveys that ask respondents to check off their marital status as one of five categories: married, divorced, separated, widowed, or single. These categories are presented as important indexes of social identity and are the only options offered. The implication of the list is that a critical aspect of the organization of personal identity is, and should be, in relation to *marriage.* This heterosexual, marriage-centric assumption is usually hidden and taken for granted. "The heteronormative assumption of this practice," Ingraham writes, "is rarely, if ever, called into question."[55] In this way, heterosexuality is routinely institutionalized and reinforced generation after generation.

These new types of sociological and other social science theorizing about sexuality and heterogender have contributed significantly to the liberation sociology tradition by accenting again the importance of societal domination as a distorting centrality in the United States. They also suggest that human diversity, not just along racial, class, and gender lines but also in regard to a variety of orientations and lifestyles, is essential to the healthy development and evolution of human societies. Much social creativity comes from diversity and the interpersonal and intergroup communication generated by it. Historically, the human species would not have survived without substantial respect for its great diversity.

ANTIRACIST SOCIAL THEORY

Another type of critical social theory with deep roots in U.S. sociology is antiracist theory. The early sociologists W. E. B. Du Bois and Anna Julia Cooper, among others, began the development of a conceptual framework probing U.S. racism as more than a matter of racial prejudice or fringe extremists. Both saw it instead as a centuries-long, deeply-lying institutionalized system of racial exclusion and violence. Cooper wrote in the 1890s of violent racist practices targeting black men and women across the country; she noted "instances of personal violence to colored women traveling in the less civilized sections of our country, where women have been forcibly ejected from cars, thrown from their seats, their garments rudely torn, their person wantonly and cruelly injured."[56] She described the "jungles of barbarism" created by white

Americans. Moreover, by the early 1900s, Du Bois was working from a conceptual perspective that all major institutions in U.S. society were structured in racial terms. He viewed this racist order in global terms, one of the first social theorists to do so. Recall Du Bois's argument that by 1900, "white supremacy was all but world-wide. Africa was dead, India conquered, Japan isolated, and China prostrate. The using of men for the benefit of masters is no new invention of modern Europe.... But Europe proposed to apply it on a scale and with an elaborateness of detail of which no former world ever dreamed."[57] Du Bois continued to develop his ideas about white supremacy and an institutionalized racist order until his death in 1963.

Writing extensively on racism and capitalism in a number of books published between the 1940s and his death in 1974, Oliver C. Cox deviated from the ideas of his University of Chicago teachers. He contributed much to the development of antiracist theory with his well-substantiated investigation of how the labor exploitation of African Americans created a structure of racialized classes. He showed that the white ruling class had worked hard to subordinate African Americans, "to proletarianize a whole people—that is to say, the whole people is looked upon as a class—whereas white proletarianization involves only a section of the white people."[58] Moreover, since the 1960s, social science analysts like Kwame Ture and Charles Hamilton have developed similar ideas and accented the centrality of *institutionalized racism* for contemporary U.S. society—those patterns of racism built into all this society's major institutions.[59]

Working on racist hierarchies and other structures of racial oppression, critical social theorists have rejected older concepts like "race relations," the phrase often used by social scientists concerned with portraying all racially defined groups as more or less responsible for the so-called race problems in countries like the United States. Such terminology is conservative in impact, for it takes the focus off whites who have created and maintained the hierarchical and exploitative system of racism since at least the early seventeenth century.[60]

The reader should recall our previous discussions of the theoretical work of Patricia Hill Collins and bell hooks on the racist construction of black women within a larger structure and culture of contemporary racism. They too examine closely and empirically the larger contextual and historical aspects of racism in the United States.

Drawing on the analyses of Du Bois and Cooper, as well as on Kwame Ture, Frantz Fanon, bell hooks, and Patricia Hill Collins, we have contributed to this development of antiracist theory in our own recent work.[61] In our conceptual analysis, we have developed the concept of systemic racism, a far-reaching framework of oppression that encompasses an array of important dimensions—the unjustly gained economic and political power of whites (historically, for example, under slavery and legal segregation), the continuing resource inequalities across the color line, and the prevailing white-racist frame with its racist ideologies, attitudes, images, emotions, and inclinations to discriminate. This system of racism has now persisted in the North American case over nearly four centuries. An important aspect of this approach is an accent on the United States as a "total-racist society," one in which most social arenas are shaped to some degree by the systemic racist realities. The macrostructure of racial oppression is reinforced by, and creates, racist ideologies and attitudes.

We have also explored the ways in which a range of "sincere fictions" created by white Americans are regularly used to reinforce racial discrimination on an everyday basis. Critical to the maintenance of systemic racism are not only the persisting prejudices—the negative ways in which whites see racialized "others"—but also the pervasive white views of whiteness, the ways in which whites positively see themselves as superior. Traditional theories of racial prejudice involve little reference to white sentiments about the white self, yet racist actions require not only a representation of the racialized other but also a conception of the white ;elf. The latter entails the creation of an array of sincere fictions, those ideological constructions that make up and reproduce the broad racial mythologies held by individual whites. Thus, white men and women often view themselves as "not racist," as "good people," even while they discriminate against African Americans and other Americans of color.[62]

The use of these concepts can aid scholars and activists to probe beneath the contemporary white denials of racism and the many contemporary myths about "race." A social theory critical of racism can help people understand the manipulated dimensions of their lives. Today, antiracist theory needs to be developed not only to lay bare the system of racial oppression but also to help in the struggle to overcome it. Antiracist theory generally attempts to facilitate human action against racist attitudes and practices. For example, in their work on racism, both Patricia Hill Collins and bell hooks have analyzed the methods by which black men and women have historically resisted racist oppression. And numerous scholars of color have examined the ways in which oppression is sometimes internalized when people of color adopt the white-racist attitudes and framing propagated within their environments—such as by the mass media—in regard to themselves. Americans of color have had to constantly create new strategies to resist both external racial oppression and the internalized oppression often fostered within themselves.[63]

Moreover, some antiracist sociologists, such as Eileen O'Brien, have developed empirical research and conceptual ideas directed at helping whites move toward assertive action against everyday racism. She has researched the strategies of two major antiracist organizations, the People's Institute for Survival and Beyond (PI) and Anti-Racist Action (ARA), which are attempting to move white Americans in the direction of antiracist action. The mostly white ARA groups include many young people and are organizing in a variety of ways against white racist activities in cities in the United States and Canada. For example, they have actively protested against neo-Nazi and Klan organizations and their numerous rallies. ARA groups have also developed other antiracist programs, including a Copwatch program attempting to reduce police brutality in several cities.[64]

The PI group, which was founded by people of color, has focused significant work on getting liberal whites to see their own racism. Various groups of whites (now in the thousands of whites) who work with mostly poor people of color, such as social workers and other government employees, come to their Undoing Racism workshops, where they are pressed to come to terms with their own paternalistic notions about the "culture of poverty" and the poor, and to examine their own racist prejudices and stereotypes. In her work, O'Brien has emphasized the importance of this PI teaching about the U.S. system of racial oppression. As she has put it, "Nearly all of us work in institutions that have historically and currently operated in racist ways. We need to acknowledge that in not actively challenging that racism, we are perpetuating it. This group is explicitly led by people of color, because it is their contention that the nature of white privilege is to unconsciously veer into that racist direction even as whites are trying to be antiracist."[65] In groups like PI, there is a conscious effort to deal with the many racial fictions of white Americans. These include ideological notions about inferior values and cultures among the poor and people of color that reproduce the self-serving myths at the level of individual whites. "It is important that even when whites affiliate with an 'antiracist' label/agenda, that they have no sincere fictions about themselves, and that they are constantly self-reflective about their own role in the movement."[66]

POSTMODERN SOCIAL THEORY

The term "postmodernism" has been used for a diverse array of social phenomena—a contemporary architectural movement, a new way of writing about contemporary life that no longer relies on "metanarratives," the historical social transformations that followed World War II, and the new conditions of a capitalism centered in information technologies. It has also been used for the supposed aftermath of the "modern" industrial age—what others have called the "consumer society," the "postindustrial society," or the "media society." Those writers and scholars who use these terms "are attempting to describe fields of political, cultural, aesthetic, scientific, and moral experiences which are distinctly different from those which were taken for granted in an earlier historical, commonly called modern or Enlightenment, phase of world history."[67]

In one way or another, postmodernism is defined in contrast to modernism, a term for the rationalist and technological culture that has expanded since the Enlightenment era of the eighteenth century. The modernist assumptions encompass the individual as the agent and creative force of society and history, the superiority of Western civilization, science as source of much truth, and a belief in social progress—views that have been basic to the development of Europe and the United States.[68] On the one hand, postmodernism often involves a radical break with this dominant modernist culture and aesthetic, which makes it important for a sociology of liberation. On the other hand, some postmodernist writers have strongly criticized the images of social liberation in the work of some social scientists for being too much a part of the modernist intellectual framework, for being tied to supposed "essentialist concepts" of human subjects that presuppose "a notion of humanity as having a fixed, unchanging identity and dynamic regardless of historical variation and social considerations such as gender, race, ethnicity, class or sexual orientation."[69]

The chaotic and diversified character of postmodern critical theory makes it difficult to assess without some selectivity and, indeed, ambiguity. Postmodernism is not *one* social theory but a complex of social theories, often of an interdisciplinary nature. Nevertheless, there are some common threads among many postmodernist writers, one of which is their challenge to what some call "foundationism"—the philosophical approach arguing that the rational, independent human subject is the foundation of ontology (being) and epistemology (how we know what we know). This foundationism views the free-thinking individual as the basic source of moral and political action. Postmodernists, instead, argue that human subjects are not autonomous creators of themselves or the worlds in which they live. Rather, they are subjects produced within a complex set of relations and are constituted within and through the moral and political arrangements around them. For postmodernists, human subjects are the effects of specific social and cultural logics.[70]

As we see it, this is a false dichotomy. Liberation-oriented sociologists want to achieve a world where human beings can endeavor creatively and move autonomously; in that sense, liberation sociologists are modernist in their ultimate aims. Yet, they are often postmodernist in their diagnoses of the troubled social worlds in which people live. Liberation social science, like all good social science, recognizes enormous differences in the capacity for agency of different social actors. Power differentials structured across racial, gender, class, and other hierarchical orders mean differences in effective social agency. A good social science recognizes the diversity within all broader social categories. Moreover, human actors are essential to a liberation analysis. No matter how determining the sociocultural order appears to be, only human beings, acting reflectively and collectively, can be said to be the inventors of social worlds. And only human beings acting reflectively and in concert can reinvent them.

We have space here to consider only a few challenges that postmodern theorizing poses to the social sciences. We can briefly discuss its implications for the sociology of liberation, as revealed in the work of several social scientists. Some postmodern theory is important for liberation projects because these theorists take seriously the fact that *experience* with reality is mediated by socially shared representations—by symbols and intersubjectivity. Human beings apprehend the reality of their own experiences, and one must take the nuanced and varying character of these experiences seriously. It is not the same thing to understand the roundness of the earth as it is to experience the death of a loved one. It is not the same thing to experience the temperature of a chemical compound as it is to experience the wind freezing our unprotected faces when we are lost on a winter day. We do not want to engage in a philosophical discussion on the nature of human experience here, but suggest that intersubjective and empathetic understanding of other human beings is critical to the human liberation project. For this understanding human empathy is decisive, for empathy is a critical human trait. That empathy has long been indispensable for survival and evolution is undeniable. Working to develop empathy across all lines within human groups, including the many lines of oppression, is necessary to human advancement in the future.

Among sociological theorists, Steven Seidman sees much that is useful for social science in postmodern thought, but also some pitfalls. Much postmodern thinking, he warns, "carries no promise of liberation—of a society free of domination. Postmodernism gives up the modernist idol of human emancipation."[71] This does not mean that all postmodernism gives up on ethical action to counter oppression. In fact, some postmodern thinkers make a strong appeal for an "ethically engaged intellectual life and pluralistic values."[72] For some, the hope of a great emancipatory transformation is replaced by the more modest aspiration of immediate and individual or localized struggles for more limited goals of social justice. At its best, postmodern thought "offers the possibility of a social analysis that takes seriously the history of cruelty and constraint in Western Modernity without surrendering to the retreat from criticalness that characterizes much current conservative and liberal social thought."[73]

Even some relatively conservative postmodern theorists have developed ideas that can be adapted effectively by liberation sociologists. For example, the French philosopher, Jean-Francois Lyotard, has underscored the intertwining of community and individual in thinking about human actions of major ethical consequence: "Thou shalt not kill thy fellow human being: To kill a human being is not to kill an animal of the species Homo Sapiens, but to kill the human community present in him as both capacity and promise. And you also kill it in yourself. To banish the stranger is to banish the community, and you banish yourself from the community thereby."[74] What is common to human beings is the image each carries in herself or himself of other people. Moreover, the human community is in the individual, and the individual is in the community. This is an important insight for understanding all types of oppression of human beings. Oppressions such as racism, classism, sexism, and heterosexism not only destroy individuals, but also destroy the social communities of which they are part.

Some feminist theorists have made effective use of postmodern insights. Donna Haraway, a materialist postmodernist analyst, has written a much-cited article, titled "A Manifesto for Cyborgs: Science, Technology and Socialist Feminism in the 1980s."[75] In the article she draws on discourse analysis to call attention to the complexities of the category of "female" as constructed in social science writings. Haraway has helped to clarify the epistemological dimensions, the ways of knowing, involved in the feminist standpoints discussed in the "standpoint theory" that we discussed earlier in the chapter.

Unquestionably, one must go beyond the postmodern concern with individual subjects, dyadic relationships, and interpersonal discourse to the much larger, imposed frameworks of social oppression. Larger-scale emancipatory visions must be articulated and pursued, beyond the individual and local level, whatever the intellectual and practical difficulties of such action. Given the life-threatening problems created by a globalizing capitalist system on planet Earth—such as global warming and its increasing threats to the atmosphere, biosphere, and sociosphere—the larger-scale emancipatory theory and research projects cannot be abandoned to a postmodern malaise and waffling on ancient philosophical issues.

Like some interpretive and ethnomethodological theory in social science, much postmodern analysis can be paralyzing, especially when it presses in the direction of making the world only into "texts" used mainly for linguistic assessment and deconstruction. For some postmodernists, the basic reality of human life is said to be language and text. Yet, there is a very substantial material world beyond all language texts, one in which people hope and empathize with others, find themselves in pain, manage to thrive or starve, and love and die—which they experience and describe with or without words. It is these omnipresent worlds of human pain and interhuman oppression that liberation sociologists seek both to understand and alleviate or eradicate.

We should add that contemporary interpretive theories, such as theories of symbolic interactionism, can also be critical of existing society, depending on which aspects of the societal context are emphasized and how those aspects are conceptualized. However, they must always go beyond "micro" descriptions and analysis. "Interpretive theorists in the more critical tradition believe that it is useful to link people's activities in everyday life to the large-scale social structures that their action creates (and that necessarily constrain action in capitalist, sexist, and racist societies)."[76] When developed along this line, interpretive theory can be an important type of critical social theory.

PUTTING LIBERATION THEORY INTO ACTION

We conclude this chapter with a brief survey of a few lives of liberation-oriented sociologists active in U.S. sociology over the past half century. The purpose is to show how critical theory becomes part of, and grows out of, lives and careers of sociologists who commit themselves to making the social world a better place. Like the lives and careers of other liberation sociologists discussed throughout this book, these lives and careers show how critical social theory can be webbed together with liberatory action. We also want to emphasize that the sociologists in our admittedly limited sample here do not stand alone, for there are a great many others just like them.

The Humanist Sociology of Alfred McClung Lee

A central figure in the liberation sociology tradition over many decades was the late Alfred McClung Lee (1908–1992). Recall from Chapter 3 that in 1951 the progressive Society for the Study of Social

Problems (SSSP) was set up with his active assistance. Lee and his associates, including his partner and talented fellow sociologist Elizabeth Briant Lee, were resisting the move to instrumental positivism in U.S. sociology and stressed the importance of dealing with serious problems facing the society, including the problems of McCarthyism and academic freedom. In 1974, the membership of the American Sociological Association elected Lee as its president in a write-in campaign promoted by sociologists involved in the 1960s and early 1970s Liberation Sociology Movement. The election of antiestablishment Lee was a watershed event signaling the resurgence of social-liberation ideas in U.S. sociology. These ideas were getting more recognition among some sociologists, bringing to the fore once again the activist and radical goals of those in the alternative sociological tradition going back to Harriet Martineau, Jane Addams, and W.E.B. Du Bois.

Lee was an early pioneer in critical social theory. Growing up in western Pennsylvania, he saw discriminatory distinctions being drawn there between the Scotch Irish and Catholic Irish, which he found to be unfair and which led him to participate in struggles of socially oppressed groups. In his view, social theory should be tied to the morality of liberating those who are thus oppressed. Such a framework affects the problems that a social scientist chooses to study. Lee called himself an "existential humanist" and probed in his work the nature of human freedom and enslavement. He linked his humanist theory with action. Thus, he was influential in the establishment of the Association for Humanist Sociology in 1976; he saw this organization as an important effort to keep the discipline of sociology "alive, relevant, and exciting for faculties and students and useful for socially constructive efforts in our communities."[77]

Writing alone or with Elizabeth Lee and other coauthors, Al Lee left behind an important body of conceptual and empirical work illustrative of a career that constantly sought the emancipation of humanity. He and his associates usually chose important political and economic topics, often those neglected by other social scientists. Recall that during the 1930s most U.S. social scientists did not research issues connected with the growing fascism in the United States and other countries. Indeed, some sociologists sympathized, openly or privately, with the increased authoritarianism.[78] However, Alfred and Elizabeth Lee were very concerned with the global rise of these fascist movements and governments and helped to organize the Institute for Propaganda Analysis. "To understand propaganda, to know how it is used in the struggles for our mind, one must constantly study propaganda of all kinds," Lee wrote in his pioneering 1952 book, *How to Understand Propaganda.*[79]

The period from the 1930s to the 1950s was one of ever growing interest in social engineering conducted under mainstream government and corporate authority. These authorities were frequently
interested in changing people's minds, either through government
propaganda designed for political purposes (for example, rabid anticommunism) or advertising on behalf of increased consumerism. Lee
and his associates viewed much of the new social engineering as an
actual or potential threat to building a truly democratic U.S. society.
Indeed, they argued that those who are targets of social oppression
must be brought into the governmental decisionmaking about their
everyday lives.

Lee recognized that the knowledge that the social sciences developed in response to the demands of government agencies, including
the military, could be useful beyond the often autocratic or imperialistic goals of typically undemocratic established institutions. This
knowledge could also be used in conceptualizing, and working for,
a more egalitarian society. Lee pressed for a theoretical and research
perspective in sociology that did *not* take oppressive social hierarchies
at face value. He was interested in how traditionally oppressive customs and mentalities could be changed by social science work. For
example, as ordinary people become better educated and gain critical
knowledge, they often come to understand that all people, whatever
their backgrounds, are equally human. People unlike ourselves are
easier to hate when we have no accurate information on their customs
and societies.[80]

In his important book on customs and human mentality, Lee argued that there was a time in Western history when speaking of changing
societal customs meant socializing "backward" peoples into "the proper
ways of life . . . to make them over into reasonable subjects or less effective
enemies. More idealistically, our panacea took the form of transforming
them through education into typical middle class Europeans."[81] In the
course of his work, Lee tackled these related social questions: For what
purposes are customs and mentality to be changed? Who is to define
these purposes and implement programs for change? What about the
unplanned or unintended consequences of social change? What methods
are most effective and acceptable in changing customs or mentality?
Lee rejected the growing propaganda machines of his day, whether
governmental or corporate, for such machines often aimed at reducing humanity to some type of political or social enslavement, however
subtle. In his view, there was a great need for a new research ethic in the
social sciences, one attuned to improving the lives of all human beings.
As Lee put it in 1958, "the only tenable reasons for seeking changes
in customs and mentality are to . . . cope with urgent and real social

developments such as overpopulation, increasingly complex technologies, urbanization, disease, secularization, international tensions, social atomization, inadequate food supplies."[82]

Lee held that sociologists should do empirical fieldwork, such as he did on racial riots and governmental propaganda, but that they must move away from the common positivistic framework that pretends to exclude human values from scientific inquiry. A critical social theory is essential, if it is one whose ultimate aim is to empower people to act. Lee tried to systematize his way of looking at the world, but not in the manner of Talcott Parsons's grand theory (see Chapter 3). In fact, he rejected the common discursive currency of sociology—the language of social roles, statuses, and functions—for one accenting hierarchy, conflict, manipulation, and exploitation. The eradication of oppression was central to his research, theory, and, indeed, life. In his many writings, Al Lee articulated the analytical and activist implications of critical theory. In one commentary just before his death in 1992, Lee wrote,

> The wonder and mysteries of human creativity, love, and venturesomeness and the threatening problems of human oppression and of sheer persistence beckon and involve those with the curiosity and courage to be called sociologists. Only those who choose to serve humanity rather than to get caught up in the scramble for all the immediate rewards of finance and status can know the pleasures and lasting rewards of such a pursuit.[83]

The Critical Sociology of Robert G. Newby

We now turn to another liberation sociologist, Robert G. Newby, who has integrated his progressive research and action with critical Marxist and black nationalist theories. Over the course of a long and productive career, Newby has been an activist sociologist and has contributed especially to our sociological understanding of the role of race and class in U.S. society.

Born in the Great Depression of the 1930s, Newby grew up in Wichita, Kansas. At home, his parents taught him a critical framing of U.S. racism, and he grew up with an active political education in the meaning of being black in the United States. Traveling a lot during his youth, Newby learned from personal experience how racially segregated the United States actually was.[84] Wichita was then segregated in many social activities, constantly inflicting the indignities of racism on its black residents. Newby attended segregated elementary schools. Since there were not enough African Americans for a separate black high school, he attended an integrated high school, where he became the head percussionist in the music program. As a young man, he participated in some of the first sit-in protests against restaurant segregation, which took place in Wichita in 1958. He has noted that this had a "profound impact on me personally. It was in these demonstrations that I was first told by a white woman that I should return to Africa."[85]

After graduation from the University of Wichita, Newby took a position as teacher in the Pontiac, Michigan, public schools. In March 1964, he joined with other NAACP members and other citizens in a march on school district offices and in a rally at city hall protesting school segregation. Going to Detroit to hear Malcolm X speak was a revelation for him: "His message was revolutionary—he exposed so many truths about how and why a system of white racism kept blacks in their subordinated position.... The major theme of the speech was its revelations of how blacks were being deceived by white organizations of political power—the Republicans, the Democratic Party, and its southern wing, the Dixiecrats."[86] When Newby and other young, more radical, members of the Pontiac NAACP were defeated in elections and replaced by more conservative members, they formed another group called the Progressive Action Committee for Equality. Newby became active in the local teachers union, in regard to the cause of local civil rights. In 1966 he was offered the position as the first regional director of the Battle Creek office of the Michigan Civil Rights Commission, where he worked on issues of discrimination in housing and education. In July 1967, he attended the Black Power Conference in Newark, New Jersey, at which leading black activists were present.[87]

Soon, Newby decided to go back to school, did some graduate work at Wayne State University, and then moved to Stanford University in 1970, where he took his Ph.D. There he became active in campus protests and got interested in debates over the Marxist and black nationalist theories used to analyze the situation of African Americans. Returning to Wayne State as a professor in 1974, Newby joined a faculty Marxist study group. He faced a protracted battle for tenure there, during which one key member of the promotion and tenure committee said that Marxists should not get tenure.[88] He also got involved in Michigan politics, and in 1984 worked for Jesse Jackson's successful Rainbow Coalition. Drawing on his significant experiences in various political movements, Newby wrote a number of penetrating sociological analyses in journals and books dealing with African American issues.

In his evolving understanding of U.S. society, Newby was increasingly using and blending both racial and class ideas in his theoretical perspective. He was coming to see that there are "no 'race-only' solutions to the situation of black people."[89] He came to see that the economic, health, and other troubling conditions of African Americans, especially those in the working class, could only be improved if the elitist capitalistic domination of U.S. society was directly confronted and the conditions for all Americans were improved. In his sociological work, Newby increasingly emphasized both racial and class issues. He criticized orthodox Marxist analysts for failing to understand the role of racism in breaking down solidarity between white and black workers, and he criticized some black sociologists for failing to recognize the role of class oppression in the conditions faced by African Americans. As he sees it, most Marxist sociologists have shown little serious interest in racial issues, except as derivative of class.[90] Yet, he also argues that so long as we have a capitalist system, we are likely to have a racist system as well: "That is the 'class' side of my commitment as an activist scholar. But I am also a 'race man,' struggling to change concretely the condition in which black people find themselves."[91]

In recent years, Newby has continued to work inside and outside the university. He has been active professionally in national associations. Thus, he has been president of the Association of Black Sociologists and the North Central Sociological Association. In both organizations, he has told us, he was "able to set forth progressive themes for the meetings."[92] He has also been active on key committees of the American Sociological Association. In his many years on the faculty of Central Michigan University, he has worked to improve the climate for students and faculty of color and has stressed the importance of racial and ethnic diversity for higher education. Thus, when a college athletic coach told his team they "should play like niggers," Newby became one of those working for his dismissal. Newby was also one of the founders of the university's important Association of Faculty and Staff of Color.[93] Active as a faculty member, Newby has also chaired the university's Affirmative Action Council, served on the board of directors of the faculty union, and served as chair of the university's academic senate. Throughout his career, Newby's academic and professional work has been shaped by the questions that have been asked by other liberation sociologists before him: "Sociology for whom?" and "Sociology for what?"

The Critical Sociology of T. R. Young

Another contemporary sociologist, the late T. R. Young, also integrated his research as a sociologist with sophisticated critical theories. Over a long career as an activist sociologist, Young contributed to changing the way sociology is done and the way it is taught. In discussion with the authors, Young noted not long before his death that numerous events in his personal biography relate to several decades of the development of liberation sociology. Young long had difficulties fitting into conventional norms of educational institutions, norms that are "fashioned such that affirmative and effective social action is very difficult, in such a way that effectively depoliticizes and dismisses even small attempts at 'liberating' sociology."[94]

Young's life story is not that of the strident troublemaker—the image of scholar-activists that is often propagated in the mass media. Instead, as in the case of Alfred Lee, his is the story of a sociologist who has tried to live a life according to principles of social justice. Significantly, Young was dismissed from his first five academic jobs because of his social justice commitments and activism. In the 1950s, his first job as a teacher at a high school in Michigan ended when at a committee meeting he proposed the gradual reduction in differences between male and female teachers' salaries. The school superintendent declared that the committee had exceeded its mandate, and at the end of the academic year, Young's contract was not renewed. Young's next position was at another high school in Michigan. Again his contract there was not renewed when he refused to join the Michigan Educational Association on the grounds that faculty members should have the right to choose between that association and a rival union.

Then, after serving time as an army draftee, Young was admitted to the master's program at the University of Michigan. After getting the degree, he secured a teaching position at a college in Iowa. He explained:

> Again, my wife and my family fit into the social life of the academic community excellently. Again, our home became a center of social life. Unfortunately, I fit in a bit too well with students—with Black students in particular. One day in April, a trio of Black students came to my office, told me that they were on their way to see the Dean about racism on campus and wanted me to go along for moral support. I did. The meeting went well. The students were respectful and persuasive, the Dean attentive and sympathetic.

But a few days later, he adds, "I was surprised to hear that the Dean was furious that I had led students to his office to make trouble." Again his contract was terminated. This time his impulse was to bridge the color line, but even this moderate action got him into trouble. His next job was at Rocky Mountain College in Montana. During the first year, he met with the college president to protest the no-raise policy for faculty. After this meeting, a raise was given to the faculty. However, after Young refused to attend the required morning chapel, his contract was not renewed.

Young's next teaching position was at Southwest Missouri State College, where his views on the burdensome character of the nuclear family for women got him into some difficulties with his chair. So, in 1960 he and his family moved to the University of Colorado, where Young got his Ph.D. He next took a job at Colorado State University, just as the radical politics of the 1960s was heating up across the country. Soon, he became involved in the civil rights movement, the women's liberation movement, and the antiwar movement. Young noted that these were "heady times and I found both intellectual and academic support for the liberation sociology that emerged by the late '60s." By 1968 students of color were organizing their own support and protest groups, and some black, Latino, and Anglo students occupied the president's office. Young acted as liaison between the students and the administration. Working with the vice president, Young developed a plan by which the student demands might be heard. The university's governing board and the protesting students accepted a plan under which new racial-ethnic courses would be added, more aggressive recruiting of students of color would be funded, and more black and Latino faculty and staff would be recruited—a plan that persisted for the next two decades.

On the day after the assassination of Dr. Martin Luther King Jr. in 1968, Young organized a King Fellowship fund and got many faculty to contribute. However, two months later, Young was notified that he would not be rehired for the next year. He wrote: "There were several reasons; first, I had set up an underground college to give minority students academic credit for their work in confronting the University; second, I had lectured on the Student-as-Nigger in the faculty lounge. Third, I had told members of the Governing Board that I intended to monitor progress on the implementation of their agreement with the Black Student Association and MECHA."

It soon became clear, however, that he would be difficult to fire this time. At the time, Young had more refereed scholarly articles than all the full professors in his department combined, was among the best teachers, and had done important service to the local community. Rather than accept this decision, Young told his chair that he had thirty days in which to reverse the decision or "all hell would break loose." The vice president with whom Young had worked in dealing with protesting students helped to reverse the decision. Some years later, the vice president told Young that that was the last time political criteria for firing faculty were used by the governing board. Over the next two decades, Young's life in academia stabilized somewhat. He wrote to us, "I did not fit in so much as the university changed to tolerate sociologists who added emancipatory knowledge and 'praxical' dimensions to their work."

As the 1960s passed, Young became more involved in developing critical theories to accelerate his and others' activities for social justice. He had no difficulty fitting into professional sociology as long as he held conventional liberal views. However, he soon became "attracted to Marxist and Critical Marxist scholarship. Conventional sociology simply did not explain either racism, sexism or class struggle in terms sensible to me." The Sociology Liberation Movement and similar groups "put together at the edges of Sociology Conferences provided an elegant theoretical perspective with which to understand racist violence in the deep South; nationalist violence in Vietnam as well as exclusionary politics in both academic and scholarly realms."

During the 1960s, many social scientists were joining critical social theory to concrete action in progressive social movements and were learning new theory from such action and involvement in local communities. Until the 1960s, Karl Marx's name was rarely heard in theory classes in sociology graduate or undergraduate departments across the United States. This was true for the graduate work done by Young at Michigan and Colorado. However, by the late 1960s, the names of Karl Marx, Herbert Marcuse, T. W. Adorno, Antonio Gramsci, and Rosa Luxemburg were becoming part of the theoretical vocabularies of some sociology graduate students and faculty members.

By the early 1970s, Young was a tenured faculty member at Colorado State University. As his work became more radical, it was rejected more often by mainstream social science journals. The *American Sociological Review* and *American Journal of Sociology* rejected everything he sent. Instead, his work found a better reception in journals such as *Sociological Inquiry, Qualitative Sociology,* and *The American Sociologist.* Young decided to make an end run around the established journals and founded the Red Feather Institute to promote critical sociological publications and conferences. Seeking to reach a broad range of sociologists, especially those just coming out of graduate school, Young began the Transforming Sociology Series of the Red Feather Institute. He went to sociology meetings to persuade authors to publish in his series and set up tables at conferences to provide copies of the independently published articles. Young wrote that "by 1980, there were over 100 papers in the Series. Those ten years were filled with hard work and great satisfaction. My wife and I built the Red Feather Lodge and in the mid-1970s held conferences three or four times a year bringing Marxists, feminists, and activists together—all patterned after the West Coast Conference." He was also facilitating conferences on critical social theories.

After his wife died in 1981, Young was devastated, and the activities of the Institute were reduced. In 1986, he resigned from Colorado State University. In the following years, Young began a series of visiting professorships, which, he notes, "brought me to new faculties with new ideas and new challenges. Gradually, my work picked up. By 1990, I was writing almost full time and teaching every other year around the country." Young was becoming a sociological "Johnny Appleseed," sowing liberation sociology ideas to sociologists across the country.

The spreading influence of the Internet attracted Young's attention, and he was one of the very first social scientists to begin publishing significant articles, journals, and books there. He developed an innovative web site for postmodern criminology, an on-line lecture series for graduate students, web sites for progressive women in sociology and for Cuban sociology, and a web site for the Red Feather Institute. Today, the Institute's site has an important collection of original materials with creative approaches to the social world (see http://uwacadweb.uwyo.edu/red_feather).[95] Young was a pioneer in the use of the Internet in spreading new sociological ideas, and he contributed very significantly to the development of critical social theories in the U.S. He was one of the first U.S. sociologists to explore the missions and methods of postmodern thought in regard to their implications for reinventing sociology. Among his Internet publications, for example, were attempts to sort out the incompatibilities and similarities between Marxist and postmodern theorists.[96]

Pushing from the Margin: The Career of Maxine Baca Zinn

A leading analyst of Latino and Latina issues in U.S. society, sociologist Maxine Baca Zinn has contributed significantly to the development of U.S. sociology in regard to issues concerning women of color. In the late 1960s, Baca Zinn began graduate work at the University of New Mexico, where she received a master's degree in sociology, and then proceeded to the University of Oregon, where she secured her Ph.D. She began her teaching career at the University of Michigan–Flint in 1975 and later held posts as a visiting scholar and professor at a number of other major universities, including the innovative Center for Research on Women at the University of Memphis.[97]

In her college courses, Baca Zinn notes, "they didn't describe social life as I experienced it."[98] So she decided to do her own work on

Mexican American women and families to show just how their lives were lived. Inspired by her life experiences, Baca Zinn has published extensively on family and gender issues, especially in regard to Mexican Americans and other Latino/a groups. For example, Baca Zinn has shown that common white stereotypes of Latinas as passive and dependent are wrong, for these women are usually at the very center of decisionmaking in their families. Drawing on her field research, Baca Zinn has criticized the commonplace blaming-the-victim perspective and pressed for a new conceptual model that is structural and takes in "the whole global picture," a model that includes explanations of the benefits to whites from subordinating people of color.[99]

In her research work, Baca Zinn has developed, with colleagues, a challenge to traditional feminist thought, which has too often accented the interests of white women. In her book, *Women of Color in U.S. Society,* edited with African American sociologist Bonnie Thornton Dill, Baca Zinn has contributed to building a new tradition of Latina feminism, a perspective that begins from the life situations of Latinas and builds on their experiences and interests.[100] She has also contributed to the development of a broader social science perspective on women of color. One conceptual problem of much social science and humanities research, including feminist research, is the positioning of white women as the gold standard for other groups of women, especially for Latinas and other women of color.[101] In Baca Zinn's view, a liberatory sociology must assess, criticize, and resist the role of conventional scholarly analysis, including much social science, in societal domination. Thus, by pressing for a full consideration in sociology and other social sciences of the interests and concerns of people of color, and for a full analysis of racial and gender systems of oppression, the social scientist is in fact engaged in acts of resistance. As Baca Zinn has noted, "integrating women of color into the mainstream of sociological work in a way that includes power relations between dominant and subordinate racial and class groups, as well as power relations between women and men, requires many forms of political and intellectual work."[102]

Like the other liberation sociologists we have considered throughout this book, Baca Zinn combines her intellectual work with activism and service to society. She prefers the term "activist scholarship" for the "transformational efforts in social analysis as well as in the institutional structures where academics carry out their work."[103] In her view, colleges, universities, and other educational institutions are important arenas in which to struggle for social justice. In these arenas liberation social scientists can challenge the restrictive perspectives of older racialized and gendered scholarship, add new knowledge from their own research, and engage in political activity to make educational institutions much more representative of the diversity of U.S. society.

Baca Zinn has been active in integrating the interests, knowledge, and perspectives of Latina/o Americans into higher education in the United States. She has played an important part in building the field of Chicano Studies and was the first Latina/o president of a regional social science association, the Western Social Science Association. As president, she worked to increase the Latino/a presence in that organization and in its journal. She has also worked to integrate this new knowledge and perspective into textbooks on family diversity, social problems, and introductory sociology. With coauthor D. Stanley Eitzen, she has argued that "textbooks need not be limited to the synthesis of dominant perspectives. Instead, texts have possibilities for constructing and transmitting liberatory knowledge."[104]

Moving to Michigan State University in 1990, Baca Zinn has continued her activist scholarship. In the mid-1990s, she was codirector of a Michigan State University summer institute of the American Sociological Association's MOST (Minority Opportunity through School Transformation), an important project designed to recruit promising students of color at the undergraduate level in sociology and to improve the recruitment of students of color in Ph.D.-granting programs. An active scholar in the Julian Samora Research Institute at Michigan State, which was created to study Latinos/as in the Midwest, she has worked to break down college structures of exclusion by recruiting graduate students from underrepresented racial-ethnic and working-class communities and by including these students, as well as progressive white students, in her research projects. As she told us, "mentoring graduate students, making them skilled, independent, and networked is activist work in settings where nondominant students have had few opportunities to become part of the networks that produce and monitor knowledge."[105]

Recovering the Feminist Past of U.S. Sociology:
The Career of Mary Jo Deegan

The careers of liberation sociologists have taken many different paths. Mary Jo Deegan, a pioneering feminist sociologist whose work we have already cited, has worked for decades to challenge discrimination against women both in U.S. society and in sociology. She has done much to bring the ideas and research work of numerous forgotten women sociologists back into mainstream discussions and research in sociology.

In the late 1960s, Deegan began graduate work at Western Michigan University with a focus on disability issues, but soon transferred to the University of Chicago. At the university's Center for Hospital Administration, she worked with Odin Anderson and Ronald M. Anderson. The only graduate student interested in qualitative research at a center doing mostly quantitative research, Deegan became interested in theory and studied with sociological theorist Talcott Parsons, cultural anthropologist Victor Turner, and religious theorist Mircea Eliade. Early on, she decided that she "wanted to be a feminist, activist, and change agent ... while the men [she studied with] wanted to be great thinkers and power brokers in academia and some of them have done so."[106] In her career, Deegan has devoted herself to the areas of disability studies, popular culture, feminist theory, and the history of sociology.

In the late 1960s, Deegan started searching for materials on the forgotten women sociologists whom she was convinced had been very important in the early development of the field of sociology. Finding very little published material, she undertook what became a long-term research project, which included searching many libraries and archives, compiling lists of women sociologists' names and bibliographies, and writing about these women sociologists and their research. As she told us, "I discovered to my amazement the enormous early sociological literature by women scholars on women and labor markets, women and unions, women and wages, and so on. I immediately asked myself two questions: (1) who were these early female sociologists, and (2) why didn't anyone ever mention them or their writings in my so-called 'best' and advanced training?"[107]

Clearly, one of the key tasks undertaken by some liberation sociologists has been to recover the critical history of the discipline, for that history has been forgotten when it has been in the interests of those white men who have historically dominated the discipline. Deegan not only uncovered and described the history of women sociologists but also tracked and resurrected some of their important theoretical ideas and empirical research.

For three decades, Deegan has answered these questions in dozens of important articles and numerous books. Much of her work has not yet been widely recognized in U.S. sociology, although some has been recognized and used in fields outside sociology. Perhaps most influential is Deegan's major book, *Jane Addams and the Men of the Chicago School, 1892–1918* (1988). This book reveals that the pen is a powerful tool for liberation sociologists, for it is pathbreaking and is beginning to have a major impact on U.S. sociologists in making them aware of the early and influential women sociologists and their pathbreaking perspective of feminist pragmatism. Deegan shows that central among these early sociologists was Jane Addams, a founder of U.S. sociology. Recall from earlier chapters that Addams was not only head resident at Chicago's influential Hull House settlement complex but also an active researcher and theoretical sociologist, as well as a founding member of the American Sociological Society.[108]

In the process of researching this early history of sociological radicalism, Deegan developed a penetrating sociology-of-knowledge approach to this history: "Sociologists who specialized in criticizing the economic structure of society and women's limitations within it were particularly subject to neglect or damning interpretations.... The early passion, political forays, and verve were abstracted from accounts of 'scientific' sociology."[109] This was also true for some of the early male sociologists, but especially true for the early women. As we have noted in earlier chapters, by the 1930s the male leadership of sociology, increasingly centered in academic departments, was moving rapidly away from the more radical and activist roots of the discipline. As Deegan has shown, "these later men therefore condemned political action for sociologists, while the ideas of the elite, in fact, permeated their work. Society as based on competition and conflict over scarce goods was a patriarchal and capitalist model of social action."[110]

Deegan has done very important research on the conceptual framework called "feminist pragmatism." Recall from Chapter 3 our discussion of the women sociologists, and a few associated male sociologists, in Chicago who developed feminist pragmatism. Pragmatism was an intellectual movement whose central idea was that the test of a concept lay in its practical significance. The feminist pragmatism of Addams and her associates emphasized a cooperative ethic, coupled with the values of liberal education and democracy. Their feminist, cooperative ethic was coupled to extensive political efforts for change in Chicago and across the country. As noted earlier, these feminist pragmatists played a very important and successful role in efforts to develop welfare-state programs supportive of families and individuals in the United States. The feminist-pragmatist ideas grew out of the strong social networks of many women sociologists and activists around the turn of the twentieth century.[111]

Deegan has shown the importance of symbolic interactionism in the thought of these early sociologists. Some, like Addams, contributed to the development of symbolic interactionism, the distinctively U.S. perspective that has rejected social determinism and viewed human beings as shaping and controlling their behavior interactively by means of socially constructed meanings.[112] Older meanings can be rejected or reconstructed by humans as social producers, and with an eye to

building better societies. Addams was an early symbolic interactionist who understood that "female" and "woman" were clearly social
constructions. She researched and analyzed the division of private
and public places for women, their struggles between family claims
and public-sphere claims. Building on the work of these early women
sociologists, Deegan has shown that symbolic interactionism is one
of the few social theories that asserts that people can create and re-
create their own lives. Thus, in its more radical form that recognizes
the importance of "macro" structures of oppression, it offers a liberatory framework for considering the present and future of women in
society. Efforts at liberating women will meet resistance, but "it is
people who create human behavior, and it is people who can change
it.... Women can do this, but only if a large enough number want to
do it, agree on definitions of what is desirable, and have access to the
means to obtain these goals."[113] Deegan thus suggests how a liberatory
theoretical framework drawing on a radical symbolic interactionism
can be incorporated into social activism on behalf of improving the
lives of ordinary people in contemporary societies.

Given the pathbreaking character of Deegan's work, it is perhaps
not surprising that there have been negative reactions on the part of
some sociologists to her research. For example, she tells of going to
an American Sociological Association meeting in 1987 and hearing
several groups of sociologists comment negatively on her book on
Jane Addams, even though it had not yet been published! She is not
alone in this experience. Other liberation sociology books and research
efforts have suffered similar gossipy and preemptive negative attacks,
which, as Deegan notes, reduce the likelihood that such scholarship
will "cross the barriers protecting mainstream ideology, gatekeeping,
and practices."[114]

Deegan has noted that liberation sociologists sometimes suffer
greatly but that they also have interesting lives "defined and expressed
very differently than those bounded by traditional and narrowly
defined careers in the discipline."[115] One of the great satisfactions
of doing liberation sociology is getting other people to see ideas and
histories that they have never seen before and to read books and materials they have not read before.

CONCLUSION

In presenting the lives and work of a few critical sociologists like
Alfred McClung Lee, Robert G. Newby, T. R. Young, Maxine Baca
Zinn, and Mary Jo Deegan, we do not intend to suggest that these

are the only sociologists who have worked on liberation theory and activist sociology over the past few decades. The other countersystem sociologists mentioned in this and previous chapters are part of that important list, as are many sociologists we have not had the space to discuss. However, these cases do suggest how, over the decades since instrumental positivism became established in U.S. sociology, the lives of particular sociologists interact not only with the development of liberation sociology but also with the academic and other important social settings surrounding them. In their careers, these sociologists illustrate a central point of liberation sociology—that lives, research projects, and theories unavoidably intersect and co-reproduce each another.

However presented, critical social theories supply liberation sociologists with ideas that are indispensable for thinking through contemporary human problems and possibilities. As all the critical theorists show, the mainstream of sociology and the other social sciences is drenched with unexamined assumptions, distorting beliefs, and even self-aggrandizing claims designed to reproduce a still oppressive status quo. Critical social theorists often focus on the social histories and social contexts of oppressive structures that limit human achievement and progress. They reject the idea of inevitable and determining permanent, cross-cultural, and natural laws of society—for societies are historically shaped and ever in the process of change. Critical social theories are grounded in the idea of science as a "thoroughly historical, philosophical, and political activity."[116] Thus, critical social theory and instrumental-positivistic theory are different in their key domain assumptions and their general outlooks.

The ideas of the critical theorists reviewed in this and previous chapters may sometimes appear rather abstract and thus irrelevant for the task of transforming the world into a more just and freer place. Yet the presumption of the irrelevance of anything this theoretical is usually misguided. We must not conceive of the relation between theory and action in a simplistic or mechanical way, as if there were a one-to-one correspondence between theory and practical activity—a correspondence in which the social scientist plays no part. For the authors of this book, this has not turned out to be the case. Often when we have been confronted by relatively abstract critical theory, we have been forced to rethink and modify our concrete and practical ideas. Critical social theories are reservoirs of important ideas, and the creativity of the actor is what accounts for their application to interpretations of specific empirical phenomena or to collective action. Indeed, much critical social theory has its roots, as we have often noted, in the thinking of "ordinary" citizens, the organic intellectuals whose thinking is shaped by much everyday experience with social oppressions and that can be revealed to all by social science research at its best.

We have noted throughout this book the importance of interdisciplinary research and perspectives in the development of critical social theories and consequent research. This interdisciplinary work, together with the growing diversity of research perspectives in sociology, bodes well for the future of the field. Patricia Hill Collins has optimistically noted that "sociology's unique social location as a contested space of knowledge construction allows us to think through new ways of doing science."[117] This is a good position to be in, as a science. Clearly, the increasing intellectual diversity in sociology and the diversity of its practitioners are virtues to be embraced. Such diversity puts sociology in a good position to deal effectively with the present and future complexities of both U.S. society and global society.

CHAPTER 8

Sociology, Present and Future: Two Sociologies

In the twenty-first century, sociology continues to ignite the imagination of countless citizens who read its books in private or in groups, as well as those who take its courses in colleges and universities around the globe. Many people continue to be drawn to sociological ideas, research, and teachings to help them make sense of the complex and difficult worlds within which they live. Indeed, since its beginning, the ideas and research of sociologists have provided excitement and insights for people in all walks of life, the world over.

Sociology is often used in a narrowly instrumental way to generate findings, such as in the statistically framed survey and demographic research that conventionally serves as a basis for some government and other official decisionmaking. In this book we have accented a broader and alternative tradition, one that accepts an array of methodological approaches and a range of critical and contending ideas. As we see it, the persisting questions are, Sociology for what? and Sociology for whom?

In this book we have emphasized, and proposed the further extension of, the critical sociological tradition that has clear-cut answers to these two questions: Sociology for making a better world, and sociology for those who struggle for their emancipation and liberation from social misery. We believe it is time for mainstream sociology to correct its skewed course so that the knowledge its practitioners generate can be placed at the service not only of government and corporate policymakers but also of those social groups and community organizations that seek to change the troubling and oppressive

233

conditions in which they live. We realize that this goal is not easy to achieve, but it is essential for social justice, and perhaps for human survival beyond this century.

From its beginnings, sociology has had internal contradictions. On the one hand, there is a deep-lying conventional and relatively conservative tradition of sociologists involved in theoretical and empirical work that generally undergirds the existing social order. On the other hand, there are progressive-reformist and revolutionary traditions of sociologists involved in theoretical and empirical work aimed at substantial social change. The classical theorists examined in Chapter 2 illustrate how these two traditions can exist even in a single sociological theorist, and how what is liberating for some can be oppressive for others. Auguste Comte, for example, proposed to change the world radically by substituting positivist-scientific thinking for theological and metaphysical thinking. Politically, however, he was a conservative who yearned for the security and social order similar to that provided earlier by the authoritarian Catholic Church, which, ironically enough, he wished to defeat. Over several generations now, the tradition of "positive science," which he proposed to change the social world, has become one of the important instruments for maintenance of the status quo.

Today much of the work connected with the social science mainstream reflects an instrumental positivism. Contemporary sociologists have their own versions of these age-old contradictions. For example, the great exemplar of U.S. sociologists, Emile Durkheim, was reconstructed a few decades after his death by Talcott Parsons and other sociologists as a positivistic theoretician of social order and consensus. However, as we have noted previously, Durkheim actually advocated a broad array of sociological methods and approaches and was a staunch supporter of France's Third Republic, which in his time was a rather *radical* force in the struggle against monarchists and the clerical establishment. As we have demonstrated, Durkheim was also a *moral* philosopher and saw that expanding social justice was essential to the future of healthy societies.

As used in this book, *liberation sociology* is a contemporary term for the old progressive and radical tradition in sociology, the approach deeply critical of existing society and its oppressive institutions and oriented to the significant reduction or elimination of social oppressions. It represents, in fact, the *real* sociology, the sociology that can help bring a more just social world. In Europe this tradition goes back to early intellectuals like Harriet Martineau, and in the United States, it goes back to Jane Addams and the women (and men) of Hull House, as well as to the work of pathbreaking black sociologists like W. E. B.

Du Bois and Anna Julia Cooper. Most were organic intellectuals representing the concerns and interests of those communities—women, African Americans, and the poor—who had mostly been excluded from the political interests of elites and from the interests of most mainstream academics. Included in this group were a few progressive white male sociologists like George Herbert Mead. And we have seen elements of this orientation to building better societies in the classical sociologists such as Emile Durkheim and Max Weber.

This countersystem tradition has been kept alive by many people and groups over more than a century. It was manifested in the creation of the Society for the Study of Social Problems (SSSP) in the 1950s and the creation of the Women's Caucus, the Association of Black Sociologists, and the Sociology Liberation Movement in the 1960s and early 1970s. This tradition has its global dimension as well. During the 1960s, many activist students, including student leaders, in protest movements in France, Germany, and the United States were sociology undergraduate or graduate students. They developed a tradition, which continues to the present day, of progressive student activists often being sociology majors in college. These activities and movements have helped keep the countersystem tradition alive within the field of sociology in the United States and in Europe.

NEW VOICES, NEW SOCIOLOGIES

Sociology, like everything human, is always in flux. At some points in its history changes have been revolutionary, and at other times evolutionary. As we move farther into the twenty-first century, we see that all social sciences are pressed hard by new voices and participants, many of whom were previously excluded or suppressed. As in the past, sociology often leads the other sciences in incorporating these progressive changes. During the 1960s, men, mostly white men, made up some 85 percent of the sociology Ph.D. recipients and sociology faculty members in the country. Today women make up the majority of new recipients of sociology Ph.D. degrees, and that proportion has grown in recent years. The percentage of women Ph.D.'s is much higher in sociology than in economics and political science, as well as the physical sciences. In addition, the proportion of sociology Ph.D.'s earned by sociologists of color has grown over this period, from a very modest percentage in the 1960s to a significant proportion of all sociology Ph.D.'s today.

Interestingly, membership in the American Sociological Association declined from 15,000 in the early 1970s to 12,000 by the mid-1980s, but then began a slow increase to more than 14,000 as of 2008.

A recent (2007) American Sociological Association national meeting had more than 6,000 participants, which set the all-time record. Today, we see that more than half of those in the field of sociology are white women and people of color, and this proportion seems to be growing year by year. These people are not simply new voices—for younger generations have always replaced earlier generations—but often represent the voices of those who were once studied only as social problems in need of official government attention. These new voices are often those who were once the silent objects of sociological study. Many thus represent the views of those suppressed and oppressed over many generations—in society generally and within the social sciences themselves.

This changing composition of those who do sociology and the other social sciences is dramatic and electrifying, for the new social scientists are making creative, provocative, and well-theorized contributions to social science knowledge. As a result of these changes in the ranks, sociology today is a field of much deeper, broader, and more multivoiced contributions to the understanding and improvement of society. These new voices, at the same time, are feared by some sociologists who have worked to enhance sociology's influence and prestige by developing a more conventional professional and "pure science" status. For these conventional sociologists, the new multivoiced theory and research are sometimes seen as a huge shift away from "scientific" sociology into a much weaker sociology, one allegedly concerned mainly with particularistic matters and lifestyle issues. Yet, these critics often exaggerate the speed and impact of this change. Their fears need to be set in context. For one thing, these professional changes have happened only gradually, over several decades.

Still, the changes are significant. Many of these relatively new sociologists are bringing important changes in the direction of a more emancipatory sociology. As we see it, this shift is not at all to be feared but should be heralded and expanded for a number of important reasons. First, the continuing growth means a great range of new people in the field of sociology, making it more representative of the country as a whole and thus more democratic. Second, this expansion of a liberation sociology generally means more intellectual power for the field. Many novel and original ideas have arisen and been pursued in field research, ideas once excluded because of the conventional understandings of the sociologists who once dominated the field. As these new voices achieve national audiences in sociology, and more generally, the expanded dialogue will greatly strengthen intellectual pluralism. Perhaps over time these previously suppressed groups will be recognized as full participants in national intellectual and political arenas.

We can note briefly a contemporary example of this new intellectual contribution to sociology. Among the relative newcomers to this emancipatory sociology is Duke University Professor Eduardo Bonilla-Silva, the winner of the 2007 American Sociological Association Lewis Coser Agenda Setter Award. The author of two influential books on U.S. racism, Bonilla-Silva recently submitted to the Sociologists Without Borders (a liberation sociology international group) listserv a brief essay about his personal experiences entitled "Eréndira in American Sociology." In the essay he tells his social science colleagues that recent months have been hard for him, because he has been working with and counseling junior faculty of color as they attempt to secure tenure in their colleges and universities. Bonilla-Silva built his essay around the powerful metaphor of the innocent Eréndira, a character in a famous novella by Gabriel García Márquez. The young Eréndira—who Bonilla-Silva equates to faculty of color in U.S. sociology departments—accidentally burns down her abuela's (grandmother's) house. In his account this abuela represents white sociology. The abuela tells Eréndira not to worry because she will be able to pay for her damage working as a prostitute. This story has been widely interpreted as an allegory for the people of Latin America represented by Eréndira and their exploitative governments represented by the abuela. In his essay Bonilla-Silva draws on fifteen years of experience in historically white universities and on numerous accounts from faculty of color in the many sociology departments he has visited to call attention to the "collective pain endured by sociologists of color." Among those painful experiences is the realization among many young sociologists of color that, after having been recruited to join a historically white department of sociology, the interest in their presence is mostly symbolic on the part of the majority of white sociologists there. There is the accompanying pain of isolation, disenfranchisement, and discriminatory disparate treatment. Bonilla-Silva concludes his essay urging "young members of Eréndira not to let Abuela get your heart.... You must not accept insults, disrespect, and white sociological nonsense. You must fight back."[1] Clearly, the demographic changes coming to sociology and the other social sciences mark only the beginning of the changes necessary for these disciplines to be considered fair and open sciences.

We saw significant evidence of the impact of new demographic pluralism in Chapters 5–7, in such important areas as feminist theory and antiracist theory, teaching, and research. Feminist scholars and antiracist scholars of color have raised many new issues about the structure and character of U.S. society, and changes therein, that have been ignored or neglected by traditional research and analysis. And it is clear that the progressive tradition in U.S. sociology has been populated not only by women and people of color but also by a considerable number of farsighted white male sociologists. From the early case of George Herbert Mead to the later examples of C. Wright Mills and Albert Lee in the 1950s and 1960s, to T. R. Young and Carl Jensen more recently, we see numerous white men playing important roles in developing the progressive and radical traditions within contemporary sociology, a sociology committed to the emancipation of groups traditionally oppressed and, indeed, to a society where "liberty and justice for all" is more than rhetoric.

RESEARCH CHALLENGES AND THE FUTURE OF SOCIOLOGY

In spite of the explosion of sociology's new voices, and the changes in research and theory noted above, too much social science research remains a type of top-down research that does not recognize social domination, exploitation, and oppression as critical social issues. Too often, the critical experiences of those suffering from such forms of oppression as racism, classism, sexism, and heterosexism are not assessed in a thoroughgoing way within the conventional outlets of mainstream sociology, such as the *American Sociological Review.* Because they typically have little access to social research or social scientists, those at or near the bottom of this society's resource and power hierarchies generally have little impact on what becomes the dominant knowledge of this society, knowledge that is used to make mainstream public policy. Clearly, the oppressing classes and the bureaucratic organizations they control often try to conceal or disguise their operations for the general public and do not seek or desire social science or other critical research on the everyday practices of social oppression. This can be seen clearly in the case of genocide in dictatorial societies such as Nazi Germany, Stalin's Soviet Union, or Pinochet's Chile, where probing social researchers did face a significant possibility of imprisonment or death. Today, in most Western countries, those probing too deeply into systems of domination and exploitation are likely to be punished in one way or another, whether by exclusion from research funding or the failure to receive tenure or promotions in the academic system or in other organizational settings. Moreover, in some countries such as El Salvador, liberation-oriented academics and theologians have been murdered by police or military forces.

Liberation sociology is a major irritant for power elites, for it seeks to render very visible the oppressive structures and processes of a society. This is an indispensable step in the eradication of social oppression. For that reason, even in a society where "freedom of speech" and "academic freedom" are acclaimed, examining the problems created by existing governments and by major national or international corporations typically requires some courage and boldness. In fact, this is the likely reason that relatively little in-depth research has been done on the ruling elites of countries like the United States.

One critical goal for liberation sociology is the collection of data that is not distorted by, or closely bound to established, and usually conservative, sociopolitical forces. There is no more significant bias in much of the sciences than the researchers' need or desire to please the rulers of the society, especially when the latter provide the funding for much research. Today much of the data produced by established organizations, as studies previously cited have shown, is manipulated or distorted to fit with the major political-economic and bureaucratic goals of those organizations. Indeed, we need more research on how the current "official data" produced by social scientists are distorted or misleading as guides for interpreting and understanding U.S. society.

There are also deeper concerns of values and morality often ignored by mainstream researchers such as the instrumental positivists. Social scientists whose vision is grounded in a concern for human liberation and human rights go beyond the research that social elites at the helm of the nation-state or multinational corporations can use to formulate major societal policies. They are concerned with implementing the long-standing ideals of liberty and justice in the larger society by means of reliable, innovative, and action-oriented social research.

Liberation Psychology and Anthropology

Of course, sociology does not stand alone. Some psychologists and anthropologists have developed a liberation orientation for their disciplines. In a 1969 keynote speech, George Miller, president of the American Psychological Association, advocated an instrumental-positivistic psychology and distinguished between the promotion of human welfare by psychologists who are social activists and the work of the positivistic psychologists.[2] In contrast, liberation psychologists have proposed a much different role for psychology.

For example, Ignacio Martín-Baró, a creative social psychologist who was murdered in El Salvador in 1989, proposed a liberation psychology that would demonstrate and critique the common and institutionalized misrepresentations of the poor and their poverty. He asserted that psychologists, as scientists of human behavior, should not only seek the welfare of the discipline of psychology but also shape psychology into a major instrument of conscientization and of debunking dominant-group myths of the poor. Martín-Baró supported activism that, buttressed by solid research data, attempts to change oppressive sociopolitical and economic structures that trespass on human welfare.[3] An example of Martín-Baró's liberation psychology is his critical analysis of the common arguments about the conformism and resignation of the Latin American poor. He argued that this social psychological image of Latin American fatalism "accurately detects the symptom but it misses in the diagnosis."[4] It misses the oppressive structures that generate most fatalism, for most Latin American societies have historically been structured so that an elite owning class oppresses the ordinary workers and the poor. In such situations fatalism is a reasonable adaptation to an extremely oppressive and militarily enforced hierarchical social order.

Some anthropologists have proposed a liberation anthropology. In 1994 the American Anthropological Association selected the theme of human rights for its annual meeting, and more sessions were dedicated to that theme than to traditional anthropological topics. Among the anthropologists who have embraced this human rights orientation is Leigh Binford. Binford has proposed a liberation anthropology that works closely with grassroots and community organizations, such as in the documentation and investigation of human rights abuses. An example can be seen in Binford's *The El Mozote Massacre,* a study of a 1981 mass murder of Salvadorans by a battalion of El Salvador's army.[5] In addition to providing an exhaustive description of events, Binford examines the political climate, the ruling oligarchy's ideology, and the military objectives that accounted for this crime against humanity. He also examines how this crime was covered up or justified by the U.S. government and by the mass media and international commissions that investigated it. Binford also describes the history and the social structure of El Mozote, the community where the massacre occurred. These aspects of the community were usually ignored in media accounts and government investigations. Here a liberation anthropologist rescues the memory of the men, women, and children whose lives were ended by this military operation. This work of liberation anthropology was generated by an anthropologist's commitment to human rights.

LIBERATION THEOLOGY: AN ANALOGOUS SITUATION

Recall "liberation theology," the powerful movement of Catholic activism for progressive change in postcolonial countries, particularly in Central and South America. In the late 1960s, major efforts toward making liberation theology central in Catholic religious commitments came to the world's attention as a result of a Latin American Bishop's Council in Colombia, where Catholic priests pressed for new initiatives to meet social justice needs in Latin America. Many priests, some other clergy, and many laypeople associated with this movement have dedicated their lives to working hard for the liberation of the poor and oppressed, which has meant being a strong voice for real political and economic change and also reforming church theology from the bottom up. However, in the early 2000s, John Paul II, then the pope of the Catholic Church, spoke out against the liberation theology movement and acted to subvert its spread in various countries by replacing activist bishops with more conventional bishops. Nevertheless, even he was influenced by liberation theology pressures in the Church to issue strong condemnations of poverty and economic oppression around the globe and to encourage Catholics to work for social reforms, albeit in non-Marxist movements. Interestingly, in many postcolonial countries the Catholic laity have supported liberation theology strongly and insisted on having activist priests committed to social change.

In recent years there has been significant cross-fertilization between liberation theology and the social sciences. For example, Ignacio Ellacuría, a Latin American liberation theologian who was murdered in 1989 in El Salvador, once wrote:

> There are social and historical structures that are the objectification of the power of sin and, also, carriers of that power against human beings, human life. And there are social and historical structures that are the objectification of grace and are carriers of power in favor of human life. The former constitute structural sin, the latter, structural grace.[6]

This comment shows how the social sciences have penetrated the thought of liberation theologians. Although the concept of sin is theological, the ideas of objectification and of social and historical structures are drawn directly from the social sciences. Central here is a rejection of the dualism between the inner experience of faith and the experience of actual participation in a given culture and society. Liberation theology overcomes the separation between "God's design and the respect for people and groups ... between revealed truth and social data, between a passive and undignified 'here' and 'now' and a happy 'afterwards.'"[7]

Similarly, liberation theologians in South Africa have rejected the dualism between the religious experience and the societal experience.

These liberation theologians have participated actively in the black African struggle for freedom from white domination in South Africa and other African countries. Pan-Africanism, the century-old political and ideological framework that accents the oneness of all people of African descent and a commitment to African liberation everywhere, is the historical context for the development of African theologians who have taken a strong stand against traditional racial colonialism, as well as against its successor, economic neocolonialism, today.[8]

The liberation sociology we propose shares with liberation theology its commitment to social justice and human rights and its taking sides with the socially oppressed. It also shares with it the rejection of the dualism that segregates the professional scientific and civic lives of its practitioners. However, liberation sociology does not seek to convert anyone to a religious or political set of beliefs. Liberation sociology can be practiced by sociologists wearing many different religious and politico-ideological labels.

Today, within U.S. sociology, there are still the old "priests" of mainstream sociology, such as those who represent the tired doctrines of instrumental positivism. They still dominate many of the established institutions, including major funding agencies and mainstream journals. However, these social science priests are constantly being challenged by the forces of change, especially those sociologists committed to a progressive sociology. Many of the new entrants into the field of sociology are overt or covert supporters of liberation sociology ideas and research strategies. They lead in calling for a new understanding of sociology's history and for a recognition that some of the earliest founders and thinkers in the field were themselves white women and African Americans. Indeed, during the first decade of sociology's development in the United States numerous sociologists of various class, racial, and gender backgrounds were committed, albeit to varying degrees, to societal reforms, including eradicating the exploitation of workers, building unions, expanding social programs for the poor and immigrants, fighting militarism, and making political and socioeconomic democracy a reality in the United States.

THE IMPORTANCE OF A BROAD HUMAN RIGHTS STANCE

The Moral Stance

As we have demonstrated throughout this book, all social research has an underlying moral stance, whether it is openly expressed or kept under cover. All interpretations and analyses of the social world carry with them the assumptions and values of those doing that work. However, for many social scientists engaged uncritically in conventional research techniques, it is de rigueur to conceal most or all of their metasociological assumptions and values. In addition to the goal of a deeper understanding of social oppression, liberation sociologists seek to take an overt moral stance toward the research process from the first formative steps. As we see it, there is great need for a renewal of the alternative social science tradition that openly embraces the moral dimensions of all human life, including that of all social research.

One problem for many contemporary sociologists, as for most classical sociologists, is that they do not develop a moral perspective that goes substantially beyond the confines of the nation-state in which they live and work. Fortunately, there are growing numbers of sociologists who are openly concerned with moral issues in sociological analysis, as well as in the larger society. Thus, "communitarian" sociologists like Robert Bellah and Amitai Etzioni have tried to bring questions of ethics and morality back into social science and public debates.[9] Generally speaking, the communitarians reject a positivistic social science that tries to ignore moral issues. In this regard, their contribution is healthy for developing both a better sociology and a better society. They are, however, critical of a too heavy accent on human rights and prefer instead to emphasize the importance of civic duties and obligations within an existing nation-state. They stress the importance of the family and of each individual's responsibility to it and to larger communities.[10] They raise important moral issues and underscore the virtues of collective concerns and values, but most social scientists working with a communitarian perspective remain centered on the traditional values of U.S. society and its existing government. Although they accent civic responsibilities, they see the world mostly from the vantage point of those who are white and affluent, while neglecting the antioppression perspectives of the poor or people of color. The poor and oppressed cannot carry out the requisite civic responsibilities in a system that systematically excludes and exploits them. Moreover, most theorists and analysts who adopt a communitarian perspective do not work aggressively to challenge the institutionalized discrimination and oppressive socioeconomic dominance of the governing elites in the United States or across the globe.

Liberation sociologists assert the importance of openly proclaiming a human morality that supports the liberation of the socially oppressed. As we see it, not only is an overt moral perspective essential to a viable liberation sociology, but that moral imperative must go beyond the confines of the existing nation-state to draw heavily on the burgeoning human rights tradition at the international level. Probing serious problems in current powerful nation-states and corporations requires a bold moral position that asserts the human rights of all citizens of the planet. Those researchers who are well supported by funding from nation-state agencies are not very likely to collect data on, or analyze critically, extant state-fostered oppression. A broad international human rights perspective can enable a social scientist to examine government manipulation or oppression more critically, and even to choose elites' manipulation or oppression as major research topics.

Unfortunately, the repeated emphasis on certain types of state-funded, quantitative-positivistic methods as the main or only way to do serious social science and the insistent teaching of these techniques and orientations to sociology undergraduates and graduate students have broad consequences for the field of sociology. A heavy stress on such procedures shapes the way that these students view the social world and thus often limits their minds and imaginations. Too often the assumptions of this "methodism" simply "reinforce an uncritical view of existing political structures and all they imply."[11]

What Human Rights Perspective?

The idea that basic human rights *transcend* the boundaries and authority of a particular society or government was articulated by Thomas Jefferson and his fellow revolutionaries. Drawing mostly on European thinkers, Jefferson in 1776 penned the provocative language, "We hold these truths to be self-evident, that all men are created equal and are endowed by their creator with certain unalienable rights ... Life, Liberty, and the pursuit of Happiness." Envisioned here are not only legal rights but also basic and broad human rights. Jefferson and his fellow revolutionaries declared that the North American minority of the British empire had rights that derive from the natural law that transcends the authority of the British nation-state. Later on, in the debates leading to the U.S. Constitution, however, many of these same members of the North American elite coupled this "rights" talk to their concerns for protecting mainly the interests and property of well-off Americans against less-privileged Americans.

In contrast, some non-European traditions do not view private property as the primary bedrock for human rights. Very important in expanding our conception of human rights traditions are the dissident rights perspectives of Native, African, and Latino/a Americans and the perspectives of women and other oppressed peoples across the globe. There are stronger human rights arguments in these traditions than in many of the elitist perspectives of theorists such as the Europeans John Locke and John Stuart Mill. For example, there is the community-centered human rights tradition of Native American groups, some of which Jefferson himself admired. Moreover, over the past several decades, an ever larger body of international agreements and laws has grown up to buttress the reality of expanding human rights on the global scene. An international perspective on human rights was clearly strengthened by the Nuremberg trials of former German Nazi government officials after World War II. The trials established the principle that "crimes against humanity" are condemned by principles higher than the laws of any given nation-state. Thus, human rights are much broader than "civil rights," since the latter are only those rights guaranteed by a particular nation-state. In this broader framework, each person is entitled to equal concern and treatment because they are human beings, *not* because they are members of a particular society.[12]

The struggle to deal with German Nazi oppression and Western imperialist oppression in many countries led to the creation of the United Nations' Universal Declaration of Human Rights. We noted earlier that this international agreement stipulates that "all human beings are born free and equal in dignity and rights" and "all are equal before the law and are entitled without any discrimination to equal protection of the law." The declaration extends these rights to everyday life: "Everyone has the right to a standard of living adequate for the health and well-being of himself and his family, including food, clothing, housing."[13]

This extraordinarily important international declaration affirms that human beings have rights independent of the particular governmental conditions in which they live and presses governments to incorporate human rights into their societies. This international rights tradition has been buttressed by a long series of subsequent international agreements, international court decisions, and court decisions within individual nations based on these agreements. Although this human rights impetus may initially have been substantially Western in its orientation, today a broad human rights perspective has been adopted by many citizen and political groups around the globe and, increasingly, by established nongovernmental agencies and by political and legal agencies in many nation-states.

At its best, this international human rights vision requires more than the integration of the formerly oppressed into a modestly adjusted societal framework. The oppressed may not be seen in most societies, but they have always been there. As they rise up periodically in liberation movements, they make evident their centrality to their societies. As this happens, it becomes clear that simply integrating them into adjusted structures that continue much of the oppression in less overt forms will not be sufficient. The ultimate goal will have to be to replace the oppressive structures and processes with totally new democratic structures grounded in a full respect for all fundamental human rights—including civic, political, family, and economic rights.

LIBERATION SOCIOLOGY: KEY DIMENSIONS

The Countersystem Perspective

Recall that the countersystem approach in social science involves social scientists stepping outside the thought patterns of a conventional instrumental-positivistic paradigm to look very critically at their own society. One good example of this can be seen in the work of Stephen Lyng, a countersystem sociologist working in the Sjoberg tradition. Lyng has pioneered in research and analysis of alternative health care systems and what they mean practically, philosophically, and politically for a United States facing continuing health care crises. Generally, those adopting a countersystem approach often question existing social structures and sometimes propose a counter set of societal arrangements. A newly envisaged countersystem can include elements of an existing society, or it can involve entirely new arrangements. Some countersystem analysts accent the importance of an external standard to judge existing societal arrangements, such as the standard in the aforementioned international vision of human rights. Other countersystem analysts accent the idea of alternative societal futures and suggest thinking about the possible range of such societal futures. Both approaches can generate discussion about the ways to create new and more just social structures and arrangements.[14]

We view liberation sociology as a countersystem approach, one that aggressively seeks the goal of human emancipation from exploitative and dominative structures. This perspective foresees a better society where most people have real compassion for human suffering and a commitment to eliminate all major forms of socially generated misery and oppression. It seeks research relevant to dealing with social miseries and oppressions as they are manifested in everyday life. A liberation sociology perspective envisions a society where people are reflective, develop empathetic compassion for human suffering, and commit themselves to changing that suffering. It creates research and analysis relevant to everyday social problems. An adequate standard for assessing existing social institutions includes a vision of more humane social arrangements, one that includes the best elements of past and present societies.

Recognizing Crises in "Normal" Systems

One of the key insights of Karl Marx was that fully human action—action that is both intelligent and moral—is possible only when people are substantially liberated from economic oppression. What type of person one can become, Marx showed at length, is significantly shaped by the social structures in which we find ourselves. The structures of modern capitalism, as Marx saw, are frequently destructive of a person's humanity.

Much social science analysis of U.S. society, its economy, and its politics reflects an ideology of status-quo maintenance that denies or hides the society's underlying contradictions and crises. One of the tragedies of any society is the failure of its people and leaders to understand the deep-lying social crises and dilemmas confronting them. For example, today there is a general denial among those in the U.S. ruling elite and among many other Americans of the major social and economic oppressions and other troubles created by an ever expanding international and bureaucratic capitalism, which is controlled largely by transnational corporations and associated government agencies guided by a narrow profit-centered ethic.

Much empirical data reveal that the United States is on a path of accentuated economic and social inequalities and probably of increasing social conflict. Thus, the social and economic contradictions of modern capitalism are becoming quite evident. Income inequality has reached a record level in recent years. Wealth inequality has increased significantly in recent decades; the wealthy have more than doubled their share of all wealth since 1970. Moreover, a great many U.S. residents still live in poverty.[15] There is no historical reason to expect the political-economic system of capitalism to last forever, yet the U.S. political elites and mass media seem relatively unconcerned. One has to turn to the alternative media, which often have smaller circulations, to get serious and sustained analysis of the crises of contemporary capitalism. (One exception may be the progressive web sites on the Internet, some of which are now accessed by hundreds of thousands of people.) One should also note that only occasionally in mainstream social science journals does one find serious discussion of the deep-lying contradictions and crises of contemporary capitalism in the United States or across the globe.

In the last few decades the failures of other political-economic systems—for example, the demise of state communism in Eastern Europe in the 1980s and 1990s—have received more attention in the U.S. media than the present political-economic contradictions and coming crises of modern capitalism. Increasing economic and social inequalities in the United States and other Western societies do get some media coverage, but typically in scattered, often brief articles with little sustained and critical analysis. Yet even these accounts of deep problems have been rationalized away by many established politicians, media commentators, and intellectuals, including some social scientists. They are sometimes even accompanied by attacks on the principles of equality and pluralism that supposedly underlie the political institutions of the United States.

For example, in the area of racial matters, many policymakers, media commentators, and mainstream social scientists have abandoned analyses of the widespread racial discrimination that persists in U.S. society, adopting instead thinly disguised racial code words such as "quotas," "reverse discrimination," "welfare queens," "street crime," and "undesirable immigrants." Claims that African Americans, Latina/os, Latin American immigrants, and other people of color are unintelligent, lazy, welfare-preferring, criminal, or culturally deficient—which marked an era in U.S. history said to have passed decades ago—have resurfaced in the past decade or two in the strongly phrased sound bites, books, articles, and political programs of some influential media pundits and neoconservative academics. We see here a recurring and vigorous defense of the highly inegalitarian status quo.

There is also a reluctance to face the central and continuing role of U.S. corporations in environmental degradation, both in the United States and across the planet. In recent decades, the levels of greenhouse gases in the earth's atmosphere have grown significantly—mainly because of fossil fuel use, deforestation, and pollution. The processes have often been triggered by, or generated by, large U.S.-based corporations, many of them transnational corporations. This global warming melts ice packs, increases coastal flooding, generates severe weather, spreads disease, and reshapes agriculture across the globe. Also as a result of human action—including that spurred by capitalistic firms and the consumerist value system they have helped over decades to generate—the earth's ozone layer is severely depleted in some critical areas, which results in a range of negative impacts.[16] Numerous leading politicians in the West, as well as a great many corporate leaders, have been unwilling to take more than modest steps to deal with this accelerating and increasingly obvious environmental destruction. Indeed, they produce speeches suggesting that the environmental crises are exaggerated—or are someone else's fault (such as the newly developing countries of China and India). Some respected environmental experts, however, are discussing the possibility that most plant and animal species, including possibly the human species, will be gone by the year 2100 or shortly thereafter. A few principled political leaders, such as Albert Gore, and numerous physical scientists, such as Jared Diamond, are now speaking out on the substantial scientific evidence on ongoing and future environmental catastrophes. As Diamond has noted, the only question is whether the ultimate civilization-threatening crises are likely to "strike our children or our grandchildren, and whether we choose to adopt now the many obvious countermeasures."[17] The data on ongoing crises suggest that intellectual defenses of the status quo inside and outside contemporary social science are yet one more way to "fiddle while Rome burns."

A Holistic Approach

Liberation sociology at its best accents interdisciplinary and holistic thinking. Originally, sociology became a separate discipline at a time when the sciences were being divided up into an array of specialties. For example, Emile Durkheim worked hard to establish sociology's independence from biology and psychology, arguing that social behavior could not be explained by the central tenets of these latter fields. Compartmentalization of ideas and methodology was useful in early struggles to establish sociology and the other social sciences as distinctive disciplines, but such efforts were political, not scientific. Marcel Mauss, Durkheim's leading disciple, thus advised his students that at their best human beings do not give themselves to observation in separate compartments fitting each discipline, but actually live all at once.[18] Thus, at its best liberation sociology accents totality and a holistic approach to the social world.

Breaking with the Nation-State Perspective

The aforementioned nation-state bias in U.S. social science means that global trends and issues are not researched as much as they need to be. The globalization of the contemporary capitalist system is engulfing all societies and most areas of organization within these societies. Global organizations, such as the World Bank and the International Monetary Fund, as well as transnational supercorporations like Exxon and IBM, are to some degree autonomous of any particular society or government. In the social sciences, much more attention needs to be given in research and analysis to these key bureaucratic actors in the global frameworks that have dramatically reshaped much of the world in recent decades.

Much of the challenge to building more humane societies that recognize the full range of human rights lies in the way in which large bureaucratized organizations perpetuate the "iron cages" of social oppression. Gideon Sjoberg has underscored the way in which political liberals tend to support government action and to be critical of corporate action, whereas neoconservatives tend to have a positive view of corporate bureaucracies and to be skeptical of government action except where they benefit. Yet, the global scene is increasingly dominated by large, highly bureaucratized corporations that function, to a varying degree, without the substantial control of any nation-state, including the United States. Such bureaucratic capitalism is a dominant, worldwide force constantly creating major problems for the world's inhabitants, especially increasing economic inequalities and ecological problems. Sjoberg notes that "as transnational organizations control agro-food systems, farmers in many developing nations are being encouraged to produce cash crops that can be sold to those who hold positions of privilege in global bureaucratic structures.... These cash crops, in turn, are replacing the production of staples for the local populace."[19] As we suggested previously, working in their own economic interests, these large transnational corporations often destroy and discard regions, countries, peoples, and environments around the globe.

As we conceive it, liberation sociology should be fundamentally opposed to the many political nationalisms that divide human beings. Sandra Harding notes that "Western sciences clearly have been and continue to be complicit with racist, colonial, and imperial projects."[20] Scientists of all types should examine their own practices in regard to their role in exploitation, domination, and oppression. Today, there are many people's movements around the globe that are fighting against colonialist, racist, classist, sexist, and heterosexist structures within societies, including manifestations of these structures in intellectual and academic institutions. In these efforts, social science can be helpful, as it is a contested zone, a place where inherited social views can be carefully examined and debated, and revolutionary new ideas asserted and promoted.[21]

If liberation sociology involves a weakening of conventional sociology within a given nation-state like the United States, that is of positive consequence, especially if that weakening means an expansion of sociology's development across the globe. As T. R. Young once put it,

> In the third world, newly industrialized countries will ... build sociology departments with indigenous scholars and more global

theories to teach ever more students about the social life worlds in which they live and the global economy in which they strive for pride of place. It is no great tragedy that American sociology has fallen on hard times if it means that the authentic self-knowledge of both rich and poor capitalist countries is thereby improved ... if it means that sociological theories are much less celebratory of the nations in which they are created and used to reproduce privilege and power.[22]

As liberation sociologists view these matters, if human beings are to have a voice in changing the conditions that exploit and oppress them, then they should have great access to the generation of the knowledge about those conditions and to the strategies for changing them.

Ongoing Reflectivity and Empathy

A potentially liberating aspect of sociology is its omnivorous observational curiosity. Sociology relies on field observations, surveys, interviews, experimentation, and historical comparisons to reach general conclusions. At their best, sociologists go into the world with a keen observing eye. Sociology can liberate when it applies humanistic concern and empathetic reason to solving serious problems afflicting human beings. Early in the history of social science, the application of reason through scientific method was once thought to bring progress; reason would make us free once we rid ourselves of ancient prejudices. Yet this promise was never delivered. Although the reason of science can be used to liberate, it has also been used to oppress.

A number of contemporary sociologists, from Jurgen Habermas and Pierre Bourdieu in Europe to Gideon Sjoberg and his associates in the United States, have argued for the importance of reflectivity— of thinking critically and deeply about the self and about the self in relation to others—in providing a basis for expanded ideas of human morality and human rights. One key theme developed in this book is that liberation sociology should be aggressively self-reflective. The idea that a human being can arrive at knowledge that is independent of all particular selves has been an assumption of intellectual activity since the time of the Ancient Greeks. Historically, the various sciences have made valiant efforts at producing this type of knowledge. Yet, for all the demonstrated ability of science to produce such knowledge, it has not been possible, even in physics, chemistry, or biology, to discount the impact of particular human beings, their biases and assumptions, and their social group interests in the form and content of knowledge. The understandings of bias that sociologists and other social scientists generate can be applied to their own situations and disciplines. This aspect of liberation sociology accents the possibility of researchers undertaking self-refection and empathy as important scientific elements of enhanced sociological knowledge.

Moreover, reflectivity, broadly conceived, is at the heart of what it means to be human; it is integral to the ability to understand, and to empathize with, the social other. As Sjoberg notes, through reflectivity, human beings learn that they "exist and thrive only through interaction with others." He adds that "reflectivity cannot be sustained without physical security and basic subsistence" and that "by recognizing reflectivity as an essential feature of human nature, one must ultimately consider just how persons often are able, or can be enabled, to take the roles of multiple divergent Others."[23] A central idea of liberation sociology is the enhancing of a critical reflectivity and of social empathy both in research and in daily life.

CONCLUSION

At least since Karl Marx, progressive sociologists have asked whether social things really are what they seem to be. Human societies are, of course, created by many people, who make frequent errors in arrangements, beliefs, and choices. Yet the current arrangements need not be allowed to stand when they destroy the lives of many people caught within them. Liberation sociology seeks to stimulate debate in the field of sociology, the other social sciences, and the larger society over what humane and fully democratic societal arrangements would look like and how they could be fully implemented.

Liberation sociologists have been rowing against the mainstream currents since sociology found its strong disciplinary identity in the late 1800s. In our view academic sociologists need to constantly resist the recurring cultural imperialism that exists both outside and inside our colleges and universities. Indeed, the conventional cultural expectations about what is "good social science" can become "a form of *symbolic violence* that relies on a relationship of constrained communication to extort submission."[24] That is, department chairs, deans, and other college administrators, as well as many established colleagues, generate this internalized symbolic violence in young, and older, sociologists by ruthlessly claiming that in their academic decisionmaking they are only applying timeless rationality and entirely depersonalized rules, when in fact they are imposing a narrow status-quo framing of both the college setting and the larger society.

Sociology can help to liberate when humanistic concern, critical reflectivity, and empathetic reason are applied to the everyday social problems that create much misery for human beings. Throughout this book we have accented a broad human rights perspective and the value of expanded humanization. This means a maximizing of human potential, self-realization, and achievement. More specifically, the aim of liberation sociology is to make sure that in classrooms more ideas are created than are brought to the classrooms by means of the ready-made ideas of textbooks and other assigned readings. Moreover, it is rather easy to demonstrate empirically that *all* social scientists mix research and moral concerns, even when they deny it. And too often their morality is that of the status quo and the extant nation-state— and is thus invisible and taken for granted. Only a modest number of social scientists have so far explicitly coupled their research styles and interests with the morality of a broad human rights perspective that reaches beyond the borders of conventional nation-states. And when they do, they often find that they are the ones who get targeted as being "biased," while those doing the work of an oppressive status quo are not challenged for their hidden assumptions. Today, the early human rights tradition of U.S. sociology needs to be strongly recalled and fully reinstituted—this time in the context of the internationally recognized human rights, rights not only to life and liberty but also to a decent standard of living and a safe environment in which to raise families. The point of liberation sociology is not only to research the social world *but to change it*. And to change it in the direction of greater fairness, social justice, and equality. The ultimate test of social science is not some type of propositional theory building but whether it sharpens our understanding and helps to build more just and democratic societies.

A just and democratic society, at both national and global levels, should be devoid of all forms of institutionalized exploitation and oppression. As we see it, this just society is not only a desirable goal for humanity but actually a *requirement* for human survival over the next century. The destructive mentality of modern capitalism, now the world's dominant economic force, is gradually destroying the planet's atmosphere, flora, and fauna; by the year 2100, if current trends continue, much of the planet will likely be uninhabitable.

Place this ongoing environmental crisis in the set of all social crises facing the world's peoples—growing economic inequality, continuing racial and ethnic oppression, high levels of patriarchal and heterosexual oppression in most countries—and you have a planet where a detached and amoral social science makes no sense. Although proposals for new and untried societal frameworks certainly involve much risk, as Ben Agger notes, "the future is a risk, a choice, framed by the past, the legacy of which is difficult to overcome. But critical social theorists, even if they cannot prove the possibility of a radical alternative to the present, are certain that the past and present do not neatly extend into the future without any slippage."[25]

In envisioning a better human future, a sociology of liberation sides with those seeking liberation from oppression. It works with people who are trying to bring changes and attempts to voice those who are oppressed. It envisions a better future for all humanity. When in the name of "objectivity" sociologists claim to envision a "neutral" or entirely relativistic future for humanity they have fallen into the absurd. Liberation sociology, unabashedly, stands for a world of increased justice and democracy.

CHAPTER 9

Epilogue: The Challenges of Teaching Liberation Sociology

Karl Marx and Frederick Engels once famously proposed that "the ideas of the ruling class are in every epoch the ruling ideas, that is, the class which is the ruling material force of society is at the same time its ruling intellectual force."[1] Sociologists who wish to teach from the liberation sociology perspective need a critical awareness of this elementary fact about society, or otherwise they will end up teaching a social science that substantially derives from, and significantly supports, the ruling ideas of society. Savvy liberation sociologists are aware that "hidden exploitation is the form taken by man's exploitation of man whenever overt, brutal exploitation is impossible," as Pierre Bourdieu once put it.[2] He also used the term "symbolic violence" for the violence that people in less powerful groups do to themselves by accepting the dominant cultural framing of those who dominate them. Thus, teachers of liberation sociology can assist their students in escaping much of this internalized violence by keeping their emancipatory mission ever in mind. The teaching of human emancipation begins with teaching students the essential role that the dominant cultural framing of society plays in the creation and maintenance by dominant groups of society's hierarchies of power and privilege.

This dominant cultural framing of society, and its array of conventional beliefs that protect these social hierarchies of power and privilege, are often disguised by a variety of strategies that Pierre Bourdieu termed strategies of "misrecognition." To communicate to college students this sociological concept of misrecognition, one of the authors devised a series of discussion questions that college students are asked to respond to in order for them to develop some awareness of how misrecognition works in everyday life.

One such discussion question asks students what they talk about with potential marriage partners. Though both partners clearly have a vested economic interest in each other's economic futures, in classroom discussions of misrecognition very few college students in fact acknowledge discussing with their partners (that is, recognizing) these crucial economic interests. Another classroom discussion explores advertising. One needs only to open a recent newspaper to realize that most "sale" advertisements emphasize savings for buyers, when the truth is that the advertising merchants actually seek to increase their never-acknowledged profits. For more than two decades we have shown to sociology classes the movie *Risky Business* (1983), a cynical movie about an upper-middle-class high school senior who through a series of comic circumstances turns into a pimp. Over two thousand students have participated over the years in the critical analysis of the movie, but *only two* have ever noted the well-off white boy's obvious transformation into a *criminal* as central to the plot of the movie. All the rest "misrecognized" this central element in the plot, and only after a second and a third viewing of the strategic scenes in the movie did they become aware of the white criminality, which they had not recognized because of their conventional positive framing of whites. Most students react in a similar way in the classroom analysis of the Disney movie, *The Lion King* (1994). Only a few students initially recognize that the central plot of that movie teaches that a society's rulers (the lions) are the *born* rulers, and that the followers (hyenas, elephants, and so forth) are *born* followers. If one adds to the critical analysis of the movie the important consideration of voices and colors (of fur) of the central animals, one can then recognize just how the movie makes use of standard U.S. racial stereotypes. Course discussions about this movie have also unearthed just how strongly many students feel about lions being, in actual fact, the "kings" of the jungle and how strong they argue that the movie is just telling an accepted truth about the natural hierarchy of the "circle of life," what Western philosophers have for centuries called the "great chain of being." Such classroom exercises make very clear to students just how much of social reality is hidden from or misrepresented to them, and how they in turn come to not recognize, that is, misrecognize, what is so plainly in front of them.

The task of the liberation sociology teacher—and we cannot emphasize this enough—is *not* to tell students what to think, but to suggest to them the *social what* that they should think about. This change from the aim of most conventional educational practice necessitates a significant change in most current relationships between teachers and students. The authors have discovered, in different settings, that numerous social science concepts can have an emancipatory effect when used to help students see what is culturally arbitrary in their society. For example, to emphasize the importance of everyday life settings, one of us has asked college students to examine the actual physical and social layout of the room in which the class—say, an introductory sociology class—is actually taking place. Students quickly realize that there is a recurring and conventional seating arrangement. Most often, the teacher is at the front, and students are in rows of chairs or desks facing the teacher. Students have learned to take this arrangement as the "natural" way for them to be educated. In such classroom discussions questions then proliferate from one unreflective college youth: "How else can one learn from a teacher?" "Are you proposing that we return to the round tables of our kindergarten days?" "Are you suggesting that all classrooms be set up with chairs in a circular shape so that students can see each others' faces and learn from each other as well as the teacher?"

Indeed, consider what might happen to educational impacts, to students, and to society if the single change of roundtable-seating for classroom arrangements were to be implemented on a large-scale in U.S. classrooms. In the overwhelming majority of classrooms, chairs or desks are neatly arranged in ways that allow the teacher to dominate physically and the janitorial staff to clean efficiently. Pressing a class for such a critical examination of what is taken for granted and submissively accepted as the normal way of doing education always creates a rich lode for self-discovery and can lead students to taking the initiative to discuss and debate important concepts learned in yet other classes. In one class a reflective student once asked us why sociology majors are taught about the social construction of reality, yet are not taught that even their sociological concepts are social constructions. In the dialogue that followed, various students came up with a long list of conventionally constructed social science dichotomies: order versus anarchy, social system versus randomness, secular versus sacred, democracy versus totalitarianism. Soon they became reflective about the artificiality and arbitrariness of many such limiting conceptual dichotomies.

A recent example of a liberation sociology approach in college teaching is that of Professor Kimberly Ducey at the University of Windsor. Recently, she used the first edition of this book as part of her creative criminology course, one oriented to a liberation social science perspective. Ducey sent us a large box of very creative class projects submitted by her students, who were often influenced by liberation sociology ideas. These projects included multifaceted methods for getting at and presenting sociological ideas and empirical findings: paintings, artisan artifacts, music, videos, and several pieces of cloth for a quilt made up of themes describing the highlights of a sociological career. Professor Ducey's gift to us of her students' class projects, and our review of them, have filled us with much hope for the future of sociology. The projects reveal a great enthusiasm not only for data collection and analysis but also for the pursuit of social justice, equality, and democracy—so much so, that our own enthusiasm for the liberation sociology effort has also been renewed. (Professor Ducey reportedly has in the works an article for the journal *Teaching Sociology* that presents details of her teaching experience with a liberation sociology approach.) Of great interest in her social science course is how, when allowed to express sociological ideas and findings in the media of their choice, students develop significant knowledge and release much creativity and originality, thereby exhibiting much more learning and insight than commonplace multiple-choice examinations and similar conventional evaluations would ever allow them to express.

These examples of students coupling some self-analysis with socio-analysis in the classroom might be multiplied endlessly from the experiences of many teachers who accent such critical thinking in the classroom. Many sociologists practice a critical and reflexive approach to teaching and research and thus know they are part of the teaching and research observations in which they engage. This significant feature of the sociology discipline opens the possibility of increased and more highly participatory teaching and research. In the examples mentioned, the social complexity of classroom interaction is learned by students as they concentrate their attention on the here-and-now world in which they live every day. Concepts such as social class, "race" and racism, gender, heterosexuality, privilege, ideology, and subjectivity can all be studied and illuminated within the boundaries of the institutional arrangements of classrooms, in which a savvy teacher can easily derive much sociologically relevant data from students about social interactions and meaning. Needless to say, the data thus derived can then be examined for representativeness and compared critically with similar data from other such settings or from other research sources.

All too often students taking social science courses get a limited, often canned, view of the social world around them. Frequently, they are provided by their teachers with a fund of social science findings that are an accumulation of facts with, at best, a modest integration of larger unifying ideas and deeper meanings. Although there are numerous exceptions to this conventional type of social scientific presentation, it remains commonplace. The attempted inculcation of assorted findings and often disconnected social facts usually fails, at least in the long run, and typically much of the content of such conventional social science courses is soon forgotten. One major reason for this large-scale forgetfulness is that exciting ideas mapping the underlying connections and critical themes are frequently missing in such social science courses.

In our capitalistic society, with its pressure to judge everything in profitability terms, even higher education is more and more "run like a business," a cliché one now hears often from college administrators. Indeed, researchers in a recent book edited by Dennis Hayes and Robin Wynward explore in some depth the "McDonaldization of higher education," which refers to the ways in which the business values of efficiency, predictability, and control by authorities are typically accented over creativity, critical thinking, and democratic exchange in the classroom.[3] Moreover, in recent decades ever more undergraduate courses, especially those in colleges and universities accenting research and grants, have been taught by graduate students, who are usually poorly remunerated for their efforts. The pressures of graduate school—or for junior faculty in similar situations of getting tenure—encourage these instructors to use introductory textbooks that are sold with manuals, collections of multiple-choice questions, teaching slides, and Powerpoint databases to facilitate the tasks of instructors. These convenient pedagogic devices encourage a type of pedagogy that is relatively unidirectional, if not authoritarian, and that requires rather modest commitments of students to learning. Among these devices multiple-choice exams (the trend is for more such exams) are especially problematical, as they discourage critical thinking, imagination, and creativity in learning course materials. In addition, most teachers in social science departments and programs—including the authors—have agreed to teach courses within the confining limits of the preestablished, conventional sociology curriculum. The standard sociology curriculum for undergraduate and graduate students is, for the most part, centered around a predefined range of topical areas, such as crime and deviance, family, demography, complex organizations, stratification, theory, and quantitative methods.

There are numerous problems with this conventional sociology curriculum. For one thing, social life is richer than what is indicated by the usual presentation of social facts within conventional sociology courses, as well as other conventional social science courses. Progressive sociologists have long suggested the need to break this orthodox mold. They often suggest new courses for the social science curriculum. Indeed, over the last century sociologists have been at the forefront in creating new academic areas of study, such as racial and ethnic studies, gay and lesbian studies, women's studies, and the study of death and aging. Moreover, instead of simply encouraging students to memorize facts, we should teach them how to study the world sociologically for themselves, to get out of the classroom and into communities to see what contemporary social life actually is like, and to be deeply critical and self-reflective in the process. For example, one possible problem with some conventional social science courses is the heavy accent in teaching about present-day social realities on older sociological findings from research that includes the opinions of people who have been dead for some years at the time of the course. A conventional statistical-research article based on ten- or twenty-year-old data is likely discussing statistical relationships and other findings for a sample that at the present moment includes, judging from U.S. mortality data, many people who are deceased.[4] As surveys age, the lack of direct access to what people actually said and thought beyond the usually very brief survey questions likely can mean less understanding of their everyday lives. In contrast, this is usually less of a problem with older qualitative studies that offer large amounts of their respondents' actual interview responses, responses that are substantial enough to be reanalyzed in a later, and perhaps different, conceptual framework.

And everyday life, as we see it, is the most important of all individual and social processes. In Spanish, there is the word *vivencia,* sometimes translated very inaccurately as just "lived experience." Vivencia actually refers to an event—one that is necessarily subjective—in a person's everyday life and is intimately tied to a related term *convivencia,* again sometimes poorly translated as "the act of living together." From this nuanced perspective, an individual can only be thought of as *living collectively* and in connection with significant others. To change the quality of our lives, thus, one needs to change the quality of our interrelations. Liberation and emancipation ideals thereby carry the connotation that the end of oppression brings into being a new collective life, a new type of living together justly and democratically. In this way the future emancipation that liberation sociology promises is not eschatological, such as the otherworldly emancipation promised by religious revelation, but is a new way of thinking in the present and immediate future, a new collective life that liberation social scientists seek to bring into being.

One of the flaws in many social science methods courses for both undergraduate and graduate students—as well as in much traditional research by social science faculty—is the recurring accent on analysis of previously collected survey and demographic data. We believe that this emphasis on other people's data, which data are usually framed by other people's assumptions and language, should often be replaced by encouraging students to get out of the college setting and research the social worlds for themselves. Sociology's great promise is to discover, imagine, and interpret the interrelationships of human beings in everyday settings—to study carefully the intricacies, pains, and wonders of the human experience.

There is yet another problem in most educational settings in countries around the globe, including the United States. As we suggested above, the educational process is typically one-way and hierarchical, if not authoritarian. Paulo Freire notes the prevalence of the "banking" concept of education, in which "knowledge is a gift bestowed by those who consider themselves knowledgeable upon those whom they consider to know nothing. Projecting an absolute ignorance onto others, a characteristic of the ideology of oppression, negates education and knowledge as a process of inquiry."[5] The banking concept tries to alter the mentality of students so that they will fit into the rigid Procrustean bed of an existing society. The major alternative is liberatory education, which is, at base, a process of mutual education with mutual respect. Freire envisions enlightened education—much like the research procedures in the best participatory action research—where the teachers are taught by the students and the students are taught by the teachers. In such educational settings there is great reciprocal and mutual learning.[6] Freire offers a clear statement about the mutual education vision of liberation sociology.

Furthermore, in the conventional social science curricula, there are few courses concerned substantially or centrally with the oppressive structures and processes that a human rights reading of society would highlight. We noted in Chapter 5 the intense debate that just *one* such course created at one of the country's premier state universities, the University of Connecticut. There major attempts were made by outsiders to derail sociology professor Noel Cazenave's attempt to teach a scholarly course that was explicitly focused on "white racism." Just the attempt to teach such a well-framed course made news in the national media, and it was attacked by white faculty members and politicians.

Indeed, those teaching about society from a strong critical perspective should be prepared to deal with the substantial energy and emotional labor that is required, both inside and outside the classroom. Such teaching requires significant preparation for the challenges that come within the classroom in getting a good hearing for ideas and evidence on issues regarded as controversial by the typically uncritical or uninformed students. The good news is that the issues and data discussed in many sociology classrooms force average students to engage, in a critical way, material that they have never had to think much about—and thus to become thoughtful participants in the surrounding society. A central and continuing difficulty is that most students come to sociology classes with a conventional and uncritical view of societal realties, one that has been drilled into their heads by parents, peers, and media. This ideological "common sense" is usually individualistic and unencumbered with a critical bent, a viewpoint that inclines them to constantly challenge even the most data-filled and substantiated analysis of matters such as class, racial, and gender inequality and oppression. Many a social science teacher has found their carefully documented arguments challenged by students who think that their homegrown "common sense" is equivalent in substance to the social science evidence presented in detail. For this reason, some liberation sociology instructors have found it to be important to begin their sociology classes with a forthright discussion of certain ground rules for class discussion and interpretations. These ground rules include getting students to suspend certain common-sense assumptions, to understand that interactive educational settings are different from conventional teaching settings, and to develop a more thoughtful view of what counts as substantial evidence for arguments about society (not including unsubstantiated views of talk-show hosts, for example).[7]

Teaching and researching from a strong liberation sociology perspective also may mean you will have to seek out "less prestigious," in conventional terms, publication outlets and academic careers. Yet there are many alternatives to the mainstream journals for such critical research and writing, such as major book publishers that we discussed earlier. Interestingly, these publishers are more interested in substantial social science writing that is readable, that has narrative, and that is interesting for the general reader than are the mainstream social science journals, whose editors assert they are interested in this broader audience but continue to publish articles that are inaccessible to all but a small elite of social science methodologists. In addition, over the last few decades numerous pathbreaking social scientists have found that smaller colleges and "less prestigious" universities are more hospitable to research deviating from the instrumental positivism and narrow topics of mainstream social science. An example is Stephen Lyng (see Chapter 8), a small college sociologist whose research on alternative medicine is pioneering and internationally known. As Ben Agger has sagely summarized the contemporary social science writing and career situation, "But if you publish work that other people want to reread, work that does not disclose itself fully upon first reading but, through its craft and sensibility, entices the reader back for a second, deeper meditation upon it, you *will* find a job somewhere, especially if you bring the same excitement to your teaching as to your writing.... There are many sociologists who share my view of sociology as a literary activity, to be pursued in order to make good ideas about social change accessible. You will not be alone!"[8]

Given the level of public resistance to sociology courses like that of Professor Cazenave, it is no wonder that there are only a modest number of courses in academia, including in sociology, that are centrally and critically focused on the various social oppressions in U.S. society or other societies across the globe. Although social oppression is dealt with as part of some social science courses—depending on the courage of instructors—there are few courses dealing systematically with such topics as white racism, sexism, class oppression, and antigay oppression under those specific titles. Even when such courses are taught, they often have more sanitized titles or are marginalized—from the point of view of many faculty and administrators—into certain academic niches such Women's Studies, Ethnic Studies, and African American Studies, rather than placed into the mainstream curricula of long-established departments.

Liberation sociology seeks to expand the range of courses offered to include courses on all forms of institutionalized exploitation, domination, and marginalization. It seeks to put students in connection with the complex realities of everyday life and the full range of experiences of human beings—including those human beings that have not as yet received adequate social science attention, those who are exploited and oppressed.

Some critics may suggest that even these improved educational procedures and curricula are of limited value in the liberation project. Certainly, they do have their limitations, for educational institutions constitute but one area of a contemporary society. It would be good if all citizens of a society had great access to settings where there was full and open learning and debate about societal problems and likely social futures. Thoroughgoing liberation pedagogy and learning should encompass all societal institutions, including the conventional media and the Internet, and not just traditional educational institutions.

Moreover, for many people, especially those who are exploited and oppressed, the beginning of liberation may lie in having their voices heard, or heard more broadly, in both learning/teaching and research settings. One of the goals of countersystem research and teaching is to help to voice the voiceless, and thereby help to assist the project of large-scale human liberation in this and other societies. In our experience, a liberation sociology teacher can provide the space for a substantially interactive and discussion-oriented learning setting, which usually adds much to the education of all those present. In such uniquely reserved societal space, students from privileged class, racial, and gender backgrounds can listen to and learn from those who are the recurring targets of stereotyping and discrimination in society, those whose everyday-world knowledge is rarely encountered in typical classroom settings. Liberation sociology teachers can provide more open learning environments in which male students hear directly what it is like for women students to suffer from sexist stereotyping and gender discrimination, or in which white students can learn much about what it means for students of color to suffer from racist stereotyping and discrimination. The liberation sociology teacher can make sure that in the classroom the voices of socially oppressed groups are given a fair hearing and, where possible, are evaluated in terms of data and analysis presented in the larger course. In this sense, liberation social science is centrally about real academic freedom and equality of discourse.

Let us conclude by considering a man who was both a liberation sociologist and one of the most important activists for social change in U.S. history, Dr. Martin Luther King, Jr. Graduating from Morehouse College in 1948, King was a sociology major who was significantly influenced by Professor Walter Chivers, a favorite sociology professor with whom King took seven sociology courses. A now mostly forgotten liberation sociologist who provided his sociology students with a savvy analysis of U.S. racism, Chivers is credited with providing major input into King's institutional analyses of U.S. racism, as well as his racial and political realism.[9] Chivers is thus a major example of the way in which a teacher of liberation sociology can have significant and lasting positive effects on society.

Inspired by his education in both sociology and theology, Dr. King gave numerous lectures and speeches in which he accented the themes of social liberation and justice. We conclude this book with two powerful statements from his speeches that indicate his progressive sociological insights. In one famous commentary, Dr. King connects the ideal of social justice to major structural changes in U.S. society: "Justice for black people will not flow into society merely from court decisions nor from fountains of political oratory. Nor will a few token changes quell all the tempestuous yearnings of millions of disadvantaged black people. White America must recognize that justice for black people cannot be achieved without radical changes in the structure of our society."[10] And in another famous speech King discussed the need to go beyond the supposedly "peaceful relations" that some asserted existed between white and black Americans to a positive situation of social justice: "We've never had true peace, we've never had positive peace, and what we're seeking now is to develop this positive peace. For we must come to see that peace is not merely the absence of some negative force; it is the presence of a positive force. True peace is not merely the absence of tension; it is the presence of justice and brotherhood."[11]

NOTES

Preface

1. See Walter Isaacson, *Einstein: His Life and Universe* (New York: Simon and Schuster, 2007).

2. Fred Polak, *The Image of the Future,* trans. and abrid. E. Boulding (San Francisco: Jossey-Bass, 1973), p. 305.

Chapter 1

1. Karl Marx, *Theses on Feuerbach,* reprinted in Karl Marx and Frederick Engels, *Selected Works,* vol. 2 (Moscow: Foreign Languages Publishing House, 1962), p. 405.

2. See Gideon Sjoberg and Leonard D. Cain, "Negative Values, Counter-system Models, and the Analysis of Social Systems," in *Institutions and Social Exchange: The Sociologies of Talcott Parsons and George C. Homan,* ed. Herman Turk and Richard L. Simpson (Indianapolis: Bobbs-Merrill, 1971), pp. 212–229; and Ted R. Vaughan, "The Crisis in Contemporary American Sociology: A Critique of the Discipline's Dominant Paradigm," in *A Critique of Contemporary American Sociology* (New York: General Hall, 1993), pp. 42–47.

3. It is now called *Critical Sociology.*

4. Berch Berberoglu, "Introduction," in *Critical Perspectives in Sociology,* ed. Berch Berberoglu (Dubuque, Iowa: Kendall/Hunt, 1991), p. xiv.

5. Ben Agger, *Critical Social Theories: An Introduction* (Boulder: Westview, 1998), p. 5.

6. "Some Comments About Project Censored and Sociology," personal communication from Carl Jensen, July 13, 1996, p. 1.

7. Ibid.

8. Ibid.

9. Carl Jensen and Project Censored, eds., *Censored: The News That Didn't Make the News and Why* (New York: Seven Stories Press, 1996), p. 35.

10. Project Censored, "Project Censored's Top 25 of 2007," httpJ/www.sonoma.edu/Project Censored/t2599.html (2007), p. 15.

11. Ibid., p. 1.

12. Ibid., p. 8.

13. Ibid., p. 8.

14. Jensen and Project Censored, eds., *Censored: the News That Didn't Make the News and Why,* p. 34.

15. Walter Cronkite, "Let the Chips Fall Where They May," in *Censored: The News That Didn't Make the News and Why,* p. 25.

16. Ibid., p. 27.

17. Peter Phillips, "Media Censorship and a Free Press in America," *Censored Alert* (newsletter), Director's Column, Spring 1998.

18. Quoted in Jensen and Project Censored, *Censored: The News That Didn't Make the News and Why,* p. 32.

19. Phillips, "Media Censorship and a Free Press in America."

20. Quoted in Frank E. Manuel and Fritzie P. Manuel, *Utopian Thought in the Western World* (Cambridge: Harvard University Press, 1979), p. 717.

21. Robert S. Lynd, *Knowledge for What?: The Place of Social Science in American Culture* (New York: Grove Press, 1964), p. 215.

22. William J. Wilson, *When Work Disappears: The World of the New Urban Poor* (New York: Knopf, 1996).

23. See Michel Foucault, *Power/Knowledge* (New York: Pantheon 1980), p. 98.

24. C. Wright Mills, *The Sociological Imagination* (New York: Oxford University Press, 1959), p. 7. Some liberation sociologists have paid a substantial price. C. Wright Mills, for example, never was promoted to the rank of full professor.

25. David L. Featherman and Robert M. Hauser, *Opportunity and Change* (New York: Academic Press, 1978).

26. Richard J. Herrnstein and Charles Murray, *The Bell Curve: Intelligence and Class Structure in American Life* (New York: Free Press, 1994); see Hernán Vera, Joe R. Feagin, and Andrew Gordon, "Superior Intellect? A Sincere Fiction of the White Self," *Journal of Negro Education* 64, 3 (Summer 1995): 295–306.

27. Alvin Gouldner, *The Coming Crisis of Western Sociology* (New York: Basic Books, 1970), p. 12.

28. Dorothy E. Smith, *The Everyday World as Problematic: A Feminist Sociology* (Boston: Northeastern University Press, 1987), p. 56.

29. Mills, *The Sociological Imagination,* p. 99.

30. Iris M. Young, *Justice and the Politics of Difference* (Princeton: Princeton University Press, 1990), pp. 38–39.

31. Ibid., p. 38.

32. Betty Friedan, *The Feminine Mystique* (New York: Dell, 1963), p. 306.

33. Ibid., p. 40.

34. Ibid., pp. 40–42.

35. Mary R. Jackman, *The Velvet Glove: Paternalism and Conflict in Gender, Class, and Race Relations* (Berkeley: University of California Press, 1994).

36. W.E.B. Du Bois, *The World and Africa* (New York: International Publishers, 1965 [1946]), p. 37.

37. For evidence on this, see Joe R. Feagin, *Racist America: Roots, Current Realities, and Future Reparations* (New York: Routledge, 2000).

38. See Gunnar Myrdal, *Objectivity in Social Research* (New York: Pantheon Books, 1969).

39. Paulo Freire, *Pedagogy of the Oppressed* (New York: Continuum, 1995), p. 26.

40. Antonio Gramsci, *Letters from Prison,* trans. Lynne Lawner (New York: Harper and Row, 1973), pp. 43–44, 183–185.

41. Walda Katz-Fishman and Jerome Scott, personal communication, November 2000; and http://www.wideopen.igc.org/projectsouth/indexl.html (retrieved Nov. 16, 2000).

42. Jerome W. Scott, personal communication, November 2000.

43. Ibid.

44. Ibid.

45. Ibid.

46. Walda Katz-Fishman, e-mail communication to authors, November 2000.

47. Ibid.

48. Ibid.

49. Philip Nyden, Anne Figert, Mark Shibley, and Darryl Burrows, "University-Community Collaborative Research: Adding Chairs at the Research Table," in *Building Community: Social Science in Action,* ed. Philip Nyden, Anne Figert, Mark Shibley, and Darryl Burrows (Thousand Oaks, Calif.: Pine Forge Press, 1997), p. 7.

50. Quoted in Sidney Liebes, Elisabet Sahtouris, and Brian Swimme, *A Walk Through Time: From Stardust to Us* (New York: Wiley, 1998), p. 204.

51. Translator's note in Freire, *Pedagogy of the Oppressed,* p. 17.

52. Freire, *Pedagogy of the Oppressed,* p. 19.

53. Ibid.

54. Sheldon S. Wolin, "Political Theory as a Vocation," *American Political Science Review* 63 (1969): 1080.

55. Karl Mannheim, *Ideology and Utopia* (New York: Harcourt, Brace and World, 1969), pp. 4–5.

56. W.E.B. Du Bois, "'To the World': Manifesto of the Second Pan-African Congress," in *W.E.B. Du Bois Pamphlets and Leaflets,* compiled by Herbert Aptheker (White Plains, N.Y.: Krauss-Thompson, 1986), as quoted by Leigh Binford, *The El Mozote Massacre* (Tucson: University of Arizona Press, 1996), p. 201.

57. Sandra Harding, "Introduction," in *The "Racial" Economy of Science: Toward a Democratic Future* (Bloomington: Indiana University Press, 1993), p. 18.

58. See Charles Lemert, *Sociology after the Crisis* (Boulder: Westview, 1995), pp. 117–118.

59. Ibid., p. 118.

60. For international human rights documents, see Department of Public Information, United Nations, *The United Nations and Human Rights, 1945–1995* (New York: United Nations, 1995), pp. 33–225.

61. Stan Bailey, e-mail communication, spring 1996.

62. See Bertell Ollman, *Alienation: Marx's Conception of Man in Capitalist Society,* 2nd ed. (Cambridge: Cambridge University Press, 1976), pp. 227–228.

63. Ibid., p. 16.

64. Chuck Collins, Chris Hartman, and Holly Sklar, *Divided Decade: Economic Disparity at the Century's Turn* (Boston: United for a Fair Economy, 1999); and Oxfam, "New Millennium: Two Futures," Oxfam Policy Papers, at http://ww.oxfam.org.uk/policy/papers (retrieved on December 30, 1999).

65. Frances F. Piven and Richard A. Cloward, *Regulating the Poor* (New York: Pantheon Books, 1971).

66. Gunnar Myrdal, *An American Dilemma* (New York: McGraw-Hill, [1944] 1964); and Leo Grebler, Joan W. Moore, and Ralph G. Guzman, *The Mexican-American People* (New York: Free Press, 1970).

67. See, for example, David A. Snow and Leon Anderson, *Down on Their Luck* (Berkeley: University of California Press, 1993).

68. Gouldner, *The Coming Crisis in Western Sociology,* p. 86.

69. Dorothy Ross, *The Origins of American Social Science* (New York: Cambridge University Press, 1991); see also Donald N. Levine, *Visions of the Sociological Tradition* (Chicago: University of Chicago Press, 1995), p. 79.

70. Levine, *Visions of the Sociological Tradition,* p. 80.

71. Harding, "Introduction," p. 17.

72. Henry A. Giroux, *Teachers as Intellectuals: Toward a Critical Pedagogy of Learning* (Granby, Mass.: Bergin and Garvey, 1988), pp. 40–45 and passim; and Abigail A. Fuller, "Academics and Social Transformation: The Radical Movement in Sociology, 1967–1975," Ph.D. dissertation, University of Colorado, Boulder, 1995, pp. 10–11.

73. Christopher G. A. Bryant, *Positivism in Social Theory and Research* (New York: St. Martin's Press, 1985), p. 133; on "abstracted empiricism," see Mills, *The Sociological Imagination,* chapter 3.

74. L. L. Bernard, "The Teaching of Sociology in the United States," *American Journal of Sociology* 15 (October 1909): 196. His italics. The sexist phrasing of this comment is particularly important given the fact that many of the early founders were women sociologists, most of whom were also progressive activists.

75. Fuller, "Academics and Social Transformation," p. 11.

76. On misunderstandings of physical science, see Paul Feyerabend, *Against Method* (London: Verson, 1975), p. 19.

77. Bryant, *Positivism in Social Theory and Research,* p. 142.

78. Wolin, "Political Theory as a Vocation," p. 1064.

79. Thomas Kuhn, *The Structure of Scientific Revolutions* (Chicago: University of Chicago Press, 1962), pp. 165–166.

80. Gouldner, *The Coming Crisis in Western Sociology,* p. 441.

81. Ben Agger, *Public Sociology: From Social Facts to Literary Acts,* 2nd ed. (Lanham, Md.: Rowman and Littlefield, 2007).

82. Michael Burawoy, "For Public Sociology," *American Sociological Review* 70 (February 2005): 4–28.

83. Ibid., pp. 9–11.

84. Agger, *Public Sociology,* p. 274. See also p. 269.

85. Burawoy, "For Public Sociology," p. 24,

86. Ibid., p. 25. See also pp. 21–24.

87. Mills, *The Sociological Imagination,* p. 187.

88. Smith, *The Everyday World as Problematic,* pp. 157–167.

89. Karl Marx, *The Eighteenth Brumaire of Louis Bonaparte,* in Karl Marx and Frederick Engels, *Selected Works* (London: Lawrence and Wishart, 1968), p. 97.

90. Mills, *The Sociological Imagination,* p. 181.

91. Quoted in Alfred M. Lee, *Sociology for the People: Toward a Caring Profession* (Syracuse: Syracuse University Press, 1988), p. 57.

Chapter 2

1. Peter Gay, *The Enlightenment: The Science of Freedom* (New York and London: W. W. Norton, 1977), p. 62.

2. Irving M. Zeitlin, *Ideology and the Development of Sociological Theory,* 6th ed. (Upper Saddle River, N.J.: Prentice-Hall, 1997), p. 4.

3. David Hume, *Treatise of Human Nature,* as quoted in Gay, *The Enlightenment,* p. 187.

4. Irving M. Zeitlin, *Ideology and the Development of Sociological Theory,* 7th ed. (Upper Saddle River, N.J.: Prentice-Hall, 2001), p. 48.

5. Max Horkheimer and Theodor W. Adorno, *Dialectic of Enlightenment* (New York: Continuum Publishing Company, 2000), p.3.

6. Gay, *The Enlightenment,* p. 555.

7. George Simpson, ed., *Auguste Comte: Sire of Sociology* (New York: Thomas Y. Crowell, 1969), p. 139.

8. Herbert Marcuse, *Reason and Revolution: Hegel and the Rise of Social Theory* (Boston: Beacon, 1968), p. 325.

9. Auguste Comte, "On the Three Stages of Social Evolution," in *Theories of Society: Foundations of Modern Sociological Theory,* ed. Talcott Parsons, Edward Shils, Kaspar D. Naegele, and Jesse R. Pitts (New York: Free Press, 1965), p. 1332; Auguste Comte, *The Positive Philosophy of Auguste Comte,* trans. and ed. Harriet Martineau (New York: AMS Press, 1974).

10. Leon Bramson, *The Political Context of Sociology* (Princeton: Princeton University Press, 1961), p. 12.

11. Ibid.

12. Zeitlin, *Ideology and the Development of Sociological Theory,* 7th ed., pp. 64–70.

13. See K. Thompson, *Auguste Comte: The Foundations of Sociology* (London: Nelson, 1976); and David Jary and Julia Jary, *Dictionary of Sociology* (New York: HarperCollins, 1991), pp. 73–75.

14. Peter Halfpenny, *Positivism and Sociology: Explaining Social Life* (London: George Allen and Unwin, 1982), p. 20.

15. See Comte, *The Positive Philosophy of Auguste Comte.*

16. Harriet Martineau, *Society in America,* 3 vols. (New York: Saunders and Otley, 1837); see also Patricia M. Lengermann and Jill Niebrugge-Brantley, "Harriet Martineau (1802–1876): The Beginnings of a Science of Society," in *The Women Founders: Sociology and Social Theory, 1830–1930,* ed. Patricia M. Lengermann and Jill Niebrugge-Brantley (Boston: McGraw-Hill, 1998), pp. 23–45.

17. Harriet Martineau, *How to Observe Morals and Manners* (New Brunswick, N.J.: Transaction Publishers, [1838] 1989), p. 73; see also Michael R. Hill, "Empiricism and Reason in Harriet Martineau's Sociology," in Harriet Martineau, *How to Observe Morals and Manners* (New Brunswick, N.J.: Transaction Publishers, 1989), pp. xv–lx.

18. Talcott Parsons, *The Structure of Social Action: A Study in Social Theory with Special Reference to a Group of Recent European Writers* (New York: Free Press, [1937] 1949), pp. 591–601.

19. Wilhelm Hennis, "The Meaning of 'Werfreiheit': On the Background and Motives of Max Weber's 'Postulate,'" *Sociological Theory* 12 (1994): 113–125.

20. Max Weber, as quoted in ibid., p. 116.

21. Max Weber, *The Methodology of Social Sciences,* trans. and ed. Edward A. Shils and Henry A. Finch (Glencoe, Ill.: Free Press, 1949), p. 72.

22. Max Weber, as quoted in Hennis, "The Meaning of 'Werfreiheit,'" p. 119.

23. Max Weber, as quoted in Ahmad Sadri, *Max Weber's Sociology of Intellectuals* (New York: Oxford University Press, 1992), p. 14.

24. Sadri, Max *Weber's Sociology of Intellectuals,* p. 16.

25. Max Weber, as quoted in ibid.

26. Max Weber, as quoted in ibid., p. 17.

27. Ibid., p. 18.

28. Gunnar Myrdal, *An American Dilemma* (New York: McGraw-Hill, [1944] 1964), vol. 2, p. 1052.

29. Ibid., p. 1057.

30. Gunnar Myrdal, *Objectivity in Social Research* (New York: Pantheon, 1969), p. 5.

31. Robert A. Jones, "The Positive Science of Ethics in France: German Influences on *De la division du travail social,*" *Sociological Forum* 9 (1994): 37–58.

32. Emile Durkheim, *The Elementary Forms of the Religious Life,* trans. Joseph W. Swain (London: Allen and Unwin, 1915).

33. Emile Durkheim, *Journal Sociologique* (Paris: Presses Universitaires de France, 1969), p. 161.

34. Ibid. Our italics.

35. Ibid.

36. Emile Durkheim, *The Division of Labor in Society* (New York: Free Press, 1933), p. 374.

37. Ibid., p. 379. Also, Emile Durkheim, *Professional Ethics and Civic Morals* (London: Routledge, [1957] 1992), p. 213.

38. Durkheim, *The Division of Labor in Society,* p. 384.

39. Ibid., p. 388.

40. Parsons, *The Structure of Social Action,* pp. 317–322; see also Talcott Parsons, *The Social System* (Glencoe, Ill.: Free Press, 1951).

41. Nicholas Timasheff, *Sociological Theory: Its Nature and Growth* (New York: Random House, 1967).

42. Don Martindale, *The Nature and Types of Sociological Theory* (Boston: Houghton Mifflin, 1960).

43. Georges Gurvitch, *Dialectique et Sociologie* (Paris: Flammarion, 1962), pp. 180–181.

44. Bertell Oilman, *Alienation: Marx's Conception of Man in Capitalist Society,* 2nd ed. (Cambridge: Cambridge University Press, 1976), p. 18.

45. Ibid., pp. 16–29.

46. C. Wright Mills, *The Sociological Imagination* (New York: Oxford University Press, 1959), p. 57.

47. See Mary Jo Deegan, *Jane Addams and the Men of the Chicago School, 1892–1918* (New Brunswick, N.J.: Transaction Books, 1988), pp. 106–107.

48. George Herbert Mead, *Mind, Self, and Society,* ed. Charles W. Morris (Chicago: University of Chicago Press, 1934), p. xxv.

49. Zeitlin, *Ideology and the Development of Sociological Theory,* 7th ed., pp. 427–428.

50. Ibid., p. 431.

51. Gideon Sjoberg and Ted R. Vaughan, "The Ethical Foundation of Sociology and the Necessity for a Human Rights Perspective," in *A Critique of Contemporary American Sociology,* ed. Ted R. Vaughan, Gideon Sjoberg, and Larry T. Reynolds (New York: General Hall, 1993), p. 135.

52. Deegan, *Jane Addams and the Men of the Chicago School,* pp. 107–111.

53. Ibid., pp. 110–118.

54. Barbara Finlay, "Lester Frank Ward as a Sociologist of Gender," *Gender and Society* 13 (April 1999): 251–257.

55. Lester F. Ward, *Pure Sociology,* 2nd ed. (London: Macmillan, [1903] 1914), p. 364.

56. Finlay, "Lester Frank Ward as a Sociologist of Gender," pp. 258–261.

57. Thomas Kuhn, *The Structure of Scientific Revolutions* (Chicago: University of Chicago Press, 1962).

58. George Ritzer, *Sociology: A Multiple Paradigm Science* (Boston: Allyn and Bacon, 1975), p. 7.

59. Kuhn, *The Structure of Scientific Revolutions,* pp. 165–166.

60. Niels H. D. Bohr, *Essays, 1958–1962: On Atomic Physics and Human Knowledge* (New York: Interscience Publishers, 1963), p. 1.

61. Ibid., p. 2.

62. Ibid.

63. Ibid.

64. Ibid., p. 4.

Chapter 3

1. Herman Schwendinger and Julia Schwendinger, *The Sociologists of the Chair: A Radical Analysis of the Formative Years of North American Sociology (1883–1922)* (New York: Basic Books, 1974), p. xix.

2. Stephen P. Turner and Jonathan H. Turner, *The Impossible Science: An Institutional Analysis of American Sociology* (Newbury Park, Calif.: Sage, 1990), p. 13.

3. Robert W. Friedrichs, A *Sociology of Sociology* (New York: Free Press, 1970), p. 73.

4. Ibid., pp. 72–73.

5. In criticizing capitalists' exploitation of Chinese laborers, Ross took a racist perspective on Chinese immigration to California. Schwendinger and Schwendinger, *The Sociologists of the Chair,* pp. 494–496.

6. Lester Ward, as quoted in Jay Rumney and Joseph Maier, *Sociology: The Science of Society* (New York: Henry Schuman, 1953), p. 167.

7. Lester F. Ward, as quoted in Schwendinger and Schwendinger, *The Sociologists of the Chair,* p. 420.

8. Mary Jo Deegan, "An American Dream: The Historical Connections Between Women, Humanism, and Sociology, 1890–1920," *Humanity and Society* 11 (August 1987): 353–365.

9. Mary Jo Deegan, "'Dear Love, Dear Love': Feminist Pragmatism and the Chicago Female World of Love and Ritual," *Gender and Society* 10 (October 1996): 590–591.

10. Mary Jo Deegan, "Gender at Hull House and the University of Chicago: The Origins and Influence of Feminist Pragmatism, 1889–2008," University of Nebraska, unpublished research manuscript, 2007.

11. Mary Jo Deegan, *Jane Addams and the Men of the Chicago School, 1892–1918* (New Brunswick, N.J.: Transaction Books, 1988), pp. 33–35.

12. Mary Jo Deegan, "A New Conscience Against Ancient Evils: The Theory and Praxis of Race Relations in Chicago, 1892–1960," University of Nebraska (Lincoln), unpublished research manuscript, 2000, p. 66.

13. Deegan, "'Dear Love, Dear Love,'" p. 592.

14. Alfred McClung Lee, "Steps Taken Toward Liberating Sociologists," in *Radical Sociologists and the Movement: Experiences, Lessons, and Legacies* (Philadelphia: Temple University Press, 1991), pp. 28–29.

15. Schwendinger and Schwendinger, *The Sociologists of the Chair,* p. 421.

16. Mary Jo Deegan, "Early Women Sociologists and the American Sociological Society: The Patterns of Exclusion and Participation," *American Sociologist* 16 (February 1981): 14–16.

17. Patricia M. Lengermann and Jill Niebrugge-Brantley, "Jane Addams (1860–1935): Ethics and Society," in *The Women Founders: Sociology and Social Theory, 1830–1930,* ed. Patricia M. Lengermann and Jill Niebrugge-Brantley (Boston: McGraw-Hill, 1998), pp. 66–72; Deegan, *Jane Addams,* pp. 42–44.

18. Jane Addams, *Democracy and Social Ethics* (New York: Macmillan, 1902), p. 6.

19. Deegan, *Jane Addams and the Men of the Chicago School,* p. 304.

20. Ibid., p. 304.

21. Addams did reject a Marxist class conflict model, preferring to accent human cooperation as seen from a pragmatic-feminist point of view.

22. Residents of Hull House, *Hull House Maps and Papers, by Residents of Hull House, a Social Settlement* (New York: Arno Press, [1895] 1970); and Mary Jo Deegan, personal communication, July 21, 2000.

23. Deegan, *Jane Addams,* p. 47.

24. Ibid., pp. 44–64.

25. Jane Addams, as quoted in Schwendinger and Schwendinger, *The Sociologists of the Chair,* p. 474.

26. Ibid., p. 475.

27. William E. B. Du Bois, *The Philadelphia Negro: A Social Study* (Millwood, N.Y.: Kraus-Thomson, [1899] 1973).

28. Turner and Turner, *The Impossible Science,* p. 15.

29. See Mary Jo Deegan, "W.E.B. Du Bois and the Women of Hull-House, 1895–1899," *American Sociologist* 19 (Winter 1988): 304–308.

30. W.E.B. Du Bois, *Some Notes on Negroes in New York City* (Atlanta, 1905), as quoted in Adolph L. Reed Jr., *W.E.B. Du Bois and American Political Thought: Fabianism and the Color Line* (Oxford: Oxford University Press, 1997), p. 44.

31. Reed, *W.E.B. Du Bois and American Political Thought,* p. 49. Reed describes Du Bois as a "positivist" social scientist, but he is using this term in the sense of a researcher who accents finding social laws, not in the detached instrumental-positivist sense we accent in this book.

32. W.E.B. Du Bois, *Dusk of Dawn: An Essay Toward an Autobiography of a Race Concept* (New Brunswick, N.J.: Transaction Books, [1940] 1984), p. 62.

33. Ibid., p. 93; Schwendinger and Schwendinger, *The Sociologists of the Chair,* p. 506.

34. Du Bois, *The Philadelphia Negro,* p. 394.

35. W.E.B. Du Bois, *Black Reconstruction in America, 1860–1880* (New York: Atheneum, [1935] 1992), p. 30.

36. W.E.B. Du Bois, *Darkwater* (1920), as reprinted in *The Oxford W.E.B. Du Bois Reader,* ed. Eric J. Sundquist (New York: Oxford, 1996), pp. 497–498.

37. Du Bois, *Dusk of Dawn,* p. 6.

38. Du Bois, *Darkwater* (1920), as reprinted in *The Oxford W.E.B. Du Bois Reader,* p. 504.

39. W.E.B. Du Bois, *The World and Africa* (New York: International Publishers, [1946] 1965), p. 37.

40. Ibid., p. 23.

41. Du Bois, *Darkwater* (1920), as reprinted in *The Oxford W.E.B. Du Bois Reader,* p. 504.

42. Du Bois, *Black Reconstruction in America, 1860–1880,* p. 10.

43. Manning Marable, *W.E.B. Du Bois: Black Radical Democrat* (Boston: Twayne, 1986), pp. 100–102.

44. See Patricia Madoo Lengermann and Jill Niebrugge-Brantley, *The Women Founders: Sociology and Social Theory, 1830–1930* (New York: McGraw-Hill, 1998).

45. Ida B. Wells-Barnett, as quoted in ibid., p. 163. We draw here on pp. 150–165.

46. Ibid., pp. 154–165.

47. Ida B. Wells-Barnett, A *Red Record* (Chicago: Donohue and Henneberry, 1895); Anna Julia Cooper, A *Voice from the South by a Black Woman from the South* (Xenia, Ohio: Aldine Press, 1892).

48. Earl Wright II, "Deferred Legacy! The Continued Marginalization of the Atlanta Sociological Laboratory," *Sociology Compass* (OnlineEarly Articles), http://www.blackwell-synergy.com/toc/soco/0/0?cookieSet=1 (retrieved December 2, 2007).

49. Ibid.

50. L. L. Bernard, "The Teaching of Sociology in the United States," *American Journal of Sociology* 15 (October 1909): 164–231.

51. For a listing, see Andrew Abbott, *Department and Discipline: Chicago Sociology at One Hundred* (Chicago: University of Chicago Press, 1999), p. 199.

52. Robert E. Park, quoted in Winifred Raushenbush, Robert E. Park: *Biography of a Sociologist* (Durham, N.C.: Duke University Press, 1979), p. 34.

53. Ibid., p. 41.

54. Robert E. Park, as quoted in ibid., p. 49.

55. Robert E. Park, as quoted in ibid., p. 50.

56. Robert E. Park, as quoted in ibid., pp. 49–50.

57. Robert E. Park, "Education in Its Relation to the Conflict and Fusion of Cultures: With Special Reference to the Problems of the Immigrant, the Negro, and Missions," *Publications of the American Sociological Society* 13: 38–63. See also Robert E. Park, *Race and Culture* (New York: Free Press, 1950), p. 387.

58. Raushenbush, *Robert E. Park,* pp. 67–84.

59. E. Franklin Frazier, as quoted in Deegan, "A New Conscience Against Ancient Evils," p. 191. We draw here on Deegan's summary of the events.

60. Ibid., pp. 188–195.

61. Valora Washington and William Harvey, *Affirmative Rhetoric, Negative Action* (Washington, D.C.: George Washington University, 1989), p. 6.

62. Robert E. Park and Ernest W. Burgess, *Introduction to the Science of Sociology* (Chicago: University of Chicago Press, 1921).

63. See Schwendinger and Schwendinger, *The Sociologists of the Chair,* pp. 388–410.

64. Stuart A. Queen and Delbert M. Mann, *Social Pathology* (New York: Thomas Y. Crowell, 1925).

65. Turner and Turner, *The Impossible Science,* pp. 46–51.

66. Raushenbush, *Robert E. Park,* p. 97.

67. Harold Gosnell, as quoted in Raushenbush, *Robert E. Park,* p. 98.

68. Abbott, *Department and Discipline,* p. 196.

69. See, for example, Joe R. Feagin, *Racist America: Roots, Current Realities, and Future Reparations* (New York: Routledge, 2000).

70. Oliver C. Cox, *Race Relations: Elements and Social Dynamics* (New York: Philosophical Library, 1976), p. 277.

71. Ibid., p. 474.

72. Ibid., p. xi.

73. Ibid., p. 22.

74. Oliver C. Cox, *Caste, Class, and Race* (Garden City, N.Y.: Doubleday, 1948), p. x.

75. Ibid., p. xvi.

76. Oliver Cromwell Cox, *The Foundations of Capitalism* (New York: Philosophical Library, 1959), p. 2.

77. Cox, *Caste, Class, and Race,* p. 462.

78. Cox, *Race Relations,* p. 21.

79. Oliver Cromwell Cox, *Capitalism and American Leadership* (New York: Philosophical Library), p. 288.

80. Bernard, "The Teaching of Sociology in the United States," p. 196.

81. See Paul F. Lazarsfeld and Morris Rosenberg, "Introduction," to Section 5, in *The Language of Social Research,* ed. Paul F. Lazarsfeld and Morris Rosenberg (New York: Free Press, 1955), pp. 389–390.

82. Abbott, *Department and Discipline,* pp. 210–211.

83. Lazarsfeld and Rosenberg, *The Language of Social Research,* pp. 15–17.

84. Ibid., p. 111.

85. Ibid. They note that this is a "somewhat facetious" way of putting the matter.

86. Arthur J. Vidich and Stanford M. Lyman, *American Sociology: Worldly Rejections of Religion and Their Directions* (New Haven: Yale University Press, 1985), p. 138.

87. Ibid., p. 145.

88. Jennifer Platt, "Research Methods and the Second Chicago School," in *A Second Chicago School: The Development of Postwar American Sociology,* ed. Gary A. Fine (Chicago: University of Chicago Press, 1995), pp. 82–107.

89. Roger C. Bannister, "Principle, Politics, Profession: American Sociologists and Fascism," in *Sociology Responds to Fascism,* ed. Stephen P. Turner and Dirk Kasler (London: Routledge, 1992), p. 189.

90. Ibid., pp. 290–291.

91. George Lundberg, *Can Science Save Us?* (New York: Longmans, Green, 1947), pp. 47–48.

92. Bannister, "Principle, Politics, Profession: American Sociologists and Fascism," p. 175.

93. Ibid., p. 205.

94. Gardner Murphy, "The Research Task of Social Psychology," presidential address to the Society for Psychological Study of Social Issues, 1938, as cited in Robert S. Lynd, *Knowledge for What? The Place of Social Science in American Culture* (New York: Grove Press, [1939] 1964), p. 18.

95. Lynd, *Knowledge for What?* p. 18.

96. Ibid., p. 18.

97. Ibid., p. 181.

98. Ibid., p. 215.

99. Ibid., p. 19.

100. Ibid., pp. 220–221.

101. Gunnar Myrdal, An *American Dilemma* (New York: McGraw-Hill, [1944] 1964), vol. 2, p. 1052.

102. Ibid., p. 1057.

103. Turner and Turner, *The Impossible Science,* pp. 109–128.

104. Ibid., pp. 134–135.

105. "National Support for Behavioral Science," pamphlet, Washington, D.C., February 1958, as reprinted in Friedrichs, *A Sociology of Sociology,* p. 88.

106. Ibid., pp. 87–89.

107. Abigail A. Fuller, "Academics and Social Transformation: The Radical Movement in Sociology, 1967–1975," Ph.D. dissertation, University of Colorado, Boulder, 1995, p. 42.

108. Turner and Turner, *The Impossible Science,* pp. 134–135.

109. See Gideon Sjoberg and Ted Vaughan, "The Bureaucratization of Sociology: Its Impact on Theory and Research," in *A Critique of Contemporary American Sociology,* ed. Ted R. Vaughan, Gideon Sjoberg, and Larry T. Reynolds (Dix Hills, N.Y. : General Hall, 1993), pp. 60–65.

110. See David L. Featherman and Robert M. Hauser, *Opportunity and Change* (New York: Academic Press, 1978).

111. J. David Knottnerus, "The Rise of the Wisconsin School of Status Attainment," in *A Critique of Contemporary American Sociology,* pp. 252–268.

112. C. Wright Mills, *The Sociological Imagination* (New York: Oxford University Press, 1959), pp. 91–92.

113. T. R. Young, e-mail communication, Progressive Sociologists Network (PSN), May 1996.

114. Turner and Turner, *The Impossible Science,* pp. 140–141,184.

115. Dick Flacks, "The Sociology Liberation Movement: Some Legacies and Lessons," in *Radical Sociologists and the Movement: Experiences, Lessons, and Legacies,* ed. Martin Oppenheimer, Martin J. Murray, and Rhonda Levine (Philadelphia: Temple University Press, 1991), pp. 18–25.

116. Friedrichs, *A Sociology of Sociology,* p. 108.

117. Reinhard Bendix, as quoted in Friedrichs, *A Sociology of Sociology,* p. 109.

118. Ben Agger, *Reading Science: A Literary, Political, and Sociological Analysis* (Dix Hills, N.Y.: General Hall, 1989), pp. 182–193.

119. George Lakoff, *Women, Fire, and Dangerous Things: What Categories Reveal About the Mind* (Chicago: University of Chicago Press, 1987), pp. 383–385.

120. Naomi Quinn, "The Cultural Basis of Metaphor," in *Beyond Metaphor: The Theory of Tropes in Anthropology,* ed. James Fernandez (Stanford: Stanford University Press, 1991), pp. 65–66.

121. Ian Craib, *Modern Social Theory: From Parsons to Habermas,* 2nd ed. (New York: St. Martin's, 1992), p. 39. His italics.

122. Kingsley Davis, "The Myths of Functional Analysis in Sociology and Anthropology," *American Sociological Review* 24 (1959): 757–773.

123. Alvin Gouldner, *The Coming Crisis of Western Sociology (New* York: Basic Books, 1970), p. 373.

124. Ibid., p. 86.

125. Talcott Parsons, *The Structure of Social Action* (New York: Free Press, [1937] 1949).

126. See Joe R. Feagin and Clairece B. Feagin, *Social Problems: A Critical Power-Conflict Perspective* (Upper Saddle River, N.J.: Prentice-Hall, 1997), p. 16.

127. Talcott Parsons, "Full Citizenship for the Negro American? A Sociological Problem," in *The Negro American,* ed. Talcott Parsons and Kenneth B. Clark (Boston: Houghton Mifflin, 1965–1966), p. 739.

128. U.S. Department of the Interior, *Public Land Statistics, 1961* (Washington, D.C.: Government Printing Office, 1961), Appendix, Table 22.

129. Trina Williams, "The Homestead Act: Our Earliest National Asset Policy," paper presented at the Center for Social Development's symposium, Inclusion in Asset Building, St. Louis, Missouri, September 21–23, 2000.

130. Craib, *Modern Social Theory,* pp. 53–54. We are indebted to T. R. Young for some insights here.

131. Gouldner, *The Coming Crisis of Western Sociology,* p. 410.

132. Lee, "Steps Taken Toward Liberating Sociologists," p. 36.

133. Ibid., p. 39.

134. Alfred M. Lee, *Sociology for Whom?* (New York: Oxford University Press, 1978), p. 216.

135. Ibid., p. 216.

Chapter 4

1. See Donald N. Levine, *Visions of the Sociological Tradition* (Chicago: University of Chicago Press, 1995), pp. 284–289.

2. See Stephen P. Turner and Jonathan H. Turner, *The Impossible Science: An Institutional Analysis of American Sociology* (Newbury Park, Calif.: Sage, 1990), pp. 140–141.

3. American Sociological Association, *The Health of Sociology (*Washington, D. C. : American Sociological Association, 2007); earlier data were calculated by American Sociological Association staff from 1992, 1995, and 1998 editions of the *Survey* of *Graduate Departments* of Sociology (Washington, D.C.: American

Sociological Association) and from National Science Foundation data. We are indebted to Roberta Spalter-Roth for assistance.

4. See Turner and Turner, *The Impossible Science,* pp. 194–196 and passim.

5. See Levine, *Visions of the Sociological Tradition,* pp. 289–290.

6. Irving L. Horowitz, "Searching for Enemies: Sociological Theories at the End of the 20th Century," *Society* (November 1995): 42.

7. Ibid.

8. On issues of racism, see, for example, Joe R. Feagin, *Racist America: Roots, Current Realities, and Future Reparations* (New York: Routledge, 2000).

9. Peter M. Blau, "Reflections on the Future of Social Problems Theory," *SSSP Social Problems Theory Division Newsletter* 4 (Summer 1975): 3, as quoted in Alfred M. Lee, *Sociology for Whom? (New* York: Oxford University Press, 1978), p. 82.

10. Lee, *Sociology for Whom?* p. 83.

11. American Sociological Association, "Trend Data on the Profession," http://www.asanet.org/cs/root/leftnav/research_and_stats/profession_trend_data/trend_data_on_the_profession (retrieved November 16, 2007). Earlier data are from tabulations by American Sociological Association staff and are from National Science Foundation, *Science and Engineering Degrees: 1966–1997* (Washington, D.C.: U.S. Government Printing Office, 1997), Tables 26,35, and 49–54.

12. American Sociological Association, "Trend Data on the Profession," http://www.asanet.org/cs/root/leftnav/research_and_stats/profession_trend_data/trend_data_on_the_profession (retrieved November 16, 2007).

13. American Sociological Association, "Trend Data on the Profession," http://www.asanet.org/cs/root/leftnav/research_and_stats/profession_trend_data/trend_data_on_the_profession (retrieved November 16, 2007); Roberta Spalter-Roth, Felice J. Levine, and Andrew Sutter, "Research Brief: The Pipeline for Faculty of Color in Sociology," *Footnotes,* newsletter of the American Sociological Association, April 1999.

14. Claire M. Renzetti, "All Things to All People or Nothing for Some: Justice, Diversity, and Democracy in Sociological Societies," *Social Problems* 54 (2007): 161–169.

15. Patricia Hill Collins, *Black Feminist Thought: Knowledge, Consciousness, and the Politics of Empowerment* (Boston: Unwin Hyman, 1990), p. 67.

16. Lee, *Sociology for Whom?* p. 80.

17. Michael R. Hill, "Epistemology, Axiology, and Ideology in Sociology," *Mid-American Review of Sociology* 9 (1984): 59–77; G. Radnitzky, *Contemporary Schools of Metascience,* 3rd ed. (Chicago: Henry Regnery, 1973), pp. xii–xiii.

18. See Gideon Sjoberg, "Reflective Methodology: The Foundations of Social Inquiry," introduction to A *Methodology for Social Research,* by Gideon Sjoberg and Roger Nett (Prospect Heights, Ill.: Waveland Press, 1997), p. xxii.

19. Jaber F. Gubrium and James A. Holstein, *The New Language of Qualitative Method* (New York: Oxford University Press, 1997), p. 5.

20. Ibid., pp. 5–6.

21. Michel Foucault, "The Discourse on Language," appendix in *The Archeology of Knowledge* (New York: Harper and Row, 1972), pp. 222–223.

22. Alvin W. Gouldner, *The Coming Crisis of Western Sociology* (New York: Basic Books, 1970), p. 41.

23. Turner and Turner, *The Impossible Science,* pp. 188–191.

24. Historically, well-funded social scientists have played a role in papering over severe problems of economic, gender, and class inequality with technical methods they proclaim to be the panaceas for social understanding. See, for example, this well-funded book: Richard J. Herrnstein and Charles Murray, *The Bell Curve: Intelligence and Class Structure in American Life* (New York: Free Press, 1994).

25. See William Alonso and Paul Starr, eds., *The Politics of Numbers* (New York: Russell Sage, 1987); Travis Hirschi, "Administrative Criminology," *Contemporary Sociology* 22 (1993): 348–350.

26. Albert J. Meehan, "The Organizational Career of Gang Statistics: The Politics of Policing Gangs," *Sociological Quarterly* 41 (2000): 364.

27. William J. Chambliss, *Power, Politics, and Crime* (Boulder: Westview, 1999), p. 35.

28. Paul Feyerabend, *Against Method* (London: Verson, 1975), p. 19.

29. Ben Agger, *Public Sociology: From Social Facts to Literary Acts,* 2nd ed. (Lanham, Md.: Rowman and Littlefield, 2007).

30. This happened to Joe Feagin when he was finally able to get a qualitative data article accepted by the *American Sociological Review* in the 1990s. The article dealt with data from in-depth interviews with African Americans on experiences with discrimination in public places. In an arduous cycle of reviews, the very quantitatively oriented *ASR* editor pressured the author to include a quantitative data table in the article as a condition for publication.

31. See Ben Agger, *Reading Science: A Literary, Political, and Sociological Analysis* (Dix Hills, N.Y.: General Hall, 1989).

32. John J. Macionis, *Sociology,* 12th ed. (Upper Saddle River, N.J.: Prentice-Hall, 2008); see also Diana Kendall, *Sociology* in Our *Times,* 2nd ed. (Belmont, Calif.: Wadsworth, 1999).

33. Levine, *Visions of the Sociological Tradition,* p. 81.

34. Edward Shils, *The Calling of Sociology and Other Essays on the Pursuit of Learning* (Chicago: University of Chicago Press, 1980), p. 15.

35. Ivan van Illich, *Disabling Professions* (London: M. Boyars Publishers, 1977).

36. Robert Blauner and David Wellman, "Toward the Decolonization of Social Research," in *The Death of White Sociology: Essays on Race and Culture,* ed. Joyce Ladner (Baltimore, Md.: Black Classic Press, [1973] 1998), p. 315.

37. Ben Agger, *Critical Social Theories: An Introduction* (Boulder: Westview, 1998), p. 4.

38. Richard Centers, *The Psychology of Social Classes: A Study of Class Consciousness* (Princeton: Princeton University Press, 1949). This study was done on what at the time was considered a nationally "representative" sample—1,097 white men.

39. Rich Fantasia, "From Class Consciousness to Culture, Action and Social Organization," *Annual Review of Sociology* 21 (1995): 270.

40. Ibid., p. 271.

41. Sjoberg, "Reflective Methodology," p. xxiv.

42. See George Marshall, "Some Remarks on the Study of Working Class Consciousness," *Politics and Society* 12 (1983): 263–301.

43. Fantasia, "From Class Consciousness to Culture, Action, and Social Organization," p. 270.

44. Ibid., p. 271.

45. See "Marx's Enquête Ouvrière," in *Karl Marx: Selected Writings in Sociology and Social Philosophy,* trans. and ed. Tom Bottomore and Maximillien Rubel (New York: McGraw-Hill, 1956), pp. 203–212.

46. Ibid., p. 203.

47. Ibid., p. 208.

48. Fantasia, "From Class Consciousness to Culture, Action, and Social Organization," p. 273.

49. C. Wright Mills, *The Sociological Imagination* (New York: Oxford University Press, 1959), p. 85.

50. Ted R. Vaughan, "The Crisis in Contemporary American Sociology: A Critique of the Discipline's Dominant Paradigm," in *A Critique of Contemporary American Sociology,* ed. Ted R. Vaughan, Gideon Sjoberg, and Larry Reynolds (Dix Hills, N.Y.: General Hall, 1993), pp. 10–53.

51. Kai Erikson, "Sociology and Contemporary Events," in *Conflict and Consensus: A Festschrift in Honor of Lewis A. Coser,* ed. Walter W. Powell and Richard Robbins (New York: Free Press, 1984), p. 306. Note, too, that this critique is in a book, not a journal article!

52. Patricia Wilner, "The Main Drift of Sociology Between 1936 and 1984," *Journal of the History of Sociology* 5 (1985): 1–20.

53. Walter Powell, "From the Editor's Desk," *Contemporary Sociology* 23 (November 1994): v–vi.

54. We are indebted here to comments from Diana Kendall.

55. Macionis, *Sociology,* p. 17.

56. Ibid., p. 19.

57. Ian Craib, *Modern Social Theory: From Parsons to Habermas,* 2nd ed. (New York: St. Martin's, 1992), p. 37.

58. Macionis, *Sociology,* p. 20.

59. See, for example, Diana Kendall, *Sociology in Our Times,* 2nd ed. (Belmont, Calif.: Wadsworth, 1999), pp. 13–17. We also draw here on personal communication with the author. See also John J. Macionis, *Sociology,* 12th ed. (Upper Saddle River, N.J.: Prentice-Hall, 2008).

60. Sjoberg, "Reflective Methodology," p. xviii.

61. Karl Marx, "Letters from the *Franco-German Yearbooks,*" in *Early Writings [of] Marx,* trans. R. Livingstone and G. Benton (London: Penguin Books, [1843] 1975), p. 209.

62. Gubrium and Holstein, *The New Language of Qualitative Method,* p. 115.

63. Michael Burawoy et al., *Ethnography Unbound: Power and Resistance in the Modern Metropolis* (Berkeley: University of California Press, 1991), pp. 271–287.

64. See W.E.B. Du Bois, *The Souls of Black Folk* (New York: Bantam Books, [1903] 1989); Jane Addams, "Charity and Social Justice," *Survey* 24 (June 11, 1910): 441–449; Jane Addams, *Newer Ideas of Peace* (New York: Macmillan, 1907); and Charlotte Perkins Gilman, *Women and Economics: A Study of the Economic Relation Between Men and Women as a Factory in Social Evolution* (Boston: Small, Maynard, 1898).

65. This was the experience of the authors in several research studies of African Americans, in which respondents were allowed to wander from the open-ended

interview schedules used to initiate discussions. See Joe R. Feagin and Melvin Sikes, *Living with Racism: The Black Middle-Class Experience* (Boston: Beacon, 1994); and Joe R. Feagin, Hernán Vera, and Nikitah Imani, *The Agony of Education* (New York: Routledge, 1996).

66. Charles Harrison, Acting Provost of the University of Pennsylvania, as quoted in David L. Lewis, *W.E.B. Du Bois: Biography of a Race* (New York: Henry Holt, 1993), p. 188. See also pp. 187–189.

67. Lewis, *W.E.B. Du Bois,* pp. 190–210; W.E.B. Du Bois, *The Philadelphia Negro* (Millwood, N.Y.; Kraus-Thomson, [1899] 1973).

68. Du Bois, *The Philadelphia Negro,* p. 394. Italics added.

69. Ibid. Italics added.

70. See, for example, Amitai Etzioni, *The Moral Dimension* (New York: Free Press, 1988); Dorothy E. Smith, *The Conceptual Process of Power* (Boston: Northeastern University Press, 1990); and Immanuel Wallerstein, *After Liberalism* (New York: New Press, 1995).

71. Hill, "Epistemology, Axiology, and Ideology in Sociology," p. 69.

72. Gideon Sjoberg and Ted Vaughan, "The Ethical Foundations of Sociology and the Necessity for a Human Rights Perspective," in *A Critique of Contemporary American Sociology,* ed. Ted R. Vaughan, Gideon Sjoberg, and Larry Reynolds (Dix Hills, N.Y.: General Hall, 1993), pp. 114–159.

73. G. William Domhoff, *Who Rules America?* (Englewood Cliffs, N.J.: Prentice-Hall, 1967); G. William Domhoff, *The Power Elite and the State: How Policy Is Made in America* (New York: Aldine, 1990; see also Joe R. Feagin, *Free Enterprise City: Houston in Political-Economic Perspective* (New Brunswick, N.J.: Rutgers University Press, 1988).

Chapter 5

1. Robert Blauner and David Wellman, "Toward the Decolonization of Social Research," in *The Death of White Sociology: Essays on Race and Culture,* ed. Joyce Ladner (Baltimore, Md.: Black Classic Press, [1973] 1998), pp. 310.

2. "What Do We Do?" http://www.industrialareasfoundation.org/iafabout/aboutwhat.htm (retrieved November 16, 2007).

3. Donald C. Reitzes and Dietrich C. Reitzes, *The Alinsky Legacy: Alive and Kicking* (Greenwich, Conn.: JAI Press, 1987), p. 2.

4. Saul D. Alinsky, *Reveille for Radicals* (Chicago: University of Chicago Press, 1946), p. 76.

5. Quoted in Bernard Doering, *The Philosopher and the Provocateur: The Correspondence of Jacques Maritain and Saul Alinsky* (Notre Dame, Ind.: University of Notre Dame Press, 1994), p. 18.

6. Hernán Vera and Michael Francis, "A Totalitarianism in Latin America: Chile's New Military Messiahs," *Third World Review* 3 (Spring 1977): 20–30.

7. Charles E. Curran, *Directions in Catholic Social Ethics* (Notre Dame, Ind.: Notre Dame University Press, 1985), p. 155.

8. Lawrence J. Engel, "The Influence of Saul Alinsky on the Campaign for Human Development," *Theological Studies* 59 (December 1998): 636; "Breaking the Cycle of Poverty," http://www.usccb.org/cchd (retrieved November 18, 2007).

9. Reitzes and Reitzes, *The Alinsky Legacy,* p. 207.

10. Cesar Chavez interview, June 19, 1984, as quoted in Reitzes and Reitzes, *The Alinsky Legacy,* p. 225.

11. Ernesto Cortes, "Reweaving the Social Fabric," at http://www.tresser.com/ernesto.htm, 2000, p. 1.

12. See Harry C. Boyte, *Community Is Possible* (New York: Harper and Row, 1984), pp. 137–159. We draw on Stella Capek and Joe R. Feagin, "Grassroots Movements in a Class Perspective," in *Research in Political Sociology,* ed. P. C. Wasburn (Greenwich, Conn.: JAI Press, 1989), pp. 27–53.

13. Mark R. Warren, "Creating a Multi-Racial Democratic Community: A Case Study of the Texas Industrial Areas Foundation," http://www.cpn.org/sections/topicskommunity/stories-studies/texas_iafl.htm, 1996, p. 3.

14. Ibid., p. 3.

15. Ibid.

16. Stanley Ziemba, "Alinsky Rules Are Still Activist's Bible," *Chicago Tribune,* June 6, 1982, pp. 1, 5, as quoted in Reitzes and Reitzes, *The Alinsky Legacy,* p. 231.

17. We follow Reitzes and Reitzes, *The Alinsky Legacy,* closely here.

18. Robert E. Park, "The City: Suggestions for the Investigation of Human Behavior in the City Environment," *American Journal of Sociology* 20 (March 1916): 577–612.

19. See Mary Jo Deegan, *Jane Addams and the Men of the Chicago School, 1892–1918* (New Brunswick, N.J.: Transaction Books, 1988), pp. 33–37.

20. John Cornwell, *Hitler's Pope: The Secret History of Pius XII* (New York: Viking, 1999).

21. Jacques Maritain, *Integral Humanism* (Notre Dame, Ind.: University of Notre Dame Press, 1973), p. 230.

22. Saul Alinsky as quoted in Doering, *The Philosopher and the Provocateur,* p. xxii.

23. Alinsky, *Reveille for Radicals,* p. 17.

24. Ibid., p. 22. Alinsky notes that to be radical, one does not need to be radical all of one's life or on all issues.

25. Ibid., p. 71.

26. Ibid., p. 66.

27. Ibid., p. 73.

28. Ibid., p. 79.

29. Saul D. Alinsky, *Rules for Radicals: A Practical Primer for Realistic Radicals* (New York: Random House, 1971), pp. 46–47.

30. Sanford D. Horwitt, *Let Them Call Me Rebel: Saul Alinsky—His Life and Legacy* (New York: Knopf, 1989), p. 532.

31. "A Sociological Technique in Clinical Criminology," *Proceedings of the Sixty-Fourth Annual Congress of the American Prison Association,* September 17–21, 1934, p. 176.

32. Horwitt, *Let Them Call Me Rebel,* p. 132.

33. Alinsky, *Reveille for Radicals,* p. 81.

34. Ibid., p. 82.

35. Ibid., p. 84.

36. Marcel Mauss, *The Gift* (London: Cohen and West, 1954), p. 1.

37. Alinsky, *Reveille for Radicals,* p. 58.

38. We draw here on Capek and Feagin, "Grassroots Movements in a Class Perspective," pp. 27–53. See also Alain Touraine, "An Introduction to the Study of Social Movements," *Social Research* 52 (Winter 1985): 749–787.

39. Harry Boyte, "Beyond Politics as Usual," in *The New Populism,* ed. Harry C. Boyte and Frank Riessman (Philadelphia: Temple University Press, 1986), pp. 3–15.

40. Robert A. Slayton, *Back of the Yards* (Chicago: University of Chicago Press, 1986), p. 196.

41. Randy Stoecker and Susan Stall, "Community Organizing or Organizing Community?" Paper presented as part of an Internet (H-Urban) Seminar on the History of Community Organizing and Community-Based Development, 1996–1997, http://comm-org.utoledo.edu/papers96/gender2.html.

42. Ibid., n.p.

43. Ibid., n.p.

44. Ibid., n.p.

45. Alinsky, *Reveille for Radicals,* p. 33.

46. Ibid., p. 40.

47. Ibid., p. 33.

48. Ibid., p. 57.

49. Ibid., p. 60.

50. Ibid., pp. 83–84.

51. Horwitt, *Let Them Call Me Rebel,* pp. 132, 529.

52. These numbers are taken from the Social Science Citation Index, Institute for Scientific Information, 2000, a Web of Science database.

53. See Martin Oppenheimer, Martin J. Murray, and Rhonda Levine, eds., *Radical Sociologists and the Movement: Experiences, Lessons, and Legacies* (Philadelphia: Temple University Press, 1991).

54. Joe R. Feagin and Hernán Vera, *White Racism: The Basics* (New York: Routledge, 1995).

55. Noel A. Cazenave, "The Militant Denial of the Existence of White Racism in Contemporary America," unpublished paper, University of Connecticut, 1996, p. 3.

56. Cazenave, "The Militant Denial of the Existence of White Racism in Contemporary America," p. 4.

57. Ibid., pp. 5–6.

58. Quoted in Katherine Farrish, "'White Racism' Course Approved," *Hartford Courant,* December 13, 1995, p. A3. See also Denise K. Magner, "'White Racism' Course Causes Skirmish at U. of Connecticut," *Chronicle of Higher Education,* January 26, 1996, p. A16.

59. Cazenave, "The Militant Denial of the Existence of White Racism in Contemporary America," p. 9.

60. Katherine Farrish, "'White Racism' Course Approved," p. A3.

61. "White Racism," *Hartford Courant,* January 12, 1996, n.p., from Xeroxed copy provided by Noel Cazenave.

62. Laurence D. Cohen, "The 'White Racism' Professor Has His Own Racial Agenda," *Hartford Courant,* February 25, 1996, p. C3.

63. Magner, "'White Racism' Course Causes Skirmish," p. A16.

64. Cazenave, "The Militant Denial of the Existence of White Racism in Contemporary America," p. 10.

65. Ibid., pp. 15, 20.

66. Noel A. Cazenave and Darlene Alvarez-Maddern, "Defending the White Race: White Male Faculty Opposition to a 'White Racism' Course," paper presented at the

Annual Meeting on Race and Ethnicity in Higher Education, Memphis, Tennessee, June 1999, p. 6. This paper has been published as Noel A. Cazenave and Darlene Alvarez-Maddern, "Defending the White Race: White Male Faculty Opposition to a 'White Racism' Course," *Race and Society* 2 (2000): 25–50.

67. Ibid., p. 6.

68. Greg Smith, "Course on Racism Stalled," *Daily Campus,* Friday, December 1, 1995, pp. 1, 4; Katherine Farrish, "White Racism Course Approved: U Conn Teacher's Proposed Class Led to Controversy," *Hartford Courant,* December 13, 1995, p. 2; Jason Jakubowski, "Uphill Battle Fails to Block Approval of Racism Course," *Daily Campus,* Friday, January 26, 1996, pp. 1, 4; and Magner, "'White Racism' Course Causes Skirmish," p. A16.

69. Cazenave and Alvarez-Maddern, "Defending the White Race," p. 14.

70. Ibid., p. 15.

71. Ibid., p. 20.

72. Frances Grandy Taylor, "'White Racism' Course Magnifies, Teaches Evolution of Bigotry," *Hartford Courant,* November 19, 1996, pp. A3, A10.

73. Cazenave and Alvarez-Maddern, "Defending the White Race," p. 21.

74. Ibid., p. 25.

75. Donald Cunnigen, ed., *Teaching Race and Ethnic Relations: Syllabi and Instructional Materials,* 3rd ed. (Washington, D.C.: American Sociological Association, 1997).

76. ¡Vote! "The Citizenship Project/El Proyecto Ciudadanía," http://newcitizen.org/aboutus.htm (2000).

77. Paul Johnston, personal communication, December 7, 1999.

78. ¡Vote! "The Citizenship Project/El Proyecto Ciudadanía."

79. Paul Johnston, personal communication, December 7, 1999.

80. Ibid.

81. Ibid.

82. Ibid. Johnston's publications are divided between academic research pieces and popular pieces. See http://members.cruzio.com/-johnston.

83. Ibid.

84. Philip Nyden, Anne Figert, Mark Shibley, and Darryl Burrows, "University-Community Collaborative Research: Adding Chairs at the Research Table," *Building Community: Social Science in Action,* ed. Philip Nyden, Anne Figert, Mark Shibley, and Darryl Burrows (Thousand Oaks, Calif.: Pine Forge Press, 1997), p. 3.

Chapter 6

1. William F. Whyte, Davydd J. Greenwood, and Peter Lazes, "Participatory Action Research: Through Practice to Science in Social Research," in *Participatory Action Research,* ed. William F. Whyte (Newbury Park, Calif.: Sage, 1991), p. 21.

2. William F. Whyte, "Introduction," in *Participatory Action Research,* ed. William F. Whyte (Newbury Park, Calif.: Sage, 1991), pp. 10–12.

3. William F. Whyte, "Conclusions," in *Participatory Action Research,* ed. William F. Whyte (Newbury Park, Calif.: Sage, 1991), p. 237.

4. Philip Nyden, Anne Figert, Mark Shibley, and Darryl Burrows, "Effective Models of Collaboration," in *Building Community: Social Science in Action,* ed.

Philip Nyden, Anne Figert, Mark Shibley, and Darryl Burrows (Thousand Oaks, Calif.: Pine Forge Press, 1997), p. 17.

5. See Paulo Freire, *Pedagogy of the Oppressed* (New York: Continuum, 1995).

6. Robert Blauner and David Wellman, "Toward the Decolonization of Social Research," in *The Death of White Sociology: Essays on Race and Culture*, ed. Joyce Ladner (Baltimore: Black Classic Press, [1973] 1998), p. 315.

7. Ibid.

8. John Gaventa, "Preface," to "Research for Social Justice: Some North-South Convergences," by Orlando Fals-Borda, *Sociological Imagination*, Part II, Special Issue of *Sociology and Social Action* 33 (1996): 1.

9. Orlando Fals-Borda, *Peasant Society in the Colombian Andes: A Sociological Study of Saucío* (Gainesville: University of Florida Press, 1955).

10. Orlando Fals-Borda, *Acción Comunal en Una Vereda Colombiana: Su* Applicación, *Sus Resultados y Su Interpretatión* (Bogota: Universidad Nacional de Colombia, Departamento de Sociología, 1960), p. 5. The quotes that follow are our translations.

11. Ibid., pp. 5, 51–52.

12. Ibid., pp. 51–52.

13. Orlando Fals-Borda, *Conocimiento y Poder Popular: Lecciones con Campesinos de Nicaragua, Mexico, Colombia* (Bogota: Siglo Veintiuno, Editores, 1985).

14. Orlando Fals-Borda and Carlos Rodriguez Brandão, *Investigación Participativa* (Montevideo: Instituto del Hombre, Ediciones de la Banda Oriental, 1987). For example, this work is quoted in M. Eugenia Sanchez and G. H. Eduardo Almeida, "Synergistic Development and Participatory Action Research," *American Sociologist* 23 (Winter 1992): 83–99.

15. Fals-Borda, "Research for Social Justice: Some North-South Convergences," 1, 5.

16. Dedication in Orlando Fals-Borda, *Historia Doble de la Costa, Tomo IV: Retorno a la Tierra* (Bogota: Carlos Valencia Editores, 1986); see also Orlando Fals-Borda, *Historia Doble de la Costa, Tomo I: Mom pox y Loba* (Bogota: Carlos Valencia Editores, 1979); Orlando Fals-Borda, *Historia Doble de la Costa, Tomo II: El President Nieto* (Bogota: Carlos Valencia Editores, 1981); Orlando Fals-Borda, *Historia Doble de la Costa, Tomo III: Resistencia en el San Jorge* (Bogota: Carlos Valencia Editores, 1984).

17. Fals-Borda, *Historia Doble de la Costa, Tomo I.*

18. Fals-Borda and Brandão, *Investigación Participativa*, p. 16.

19. Ibid., p. 17.

20. Ibid., p. 12.

21. Fals-Borda, "Research for Social Justice: Some North-South Convergences," p. 5.

22. Ibid., p. 5.

23. Davydd J. Greenwood and Morten Levin, *Introduction to Action Research: Social Research for Social Change* (Thousand Oaks, Calif.: Sage, 1998), p. 180.

24. Hernán Vera, "On Being Treated Like a Person: The Client's View on High-Quality Care in Santiago, Chile," *Studies in Family Planning* 24 (1993): 1–10.

25. Maria Eugenia Sanchez and F. H. Eduardo Almeida, "Synergistic Development and Participatory Action Research in a Nahuat Community," *American Sociologist* 23 (Winter 1992): 83–99.

26. Ibid., p. 91.

27. Blas Soto Islas, Felipe Gutierrez Sandoval, and Aguilar Lopez Anastacio, "A Global Experience of Self Promotion (voluntary association): The Case of San Miguel de Tzincapan," *Wisconsin Sociologist* 22 (1985): 129–132, as quoted in Sanchez and Almeida, "Synergistic Development and Participatory Action Research in a Nahuat Community," p. 96.

28. Sanchez and Almeida, "Synergistic Development and Participatory Action Research in a Nahuat Community," p. 97.

29. Rakesh Rajani and Mustafa Kudrati, "The Varieties of Sexual Experience of the Street Children of Mwanza, Tanzania," in *Learning About Sexuality: A Practical Beginning,* ed. Sondra Zeidenstein and Kirsten Moore (New York: Population Council International Women's Health Coalitions, 1996), pp. 301–323.

30. Ibid., p. 303.

31. Ibid., pp. 304–306.

32. Ibid., p. 315.

33. Peter H. Mettler and Thomas Baumgartner, "Large-Scale Participatory Co-Shaping of Technological Developments," *Futures* 30 (1998): 535–554.

34. Ibid., pp. 546–547.

35. Richard E. Walton and Michael E. Gaffney, "Research, Action, and Participation: The Merchant Shipping Case," in *Participatory Action Research,* ed. William F. Whyte (Newbury Park, Calif.: Sage, 1991), p. 99.

36. Ibid., p. 102.

37. Ibid., pp. 103–104.

38. Gregory D. Squires and Dan Willett, "The Fair Lending Coalition: Organizing Access to Capital in Milwaukee," in *Building Community: Social Science in Action,* ed. Philip Nyden, Anne Figert, Mark Shibley, and Darryl Burrows (Thousand Oaks, Calif.: Pine Forge Press, 1997), pp. 52–54.

39. Ibid., p. 56.

40. Philip Nyden, Joanne Adams, and Kim Zalent, "Creating and Sustaining Racially and Ethnically Diverse Communities," in *Building Community: Social Science in Action,* ed. Philip Nyden, Anne Figert, Mark Shibley, and Darryl Burrows (Thousand Oaks, Calif.: Pine Forge Press, 1997), pp. 32–35.

41. Ibid; ONE, "Victories," http://www.onechicago.org/victories.htm (retrieved November 19, 2007).

42. Ibid., pp. 33–36.

43. Gregory D. Squires, "Do Subprime Loans Create Subprime Cities? Inequality and Access to Financial Services," Briefing Paper, Economic Policy Institute, 2007.

44. Robert D. Bullard, "Dismantling Environmental Racism in the Policy Arena: The Role of Collaborative Social Research," in *Building Community: Social Science in Action,* ed. Philip Nyden, Anne Figert, Mark Shibley, and Darryl Burrows (Thousand Oaks, Calif.: Pine Forge Press, 1997), pp. 67–68; see also Robert D. Bullard, *Dumping in Dixie: Race, Class, and Environmental Quality* (Boulder: Westview, 1990).

45. Bullard, "Dismantling Environmental Racism in the Policy Arena," pp. 67–68.

46. Ibid., p. 72; see also Robert D. Bullard, *Growing Smarter: Achieving Livable Communities, Environmental Justice, and Regional Equity* (Cambridge: MIT Press, 2007); and Robert D. Bullard, *The Black Metropolis in the Twenty-First*

Century: Race, Power, and the Politics of Place (New York: Rowman and Littlefield, 2007).

47. Nancy A. Matthews and Anne Parry, "Grassroots Approaches to Violence Prevention: Rainbow House's Choosing Non-Violence Institute," in *Building Community: Social Science in Action,* ed. Philip Nyden, Anne Figert, Mark Shibley, and Darryl Burrows (Thousand Oaks, Calif.: Pine Forge Press, 1997), pp. 190–192.

48. Ibid., p. 194.

49. See, for example, the special issue: "Feminism, Restorative Justice, and Violence against Women," *Violence Against Women* 11 (May 2005): 563–730.

50. Nyden, Figert, Shibley, and Burrows, "Effective Models of Collaboration," pp. 16–17.

51. Ibid., pp. 25–26.

52. Greenwood and Levin, *Introduction to Action Research: Social Research for Social Change,* p. 181.

53. Philip Nyden, Anne Figert, Mark Shibley, and Darryl Burrows, "Conclusion: Collaboration Gives Hope and Voice in an Age of Disillusionment," in *Building Community: Social Science in Action,* ed. Philip Nyden, Anne Figert, Mark Shibley, and Darryl Burrows (Thousand Oaks, Calif.: Pine Forge Press, 1997), p. 240.

Chapter 7

1. C. Wright Mills, *The Sociological Imagination* (New York: Oxford University Press, 1959), p. 63.

2. Alfred McClung Lee, *Sociology for Whom?* (New York: Oxford University Press, 1978), p. 80.

3. Talcott Parsons and Edward A. Shils, "Values, Motives, and Systems of Action," in *Toward a General Theory of Action: Theoretical Foundations for the Social Sciences,* ed. Talcott Parsons and Edward A. Shils (New York: Harper Torchbooks, 1965), p. 54.

4. Talcott Parsons, Edward A. Shils, Gordon W. Allport, Clyde Kluckhohn, Henry A. Murray, Robert R. Sears, Richard C. Sheldon, Samuel A. T. Stouffer, and Edward C. Tolmon, "Some Fundamental Categories of the Theory of Action: A General Statement," in *Toward a General Theory of Action,* ed. Talcott Parsons and Edward A. Shils (New York: Harper Torchbooks, 1965), p. 3.

5. Talcott Parsons, *The Structure of Social Action: A Study in Social Theory with Special Reference to a Group of Recent European Writers* (New York: Free Press, [1937] 1949), pp. 720–730.

6. Mills, *The Sociological Imagination,* p. 49.

7. bell hooks, "Intellectual Life: In and Beyond the Academy," *Z Magazine,* November 1995, p. 28.

8. Richard and Gerald T. Flacks, "Radical Sociology: The Emergence of Neo-Marxian Perspectives in U.S. Sociology," *Annual Review of Sociology* 4 (1978): 193–233.

9. Mills, *The Sociological Imagination,* p. 7.

10. Here we are using composite examples from a number of cases we have personally seen, as well as some we have read about.

11. See Michael Lerner, *Jewish Renewal: A Path to Healing and Transformation* (New York: Harper Perennial, 1994), p. xviii.

12. Robert W. Friedrichs, *A Sociology of Sociology* (New York: Free Press, 1970), p. 65.

13. Donald E. Comstock, "A Method for Critical Research: Investigating the World to Change It," in *Archives of the Transforming Sociology Series of the Red Feather Institute for Advanced Studies in Sociology* (1980), at http://www.tryoung.com.

14. Martin Jay, *The Dialectical Imagination: A History of the Frankfurt School and the Institute of Social Research, 1923–1950* (Boston: Little, Brown, 1973), p. 253; see also Calvin J. Larson, *Sociological Theory: From the Enlightenment to the Present* (Bayside, N.Y.: General Hall, 1986).

15. Tom Bottomore, "Marxism and Sociology," in *A History of Sociological Analysis,* ed. Tom Bottomore and Robert Nisbet (New York: Basic Books, 1978), p. 133. Bottomore cites a series of articles by Horkheimer.

16. Max Horkheimer and Theodor W. Adorno, *Dialectic of Enlightenment* (New York: Continuum Publishing Company, 2000), p. 3. See also p. xiiiff.

17. Jurgen Habermas, *Knowledge and Human Interests* (Boston: Beacon Press, 1971), p. 356.

18. Jurgen Habermas, "The Analytical Theory of Science and Dialectics," in *The Positivist Dispute in German Sociology, as* cited in Larson, *Sociological Theory,* p. 187.

19. Ibid., p. 189.

20. Jurgen Habermas, "Modernity Versus Postmodernity," in *Culture and Society: Contemporary Debates,* ed. Jeffrey C. Alexander and Steven Seidman (Cambridge, U.K.: Cambridge University Press, 1990), p. 353.

21. Ibid.

22. Ibid.

23. Daniel Bell, *The Coming of Post-Industrial Society* (New York: Basic Books, 1973), p. 453.

24. Bottomore, "Marxism and Sociology," p. 134.

25. Larson, *Sociological Theory,* p. 189.

26. See Bertell Oilman, *Dialectical Investigations* (New York: Routledge, 1993), pp. 42–45.

27. Jurgen Habermas, *The Philosophical Discourse of Modernity: Twelve Lectures,* trans. Frederick Lawrence (Cambridge: MIT Press, 1987), pp. vii–xvii and passim.

28. Jurgen Habermas, *The Theory of Communicative Action,* vol. 1, *Reason and the Rationalization of Society* (Boston: Beacon Press, 1984), pp. 305–387.

29. Richard Munch, *Sociological Theory: Developments Since the 1960s* (Chicago: Nelson Hall, 1993), pp. 240–241.

30. Habermas, *The Theory of Communicative Action,* p. 10.

31. Larson, *Sociological Theory,* p. 186.

32. David M. Rasmussen, *Reading Habermas* (Cambridge, U.K.: Basil Blackwell, 1990), p. 34.

33. Habermas, *The Theory of Communicative Action,* p. 398.

34. Erving Goffman, "The Nature of Deference and Demeanor," *American Anthropologist* 58 (1956): 477.

35. See Erving Goffman, *The Presentation of Self in Everyday Life* (Garden City, N.Y.: Anchor Books, 1959); Erving Goffman, *Behavior in Public Places: Notes on the Social Organization of Gatherings* (New York: Free Press, 1963).

36. Patricia M. Lengerman and Jill Niebrugge-Brantley, "Feminist Sociological Theory: The Near-Future Prospects," in *Frontiers in Social Theory,* ed. George Ritzer (New York: Columbia University Press, 1990), p. 317.

37. Judith Stacey and Barrie Thorne, "Is Sociology Still Missing Its Feminist Revolution?" *Perspectives: The ASA Theory Section Newsletter* 18 (Summer 1996): 1.

38. See Catharine A. MacKinnon, *Toward a Feminist Theory of the State* (Cambridge: Harvard University Press, 1989), pp. 2–10.

39. Dorothy E. Smith, *The Conceptual Practices of Power* (Boston: Northeastern University Press, 1990), p. 11.

40. Ibid., p. 12.

41. Ibid., p. 13.

42. Ibid., p. 199.

43. See George Ritzer, *Modern Social Theory* (New York: McGraw-Hill, 1996), pp. 328–329.

44. Claire M. Renzetti, "Confessions of a Reformed Positivist: Feminist Participatory Research as Good Social Science," in *Researching Sexual Violence against Women: Methodological and Personal Perspectives* (Thousand Oaks, Calif.: Sage, 1997), p. 142.

45. bell hooks, *Outlaw Culture* (New York: Routledge, 1994); see also bell hooks, *Feminist Theory: From Margin to Center* (Boston: South End Press, 1984), pp. 6–51.

46. bell hooks, "Sexism and Misogyny: Who Takes the Rap?" *Z Magazine,* February 1994, pp. 26–29.

47. Patricia Hill Collins, *Black Feminist Thought: Knowledge, Consciousness, and the Politics of Empowerment* (Boston: Unwin Hyman, 1990), p. 67.

48. Patricia Hill Collins, *Fighting Words: Black Women and the Search for Justice* (Minneapolis: University of Minnesota Press, 1998), pp. xi–xii.

49. Ibid., p. 96.

50. Ibid., p. 199.

51. Ki Namaste, "The Politics of Inside/Out: Queer Theory, Poststructuralism, and a Sociological Approach to Sexuality," *Sociological Theory* 12 (July 1994): 220–231.

52. Chrys Ingraham, "The Heterosexual Imaginary: Feminist Sociology and Theories of Gender," *Sociological Theory* 12 (July 1994): 203–219.

53. Ibid., p. 204.

54. See Smith, *The Conceptual Practices of Power,* p. 13.

55. Ingraham, "The Heterosexual Imaginary," p. 211.

56. Charles Lemert and Esme Bhan, *The Voice of Anna Julia Cooper* (Lanham, Md.: Rowman and Littlefield, 1998), p. 93.

57. W.E.B. Du Bois, *Darkwater* (1920), as reprinted in *The Oxford W.E.B. Du Bois Reader,* ed. Eric J. Sundquist (New York: Oxford, 1996), p. 504.

58. Oliver C. Cox, *Caste, Class, and Race* (Garden City, N.Y.: Doubleday, 1948), p. 344. In this section we draw on Joe R. Feagin, *Racist America: Roots, Current Realities, and Future Reparations* (New York: Routledge, 2000), chapters 1–2.

59. Stokely Carmichael [Kwame Ture] and Charles V. Hamilton, *Black Power: The Politics of Liberation in America* (New York: Vintage, 1967).

60. See Joe R. Feagin and Hernán Vera, *White Racism: The Basics* (New York: Routledge, 1995).

61. See Feagin, *Racist America,* chapters 1–2; and Feagin and Vera, *White Racism,* chapter 1.

62. See Feagin and Vera, *White Racism,* chapter 7.

63. See bell hooks, *Killing Rage* (New York: Henry Holt, 1995), p. 201.

64. Eileen O'Brien, "Whites Doing Antiracism: Discourse, Practice, Emotion, and Organizations," doctoral dissertation, University of Florida, 1999; Feagin, *Racist America,* pp. 255–257.

65. Eileen O'Brien, personal communication, November 11, 2000.

66. Ibid.

67. Norman K. Denzin, *Images of Postmodern Society: Social Theory and Contemporary Cinema* (Newbury Park, Calif.: Sage, 1991), p. 180.

68. Steven Seidman, "Introduction," in *The Postmodern Turn: New Perspective on Social Theory,* ed. Steven Seidman (Cambridge: Cambridge University Press, 1994), p. 1.

69. Steven Seidman, "The End of Sociological Theory," *Sociological Theory* 9 (Fall 1991): 140.

70. See George Ritzer, *Postmodern Social Theory* (New York: McGraw-Hill, 1997), p. xvii.

71. Seidman, "The End of Sociological Theory," p. 131.

72. Robert J. Antonio, "Postmodern Storytelling Versus Pragmatic Truth-Seeking: The Discursive Bases of Social Theory," *Sociological Theory* 9 (Fall 1991): 161.

73. Seidman, "The End of Sociological Theory," p. 131.

74. Jean-Francois Lyotard, "The Other's Rights," in *On Human Rights: The Oxford Amnesty Lectures,* ed. Stephen Shute and Susan Hurley (New York: Basic Books, 1993), p. 136.

75. Donna Haraway, "A Manifesto for Cyborgs: Science, Technology and Socialist Feminism in the 1980s," in *Feminism/Postmodernism,* ed. Linda J. Nicholson (London: Routledge, 1990), pp. 190–234.

76. See Ben Agger, *Critical Social Theories: An Introduction* (Boulder: Westview, 1998), p. 31.

77. Alfred McClung Lee, "Steps Taken Toward Liberating Sociologists," in *Radical Sociologists and the Movement: Experiences, Lessons, and Legacies,* ed. Martin Oppenheimer, Martin J. Murray, and Rhonda Levine (Philadelphia: Temple University Press, 1991), p. 39. We draw here on the article.

78. See Roger C. Bannister, "Principle, Politics, Profession: American Sociologists and Fascism," in *Sociology Responds to Fascism,* ed. Stephen P. Turner and Dirk Kasler (London: Routledge, 1992), p. 189.

79. Alfred M. Lee, *How to Understand Propaganda* (New York: Rinehart, 1952), p. viii.

80. Alfred M. Lee, *How Customs and Mentality Can Be Changed* (The Hague: Uitgeverij Van Keulen N.V., 1958), pp. 1–2.

81. Ibid., p. 1.

82. Ibid., p. 3.

83. Lee, *Sociology for Whom?* pp. 16–17.

84. Robert G. Newby, "The Making of a Class-Conscious 'Race Man': Reflections on Thirty Years of Struggle," in *Radical Sociologists and the Movement: Experiences, Lessons, and Legacies,* ed. Martin Oppenheimer, Martin J. Murray, and Rhonda Levine (Philadelphia: Temple University Press, 1991), pp. 159–163. This section on Newby draws heavily on this article.

85. Ibid., p. 161.

86. Ibid., pp. 168–169.

87. Ibid., pp. 70–72.

88. Ibid., p. 176.

89. Ibid., p. 177.

90. Ibid., p. 178.

91. Ibid., p. 178.

92. Robert Newby, e-mail communication, December 4, 2000.

93. Ibid.

94. T. R. Young, personal communication, January 2000. In this section all quotes from Young and all information on his life are from this communication, unless otherwise indicated.

95. See http://www.tryoung.com.

96. See T. R. Young, "Marx and the Postmodern: Compatibilities and Contrarities," *Archives of the Transforming Sociology Series of the Red Feather Institute* (1991), at http://www.tryoung.com; and T. R. Young, "Reinventing Sociology: Missions and Methods for Postmodern Sociologists," *Archives of the Transforming Sociology Series of the Red Feather Institute* (1993), at http://www.tryoung.com.

97. Yleana Martinez, "Maxine Baca Zinn," in *Latinas: Women of Achievement,* ed. Diane Telgen and Jim Kamp (Detroit: Visible Ink Press, 1996), p. 33.

98. Ibid., p. 31.

99. Ibid., p. 34.

100. Maxine Baca Zinn and Bonnie Thornton Dill, eds., *Women of Color in U.S. Society* (Philadelphia: Temple University Press, 1994).

101. This is from a biographical statement at http://www.chicanas.com/chingonas.html.

102. Maxine Baca Zinn, e-mail communication, December 3, 2000.

103. Ibid.

104. Ibid.

105. Ibid.

106. Mary Jo Deegan, personal communication, July 18, 2000.

107. Ibid.

108. Mary Jo Deegan, *Jane Addams and the Men of the Chicago School, 1892–1918* (New Brunswick, N.J.: Transaction Books, 1988).

109. Ibid., p. 2.

110. Ibid., p. 304.

111. Mary Jo Deegan, "'Dear Love, Dear Love': Feminist Pragmatism and the Chicago Female World of Love and Ritual," *Gender and Society* 10 (October 1996): 590–607.

112. Mary Jo Deegan, "Symbolic Interaction and the Study of Women: An Introduction," in *Women and Symbolic Interaction,* ed. Mary Jo Deegan and Michael R. Hill (Boston: Allen and Unwin, 1987), pp. 3–15.

113. Ibid., p. 13.

114. Mary Jo Deegan, personal communication, July 18, 2000.

115. Ibid.

116. Agger, *Critical Social Theories,* p. 6.

117. Patricia Hill Collins, "On Book Exhibits and New Complexities: Reflections on Sociology as Science," *Contemporary Sociology* 27 (January 1998): 10.

Chapter 8

1. Eduardo Bonilla-Silva, "Eréndira in American Sociology," SSF Listserv, November 2, 2007 (retrieved November 2, 2007).

2. George Miller, "Psychology as an Instrument at the Service of Human Welfare," *American Psychologist* 21 (1969): 1063–1075.

3. Ignacio Martín-Baró, *Writings for a Liberation Psychology,* ed. Adrianne Aron, Shawn Come, and Elliot Mishler (Cambridge: Harvard University Press, 1994).

4. Ignacio Martín-Baró, "El Latino Indolente," in Ignacio Martín-Baró, *Psicología de la Liberatión,* ed. Amalio Blanco (Madrid: Editorial Trotta, 1998), p. 91. See also pp. 73–101.

5. Leigh Binford, *The El Mozote Massacre: Anthropology and Human Rights* (Tucson: University of Arizona Press, 1996), pp. 199–203.

6. Ignacio Ellacuría, quoted in Ignacio Martín-Baró, *Psicología de la Liberación,* ed. Amalio Blanco (Madrid: Editorial Trotta, 1998), p. 27. Our translation.

7. Amalio Blanco, "Introduction," in Ignacio Martín-Baró, *Psicología de la Liberación,* ed. Amalio Blanco (Madrid: Editorial Trotta, 1998), p. 27.

8. Emmanuel Martey, *African Theology: Inculturation and Liberation* (Maryknoll, N.Y.: Orbis, 1993), p. 11.

9. See Robert N. Bellah et al., *The Good Society* (New York: Knopf, 1991); Amitai Etzioni, *The Spirit of Community: The Reinvention of American Society* (New York: Simon and Schuster, 1993).

10. See Etzioni, *The Spirit of Community.*

11. Sheldon S. Wolin, "Political Theory as a Vocation," *American Political Science Review* 63 (1969): 1064.

12. See Gideon Sjoberg, Elizabeth Gill, Norma Williams, and Kathryn E. Kuhn, "Ethics, Human Rights, and Sociological Inquiry: Genocide, Politicide, and Other Issues of Organizational Power," *American Sociologist* 26 (Spring 1995): 11–13.

13. For this and related international human rights documents, see Department of Public Information, United Nations, *The United Nations and Human Rights, 1945–1995* (New York: United Nations, 1995), pp. 33–225.

14. Stephen Lyng, *Holistic Health and Biomedical Medicine: A Countersytem Analysis* (Albany, N.Y.: SUNY Press, 1990); and Ted R. Vaughan, "The Crisis in Contemporary American Sociology: A Critique of the Discipline's Dominant Paradigm," in *A Critique of Contemporary American Sociology* (New York: General Hall, 1993), p. 47.

15. Chuck Collins, Chris Hartman, and Holly Sklar, *Divided Decade: Economic Disparity at the Century's Turn* (Boston: United for a Fair Economy, 1999), http://www.stw.org/my_html/Divided.html (retrieved December 1999).

16. See Michael M. Bell, *An Invitation to Environmental Sociology* (Thousand Oaks, Calif.: Pine Forge Press, 1998).

17. Jared Diamond, *The Third Chimpanzee: The Evolution and Future of the Human Animal* (New York: HarperCollins, 1992), p. 362.

18. See Marcel Mauss, *The Gift* (London: Cohen and West, 1954).

19. Gideon Sjoberg, "The Human Rights Challenge to Communitarianism: Formal Organizations and Race and Ethnicity," in *Macro Socio-Economics: From Theory to Activism,* ed. David Sciulli (Armonk, N.Y.: M. E. Sharpe, 1996), p. 287.

20. Sandra Harding, "Introduction," in *The 'Racial' Economy of Science: Toward a Democratic Future* (Bloomington: Indiana University Press, 1993), p. 3.

21. Ibid., pp. 12–16.

22. T. R. Young, e-mail communication.

23. Sjoberg, "The Human Rights Challenge to Communitarianism," pp. 281–282.

24. Pierre Bourdieu and Loic Wacquant, "New Liberal Speak: Notes on the New Planetary Vulgate," trans. David Macy, *Radical Philosophy* (Jan–Feb 2001), http://www.radicalphilosophy.com/default.asp?channel_id=2187&editorial_id=9956 (retrieved December 2, 2007).

25. Ben Agger, *Public Sociology: From Social Facts to Literary Acts* (First edition; Lanham, Md.: Rowman and Littlefield, 2000), p. 9. See also the second edition (2007).

Chapter 9

1. Karl Marx and Frederick Engels, "The German Ideology," in Robert C. Tucker, ed., *The Marx and Engels Reader* (New York: W. W. Norton, 1978), p.154.

2. Pierre Bourdieu, *Outline of Theory of Practice* (Cambridge: Cambridge University Press, 1977), p. 192.

3. Dennis Hayes and Robin Wynward, eds., *The McDonaldization of Higher Education* (Westport, Conn.: Greenwood Press, 2002).

4. The 2006 provisional noninfant mortality rate in the United States is 8.1 per thousand, which over 10 years represents about 81 people per thousand. "Births, Marriages, Divorces, and Deaths: Provisional Data for 2006," *National Vital Statistics Reports* (NVSR), Volume 55, August 28, 2007.

5. Paulo Freire, *Pedagogy of the Oppressed* (New York: Continuum, 1995), p. 53.

6. Ibid., p. 55.

7. We are indebted here to critical comments by Jennifer Mueller.

8. Ben Agger, *Public Sociology: From Social Facts to Literary Acts* (Lanham, Md.: Rowman and Littlefield, 2000), p. 266.

9. Michael G. Long, *Against Us, But for Us: Martin Luther King, Jr. and the State* (Macon, Ga.: Mercer University Press, 2002), pp. 29–30.

10. James M. Washington, ed., *A Testament of Hope: The Essential Writings and Speeches of Martin Luther King* (New York: HarperCollins, 1991), p. 314.

11. Ibid., pp. 50–51.

INDEX

ABOUT THE AUTHORS

Joe Feagin is the Ella C. McFadden Professor in Sociology at Texas A & M University and has served as the Scholar in Residence at the U.S. Commission on Civil Rights. He has written fifty-three books including *Ghetto Revolts: The Politics of Violence in American Cities* (MacMillan 1973), which was nominated for a Pulitzer Prize. He is the 2006 recipient of a Harvard Alumni Association achievement award and was the 1999–2000 president of the American Sociological Association.

Hernán Vera is Professor Emeritus at the University of Florida–Gainesville and a leading scholar in U.S. racial and ethnic relations. His books include *Screen Saviors: Hollywood Fictions of Whiteness.*